LAW  THE

"Nature is the guide, the silent flow of traditional events, the majestic order of the seasons and the sky; it is the Tao, or the Way, exemplified and embodied in every brook and rock and star; it is that impartial, impersonal and yet rational law of things to which the law of conduct must conform if men desire to live in wisdom and peace. This law of things is the Tao or way of the universe, just as the law of conduct is the Tao or way of life; in truth, both Taos are one, and human life, in its essential and wholesome rhythm, is part of the rhythm of the world. In that cosmic Tao all the laws of nature are united and form together the substance of all reality; in it all natural forms and varieties find a proper place, and all apparent diversities and contradictions meet, the Absolute in which all particulars are resolved into one unity."

"All things in nature work silently. They come into being and possess nothing. They fulfill their function and make no claim. All things alike do their work, and then we see them subside. When they have reached their bloom, each returns to its origin. Returning to their origin means rest, or fulfillment of destiny. This reversion is eternal Law. To know that Law is wisdom."

Lao-tze

INTRODUCTION

IRVING BABBITT

The imperialism that made the Romans masters of the world is not the same kind as that which prevailed when they cringed beneath a Tiberius or a Nero. It is possible to trace the process by which the order finally took on a decadent cast. The critical period for Rome was the moment of triumph when the leaders of the state no longer felt the restraining influence of dangerous rivals like Carthage. At the same time, they were beginning to throw off the traditional controls of the Republic. The result of all this emancipation was that men's desires became immense, with the significant symptom being the inordinate growth of luxury. A still graver symptom, however, was the appearance of these leaders who were ever more ruthless in their pursuit either of personal advantage or that of some class or faction. The new spirit that was undermining the Roman constitution manifested itself even less, as Cicero notes, in acts of injustice and cruelty to the vanquished peoples, than in the rage of civil strife. It can scarcely be maintained of the Romans who thus precipitated the decadence that they any longer exercised to any degree the will to refrain. The right opponents of these anarchists were the individuals who had qualified for true leadership by setting bounds to their expansive lusts, especially the lust of domination. Rome declined because she failed to produce individuals of this type in sufficient numbers.

Certain analogies may be discovered between this Roman dilemma and the dilemma with which we are now confronted in America. We, too, seem to have reached the acme of our power and are at the same time discarding the standards of the past. There is an increasing role in our national life of groups with highly unethical leaders who seek to advance the material interests of their clients at the expense of the whole community. Will and appetite have had their way unchecked in a great part of the world; humanism fights a rearguard action in America; democracy sinks beneath tribulations, and leaders with the proper imagination are few. It has proved to be more than just a passing phase and thus portends the end of our constitutional liberties and the rise of decadent Authority. We are not just on a descending curve but a fatal one. But if one is to get at the root of the matter, he must turn from the merely peripheral manifestations of the push to power and explore the inner life of the individual.

What is specifically human in man is a certain quality of will, one that is felt in relation to his ordinary self as the will to refrain. The idea of humility, the idea that man needs to defer to a higher will, came into Europe with an Oriental religion-Christianity. This idea has been losing ground in almost exact ratio to the decline of Christianity as a controlling faith. Inasmuch as the recognition of the supremacy of the will seems to be imperative in any wise view of life, I side with the Christian against those who are inclined to give first place to the emotions. I differ from the Christian in that my interest in the higher will and the power of veto it exercises over man's expansive desires is humanistic rather than religious. It is concerned with the law of measure that should govern man in his secular relations, particularly his political ones. Deny the validity of this opposition and the inner life tends in the same measure to disappear. When one heeds the admonitions of the inner monitor the result is character and happiness. This is one of the great paradoxes of life. The true leader is the man of character, and the ultimate root of character is humility. A chief source of Christian humility was the conviction that man is unable by his own resources to achieve any such truth, the conviction, above all, that mere reason cannot prevail over the deceits of the senses.

The disparagement of following our senses is found as far back as Plato. He hopes to attain a truth that is "firm and not pulled around this way and that by our fancy." Later, to the Stoic, it seemed both feasible and imperative that reason should hold sway over all the impressions that beat upon the gateway of the senses and make a severe selection among them. "How easy a thing it is," says Marcus Aurelius, "to put away and blot out every fancy that is disturbing or alien, and to be at once in perfect peace." The Stoic based his optimism on faith in his reason. To *know* the right thing was tantamount to doing it. Reason and will tended to become identical. The whole question was closely allied to the Platonic and Socratic identification of knowledge and virtue, and thus to the relation of intellect and will. Similarly, no tendency is more marked in the Cartesian system than to conceive reason as it were mathematically and logically of the truth and reality of both the human and the natural order. To adjust one's will to God or nature is equivalent to adjusting it to reason. The Reason that the Stoic took as his guiding principle was conceived as being one with reality. Right reason and will are indeed identical. We achieve character, personality and manners in order to make our lives an art and to bring our souls into relation with the whole scheme of things, which is Natural Law.

Persons were not lacking in ancient Athens who saw the perils of an anarchial individualism. Socrates, along with Plato and Aristotle were seeking to build up traditional standards more in accord with the critical spirit. The Greeks, on their emancipation from traditional standards, slipped rapidly into mere rationalism, and that, whether in the form of Stoicism or Epicureanism, showed its inability to control the expansive lusts of the human heart. Stoicism sought to achieve a principle of union among men that would have universal validity; it sought, in other words, to do the work of religion. It saw this universal principle in Reason and proclaimed at the same time that to live according to Reason was to live according to nature. The Stoic assumed that man's reason could prevail unaided over his outer impressions and expansive desires. Right action would follow right knowledge. The effort on the whole was a failure and it may be maintained that Western civilization is still suffering from that failure-of character to measure up to the mind. Greeks employed many fine phrases but the law that actually tended to prevail was the law of force.

We need to remember how much of the Christian tradition itself goes back not to Judea but to Greece and Rome. It has been asserted that Saint Augustine is the Christian Plato and Saint

Thomas Aquinas the Christian Aristotle. In a certain sense Plato and Aristotle are in their true spirit nearer to us than to the men of the Middle Ages-to be critical in one's outlook on life is to be modern while the medieval view of life rests on the belief in supernatural revelation. Aristotle specifically remains the chief example of a thinker who treated in a critical and humanistic way the problems of government. Before writing his *Politics,* he had made detailed studies of the history and constitutions of over one hundred and fifty city-states, and in general rests his conclusions upon a great body of actual political experience. We have been further enlightened about certain problems by an enormous mass of further lessons from both the East and the West that he did not have at his command. Even if there is no God and no positive revelation man might be guided aright in political matters by the law of nature conceived as the law of right reason. Anyone can convince himself of the startling relevancy of Aristotle's *Politics* to existing conditions, especially now that we have slipped our constitutional moorings and are drifting towards direct or unlimited democracy. There are passages as modern as the morning news report. Rome later ran through a similar cycle: a constitutional republic resting ultimately on religious control gradually gave way to an egalitarian democracy which in turn passed through the usual incidents of class war to arrive at a decadent totalitarian state.

The feudal government of the ancient city-state was allied with traditional religious forms, and that government changed when the hierarchy that traditional religion had established, first of all in the family, and then in the state, was gradually undermined by individualism and then egalitarian tendencies. The Church had succeeded in creating symbols that in a very literal sense united men from the top to the bottom of society in the same spiritual hopes and fears. Everyone might enter a great cathedral and see depicted on one hand the torments of the damned and on the other the bliss of paradise. As a result of this imaginative control exercised over all classes, the church did not need the support of physical force: purely spiritual penalties, especially excommunication, sufficed. But controlling men by an appeal to their religious hopes and fears without any need of physical compulsion seems to us a veritable spiritual tyranny. The older religious control has given away for several centuries past to centrifugal tendencies, and the danger is now manifest that in the absence of any new integrating principle, what may triumph in our modern world, as it finally triumphed in the ancient world, is the principle of naked force. The yielding of religious control to a political order based on naked force led to the decline of every ancient civilization.

To be genuinely humanistic one must assert in the form of free moral choice a power in the heart of the individual that may lift him above his physical nature. Diderot and other Encyclopedists set out deliberately to substitute the kingdom of man for the traditional kingdom of God. The substitution of the idea of Law for the idea of Providence is not a chimerical undertaking. Such humanists believe that man is a distinct being, governed by laws peculiar to his nature: there is a Law for man and there is Law for things. Man stands higher than the beasts that perish because he recognizes and obeys these laws of his nature. The disciplinary arts of humanity teach him to put checks upon his will and his appetite. Those checks are provided by reason, the higher reason which grows out of a respect for the wisdom of our ancestors and out of the endeavor to apprehend order in the person and order in the Republic. Its enemies are the sentimentalist, who would subject man to the forces of impulse and passion; the pragmatic materialist, who would treat man as a mere edified ape; and the leveling enthusiast, who would reduce human personality to a collective mediocrity. The world is sinking into unreason; it is only the humane tradition and ethical discipline which keeps us civilized and maintains a decent but fragile social framework. Humane studies are those which teach a man his dignity and his rights and duties. Opposed to the humanist is the humanitarian who believes only in material gain and the emancipation from moral obligations, the substitute of moral self-restraint with the worship of one's reckless self, and the narcissism and appetite which oppress our time. He hungers for the gratification of all in an equality of condition impossible to realize.

The basis for the humane inner life is the opposition between a lower and a higher will. The higher will cannot act at random; it must have standards. Formerly the standards were supplied by tradition. The man who accepted Christian tradition, for example, was in no doubt as to the kind and degree of discipline he needed to impose on his lower nature. He thus achieved some measure of moral unity with himself and with other men who accepted the same discipline. The church as an actual institution had such a monopoly on the higher life of man that to seek, like Machiavelli, to give the state a basis independent of the church was to run the risk of giving it a basis independent of morality. The rules of ordinary morality may hold in the relations between man and man but have only a secondary pace in the relations between state and man. The virtue of the Machiavellian political leader has little in common with humanistic virtue and nothing at all with religious virtue. The malevolent ruler above all should have no conscience apart from the state and its material aggrandizement. Any person who consents to become a passive instrument to the point of practicing a morality different from that which should rule the individual is in the Machiavellian tradition. He embodies, more completely than anyone else, the realistic tradition in European politics. If the Progressive is to have similar standards, they are in direct ratio to the completeness of his break with the traditional unifications of life. But judgment sooner or later overtakes those who transgress the moral law. Without asserting that public and private morality should coincide precisely at all points, one may affirm that it is chimerical to set up a dual code; to suppose that men can be ruthless in the service of country and at the same time upright as individuals. It is a defeat for civilization, which ultimately depends on a maintenance of standards, that it cannot be brought to a cogent judgment and criticism of such a philosophy. The Progressive decline of standards has brought nothing but the current anarchy. No amount of devotion to society and its supposed interests can take the place of this inner obeisance of the spirit to standards.

If one is to refute Machiavelli and Hobbes one must show that there is some universal principle that tends to unite men even across national frontiers, a principle which continues to act even when their egoistic impulses are no longer controlled by the laws of some particular state supported by its organized force. The inner life of man is the recognition in some form or another of a force that moves in an opposite direction from the outer impressions and expansive desires that together make up his ordinary self. The political reflex of this process was the passage, in time, of a Europe that was unified in theory by the Roman theocracy and Law, to a Europe made up of great territorial nationalities governed by international law. Within the bounds of each separate nationality the essential aspect of this secular process was the passage from divine right to popular right, from the sovereignty of God to the sovereignty of the people. In this long period of transition supernaturalist and naturalistic views were blended in almost every possible proportion-see Aquinas, Averroes and Maimonides.

Whether one starts with a state of nature in which men are conceived as mere isolated units, and then imagines a contract of some kind by which they pass from that state of nature into society, or whether one asserts with Aristotle that man is a political animal, and it is therefore natural for him to live in society, one needs in either case to define with some care the functioning principle of cohesion among men. According to the Christian it is submission to the will of God; to others it is a bond of union among men in a "rule of reason," and the association of this rule of reason with nature is not Christian, but Stoical. The notion of a state of nature and of a law of nature antecedent to positive law and organized society emerged in classical antiquity, and survived throughout the Middle Ages, largely as a result of the infiltration of the Stoical influence into Roman law. It was reinforced again by the direct return of the Renaissance to the Stoical and other similar ancient humanist sources. Among Church fathers there was a tendency to identify the supposed state of nature with the state of man before the Fall, and to associate this not only with the bliss of ignorance, but give this state a communistic coloring, associating at the same time man's lapse from innocence with the rise of private property. The period that extends from the Renaissance to the eighteenth century was marked by the progressive emancipation of the individual from outer authority and the supernatural beliefs that this Authority sought to impose.

The problem of personal will is closely bound up with the problem of standards, for it is impossible to achieve standards unless one can discover in life somewhere an abiding unity with which to measure its variety and change. While absolute unity and reality must ever elude us and the absolute in general must be dismissed as a metaphysical dream, we may still discover to what degree any particular view of life is sanctioned or repudiated by the nature of things and rate it accordingly as more or less real. To determine the quality of our view we need to supplement the power in man that perceives and conceives with the power of discrimination. In emphasizing the importance of the power in man that discriminates, that works on the actual material of experience, the only thing that finally counts in the world is a concentration on the facts of Natural Law.

The origins of the tendency to interpret more optimistically the state of nature, defined by Hobbes as liberty, equality and war, *was* the revival of Stoical philosophy and the Stoical views regarding natural law and *jus gentium* that had been incorporated in Roman law. Even more so was the positive and critical method by which scientific discoveries and progress had been achieved, a method in direct conflict with the dogmas and uncritical affirmations of religion. The underlying driving power behind the return to nature from the Renaissance forward was the rise of the new astronomy and the growing triumphs of physical science. Scientific advances were making increasingly possible the satisfaction of men's newly released desires. It was gradually developing a vast machinery designed to minister to man's material comfort and convenience and destined to culminate in the Industrial Revolution. Considered, though, from the point of view of the individual the multiplication of wants is bad. This expansion, with its concomitant growth of luxury, would bring with it the growth of vice and selfishness, just as it had in Rome.

It goes without saying that the partisans of "progress" have not admitted their spiritual blindness. They have accepted as substitutes for the traditional standards, and the moral unity that these standards tended to promote, certain new unifications of life that display great imagination, but an imagination that had not been sufficiently tested from the point of view of reality. These new schemes for unifying men were deliberately erected on the ruins of discrimination. Anyone who takes seriously the creations of this type, an imagination not disciplined to the human or natural law, but free to wander wild in its own realm of chimeras, falls into mere conceit or vain imagining. Conceit has always been the specifically human malady, but never, perhaps, more so than today. The outstanding trait of the men of our period may seem in retrospect to have been the facility with which they put forth untried conceits as "ideals," ideals that when put to the test have turned out to be only disastrous daydreams. Why should men progress unless it can be shown that they are progressing toward civilization and not barbarism? An age that thinks it is progressing toward an undefinable, yet somehow desirable, social justice finds instead it is progressing towards moral and economic collapse.

When studied with any degree of thoroughness, the economic problem will be found to run into the political problem, the political problem in turn into the philosophical problem, and the philosophical problem to be indissolubly bound up with the moral problem. This book is one of a series in which I try to bring out the deeper implications of the modern Progressive movement. Though devoted to different topics the volumes are bound together by their pre-occupation with the collectivist trend. Among the men of the Eighteenth century who prepared the way for the world in which we now live stands, in the pre-eminent place, Jean-Jacque Rousseau. He is first among the theorists for radical democracy and the most eminent of those to attack civilization. We are living in a world that in certain important aspects has gone wrong on first principles, which is another way of saying that we are living in a world that has been betrayed by its leaders. There will always be good and bad leaders, and democracy becomes a menace to civilization when it seeks to evade this truth. The notion that a substitute for leadership may be found in numerical majorities that are supposed to reflect Rousseau's "general will" is a particularly pernicious conceit. Rousseau did not call on individual men to repent and amend each his own wicked existence, that they might be saved; but called on men to amend each the whole world's wicked existence and be saved by making a social contract. To the social contract, unlimited sovereignty, and the state of nature we must add natural rights if we wish to complete the list of abstract and metaphysical conceptions that have dominated much of political thinking since Rousseau.

It has been the constant experience of man that mere rationalism leaves him unsatisfied. Man craves an enthusiasm that will lift him out of his merely rational self. Cold reason has never done anything illustrious. The battle that has been in progress since the end of the eighteenth century, though, is a battle between the rational spirit of Edmund Burke and the irrational spirit of Rousseau. This leftist substitution of social reform for self-reform involves the turning away from the more immediate to the less immediate. I am unable to discover truths of any form in the philosophies now fashionable; I have been led to prefer to the wisdom of the age of Rousseau, Burke's wisdom of the ages.

With Rousseau's social contract, the virtues of liberty, equality and fraternity no longer reside in the individual but in the general will. All the clauses of this contract reduce themselves to one: the total alienation of every associate, with the submission of all his rights, including property, to the whole community. But what guarantee is the individual to have that the community will not then abuse this unlimited control that he has granted it over his person and property? On all ordinary occasions the general will means a numerical majority at any moment. An individual or minority of individuals has no appeal from the decision of the majority in its interpretation of the general will. In exercising constraint upon him, the majority is simply "forcing him to be free." The state, as embodied in the general will is subject to no control at all, save force. Rousseau transfers to the people the doctrine that the king can do no wrong. Practically, the general will is lawless; the sovereign people is responsible to no one. It is Authority. It is the arbitrary will, restrained by no obligations. The popular will is the successor of the divine will, from which everything derived in the medieval theocracy, and from which is now derived collectivism. The Rousseau who has been influential is always Rousseau the extremist, the Rousseau of unflinching collectivism, the Rousseau whose methods seek nothing less than divesting the individual as completely as possible of any natural virtue in order that he may acquire the virtue of the submissive citizen.

According to Rousseau the source of social evils was the invention of private property-the appearance of which caused the disappearance of equality-of industry, which only brings misery-and of institutions, which introduce vice and error to man's constitution, and those who administer those institutions. With him the inner conflicts between good and evil are transferred from the individual to society. The inevitable effect of Rousseau's writings is to make, through flattery, the poor man proud, and at the same time make him feel that he is the victim of a conspiracy. The man at the bottom of the existing social order is flattered by being told that he is more virtuous, more fully possessed of the spontaneous goodness of the state of nature than the man at the top.

The establishment of society and laws made it possible to change "an adroit usurpation (private property) into an irrevocable right, and for the profit of a few ambitious persons subjected henceforth the whole of humankind to toil, servitude, and wretchedness." One need scarcely be surprised that this and similar passages of his

Second Discourse should still be a direct source of inspiration to the bomb-throwing anarchist, even this far removed from the guillotine and the French Revolution. What one hears throughout his writing is an envious plebian fomenting hatred and class warfare; it is the idea that the rich and happy of the world are so at the expense of others, as though that happiness has been usurped from their own. The agitator makes his chief appeal to it when he stirs the multitude by his pictures of the felicity that is to supervene upon destruction of the existing social order. "The people constitute the human race and all that is not the people is parasitic and scarcely deserves to be counted were it not for the harm it does." Perhaps no doctrine has been more cunningly devised to fill the poor man and the plebian with self-righteous pride, and at the same time inflame him with hatred and suspicion of those who enjoy any social or economic superiority. Rousseau's premise of a fictitious state of nature led him to conclusions that justify emotional revolt against everything established, that are indeed enough to make "the very stones of Rome to rise and mutiny." Unfortunately, when the real refuses to vanish in favor of the ideal, it is easy to persuade the simpleminded that the failure is due not to the ideal itself, but to some conspiracy.

The universal brotherhood imagined by Rousseau and today's Progressives instead becomes a growing mania of suspicion. Just as the earliest victims of the French Revolution were the members of the privileged classes who had been so zealous in promoting the new philosophy, so will the parlor socialists who have invited the far Left into their Party. The opposition between virtuous and vicious individuals that has been established is even less than has been established between whole classes. The judging of men by their social grouping rather than their personal merits and demerits has been implicit in the logic of the Progressive movement from the French to the Russian Revolution. In France Robespierre and Saint-Jus were ready to violently eliminate whole social strata that seemed to them to be made up of parasites and conspirators, in order that they might adjust the actual France to the Sparta of their dreams. From the start the French Revolution took on the character of a universal crusade. The first principles it assumed made practically all existing governments seem illegitimate. The various peoples were invited to overthrow these governments, based upon usurpation, and, having recovered their original rights, to join with France in a glorious fraternity. France was to be the Christ of Nations. But the last stage of Progressivism is homicidal mania. In the name of an ideal general will, of which Progressives profess only to be the organ, they are ready to tyrannically impose their will on the actual people. The net result is not to get rid of corrupt leadership, but to produce an inferior and even insane Authoritative type.

In practice, the enormous mass of interlocking machinery purported to promote the greatest good of the greatest number has been pressed into service of the will to power of individuals and social groups, even nationalities. The preoccupation with the masses had for their aim the physical, intellectual and moral amelioration of the poorest and most numerous classes. Yet the chief victims have been the very masses whom both Rousseau and other reformers have professed themselves so eager to benefit. The most palpable error of the era is the confusion of mechanical and material progress with moral progress. Physical science is excellent in its own place, but when supreme moral issues are involved, it is only a multiplying device. If there is rightness at the center, it will no doubt multiply the rightness. If, on the other hand, there is any central error, the peripheral repercussion will be terrific. It would mean a return of the law of cunning and the law of force on a scale to which the past has seen no parallel. The present situation is one of unexampled gravity.

Christianity in its medieval form did secure for Europe no small degree of spiritual unity and cohesion. With those who still cling to the principle of a necessary outer authority I have no quarrel. The loss of this older European unity in favor of Progressivism has meant to minister to man's power and utility. But their substitute for the spiritual unity of the old order, when tried experimentally, according to their own principles, has failed disastrously. The results of the material success and concomitant spiritual failure makes it obvious that somewhere the power of man ran very much ahead of his wisdom. The outlook might look more cheery if there were any signs that men were seeking seriously to make up his deficiency on the side of wisdom. On the contrary, the Progressive is reaching out almost automatically for more and more power. The breakdown of traditional controls combined with the failure thus far to supply any adequate substitute is simply creating fools and madmen.

One can at last understand the point of view of those who decide to stand in the ancient ways and to assume towards much of what is deemed Progressive nowadays an attitude frankly dismissive. To be sure, the man who turns nowadays to the past for instruction is likely to be regarded as more or less a reactionary. One should "oppose to the aberrations of the hour the mass of universal history," from which can be derived the standards to judge those aberrations. A more familiar type is that of the Progressive who has repudiated the past, barely tolerates the present and is at home imaginatively only in the future. But a true, disciplined vision is needed if one is to profit by experience. Experience keeps a hard school, but fools will learn in no other. The type of vision that can bring to bear the experience of the remoter past upon our Democratic-Progressive era is not easy to attain but is very necessary if one is to appeal to history at all. If history were only a whirl of unrelated happenings that did not exhibit the workings of any central human law, one would have a right to dismiss any attempt to judge the present in the light of past experience. But it is not as easy as purging the illusions of men with the aid of reason and putting life once and for all into formulas.

The Left, in getting rid of conventions has also got rid of standards and abandoned itself to the mere flux of impressions. The problem of standards would be simple if all we had to do is oppose to anarchial liberty a sound set of general principles. So much experience has accumulated in both East and West that it should seem possible for those who are seeking to maintain standards and to fight Progressivism to come together, not only as to their general principles, but as to the main cases that arise in the application of them. But life resolves itself into a series of particular emergencies, and it is not always easy to bridge the gap between these emergencies and the general principle. It has been held by both Aristotle and Confucius that one should be guided in one's application of general principle by the law of measure.

The remedy for the failure of men at the top to curb their desires does not lie, as the Progressives would have us believe, in inflaming the desires of the man at the bottom, nor again in substituting for real justice some phantasmagoria of social justice. As the result of such a substitution one will presently turn from the punishment of the individual offender to an attack on the institution of property itself; and a war on capital will speedily degenerate into a war on thrift and industry in favor of laziness and incompetence, and finally into schemes of confiscation that profess to be idealistic and in fact are subversive of common honesty.

Among all the forms of dishonesty that assume this idealistic mask, perhaps none is more diabolically effective in unsettling the bases of civilized life than those that involve a tampering with the monetary standard. If property stands for work and if money is the conventional symbol of property, the ends of justice tend to be subverted if this symbol fluctuates wildly in value; thrift and foresight become meaningless; no man can be sure that he will receive according to his works. The various idealistic schemes that are being put forward by the Progressives, whether economic or political, are undermining the confidence that is the necessary basis of credit and exchange: so that the whole elaborate structure that has been reared by the industrial revolution is in danger of collapse.

The ordinary laboring man may not be able to see that the "levy upon capital" for which he is urged to vote in the name of social justice, will finally recoil upon himself. It is not yet clear that it is going to be possible to combine universal suffrage with the degree of safety for the institution of property that genuine justice and genuine civilization both require. Can those who tax in the name of the sovereign people be counted on to tax more equitably than those who alleged royal sovereignty?

The remedy for luxury and self-indulgence that have tended to increase with the breakdown of traditional standards-true simplicity of life-must be attained by the limitation of desire, while what Progressivism offers man might "devour creation without being satisfied." Freedom is better associated with an inner control. True liberty cannot be founded on indolence; it is something that must be won by high-handed struggle, one that takes place primarily in oneself and not in the outer world. We have conversely heard asserted the abstract right of whole populations to self-determination before they have achieved any degree of moral development. To put forward a right of this kind is to sink to the ultimate depth of humanitarian self-deception. To act according to the ethical will is to pull back, limit and select. The intellect must be present, and by that is meant the power in man that analyzes and discriminates, and traces causes and effects; for this power alone can determine whether the unity the mind has established among the facts is real or whether it exists only in some other realm.

Civilization is something must be deliberately willed; it is not something that gushes up from the depths of the unconscious. If there is a question of drift, there is only one direction in which one can drift and that is toward barbarism. The far-off event toward which all of Progressivism moves is the domination of the laboring class, with the understanding that the laboring class itself is to be dominated by the Lenin and Stalin of the day. The Left leaves desolation in its wake and calls it Progress. With the Progressive weakening of our traditional standards, the inability of the Left to supply any adequate substitute for the notion of unity is becoming apparent. We have reached the stage of the decadent Romans who, according to Livy, were unable to endure the evils from which they were suffering, and also the remedies for those evils. If men can really come together only in humble obeisance to something set above their ordinary selves, then the great temple of humanity which the Progressives profess to be erecting will be found to have been built on shifting sands.

The Progressive experiment shows signs of breaking down; the explanation is surely that it has failed thus far to achieve adequate equivalents for the traditional controls. Instead of setting up genuine standards, pulling back and then selecting with reference to them, disciplining his temperamental self, the men who profess to be modern have turned selection over to emotion and sought to substitute for the working of the ethical will a diffuse, unselective sympathy. This tendency to put on sympathy a burden that it cannot bear and at the same time to sacrifice a truly human hierarchy and scale of values to the principle of equality has been especially marked in the historical Progressive movement, nowhere more so perhaps than in the American Democrat Party.

The net result of the Progressive movement is a huge mass of standardized mediocrity; we are in danger of producing in the name of democracy one of the most trifling brands of the human species that the world has seen. What follows the decline of standards, and the disappearance of leaders is not some egalitarian paradise but inferior types of moral leadership. Democracy is an aristocracy of blackguards. As I watch America speed with invincible optimism down the road to destruction, I see the greatest tragedy in the history of mankind. If Democracy means simply the attempt to eliminate the qualitative and selective principle in favor of some general will then Rousseau will have succeeded.

If we go back to the beginning of our institutions, we find that America stood from the start for two different views of government that have their origin in different views of liberty and ultimately of human nature. The view that is set forth in the Declaration of Independence assumes that man has certain abstract rights; this idea is properly associated with Jefferson. The view that inspired our Constitution, as explained in the *Federalist,* is represented by Alexander Hamilton. The Jeffersonian liberal has faith in the goodness of the natural man, and so tends to overlook the need of a veto power in the individual or in the state. The men of whom I take Hamilton to be the type are less expansive in their attitudes. Just as man has a higher self that acts restrictively on his ordinary self, so, they hold, the state should have a higher or permanent self, appropriately embodied in institutions that should set bounds to its ordinary self, expressed by the popular will. Inner control upon the expansion of man's natural impulse is the indispensable check on democracy in keeping the balance between external control and the self. The idea that the state should have a permanent or higher self (the Senate and Executive) that is felt as a veto power upon its ordinary self (the Congress representing the people), rests ultimately upon the assertion of a similar dualism in the individual.

The best that the great teachers of antiquity can do for us is to help us to discover what is already present in ourselves. From this point of view, they are well-nigh indispensable. Those who attack the principle of self-control in human nature are attacking the wisdom of the ages and all its authentic representatives in both East and West. The belief in moral responsibility must be based on a belief in the possibility of an inner working of some kind with reference to standards. There is an opposition of first principles between those who maintain that the popular will should prevail, but only after it has been purified of what is merely impulsive and ephemeral, and those who maintain that this will should prevail immediately and unrestrictedly. The American experiment in democracy has from the outset been ambiguous and will remain so until the irrepressible conflict that is now looming has been concluded.

It is fortunate that the very word sovereignty does not occur in our Constitution. The men who made it were for granting a certain limited power here and another limited power somewhere else, and absolute power nowhere. The best scheme of government they conceived to be a system of checks and balances. They did not, however, look on the partial powers they bestowed as being on the same level. They were aware that true liberty requires a hierarchy and a subordination, that there must be something central in a state to which final appeal may be made in case of conflict. The complaint has been made that they left certain ambiguities in the articles that finally had to be clarified on the battlefield. But if they had been more explicit it is not probable that they would have been able to establish a union at all.

John Marshall deserves special praise for the clearness with which he saw that the final center of control in the type of government that was being founded; if control was to have an ethical basis and not be another name for force, it must be vested in the judiciary, particularly in the Supreme Court. This court, especially in its most important function, that of interpreting the Constitution, must, he perceived, embody more than any other institution the higher or permanent self of the state. With a sound and independent judiciary, above all a sound and independent supreme bench, liberty and democracy may after all be able to coexist. Personal liberty and the security of private property, which is almost inseparable from it, were to be closely bound up with the fortunes of the Supreme Court.

Prior to the Civil War the Jeffersonian doctrine was developed with logical rigor by Calhoun whereas the opposite view was carried through no less uncompromisingly by the abolitionists. The result, instead of being settled on ethical lines, had to be submitted to the arbitration of force. The man who grasps the full import of the conflict between the liberty of the unionist and that of the Jeffersonian has been put into possession of the key that unlocks American history. There is no clearer proof of an uncritical discrimination than when expressing piety towards both Jefferson and Marshall, as each stood for incompatible things. John Quincy Adams said: "Marshall has cemented the Union which the crafty and quixotic democracy of Jefferson had a perpetual tendency to dissolve."

By his preoccupation with the question of the union, Lincoln was the true successor of Hamilton and Marshall. The type of constitutional liberty that we owe these men is one of the greatest blessings vouchsafed to any people. And yet we are in danger of losing it. Our present drift away from constitutional freedom can be understood only with reference to the Progressive crumbling of traditional standards and the rise of a philosophy, that, in its treatment of specifically human problems has been utilitarian, in the way that Christianity gave way to humanitarianism.

Progressivism has undermined in no small measure the unifying influences of the past-the Church, the family, and a traditional education. Sentimental idealism has tended to take the place of religion. The Progressive does not seek to get at evil in the heart of the individual, so that he is finally forced to resort to outer regulation. The basis on which the whole structure of the new ethics has been reared is the assumption that the significant struggle between good and evil is not in the individual but in society. Man is morally responsible but is always trying to dodge that responsibility; what he suffers is not fate but a spiritual supineness. His self-flattery is closely related in turn to his moral indolence. The essence of man's spiritual indolence is that he does not wish to look up to standards and discipline himself with reference to them. Man does not want an adjustment of his natural will to some higher one, because of the moral effort it implies. He wills the ends, because they are clearly desirable, but he does not will the means because they are difficult and disciplinary. If one agrees, this then transfers the work of morality to the outer world.

Livy is a bit idyllic when he exclaims: "Where will you find in one man this modesty and uprightness and loftiness of spirit that then belonged to a whole people?" If one compares the Rome of the Republic with the Rome of the Empire one is conscious of a real decline. The Senate that had seemed to Cineas, the adviser of Pyrrhus, an assembly of demigods, had become by the time of Tiberius a gathering of cringing sycophants. Horace was uttering only the sober truth when he proclaimed the progressive degeneracy of the Romans of his time. The most significant symptom of this degeneracy seemed to him and other observers to be the relaxation of the bonds of the family. The family is the natural biological group, the normal milieu of shared experiences, community of interests and integration of personality. But the moral and educational functions of the family are more and more entrusted to external, depersonalized government agencies which simulate the form of familial function, but which are entirely devoid of its content. "In youth as in age, in work as in play, in physical care as in education and morals, there remains a vital function which only such a face-to-face relation as the biological family can fulfill. No artifice of the social scientist or community agency can replace this relationship as a medium for the development and integration of human personality. The life of the family is the life which actual fathers, mothers and children live in one another's company. Unless there are opportunities for individuals to grow and to realize their potentialities through free contact with one another, the most highly perfected pattern of the sociologist will be only an empty formula." The benefits of families long ago surrendered to the Progressive order, whose patterns of conduct are incompatible with the conditions necessary to the stability and integrity of family life. The institution of various palliative measures by Progressives may serve to postpone the hour of reckoning, may stabilize conditions for a time, but requires considerable optimism to believe them a long-term solution. The most that is offered to the poor is the bleak assurance that no serious physiological want will overtake him; but the men, women and children will have no humanized living, their being caught in the throes of therapeutic government. But getting and consuming is more than just the process of production. Those with meaningful work would not have to look forward to the demoralizing aspect of the dole, allowing them to knit together the fragments of lives now broken on the wheel of what we call humanitarian compassion. We must have the courage to submit the humanitarian zeal to a closer scrutiny. The Progressives never ask whether a man is an underdog because he has already had his opportunity and failed to use it as a result of his own misconduct, indolence and inattention.

The just man is he who, as a result of his moral choices based on due deliberation, choices in which he is moved primarily by a regard for his own happiness, has quelled the unruly impulses of his lower nature and so attained to some degree of unity with himself. At the same time, as with religion, he will find that he is moving toward a common center with others who have been carrying through a similar task of self-conquest. A state that is controlled by men who have been minding their own business will be a just state that will also mind its own business; it will be of service, not by meddling in commercial or economic affairs but by setting a good example. A state of this kind may hope to find a basis of understanding with any other state that is also ethically controlled.

The maintenance of our constitutional tradition is indissolubly bound up with the maintenance of standards. The democratic contention that everybody should have a chance is excellent provided it means that everybody is to have the chance to measure up to high standards. If the democratic extension of opportunity is, on the other hand, made a pretext for lowering standards, democracy is, insofar, incompatible with civilization. One might be more confident of the outcome of the struggle if the problem of standards was being dealt with more adequately in our education system. The tendency is to discard standards in favor of ideals, and these ideals recognize very imperfectly that man needs to be disciplined to a law of his own, distinct from the law of physical nature.

The ethos of the larger community is derived from habit. If a community is to transmit certain kinds of habits to its young, it must normally come to some kind of agreement as to what habits are desirable; it must in the literal meaning of that word achieve a convention. Without a convention of some kind, it is hard to see how the experience of the past can be brought to bear on the present. The civilization of a community and ultimately the government of which it is capable is closely related to the type of education on which it has agreed. "The best laws," says Aristotle, "will be of no avail unless the young are trained by habit and education in the spirit of the constitution." Aristotle complained that this great principle was being violated in his time. Is it being observed in ours? Assuming that what we wish to preserve is a federal and constitutional republic, are we training up a class of leaders whose ethos is in intimate accord with this type of government? The answer is obviously no. The old education with its classical element was training for wisdom and character. The new education suggests a radical break with our traditional ethos. It is training for service and power. It is not in any sense supplying us with standards. To have standards means practically to select and reject; and this means one must discipline one's feelings to some ethical center. If the discipline is to be effective so that a man will discern the right things, it is necessary that it should become a matter of habit, and that almost from infancy. One cannot wait until the child has reached the so-called age of reason, until he is in position to do his own selecting, for in the meanwhile he may have developed bad habits. This is the true prison in danger of closing in on children.

Man is caught between two infinities, one of smallness and one of magnitude, and despite his education he is equally unable to fully grasp either, so that the essence of things eludes him and may forever elude him. If at any time he thinks he has found a firm foundation on which to rear a tower, this foundation suddenly fails him, and he has no assurance that his knowledge is real knowledge or anything more than a dream. But the most humbling aspect of man is this inability of unaided reason to effectively control his outer impressions and expansive desires. He does not want to be limited in his dominant desire, whatever that may be. He wishes to be free to pursue his folly, as Erasmus would say, and finally discovers the limits established in the nature of things by the somewhat painful process of colliding with them. In short, he harbors incompatible desires and so listens eagerly to those who encourage him to think that it is possible to have the good thing without paying the appointed price. The self-flattery that encourages the huddling together of incompatible desires has never been pushed further than in the instant gratification of the Progressive movement. One is forced to conclude that an outstanding human trait is a prodigious and pathetic gullibility. The chief corrective of gullibility is a strong dose of reality.

No one is more reckless in his attacks on personal liberty than the apostle of the aforementioned "service." He is prone in his furtherance of his schemes of "uplift" not only to ascribe unlimited sovereignty to society but as against the individual. Progressives do not reveal an adequate sense of the nature of obligation and of the special type of effort it imposes. As a result of their shallowness, they are in danger of substituting for real justice the fantasy of social justice. Social justice means in practice class justice, which means class war, and that, if we are to go by the experience of past and present, means disaster. The inadequacy of social justice, with its tendency to undermine the moral responsibility of the individual and at the same time obscure the need for standards and leadership, to count practically justice in the abstract, and ignore the just man, is the determiner of its bad outcomes. Some of the inequalities that the collectivist criticizes are no doubt the result of unethical competition but the remedy for these inequalities is surely not the pursuit of such chimeras as social or economic equality, at the risk of sacrificing the one form of equality that is valuable: equality before the Law. We are gradually being deprived of our liberties on the ground that their sacrifice is necessary to the good of society. If we attend carefully to the psychology of the persons who manifest such an eagerness to serve us, we shall find that they are even more eager to control us. There is a growing will to power. Progressives seem to be turning more and more to social "service", which means they have been substituting for the truths of the inner life various causes and movements, reforms and crusades. In their schemes for service, they are led to make light of the constitutional checks on their authority and reach out for unlimited Authority.

It is evident that we are not coping adequately with the special problem of democracy; that we are combining the strength of giants with the critical intelligence of children. If regeneration were to gain a hold, the followers of Progressive leaders would finally be forced to ask themselves whether the ideals with which they were being beguiled really mean anything, or at all events anything more than the masking in fine phrases of the desire to get one's hand into the other citizen's pocket. Sham spirituality is especially promoted by the blurring of distinctions, which is itself promoted by a tampering of general terms, a specialty of the Left.

The moral realist will pay no more attention to the fine phrases in which ideals of their kind are clothed and refuse to shift, in the name of sympathy or social justice, or on any other ground, the struggle between good and evil from the individual to society. If we restore the moral struggle to the individual, we are brought back at once to the assertion of the truths of the inner life. It is humanitarianism crusading as a substitute for the inner life which is breaking down. One suspects that the popularity of the gospel of service is due to the fact that it is flattering to unregenerate human nature. It is pleasant to think that one may dispense with the inner obeisance of the spirit to standards, provided one be eager to do something for humanity. We are rapidly becoming a nation of humanitarian crusaders. We must develop a sounder type of vision than that of the Progressive "reformers." It is growing too evident that the drift toward license is being accelerated rather than arrested by their multiplication of "reformative" laws. The first step is to perceive that the alternative to a constitutional liberty is not a legalistic millennium, but a triumph of anarchy followed by a triumph of force. The time will come when a predominant element in our population, having grown more and more impatient of the ballot box and representative government, of constitutional limitations and judicial control, will display a growing eagerness for direct action.

The conception of liberty found in Roman law reflects Stoic rationalism, and like all Greek and Roman political philosophy, is ready to sacrifice in an unwarranted measure the individual to the state. By the *lex regia* the Roman people made over its unbounded power to the emperor. The reasons for this bear investigation and comparison to our present circumstances. At the instigation of the demagogues the Roman people had refused to limit themselves and had at the same time tended toward the type of equality that is won at the expense of quality and the due subordination to standards that quality always requires. So far as our modern democracies are pursuing a merely quantitative equality, their fate would seem to be foreshadowed by this Roman development. The moment comes, when the concentration of power in the hands of one man is felt as a relief from the irresponsible tyranny of the mob. This is the process by which a radical democracy passes over into what is a decadent, tyrannical imperialism.

The Progressive is tending to conceive of the state in a more and more absolute fashion. There can be no retreat. He feels that its power should suffer no restriction when it is seeking to promote what they feel is socially useful, the greatest good of the greatest number. The underlying fallacy of the Progressive is that he conceives of the greatest good and of happiness in general in terms of pleasure or else in terms of a merely outer working. But a man bent on self-improvement passes, as he mounts the scale, from an outer to an inner working. The individual is to impose progressively his developing ethical will, affirmed as an immediate fact of consciousness, upon his outgoing desires. By restraint and control the wise man makes for himself "an island which no flood may overwhelm," in Buddha's terms. Society is bound to protect itself against the unrestraint of the individual, but if it is not to push this necessary assertion of its authority to an oppressive extreme, it needs to take cognizance not only of outer working but encourage an inner working that is the final source of sound individualism. A sound individualist must have standards obtained, not by leaning on an outer authority but by the cooperation of his intellect and imagination. The standards he has thus secured he will proceed to press into the service of the ethical will. If a man is to be self-reliant, he must have sound standards and then be free to act on them. To secure the standards he needs intellect and to act on them he needs will. If we are to gain any hold on the present situation, we need to develop a little moral gravity and intellectual seriousness. We shall then see the strength of traditional doctrines as compared with the modernist position when faced with the facts of evil.

Christianity supplied what was lacking in Greek philosophy. It set up doctrines that humbled reason and created symbols that controlled man's imagination and through the imagination controlled his will. By its separation of the things of God and the things of Caesar, Christianity established a domain of personal liberty and free conscience, in which the individual might take refuge from the encroachments of the omnipotent state. On this basis it was possible to reconstruct European civilization after the Greco-Roman collapse in the midst of barbarian invasions. But this work was accomplished at the expense of the critical spirit and resulted in the triumph of a humbling Authority "anterior, exterior and superior" to the individual. When the higher will is conceived as divine and revealed, the effect is to force human life into a rigid and definitive mold. Men were asked to believe a thing because it was absurd, and ignorance was declared to be the mother of devotion. The church was enabled to carry on all the more effectively the work of regeneration from the fact that men had ceased to be self-reliant and ceased like the Socratic Greek to rely on the intellect. Rousseau asks: "is righteousness, then, the daughter of ignorance?" It is plain that Rousseau does not propose to leave the individual any such refuge.

The real emancipation of the intellect got under way with the Renaissance. Men were becoming self-reliant again and in almost the same measure were losing their humility. They were inclining once more, like the ancient Greeks, to look on life primarily as a problem of knowledge. Only the knowledge they sought was not the ethical knowledge at which Socrates aimed but knowledge of the natural order. Ethical knowledge had come to be indissolubly associated with incomprehensible dogmas. An acute conflict was inevitable in the hearts of men, between the old humility and the new spirit of intellectual inquiry.

The later Reformation, by its underlying postulates, sought to recover the authentic Christian doctrine that seemed to have been perverted by the Roman theocracy. It urged the individual to take a critical attitude toward this theocracy, urging him at first to exercise the right of private judgment, which is to encourage him to be self-reliant. But the Pauline and Augustinian forms that Calvin and Luther sought to revive were ultimately designed to make man feel his utter and helpless dependence on the divine will. Under the religious order spiritual control had its final source and sanction in the doctrine of grace. It may be said of Progressives, as it was of Christianity's extreme partisans, that they have simply repudiated self-reliance.

Traditional education aimed to produce leaders whose basis of leadership was not commercial or industrial efficacy but wisdom. Can anything so purely expansive as service supply an adequate counterpoise to the pursuit of unethical power? Can the proper counterpoise be more likely sought in the cultivation of the principle of inner control, first of all in the individual, the family, and finally in the state? There is a real relation between the older educational standards that thus acted restrictively on the temperament of the individual and the older political standard embodied in institutions like the Constitution, the Senate and Supreme Court, that serve as a check on the ordinary or impulsive will of the people. We have been permitting Progressives and their ilk an influence on our education that amounts in the aggregate to a national calamity; we need educational leaders who will have less to say about service and more to say of culture and civilization. Idealism is firmly entrenched in this country, especially in academic circles, where it seems to be held more confidently and smugly with each succeeding year. The gap between what men do and what they ought to do is turning out to be even wider than in Machiavelli's time.

The new education does not meet the Aristotelian requirement: it is not in intimate correspondence with our form of government. If the veto power disappears from our individual formation of character, there is no reason to anticipate that it will long survive in the state. The spirit of the leaders will not be that which should preside over a Constitutional Republic. The older education was based on the belief that men need to be disciplined to some ethical center. The Left contrarily assumes that men can come together expansively and on the level of their ordinary selves. All standards are suspect. They oppose a definite curriculum which aims at some humanistic discipline which might inhibit an individual to freely develop his bent or temperamental proclivity. The standard or common measure is compromised by the assertion of this supposed right, and in about the same measure the effort and spirit of emulation that the standard stimulates disappear.

Burke wrote: "They are so taken up with the rights of man that they have totally forgotten his nature." Under cover of getting rid of prejudice they would strip man of all the habits and concrete relationships and networks of historical circumstance in which he is actually implicated and finally leave him shivering "in all the nakedness and solitude of metaphysical abstraction." In his attack on the enemies of prejudice, by which was meant practically everything that is traditional and prescriptive, Burke showed that the traditional forms are in no small measure the long-funded experience of any particular community, without which the state loses historical continuity, its permanent self that unites its present with its past and future.

The imagination has been drawn away more and more from the element of unity in things to the element of diversity. As a result of the type of progress that has been proclaimed, everything good has come to be associated with novelty and change, with the piling up of discovery on discovery. Life, thus viewed, no longer involves any reverence for some center or oneness, but is conceived as an infinite and indefinite expansion of wonder and curiosity. As a result of all this intoxication with change, the world is moving toward some far-off event. That event is Rousseau's state of nature requiring no serious moral effort or self-discipline on the part of the individual.

The star of Burke is manifestly fading while a great part of Rousseau's teachings is passing into contemporary politics. The main purpose of the Progressives seems to "ruin the great work of time." The Progressive is assuming that his age is so unique that all past experience has become obsolete. As loyalty to the great traditions declined, the path was prepared for the utilitarian industrial revolution. The battle for prejudice and prescription-a "wisdom above reflection" -has already been lost. It is no longer possible to wave aside the modernists as the mere noisy insects of the hour. Yet Burke will be cherished as long as anyone survives in the world who has a perception of the nature of true liberty. Burke's final emphasis is not on the state but the individual. In getting the standards by which the individual may hope to surpass his ordinary self, and achieve humanism, he would have him lean heavily on prescription. He would not set the individual to trading on his own private stock of knowledge; rather, he would have him respect the general sense, the accumulated experience of the past that has become embodied in the habits and usages that are otherwise dismissed as prejudice. According to Burke, the basis for right conduct is not just reasoning but experience, and experience much wider than that of the individual, the secure possession of which can result only from the early acquisitions of right habits. A man may realize in his ancestors a standard of virtue and wisdom beyond the vulgar practice of the hour; so that he may be enabled to rise with the example to whose imitation he has aspired.

Burke's writings had their best effect on England and America; it was Rousseau who exercised the strongest influence in France. He held that absolute political equality was the essential condition of political freedom, and that no diversities of power, or representations of classes, or of interests, would be suffered to exist in the Constitution. Every man should have a vote and a vote of the same value. The French Constitution of 1793 completed his vision of democratic equality. It was under this system-the most bloody and tyrannical assembly of which history has any record-that the Convention was elected. The year when this Constitution was enacted was one of the most tragic in French history. It was the year when the ancient monarchy was overthrown; when the King and Queen were brought to the scaffold; when the flower of the French nation were mown down by the guillotine or scattered as ruined exiles over Europe; when the war with England began which raged with scant intermission for more than twenty years. In strong reaction to the horrors of the Revolution France moved on by steady stages to the absolute despotism of Napoleon. It is curious and melancholy to observe how Rousseau's doctrine of the omnipotence of numbers and the supreme value of political equality is displacing in the United States all the old axioms upon which American liberty once rested. It is virtually disfranchising loyalty, property and intelligence, along with any last chance at self-government.

The forms and traditions that Burke defends, on the ground that they are not arbitrary but are convenient summing up of a vast body of past experience, which draws the individual back to an ethical center, supplies in turn a standard with reference to which the individual may set bounds to the lawless expansion of his natural self. Burke's conception of liberty is the nice adjustment between the taking on of inner control and the throwing off of outer control. This adjustment between inner and outer control, which concerns primarily the individual, determines at the last degree to which any community is capable of political liberty. "To form a free government-that is, to temper together these opposite elements of liberty and restraint in one consistent work, requires much thought, deep reflection, and sagacious, powerful and combining minds."

It is well to open one's mind only as a preparation for the supreme act of judgment and selection. What makes the Socratic group at Athens and the scientific investigator today seem so respectable, when compared with the emotionalist, is that they ask, first of all, not whether a man is sincere, but whether he is right or wrong. Truth is less congenial to human nature than error, because it imposes limitations, whereas error does not.

CHAPTER ONE- A SHORT HISTORY OF HISTORY

ISABEL PATERSON
ROSE WILDER LANE

"You told my father, Shah Jehan, that you would teach me philosophy. 'Tis true, I remember very well, that you have entertained us for many years with airy questions of things that afford no satisfaction at all to the mind, and are of no use in human society, empty notions and mere fancies, that have only this in them, that they are very hard to understand and very easy to forget…I still remember, that after you had thus amused me, I know not how long, with your fine philosophy, all I retained of it was a multitude of barbarous and dark words, proper to bewilder, perplex and tire out the best wits, and only invented the better to cover the vanity and ignorance of men like yourself, that you would make us believe that you know all, and that under those obscure and ambiguous words are hidden great mysteries which you alone are capable to understand."

"If you had instead seasoned me with that philosophy which formeth the mind to ratiocination, and insensibly accustoms it to be satisfied with nothing but solid reasons, if you had given me those excellent precepts and doctrines which raise the soul above the assaults of fortune, and reduce her to an unshakable and always equal temper, and permit her not to be lifted up by prosperity nor debased by adversity; if you had taken care to give me the knowledge of what we are and what are the first principles of things, and had assisted me in forming in my mind a fit idea of the greatness of the universe, and of the admirable order and motion of the parts thereof; if you had taught me how to distinguish all the states of the world; well to understand their strengths, their way of fighting, their customs, religions, governments and interests; to observe their rise, progress and decay; and whence, how, and by what accidents and errors those great changes and revolutions of empires and kingdoms have happened. If, I say you had instilled into me this kind of philosophy, I should think myself incomparably more obliged to you than Alexander was to his Aristotle and believe it my duty to recompense you otherwise than he did him."

Aurangzeb (1618-1707), sixth Mughal emperor (India) to his former tutor

"To one small people, covering in its original seat no more than a handsbreadth of territory, it was given to create the principle of Progress, of movement onwards and not backwards or downwards, of destruction tending to construction. That people were the Greeks. Except for the blind forces of Nature, nothing moves in this world which is not Greek in its origin. A ferment spreading from the source has vitalized all the great advancing races of mankind, penetrating from one to another, and producing results accordant with its hidden and latent genius, and results of course often far greater than any exhibited by Greece itself."

Sir Henry Sumner Maine

All historians seek a philosophy of history: the recorded effort of man to reduce the multiplicity of past events to a measure of unity by looking for some pervading purpose and significance, some law of sequence and causation, some illumination for the present and the future. To the early Greeks man and the human race were episodes in the world-process, which repeated itself forever according to like laws. Greek thinkers attempted to discover the nature of the abiding essence which manifested itself in these eternal cycles. They had no philosophy of history as of yet, saw no meaning in history as such. A philosophy of history attempts to impose order on the mixed and incoherent content of time; alternatively, some may prefer to reconstruct this particular scene or that unrelated period. Some prefer the Renaissance, some like better the Periclean age; others are Platonists, Aristotelians, Stoics or Epicureans. It was not until the Hellenistic-Roman period that a definite philosophy of history appeared, based upon the doctrines of Christianity. Man was regarded as a personality endowed with freedom but convicted of sin; his earthly sojourn was a period in which he should purge himself of that sin through faith, in order to return to heaven at the end of life. The doctrine of the temporal finitude of the earth, with corporeal resurrection, as a culmination, marks probably the first attempt on the part of man to conceive the flux of events historically or teleologically. Europe owes to Christianity, even today, the small species of unity that has survived among its members. But this teleology has no affinity with our modern progress, for it was based upon a belief in the innate depravity of man's nature and upon a denial of all value to earthly existence. Still, some look hopefully to Christianity and its two Testaments, with their very ancient and obscure origins, and their muddled contents. That even after two wars in which the men of the two chief Protestant countries were blowing each other up with high explosives, at the same time they sought to starve one another's women and children en masse. All such teleologies are replete with as much accident and uncertainty as the time we ourselves are living in. Voltaire, the wisest man of his age, said "I want to know what were the steps by which men passed from barbarism to civilization." The change from primitive to civilized man is here presented as a slow development with certain intermediary stages forming a more logical philosophy of history. Our observations will allow some insight concerning the question.

In 325 BC a Greek colonial navigator sailed from the port of Massilia (Marseilles) through the Straights of Gibraltar, past Sagres Point, up the coast of Spain and France, around the British Isles, and possibly as far as Iceland, then called Ultima Thule. Others had preceded him: it had been the trade route of Phoenician merchant ships for centuries-tin from Cornwall and amber from the Baltic were delivered to the markets in the East for the profit of Carthage, which drew its riches from its position as intermediary. When Pytheas made his voyage, the Punic Wars and the Roman Empire were still in the future. The midland waterway between the great continents of classical antiquity-Europe, Asia and Africa-spawned a thousand years of wars running through the history of the Phoenicians. The swirl of these conflicts always led in one direction which, in the extant view of geography made no sense, for it pointed toward the open ocean.

It was the Phoenicians who built Solomon's Palace, and later the Temple, supplying materials, transport and skilled labor-cedars hewed to measure in Lebanon, stone dressed at the quarry and elaborate metal work wrought to specifications-so that the royal house was raised, according to scripture, "without the sound of hammer or axe or any tool of iron." When Solomon sent out ships of his own, they went out under Phoenician convoy. Their sphere of authority shifted progressively from Sidon and Tyre to their last capital city, central on a line from Syria to Spain. Carthage, their final and supreme achievement, was located at a position between sea and desert, at the nexus of the trading energy of three continents.

With the Greeks they had held their own fairly well in the ongoing fight. Neither side proved capable of keeping their colonies in strict confederation; the subsidiary cities changed sides under pressure and made their own treaties when they dared. Some element in each system was lacking, to hold them together. The conflict of Greece and Carthage may properly be called a trade war. They were in competition for stations, goods, charters, and customers. Possibly Rome, at that time, was a permanent settlement as a local trading center but was otherwise comparatively negligible. For international trade Rome was badly placed. But commerce and contractual relations were present and were inextricably interwoven into Rome's later political success.

Compared to Greece, just then Carthage was probably ahead in economic organization and technical knowledge and had the greatest number of ships under single command, monopolizing the most extensive provinces rich in natural resources-especially Hispania. Within fifty years, Rome, thrust between the two, commenced the long, bitter effort that broke the Phoenician power, razed the walls of Carthage, and left the site a waste. Nor did the Greeks benefit by the ruin of their mighty antagonist-the subjection of Greece was to follow at nearly the same time.

What happened when Carthage was destroyed was of immense and permanent importance. It portended the rise of Europe, and the subsidence, in the balance of world power, of the Eastern Hemisphere. The process had been brought thus far by the Phoenicians and could only be further effected through Rome. Pytheas opened the door. He is remembered over others because he was a scientist and merchant adventurer who wrote a narrative of his voyage, often quoted by Strabo. Pytheas made valuable contributions to the exact mathematical science of astronomy, applied in navigation; he was able to make his exploration and safe return while the Carthaginians were under attack from Syracuse, leaving the Straits insufficiently guarded. He was disparaged, as his observations contradicted orthodox theory. Pytheas was accused of lying about what he saw with his own eyes, by men who had never been there at all. He faced a political ban while alive and censure after his death. He had shown the way, where the Phoenicians, for all their shrewdness and hardihood and their factual priority, did not; because he was endowed with the rare combination of disinterested curiosity, speculative intellect, and active enterprise, qualities which impelled him to slip through an official barrier of the utmost rigor, protected by both myth and naval power, to try the chances of the unknown. Pytheas ranks among the notable discoverers, along with Galileo, as an example of the free mind. He could not know he was looking toward America.

Limiting the flow of trade had otherwise backed the Phoenicians up against the deserts of Africa, while Rome represented the head of the channeled forces. Nations are not powerful because they possess, like Carthage, wide lands, safe ports, large navies, huge armies, fortifications, stores, money, and credit. They acquire and sustain these advantages because they are powerful, having devised on correct principles the political structure which allows the process of growth to take its proper course. The question is how? The available outlets to either benefit or destruction are always the same. Economic determinism failed, sea-power failed, Hannibal's land invasion failed; in the second century BC Carthage and Greece themselves fell. In the modern era a wrong move is even more appalling, in the extent of its consequences, as evidenced in two world wars.

In historical perspective, the Phoenicians are unique; though they had a tremendous and active part in the events of their time, it was that of antagonist. On the instant of their disappearance, they faded into unreality, leaving little residue. We do not feel they bequeathed us anything substantial, to become incorporate with our bones, woven into the texture of our lives. This is more paradoxical, since our inheritance from Greece and Rome consists of abstractions; while the Phoenicians were practical and did succeed with a kind of international organization. Above all, they touched the points where our vital ideas originated. Their activity stimulated Greece to inquiry and forced Rome to expand; they erected the Temple at Jerusalem and took in pledge the humble villages of Galilee. They were carriers and catalysts. Yet we seem to always start *de novo* with Greece and Rome. The Phoenicians were a phenomenon which their political mechanism could not accommodate. In human affairs all that survives is what men think. As a nation, the Phoenicians disintegrated from the impact of new ideas.

The art of Greece was self-contained and static. Their sculpture was fixed in an immutable perfection of a chosen type. It escapes limitation, in countless statues, by the timeless quality of a moment of beauty saved and set apart in defiance of the eternal flux. In their social system the Greeks were also at a dead end. Their divinities enjoined no moral order, representing rather the indifferent caprice of nature toward man. The gods had become remote; for educated men they were relegated to poetic fancy. As a consequence, the Greeks tended to regard the universe as pure phenomena. The Athenians, being open to commerce, for a time took license to think. Trade and travel enabled them to make comparative observations; they were eager to hear new things. The idea they evolved, taken by itself, was a solvent of such institutions as they possessed; it aggravated the peril in which they stood by further attenuating the social fabric. Yet they formulated it courageously; and it was their contribution to the future. Pytheas embodied it. The Greeks had the idea of Science.

Most advanced societies established on tradition see knowledge as given and final; hence further investigation is apt to be forbidden as impious. The Greeks had their premonitory fables of Prometheus and Icarus. They nevertheless perceived that all knowledge might be interconnected and capable of indefinite enlargement by rational inquiry. They examined the processes of the intellect, sharpened and tested their minds, to concentrate on generalizations and search for axioms. Inconsistently, they expressed contempt for practical application. The application of science to production requires assured possession of private property, free labor, and time enough to return benefits for the effort and capital expended. With the Greeks, the hopeless instability of democracy allowed no security of the individual against the mass or of the nation against external attack. Yet this extraordinary denial may have some use in the circumstances, by stressing the intrinsic value of thought. But the implication the Greeks put aside was ultimately inescapable. Science is the rule of reason. It is the clear seeing, exact recording, impartial testing, and slow accumulation of a knowledge objective enough to generate prediction and control. Instead of being resigned to an inexorable, repeating destiny or blind chance, it might be possible, by discerning the causation of events, to order them at will, and bring about what men desire. An abstraction can move a mountain; nothing can withstand an idea. The Greeks had found the lever.

While Greece philosophized, Rome overpowered them. This would seem a victory of gross substance, a refutation of the concealed premise of the superiority of mind over matter. But Rome had itself evolved an abstraction, a political concept, which was likewise among the universals. Rome had the idea of Law. All nations have had laws; the most primitive savages were bound by custom, and a binding custom is a law. Primitive people thought their laws were permanent even though perhaps arbitrary. The effective meaning was that custom may alter only by imperceptible degrees, if it is to remain valid. What may happen by war, pestilence or migration, or even by innovations otherwise beneficial, is a period of confusion, in which habit is interrupted and expedients tried. Since custom cannot meet change quickly, and above an elementary level of culture there will be occasional necessity for deciding a course of action which must affect the group, an informal council and leader comprised the next obvious development. The simultaneous evolution, alongside of secular government, of a priesthood, with moral authority, was also to be observed. Division of powers, or opposed agencies of moral authority and physical power, were necessary in the institution of government to secure stability. But all of these forms of association were effective only in appropriate conditions and had their innate defects. Custom could not deal with the unexpected. Inspired leadership will not serve with organized institutions. Monarchy becomes despotic. Each type of association is suitable to certain circumstances but will either break down or become fused into rigidity when it is asked to do more than it was intended to accommodate. At that point, reason must define the prime source of Authority, to invest it with a viable form.

By such a sequence Rome became a political laboratory. What went into the crucible must be deduced from the myths, legends, traditions and institutions which took shape in the obscure centuries of the city's early history. Having its inception in trade, using money and holding land as private property; these were elements of an advanced civilization. Rome was more or less an open city, admitting refugees, immigrants and exiles, bringing varied customs which must be reconciled under general rules. Distinctively, one had to be born a Greek, but one could become a Roman. Being already far advanced beyond custom and leadership, and aware of the incompetence of democracy, the Romans were obliged to solve the problem of government, in rational terms, working with what they had.

The family as the social unit, offset by Contract law in respect of property, made the individual Patriarchs the political unit. There were clans of ancient local stock comprising an aristocracy and a large miscellaneous population, the plebians. From the beginning the city of Rome was a federation, comprised of permanent bases and structure, the elements of architecture. The civic tribes, the patrician families and the members of the Senate were the arches and keystones. The individual citizen's double fealty, to family and state, gave the overlap of the courses. They established rotation in consular office, restricted to a fixed and short tenure, in which the office-seeker was not eligible for re-election. That provision was sound, for the sole object of setting a term is to get the incumbent out. The Romans also watched their generals closely, forbidding even a victorious one from re-entering the city without formal permission. Political offices were mainly vested in the aristocracy, and were partly elective, partly appointive. As both voters and officeholders were owners of property, they had a solid interest in keeping the nation a going concern, with a concomitant obligation for defense. But the unique stroke of political genius was that the Roman state made provision not only for delay but for positive deadlock. The power of the plebs, through their tribunes, was outright obstruction. The tribunes could not initiate any measure, but they could stop the works, and their persons were sacred. Nothing is more essential to the welfare of a nation than the countercheck on government, by legitimate means. The Roman system became possible by defining the source of authority; its stresses became strength, and control was ensured by separating the function of the executive agency and the veto. The Romans possessed from very early times the conception of *jus,* which is wider than that of positive law laid down by authority and denotes an order morally binding on the members of the community, both human and divine. This idea of Law, as an abstract concept, was not predicated by custom, leadership, council or king; nor was it compatible with democracy. With all these, Authority was arbitrary, being either given in the particular custom, or lodged in persons by precedence (parenthood or seniority) or assigned to numbers. The Romans affirmed a moral order in the universe itself.

Needless to say, the actuality fell far short of the ideal. Penalties in Roman law were excessive and cruel. Slavery and class privileges were legal institutions; they cannot exist otherwise. Equality before the law was limited to freemen; a debtor risked slavery. But to sentimentalize Roman law and gloss over its harsh and faulty aspects is to miss the point. Its solid virtue was its mere existence, since at worst it proved preferable to the unpredictable will of either king or people. The quality of Roman law was that it was dependable. In Roman law a man must be charged with a specified act having known penalties, and convicted on something more positive than opinion, to incur sentence. The famous example of the Apostle Paul invoking his rights as a Roman citizen, in making an appeal to Caesar showed that a poor street preacher, of the working class, under arrest, and with enemies in high places, had only to claim his civil rights and none could deny him. Here the whole historic *process* becomes apparent in its imperial fulfillment.

The value of the idea of Law in its primary use of framing legislation is clear. It sets moral sanctions above force, while recognizing human fallibility. Men made the statutes; and it was understood that a statute might be inequitable or ill advised, but a bad law reflected on the legislators who made it. Statutes were open to change, without impairing the majesty of the Law in principle. The means of repeal or alteration were provided, without recourse to violence. Thus, the idea of Law answered to Reason. Finally, the Law posited that a man had rights that must be respected, and which he could forfeit only by his own act. Though not all men were free, the condition of a free man had been defined. And since freedom was found to be inherent in the order of the universe, logic must ask in time why all men were not free.

The practical employment of the concept of Law in founding the Empire began with international relations. Their habit of mind made the Romans more reliable in keeping treaties and more steadfast against reverses, and therefore made their alliance desired. Legal clarity could likewise serve to specify bearable terms to those conquered. Citizenship was formulated as a legal condition rather than an accident of birth and could be bestowed on the people of another nation. The former local governments could be left with subsidiary authority; no change of custom was forced upon the people; and the risk of revolt was minimized. Under stress, the citizens as individuals could cling to Rome for protection against local tyranny, as Paul did in Jerusalem; for Roman law was super-territorial, like canon law in the Middle Ages.

Time and distance are the two factors which necessitate formal government. Each type is suited to certain time-space relations of individuals to one another and to their environment. The appropriate scope or dimension becomes evident in territorial size estimated with the co-efficient of the speed of transport and communication. When confined to its appropriate area, the political structure of the Roman Republic was the strongest that had yet been devised. In the end, though, even the arm of Roman law was unequal to the geographic reach and retractive action was demanded by such an unprecedented spread of the field. Rome was literally torn apart in the civil wars of the Triumvirate, and the Republic did perish.

The Empire was formed by a community that produced its own livelihood, including the personnel and maintenance of the army; energy originated within. It could meet extraordinary demands in war because the normal expenses of the state were moderate. As the Empire grew the energy came from outside as money flowed into Rome from external sources. To adapt the disrupted mechanism of Rome to the new potentials the internal parts had to be adjusted again by a semi-automatic nexus and distributor. The new position was something like a crude fuse plug, which may blow out but provides a measure of safety in certain contingencies. If one failed, another was thrown in the gap by the turn of events. A man could be the emperor, as long as he lasted. He had to take the incoming current and re-distribute it outward. Various men-Caesar, Cicero and Antony-died by violence, which was their natural end, since they represented the instruments in collision: the army, the Senate, and the Roman populace. They took the impact, which Augustus nullified by representing no particular part. He broke the patricians by proscription, put the army on a professional basis, paid off the plebs with the dole, and organized a bureaucracy which furnished perquisites for the upper and middle class.

The emperor, contrarily, was less safe than the least of his subjects. Whenever an emperor lacked intelligence to comprehend the reality of his situation, the raw forces broke loose and crushed him; in plain words, he was killed. Domestic and political murder were the imperial tutors, instructing the emperor exactly where his power had its limits. The horrible abuses inherent in such a system-political graft, the demoralization of the dole, the increase of slave labor taken from punitive border wars, and the degradation of personal economic and political responsibility, due to the influx of money to Rome-indicate that the ordinary man must have had a compensating reason to persuade him to tolerate such evils. That compensation was that Roman policies allowed the flow of commerce, the exchange of surplus products to travel over well-constructed roads and bridges, with no exclusive barriers, and no grants of formal monopoly. Roman law affirmed private property, and this affirmed individualism. The great stream of commerce was unceasing. The bureaucracy took steady toll on it in taxes, enough to run the government, but for a time left the channels open. The Law was the insulating medium for the live current. On the whole life and property were secure under Roman law; citizenship was a solid asset even to a poor man. One could say "I am a Roman" though he had never seen Rome.

The manifest corruption of imperial Rome, and the apparently despotic prerogative of the emperor, seem to deny the basic premise of moral authority residing in the concept of Law. Since the power of the emperor had no express restrictions, it must be called absolute. But an empire can only exist if it offers to the world some negotiable benefit in exchange for tribute. Roman law was that export. Roman civil authority was supreme, as with Paul, when the man of the sword was "afraid" before his prisoner. Nations obtained the Law, but weighed against arbitrary rule, it was thought to be worth the great cost. Local officials dared not deal arbitrarily with a humble citizen because they might have been reported to the emperor as fomenting a plot against Rome's power. This is what the Carthaginians did not have to offer and did not understand when they saw it; they never knew what hit them.

From the beginning of the Empire to its destruction, the ratio of production to population diminished, while unemployment increased and became chronic. In the imperial set-up, Rome was strictly a consumer of material goods. The energy which sustained the empire as a going concern came from the provinces outside the imperial city. What Rome did for them, as compared to any other known form of government was to do nothing; the margin of benefit consisted in the limitation of government. The political power being withheld from economic activity, production was thus left to private management. The government of Rome was better than its predecessors because Rome governed less. The stream of energy welled from innumerable springs flowing into the great exchange routes. But when the enterprisers of any nation tapped a source of trade, forthwith they sought to use political power to impound the resultant flow completely. Egypt was fossilized by government ownership of the land and slavery; the absolute power of government made the country easy prey for invaders. Athenians tried to impose monopolies of commerce on their island colonies. Carthage was a static corporative state. Precisely because of the collectivism forced on Egyptians, fertile fields turned to desert. Precisely because Pericles wanted to upgrade the appearance of Athens, by appropriating the treasury collected at Delos, Greece was weakened, lost its islands and was invaded by Xerxes and later Rome. Precisely because Carthage contrived to clamp a monopoly on the main channel of trade with Europe, it was swept away. But the Romans, having been engaged with the great problem of the proper political principle, were predisposed to allow the stream of trade to follow its natural course. The Pax Romana of Augustus Caesar was designed to last forever. In time, though, the exactions of the bureaucracy increased, and the number of officials multiplied. More and more of the flow was diverted from production into the political mechanism. When Diocletian perfected it, the economy was so thoroughly planned and so well administered, that farmers could no longer farm nor workers work. In an exchange of goods, the producers must get back enough profit to enable them to keep on producing and working up the raw materials and providing transport. In the later Roman Empire, the bureaucrats took such a large cut, at length, scarcely anything went through the complete circuit. Receiving less and less in exchange for their products, the producers made less, since they would get no fair return; in fact, effort from which there is no net return automatically must cease. Farmers consumed their own products instead of putting them into exchange. Government took care of them on the little relief that taxes could provide, until the increasing taxes pushed so many more workers onto the rolls that there was not enough production left to pay the taxes. With that all trade began to dry up. The bureaucrats inevitably came down on the producers, with the object of sequestering productive energy directly at the source, by a coercive, planned economy. No one could change his residence or occupation without permission. The currency was debased. Prices and wages were fixed until there was nothing to sell and no work to be had. Sealed at the source, the level of production sank until it was no longer sufficient to operate the economy. The building of the Roman Wall in Britain marked the high point; thereafter the Legions were withdrawn due to the impossibility of maintaining supplies and reinforcements. The tax-eaters had absorbed it all. The Goths, the Huns and Vandals followed along the main trade routes until ultimately reaching Rome. The Roman Empire with its world peace collapsed into the Dark Ages. Rome, having suffered material defeat, sent her dogmas instead of her legions into the provinces. To this spiritual Rome, medieval and modern Europe has owed what small equivalent it enjoyed of the remaining *Pax Romana.* The ultimate binding element in the medieval order was subordination to the divine will and its earthly representatives, most notably the pope. The latter Middle Ages and the Renaissance saw a weakening of this principle of union and the rise of great territorial nationalities.

In analyzing or describing the successive stages and forms of association men have devised, we can continue our metaphor, giving to the representational order the name of architecture, and to the political agency in action the name of mechanism. The structure must accommodate the mechanism, and each must correspond respectively to the type of culture and the economic system. These forms and mechanisms do not occur and assemble themselves fortuitously by material determinism. They are created by conscious intelligence in the light of experience. Naturally progress tends to be uneven; prolonged failure to adjust to and maintain the new developments is the cause of the decline of nations. Production methods will catch up with advanced political ideas; whereas if an advanced physical economy develops within a political framework that cannot accommodate it, production must either be choked down or it will destroy the political entity, the economy being subverted to the wrong ends.

....

A previous book by this writer largely traces the European past: Pagan Greece and pagan Rome, the transformation of the Empire to The Church during the Dark Ages; the Renaissance, the Reformation, the Enlightenment, the Age of Discovery. During the stagnation of Europe, a world was actually bright with a brilliant civilization, more akin to the later American one and more fruitful than any other in the past. Millions of people, believing that all men were equal and free, created that civilization and kept on creating it for eight hundred years. To them the world owes modern science-mathematics, astronomy, navigation, medicine, surgery and scientific agriculture. To them the world directly owes the discovery and exploration of the Americas. These men were of all races and colors and classes, of all former cultures and many religions. They were not Romans. Europeans called them Saracens.

From Aristotle on, no known century has ever lacked scientists. Whenever Authority was weak, men opened schools of science, until a more efficient ruler suppressed them. Scientists could stop their work or leave. Many went to Persia. While the Byzantine Empire's energy was failing the Muslims swept across much of the known world-India, Arabia, Syria, Palestine, Egypt and all northern Africa to the Atlantic, Gibraltar and Spain, southern France and Italy, and the Balearic and Italian islands. The men who lived here no longer believed in pagan gods. They knew they were free. The natural aim of human energy is to make this earth habitable for human beings. When no false belief obstructs human energy at its source in the individual, men attack this earth to adapt it to human needs and desires. They need scientific knowledge, which is knowledge of the material world. The refugee scientists-respected, admired and listened to-opened their schools from Baghdad to Grenada. A Saracen university had no curriculum or examinations; they were simply institutions of learning. One went to universities to learn whatever he wanted to know. Students wanted science-Aristotle, Galen and Euclid, and every scrap of knowledge that had been added to theirs. Success depended on the demand for the knowledge each had. Fees were agreed upon privately between teacher and student.

The Greeks and Romans had seen in India the Hindu symbols of numbers. But the Saracens were the first to grasp the importance of the concept of zero. Without zero, there could be no mathematics. Without zero there would be no engineering, no chemistry, no astronomy, no measurement of substance or space. There would not be modern science or the modern world without the zero. Having zero, the Saracens developed arithmetic, adding algebra and quadratics. To Euclid's ideas, they added plane and spherical geometry. Applying this mathematics to the skies they produced astronomy. Across three continents they built observatories. They invented the sextant and the magnetic compass, accurately calculated latitude and attempted longitude. They deduced the shape and the dual movement of the spinning earth-around its axis, and around the sun-and they measured its size. The Saracens gave the Europeans the portolani, and the maps and charts that Columbus took with him on his voyages.

The Saracens translated Galen's works into Arabic. They did a lot of their own original research in medicine and surgery. They used practically the entire American pharmacopoeia of today. They built medical schools and hospitals, including one at Salerno. They discovered local anesthesia. Both Milan and Venice were thriving commercial cities, entirely from trade with the Saracens. The Renaissance had its origins partly from the Italian's contacts with Saracen civilization.

In Spain the Saracens built great centers of science and art and commerce-Cordova, Granada, Seville. Students from the East came to universities in Spain and from Spain students went to Baghdad and Delhi. The Saracen world was peaceful for a time, until Pope Urban the Second sent a half-million fanatics to attack them in Palestine. He called upon them to save the tomb of Christ, gave complete forgiveness of all sins to every man, along with instant entrance to paradise, for anyone killed along the way. Saracens had long set a guard at the Church of the Holy Sepulcher. For more than a thousand years a Moslem had stood there to keep Christians from killing members of rival sects at the tomb of Christ. The Crusaders crossed the Bosporus, unsuccessfully besieged Nicaea and Antioch, then went on to Jerusalem. Of the 426,000 Crusaders who entered the country, only 30,000 reached Palestine. After five weeks they took Jerusalem and slaughtered everyone they found. Five hundred years after the Crusades, Protestants and Catholics were fleeing to the American wilderness to escape from a similar European fanaticism.

The Crusaders were befuddled by what they found-silks, linens, leathers, cushions, carpets, unknown metals, strange utensils. They did not know what an oil lamp was. They had never heard of sugar. They had not seen cosmetics. Tile floors, walls and ceilings of mosaics. Glass. It was a country of magicians. On the subject of cleanliness, the Saracens were fanatics. Fountains were everywhere; one could not go to prayer without first bathing. Not an acre of arable land ever rested in the Saracen world. Their farmers fertilized, deep-and contour-plowed, irrigated and rotated their crops. They poured their produce into markets and took in return such a wealth of goods as the world had never seen before. We eat, our cars run, our streets are paved, our houses are furnished, and our bodies clothed with things the Saracens created.

There were many methods of controlling by mutual consent, all these activities of that busy civilization spanning three continents, with trade, discovering and increasing scientific knowledge, creating and distributing an unprecedented wealth of goods and of knowledge, literature, art, architecture-constantly improving all living conditions. Men were spending enormous sums of money in building roads and observatories and universities and hospitals and mosques and fountains and public garden. Scholars were collecting and exchanging manuscripts and books; architects were creating the world's most beautiful buildings. Traders were managing businesses extending thousands of miles.

Italians, through trade, were constantly meeting these men of greater knowledge and wider experience than theirs, richer, better dressed and fed, cleaner and better groomed; men who thought and acted quickly, and independently. The Saracens had better methods of navigating ships, quicker ways of computing costs and adding bills. With incredible swiftness, they dispatched their business affairs over great distances. Look for the people who communicate quickly with others over long distances, people who attack space and time and create a vibrant civilization. Two peoples have done this: the Saracens and Americans. They shared a common human situation on earth, a common human nature, and both once lived in conditions that did not prevent them from using their natural freedom.

The Saracen civilization ceased to exist. Why? No single organization, religious, political or social, extended over that civilization. There was no Law. There is a natural necessity for a civil law, a code, explicitly stated, written and known; an impersonal thing, existing outside all men, as a point of reference to which any man can refer and appeal. Not any form of control, for each controls himself; but Law, acting as a third party in relationships between living persons; an impersonal witness to contracts, a registrar of promises and deeds, of ownership and transfers of property, a not-living standard existing in visible form, by which men's acts can be judged and to which men's minds can cling.

When the Turks struck their civilization, the Moslems forgot the God of Abraham, Christ and Mohammed. They came again to think of God as Authority, controlling men. They could find no other explanation for the ruin of their world. The Saracens and the Turks who had conquered them sank into stagnation. Moslems had gone back to the static, changeless universe and the controlling Authority. They had escaped from the responsibility of freedom. They submitted to the Unknowable, as Spartans submitted to the Law of Lycurgus, as communists and fascists submit to the Party, and as some Americans believe that individuals should and must submit to an enforced Social Good, to the Will of the Majority, to a Planned Economy. Authority rests upon the belief that nothing is being created. The whole idea of Authority controlling the universe depends on men seeing the universe as completed, finished, motionless and changeless. If the universe is not completed and static; if instead Dynamic Energy is creatively operating; then things impossible at this instant will exist in a coming one, then all things are changing into new, unprecedented things, tomorrow cannot be known today, and nothing that exists today can control tomorrow. No mind on the Left dares admit the thought that Reality is Creative Energy, that change is in the very nature of things. When Authority learned that this earth spins in space, their minds and souls recoiled in horror. Neither could it look for the East in the West; that would admit that the round earth spins in space; that would admit that the principle of the universe is Energy, Change and Progress.

The Reconquista released the living human energy of the Saracen's world into European history. Explorers of the New World came from Spain. Only from Spain. For one century after the fall of Grenada Spaniards were less submissive to Authority than any other Europeans. During that century Spaniards explored and conquered the New World and much of Europe. One century later Spanish energy was not able to get food enough to keep Spaniards alive. All the energy of Saracen civilization that had been creative was turned, by the lure of unknown lands, and the Authority of new Kings, into conquest and war. Authority burned the libraries; reading, writing or speaking Arabic was forbidden. The freedom of thought in Spain was more appalling than anyone had suspected. All the force of the State was barely able to suppress it. It was the end of Spain. No one was left who knew that men were free. Human energy in Spain simply ceased to work. Spaniards flocked to the cities where the Church and King would feed them. Again and again in history this happened. During Rome's decline farms were abandoned for the grain dole; during the twentieth century Americans did the same; at the same time Russian peasants crowded into cities-for food. In Spain villages were dwindling, the Government could not get a dribble of taxes from the provinces, property flowed to the Church; it was said that the Catholicism was devouring the country. There was security in the Church, for mind and soul and body. Spaniards wanted that security, the security that children have a right to expect from any Authority they obey. For nearly eight hundred years human energy in Spain had produced such an abundance of food, comforts and luxuries as the world had never before imagined. After Granada fell, energy continued to operate upon the New World and Europe, until the people could no longer support the Government, and they died of starvation. Spain had practically ceased to exist.

Under the Authority of the Church, Europeans developed the feudal system to its perfection. For the first time personal duties and by consequence personal rights were linked to the ownership of land. Whatever be the proper view of its origin and legal nature, the best mode of vividly picturing to ourselves the feudal organization is to begin with the basis, to consider the relation of the tenant to the patch of soil which created and limited his services, and then to mount up, through narrowing circles of super-feudation, till we approximate to the apex of the system. In the nature of things there must necessarily be a culminating domination somewhere, and that authority was increasingly assigned to the supposed successor of the Caesars of the West, attributed to the See of Rome. The Church was interlocked with feudalism by the system of land tenure on its immense properties, and so had a vested interest in the status quo. Similarly, the original Authority of the English monarchy derived wholly from the feudal order, so the interest was similar in preserving that economic system. It was said to be the highest and the best civilization our race had known, conformable to the instinct of the European, fulfilling his nature, and giving him that happiness which is the end of man. In the feudal system the individual hardly existed, even in his own mind. He lived in two worlds. In the invisible world all souls were equal. And the spiritual world *was* the real world. Men thought the world they inhabited was temporary. He would discard his body soon and step into that real world. In this world everyone had their place and was neatly kept in it. Born a peasant, a man *was* a peasant. He could make no effort to be anything else. He could take no risks, suffer no failure; he had no responsibility whatever for his own fortunes. The serf was fastened to the land he worked; he could not leave it, nor lose his place on it. Everyone else was also secure, in his own class. Each owed a certain duty and received certain protections. They created all sorts of exceptions but patiently fitted these into the system. Every human relationship was worked out minutely.

The feudal system's equilibrium, that had been so perfect through the 12th century, was threatened by the troubling questions in men's minds. The Church was more and more suppressing the new heresies. Outside the Church the class structure was one that men could not create or endure unless they were convinced that the universe was static. They could not have born its stagnation, if they had suspected that progress was possible. They would have rebelled, had they not thought this world was only a prelude, from which they were going to go to Heaven. If you held the pagan belief that some Authority controls individuals and the feudal belief that God places each person in his proper place in the temporal world, you naturally believe that a King has a God-given right to rule his subjects. The balance of rights and duties among the classes was gone when Europeans began to believe in the Divine Right of Kings. But the other feudal beliefs remained; the idea that the universe is changeless, the belief in Authority, the belief in classes, the belief that there must be a social system administered by Government, and that Government must make everyone secure. But the more earnestly the King tried to enforce social order and the control of production which his ministers planned, the less his subjects were able to produce. And the Government progressively consumed more and more of the wealth that the subjects *did* produce, and constantly subtracted more and more energy from the productive capacity of the nation. The

Church, the nobles and the merchants eventually combined against King John with the Charter in 1215.

When Kings broke the feudal system, they then needed some ground to stand on, so they and their supporters invented the Nation. The Nation is nothing but simple Force. The only thing that permits any of these Nations to exist is the belief in the minds of all persons that Government naturally controls their business, their work, their news, their religion, their personal habits. The ancient belief in Authority is the whole basis of Nations that do exist. The people of Europe have never questioned Authority. Their only outcry has been that Authority does not control them properly. Socialist, Communist, Fascist, National Socialist, Social Democrat, Democrat Socialist-all demand that Government make a better system, that Government control the men who produce and distribute goods, that Government create security for men on this earth. The basis of all this thinking is ignorance of creative energy; it is ignorance of the real nature of human beings; it is the ancient, pagan superstition that Authority controls a static, limited universe. The belief is at least six thousand years old. Acting on this belief, human beings have tried every one of these ideas now advanced as revolutionary; they have tried every way of making a human world in which human energy can work at its natural job of making this earth habitable for human beings, and never in one of those centuries have they succeeded in using their energies well enough to get them all enough to eat. Yet they keep trying, because individuals control human energy in accordance with their religious faith, whatever it may be. And belief in Authority controlling a fixed, limited, changeless universe is the pagan religion. If this were true then a world controlled by some kind of Authority would have worked, at least once, at least fairly well, during six thousand years of trying.

When for all that time human energy does not work well enough to get from the earth the food to keep humans alive, it does not work because men fail to use their energy in accordance with their nature. But they do not question their infantile belief because they can always blame the Authority. The history of every group of men who ever obeyed a living Authority is also a history of revolts against all forms of Government. They revolt against a King and replace him with another. In time they revolt against monarchy itself; they set up another *kind* of living Authority. For centuries they revolt against that kind and set up *another*. An Old-World revolution is only a movement around a motionless center; it never breaks out of the circle. Firm in the center is belief in Authority. They replace the priest by a king, the king by an oligarchy, the oligarchs by a despot, the despot by an aristocracy, the aristocrats by a majority, the majority by a tyrant, the tyrant by oligarchs, the oligarchy by a king, the king by a parliament-there's six thousand years of it, in every language. All these kinds have been tried, too, in every possible combination-try to think of one, and somewhere it has been tried. Each might work for a while, except that the people did not get enough to eat. Whenever you look at Pharaoh's subjects, obeying a living God, or at Athenian Greeks obeying a majority, or Romans taxed to their last extent, you see the same result: people did not get enough to eat.

Plato was a philosopher. He worked out in monstrous detail an ideal system, a totalitarian state, in which every human impulse was absolutely controlled. Alexander was a military despot, so was Napoleon, so were Hitler, Stalin and Mao. If men and women do not want to live like that, then this is a fact: human energy does not work as human beings want it to work, under any kind of Authority that men are able to imagine or devise. Take any few hundred years of Old-World experience and you see a succession of convulsive efforts and collapses, as if living things were roped down and struggling. This is precisely what was happening. Human energy could not get to work at its natural job of providing for human needs, because whenever men began to develop farming and crafts and trade, the Government stopped them. The struggle went on for centuries. Leader after leader, philosophers and even warriors kept insisting upon the fact of individual self-control, individual freedom. But people soon tire and want to escape from the relentless responsibility of freedom. And when they realize what is being done to them there is little consolation in the fact that it is by an Authority that they have chosen themselves.

Vast quantities of raw materials have always been available to human beings. Two thousand years ago when Caesar went into Gaul, Europe was just as rich as the American continent a century ago. It was not the material, but the uses that human energy made of them, that created this new world. The plain fact is that human energy operates more effectively in America than anywhere else on the planet. It operates to make human lives safer, healthier, longer, more comfortable and more enjoyable. Since this is what men have always wanted, obviously some obstacle kept them from using their energies effectively, until this country was formed. For sixty known centuries men have lived on this earth. Their desire has been just as strong as ours. They have had enough energy to make the earth at least habitable for human beings. Their intelligence has been great. Why then did they walk, and carry goods on their back, for six thousand years, and suddenly in one century make unprecedented advances? For all that time human beings used their energies in unsuccessful efforts to get wretched shelter and meager food. Then in one small part of earth, a few men used their energies so effectively that in three generations was created an entirely new world. American made a stupendous attack on space and distance: steamships, railroads, autos, airplanes, rockets. And on time: telegraph, telephones, radio, television, the internet. What explains this?

Perhaps it is tough on human beings that no Authority exists to take care of them. That is a brutal fact. It is a tough job to be free. But six thousand years of trying to escape the fact was tougher. The free exercise of human rights created the New World. Stop this exercise, shed individual responsibility and individual freedom, submit to Authoritative control of ordinary human affairs, and this whole new world of economic abundance, the unprecedented wealth of food, shelter, health, comforts; this world of swift transportation and communication, this dynamic complex of productive human energies will no longer continue to be created or improved, and will cease to exist. Relinquish the free use of individual energies and the defenses of human life must vanish as the walls of Athens and the galleys of Rome vanished. This whole modern world must disappear as completely as the Saracen's world disappeared. Every effect ceases when its cause no longer operates. This whole modern civilization must cease to exist if individual Americans forget the fact of individual liberty and abandon the exercise of individual self-control and individual responsibility that creates it. Americans who have no knowledge of history take the present for granted. When they imagine that a control exists which can be used over individuals, to make a better world according to their plan, they are falling into the ancient delusion that every dictator has as well. Nothing but human energy, working freely under its natural, individual control, can keep on creating this new world and keep it existing.

Mussolini wanted to bring back the grandeur of Rome. Hitler tried to re-establish the Holy Roman Empire of the 16th century. Radical Islam wants to return to the seventh century and Mohammed's dreams. Present defenders of a tyranny older than history imagine that they can go back to the time before America was discovered. And *they* claim they are the Progressives. Unable to understand this New World, the counterrevolutionaries use free men's discoveries, their inventions, their techniques and their tools to tear this network of dynamic productive energies to pieces and destroy the freedom that creates it.

Freedom is not a permission granted by any Authority. Freedom is a fact. It is in the nature of every living person, as gravitation is in the nature of the planet. Freedom is the individual control of human energy. It cannot be separated from life. Liberty is inalienable. I cannot transfer control of my life to anyone else. This fact is not recognized when individuals submit to an Authority that *grants* them "freedoms.' Implicit in that is the belief that persons are *not* free, that adult men and women must be controlled and cared for, as children are, and that, like children, they are naturally dependent and obedient to an Authority that is responsible for their acts and welfare. Any Authority that can grant freedom can withdraw it. So long as they live, men are self-controlling and responsible for what they do. Ignorance is no escape from the fact. The Left simply works to de-moralize the country to the point where it will submit to anything.

This is our planet, whirling in sunlit space, enveloped in gases, inhabited by living creatures. Every living creature has the desire to continue to live. Men are alive on this earth only because the imperative human desire is to attack the enemies of human life. What is the meaning of this American Republic in history, but an unprecedented fury of human energy, attacking the non-human world, and making this earth more habitable for human beings?

CHAPTER TWO-ANCIENT LAW

SIR HENRY SUMNER MAINE
IRVING BABBITT

"You have landed estates as large as the Romans', combined with commercial enterprise such as Carthage and Venice united never equaled. And you remember that this country, with its strong contrasts, is not governed by force; it is not governed by standing armies; it is governed by a most singular series of traditionary influences, which generation after generation cherishes because it knows that they embalm custom and represent Law. If you destroy that state of society, remember this-the country cannot begin again."

Benjamin Disraeli, writing of England

"The people were taught, by Solon, that the strength of a free state consists in its laws; that laws are nothing, unless they be obeyed; that laws will not be obeyed, unless honor be given to the obedient, and punishment inflicted on transgressors; that the laws are not to be subjected to the government, but the government to the laws."

Burgh, *Political Disquisitions,* 1775

"An ignorant man, who is not fool enough to meddle with his clock, is however sufficiently confident to think he can safely take to pieces, and put together at his pleasure, a moral machine of another guise, importance and complexity, composed of other wheels, and springs, and balances, and counter-acting and co-operating powers…their delusive good intention is no sort of excuse for their presumption."

Edmund Burke

Twenty-three hundred years ago there were scientists. Before Rome was an outlaw's camp in the far west, Aristotle was saying. "If a man grasps truths that cannot be other than they are, in the way which he grasps the definitions through which demonstrations take place, he will not have opinion, but knowledge." Throughout the history of thought, from Aristotle onward, men have tried to develop systems of ratiocination that are self-contained; that move, step-by-step, by links of logic, gathering first inductive then deductive and empirical evidence in order to derive and prove theories. Such men always tried to reduce the process of thought to the compass of the individual brain, with its own experience and structure, governed by physical laws. But matter is predictable and calculable only because it is dead and its future preordained. Thus, the laws of physics. But the human mind is no longer autonomous nor limited by its small fund of individual experience. The human mind reaches out to grasp the objects beyond it and is ultimately governed by the things it recollects and reflects. Through books, the internet, and other people, men can reach new truths, glimpse new ideas and merge what he knows with that, extending his knowledge backward to its origins and forward to what may be new applications. A man can study the experiences of the wisest men of the past and examine the actual political experience of the people-then put it into their own law and governmental policy and see whether or not it is conducive to the welfare of the state and the citizenry. Through the strengthening of empirical knowledge, the foundations of society can be improved. The advances of invention, the varieties of economic organization, the experiments in government, the aspirations of religion, the changes in morals and manners, the development of the sciences and the wisdom of philosophy all contribute.

Any science seeking to investigate an area of reality must start by identifying the main factors and basic underlying forces in their simplest form; this first simple image is then filled out, improved and made more complex as further details, secondary causes and less direct influences are brought in to correct it and broaden its understanding, so that it approximates more and more closely to reality. We understand that the final picture is much more complex, and that many problems remain to be resolved before we comprehend it; we must, to some extent await the lessons of experience in order to do so. The eminence of a scientist is measured by the true vision he possesses in connection with the field of facts to which he fixes his attention. What may come to him in a flash of insight he is careful to check up and test experimentally by every means in his power. His success is due to the correct relation he has established between the part of himself that perceives, the part that conceives, and the part that discriminates. Any other than a cause-and-effect philosophy is likely to fall into sheer unreality; inasmuch as reality means law and law means that as a matter of positive observation there is a constant association between certain phenomena either in time or in space-an association that exists quite apart from the desires or opinions of the individual. If there is not a human law that is thus objective, so that the person who violates it exposes himself to certain consequences, then the human law is not worth going in search of. The necessity of taking the body of Roman Law, bearing in its earliest portion the traces of the most remote antiquity, and yet supplying from its later usage the staple of the civil institutions by which modern society is even now controlled, compelled this author to write an entirely separate book, and then to draw from it what may appear to be a disproportionate number of examples for use in this one.

One of the ambitions of these books is to provide new and more manageable definitions of Nature and of its Law; it is indisputable that the conception, in passing through the long series of writers on Public Law, has gathered round it a large accretion, consisting of fragments of ideas derived from nearly every theory of ethics which has in its turn taken possession of the various schools of thought. A series of explicit statements, recognizing and adopting these conjectural theories of a natural state, and of a system of principles congenial to it, has been continued with but brief interruption from the oldest days up to our own. These men differed as to the characteristics of the pre-social state, and as to the abnormal action by which men lifted themselves out of it into that social organization with which we are acquainted, but they agreed in thinking that a great chasm separated man in his primitive condition from man in society, and we cannot doubt that they borrowed, consciously or unconsciously, ultimately from the Romans. If the phenomena of Law be regarded as one vast complex it is not surprising that even the best mind would evade the task set for itself by falling back on a conjecture which, plausibly interpreted, seems to reconcile everything, or else it would abjure in despair the labor of systemization. So, if we can determine the early forms of jural conceptions, we may subsequently show all the forms in which the law has exhibited itself. The rudimentary ideas are to the jurist what the primary crusts of the earth are to the geologist. Modern legal forms, conceptions and codes are the outgrowth of the slow and gradual development of Ancient Law.

Maine's *Ancient Law* is frequently compared with Darwin's *Origin of Species.* The mistake which the Left commits is analogous to the error of one who, in investigating the laws of the material universe, should commence by contemplating the existing physical world as a whole, instead of beginning, as did Darwin, with the particles which are its simplest ingredients. It would seem we should commence with the simplest social forms in a state as near as possible to their rudimentary condition; we should first penetrate as far as we can in the history of primitive societies. No pain will have been wasted in ascertaining the germs out of which has assuredly been unfolded every form of moral restraint which controls our actions and shapes our conduct at the present moment.

The earliest intellectual exercise to which a young nation devotes itself *is* the study of its laws. As soon as the mind makes its first conscious efforts toward generalization, the concerns of everyday life are the first to press for inclusion within general rules and comprehensive formulas. At the outset this pursuit was unbounded, but a new stage of intellectual progress began with the Augustan age. The brief span of literature glorifying the ancient virtues of Rome was suddenly closed under a variety of influences and ancient intellect was forcibly thrust back into its old courses. As soon as the Romans ceased to sit at the feet of the Greeks and began to ponder out a theology of their own, the theology proved to be permeated with forensic ideas and couched in a forensic phraseology.

From the earliest times forward, all societies have possessed concepts of higher ideals to which positive law and its applications ought to conform. While the Greek Homeric poems no doubt exaggerated features of that age-the prowess of warriors and the potency of gods, there is no reason to believe that it tampered with moral or metaphysical conceptions which were not yet the subjects of conscious discussion. In this respect the Homeric literature is far more trustworthy than those relatively later documents which pretend to give an account of times similarly early, but which were compiled under philosophical or theological influences. Plato's Ideas were another example. These early forms of jural conception potentially contain all the forms in which law has subsequently exhibited itself. Rather than overwhelming the settled prescriptions or rules of society by an ad hoc superimposition of conflict, or worse, stifling the progress of civilization entirely by looking more to the past than the future, Roman Law avoided both pitfalls. Assembled from actual laws on the books of contemporary states into one law capable of universal administration, the higher law was not perceived as standing in an antagonistic relationship to the positive law and could best be discovered or approximated through evolutionary refinement, a gradual process that would eventually yield up the underlying principles of diverse and disparate positive laws.

In the primitive condition of mankind men could only account for sustained or periodically recurring actions by supposing a personal agent. The wind blowing, the sun rising and the earth yielding its increase were caused by divine persons. As, then, in the physical world, so in the moral. There was the persuasion in the human mind, which clung so long and so tenaciously, of a divine influence underlying and supporting every relation of life and social institution. In the early rudiments of law and political thought, symptoms of this belief meet us on all sides. A divine king was supposed to consecrate and keep together all the cardinal institutions of those times-the State, the Race, and the Family. Men, grouped together in the different relations which those institutions imply, were bound to periodically celebrate rites and rituals, purifications and expiations, which appear intended to deprecate punishment for involuntary or neglectful disrespect. It is certain that in this infancy of mankind no sort of legislature, not even a distinct author of law, was conceived of or contemplated. Law had scarcely reached the footing of custom; it was still more a habit. Every man, living the greater part of his life under patriarchal despotism, was practically controlled in his actions not by a regimen of law but one of arbitrary caprice.

Kingship depended on divinely given prerogative, as well as personal strength, courage and wisdom. As the impression of the monarch's sacredness weakened, and feeble members occurred in the series of hereditary kings, royal power decayed and at last gave way to the dominion of aristocracies. In Greece, Italy and Asia Minor, the dominant orders consisted of a number of families united by a relationship of blood who approached political oligarchy. The king became a mere functionary, such as the Archon at Athens, while the aristocracy was universally the depository and administrators of the law. The connection of ideas which caused the judgments of the patriarchal chieftain to be attributed to super-human dictation still showed itself in the claim of a divine origin for the entire body of rules, or for certain parts of it, but the progress of thought no longer permitted the solution of particular disputes to be explained by supposing an extra-human interposition. What the oligarchy next claimed was to monopolize the *knowledge* of the laws, to have the exclusive possession of the principles by which quarrels were decided. Customs or Observances now existed as a substantive aggregate and were assumed to be precisely known to the aristocratic order. Before the invention of writing an aristocracy invested with judicial privileges formed the only expedient by which accurate preservation of the customs of the people could be approximated. Their genuineness was insured as far as possible by confiding them to the recollection of this limited portion of the community. On the assumption that there was a large mass of civil and criminal rules known exclusively to judges, and after the courts began to base new judgments on recorded cases, the law which was administered became customary written law. Aristocracies sometimes seem to have abused their monopoly of legal knowledge; at any event their exclusive possession was a formidable impediment to popular movements such as those of the Plebians in Rome.

The usages which a particular community is found to have adopted in its infancy and in its primitive seats are generally those which are on the whole best suited to promote its physical and moral well-being; and, if they are retained in their integrity until new social wants have taught new practices, the upward march of society is almost certain. Changes in unwritten usages were spontaneously developed, dictated by feelings and modes of thought, which slowly altered the customs of any community. Once, though, primitive law was embodied in a code we could trace the course of legal modification to the conscious desire of improvement. With the onset of written codes, the distinction between stationary and progressive societies begins to make itself felt. It is difficult for a citizen of the contemporary world to understand that the civilization which surrounds one in a free society is a rare exception in history. The stationary condition of the human race is the rule, and the advancing one the exception. To understand the difference requires an accurate knowledge of Roman law in all its principal stages. Roman jurisprudence has the longest known history of any set of human institutions; from its commencement it was progressively modified for the better, and the course of improvement was continued through periods at which the rest of human thought and action materially stagnated.

But unhappily there is also a law of development which ever threatens to operate upon unwritten usage. A barbarous society practicing a body of customs is exposed to special dangers which may be absolutely fatal to its progress in civilization. While the customs are obeyed by the masses, they are in any case are incapable of understanding the ground of their expediency and inevitably superstitious reasons are invented for their permanence. A process then commences which may be shortly described by saying that usage which is reasonable generates usage which is unreasonable. Prohibitions and ordinances, originally confined to a single description of acts are made to apply to all acts of the same class, because a man menaced with the anger of the gods for doing one thing, feels a natural terror in doing any other thing which is remotely like it. Irrational imitation engrafts in it an immense apparatus of cruel absurdities. From these corruptions a written Code protected the Romans. The question was not so much whether there should be a code at all, but when in the relative progress of each community it was adopted. Thus, the point on which turned the history of any race was at what period, at what stage of their social progress, they should have their laws put into writing. With Rome it was compiled when the usage was still wholesome-the Plebians or popular element assailed the oligarchy early in the history of the Republic. If the Twelve Tables had not been published when they were the Romans might have been condemned to a feebler civilization and, with the interruption of jurisprudence created by feudalism, might have prevented any modern law from being traceable to one or more of the antique fountainheads.

The Twelve Tables of Rome were the most famous example of a Code. Laws engraved on bronze and published to the people took the place of usages deposited and known only in the recollection of a privileged oligarchy. Inscribed tablets were seen to be a better security for the law's accurate preservation, than the memory of a number of persons, however strengthened by habitual exercise. The Tables did exhibit some progressive traces of systematic arrangement garnered from the Attic Code of Solon and even earlier from the laws of Draco; religious, civil and moral ordinances were mingled without any regard to their essential character, as separating law from morality and religion from law belong to the later stages of mental progress. The opportunity of increasing and consolidating power was still too tempting to be resisted by religious oligarchies. Roman society was only recently emerging from that intellectual condition in which civil obligation and religious duty were confounded. The value of the Tables did not lie in the terms but in their publicity, and in the knowledge which they furnished to everyone, as to what he was to do, and what not to do. Another of the chief advantages which the Twelve Tables and similar codes conferred on societies which obtained them was the protection which they afforded against the frauds of the privileged oligarchy and against the spontaneous depravation and debasement of the national institutions.

The rudiments of the social state can be known through accounts of contemporary observers of civilizations less advanced than their own; Tacitus made the most of such an opportunity. As societies do not advance concurrently, but at different rates of progress, there are epochs at which such men, trained to the habits of methodical observation, have really been in a position to watch and describe the infancy of mankind. If we confine our attention to those fragments of ancient institutions which cannot reasonably be supposed to have been altered with time, as with Homer, we are able to gain a clearer conception of certain great characteristics of the society to which they originally belonged. Using our knowledge of antique systems of laws allows us to discriminate between those which are truly archaic from those which have been affected by the prejudices, interests or ignorance or the compiler. The effect of the evidence derived from comparative jurisprudence is to establish that view of the primeval condition of the human race which is known as Patriarchy, the eldest male parent or ascendant, who was absolutely supreme in his household, and whose members were considered by Roman Law as a unity-in-person. An aggregation of Family groups in some wider organization-a system of concentric circles which gradually expand from the same point such as a House or Tribe-looks like the immature germ of a state or commonwealth, and an order of rights superior to those of family relation. The unit of ancient society was the Family, of a modern society the Individual. The history of political ideas therefore began with the assumption that kinship in blood or adoption was the sole possible ground of community in political functions; nowhere yet was the idea of geographical contiguity the basis of common political action.

The arguments in favor of the patriarchal view of government have never been adequately set forth; we must, if we go by the actual experience of mankind, conclude that the patriarchal conception has enormous elements of strength. The Greek and Roman city-states were derived from the religion of the family. Men were born, not free and equal, but subjects, first of all to their parents, which in turn, served as a model for that of the king. Powers of the Patriarch over the persons of his family were extensive-divorce, sale, and even life or death-but the father's rights over the son's property were absolute. The father was entitled to take the whole of the son's acquisitions, and to enjoy the benefits of his contracts, without being entangled in any compensating liability. Caracalla (188-217) conferred Roman citizenship on the whole of his subjects-African, Spaniard, Gaul, Briton, and Jew-enormously enlarging the sphere of the Patria Potesta, a step tightening the family relation throughout the empire, and as a beneficial agency, one which ought to be kept more in view today.

The social organization of the clan, the family, the city-state, and the religious brotherhood, is essentially a band of individuals held together by certain practices which, it is assumed, will be of mutual benefit to its members. The tribe lives and acts in common, and its actions are motivated by a complete knowledge of what is permitted and what is forbidden. These customs-religious, social and moral-are the unwritten but unbreakable laws of the community. They represent the unconscious demands of that community embodied in definite practice-and all their actions must respond to them. We cannot understand the early Greeks or any other race of early antiquity without first understanding such customs which supply balance to the community observing them.

The truth is that the stable parts of the older stages of the race have obstinately defied the influences that have elsewhere had ill effects are our mental, moral and physical constitutions, and the resistance that it opposes to change is such that, though the variations of human society in a portion of the world are plain enough, they are neither so rapid nor so extensive that their amount, character, and general direction cannot be ascertained. The true enigma of the Patria Potesta resides in the slowness with which these proprietary privileges were curtailed and seriously diminished, with the entire civilized world being brought within their sphere. Constantine, and later Justinian, effectively reduced the property a son received from his mother, or that earned by the son himself, to only a usufruct, or life-interest of the father. The social legislation termed Plaetoria sought to place male Orphans, who had lost all male adults in their lineage, under the class of guardians called Curatores, whose sanctions were required to validate their acts or contracts, until they reached their majority at twenty--five years of age, as employed in Roman Law.

In communities situated under ancient jurisprudence, the legislation of assemblies and the jurisdiction of the Courts reached only to the heads of families; to every other individual the rule of conduct was the law of his home, of which his Parent was the legislator. The Family was in essence a Corporation, the Patriarch was its representative, or Public officer. He enjoyed rights and stood under duties which in the eye of the law were quite as much those of the Family as his own. Were the person representing the collective body to die, his demise would be immaterial-the person responsible to municipal jurisdiction would simply bear a different name. The rights and obligations which attached to the deceased head of the house would attach, without breach of continuity, to his successor, and the Family would continue on as before. Testamentary succession was in effect the prolongation of a man's legal existence in his heir and sustained the corporate aspect of the Family. The Law of Persons, which was nothing else than the Law of Status, would be restricted to the smallest limits as long as all forms of status were merged in common subjection to Paternal Power, as long as the Wife had no rights against her husband, the son none against his father, and the infant Ward none against the Agnates who were his guardians. Similarly, the rules relating to Property and Succession could never be plentiful, so long as land and goods devolved within the Family. But the greatest gap in ancient civil law would always be caused by the absence of Contract, which some archaic codes do not mention at all.

What passed from the Testator to the Heir was indeed the Family, the aggregate of rights and duties contained in the Patria Potesta. Original wills and testaments were therefore a proceeding by which the devolution of the Family was regulated. It was a mode of declaring who was to have the chieftainship, in succession to the Testator. Ancient Law knew next to nothing of Individuals, only Families. So far as we have recognizable traces of it, society rested on the Family and in particular upon the patriarchal power of the father to whom all were absolutely subject. All the members of the Family, except its head, were in a condition of *status:* they had no power to acquire property, or to bequeath it, or to enter into contracts in relation to it. The life of each citizen was not regarded as limited by birth and death; it was but a continuation of the existence of his forefathers, and it would be prolonged in the existence of his descendants. The separation of the Law of Persons from that of Things had no meaning in the infancy of law; their distinction is appropriate only to later jurisprudence. The history of jurisprudence must be followed in its whole course, if we are to understand how gradually and tardily society dissolved itself into the component atoms of which it is now constituted-by what insensible gradations the relation of man to man substituted itself for the relation of the individual to his family and of families to each other. The sphere of civil law tended to steadily enlarge itself; at every point of progress a greater number of personal rights and a larger amount of property were removed from the domestic forum to the cognizance of the public tribunals. The ordinances of the government gradually obtained the same efficacy in private concerns as in matters of state and were no longer to be overridden by a despot before each hearthstone. In time the idea of Roman universal succession meant that the qualities and characteristics of the family corporation were gradually invested with the individual citizen. The gradual substitution of the Individual for the Family was effected most conspicuously by the development of the idea of *Contract*-the capacity of the individual to enter into independent agreements with strangers to his family-group to which he was legally bound. The most important passage in the history of Private Property is its gradual separation from the co-ownership of kinsmen.

The movement of progressive societies has been uniform in one respect. Through all its course it has been distinguished by the gradual dissolution of family dependency and the growth of individual obligation in its place. The Individual was steadily substituted for the Family as the unit of which civil laws take account. The eventual transformation of Roman jurisprudence by Natural Law bequeathed the impression that individual ownership was the normal state of proprietary right, and that communal ownership by groups of men was only a rare exception.

Accomplished by societies at various rates of celerity, no matter what the pace, the change has not been subject to reaction or recoil, and any retardation will be found to have been occasioned through the absorption of ideas from some entirely foreign source. Nor is it difficult to see what is the tie between man and man which replaces by degrees those forms of reciprocity in rights and duties which have their origin in the Family. It is Contract. Starting, as from one terminus of history, from a condition of society in which all the relations of Persons are summed up in the relations of Family, we seem to have steadily moved towards a phase of social order in which all these relations arise from the free agreement of Individuals. Thus, the status of slave disappeared, to be superseded by the contractual relation of servant to employer. For the Female, all the relations she may form were now relations of contract. The child before reaching his majority, those adjudged unsound of mind, those under guardianship were still regulated by the Law of Persons, on the single ground that they did not possess the faculty of forming a judgment on their own interests; in other words, that they are wanting in the first essential of an engagement by Contract. All the forms of Status taken notice of in the Law of Persons were derived from the powers and privileges anciently residing in the Patriarch of the Family. If we employ Status to signify these personal conditions only and avoid applying the term to such conditions as are the immediate or remote result of an agreement, we may say that the movement of advancing societies has hitherto been a movement from Status to Contract.

The point which has to be comprehended in the constitution of primitive societies is that the individual originally created for himself few or no rights, and few or no duties. The rules which he obeyed were derived first from the station into which he was born, and next from the imperative commands addressed to him by the chief of the household of which he formed a part. Such a system left the very smallest room for Contract. Old law, especially feudal, fixed a man's social position irreversibly at his birth; modern law allows him to create it for himself by convention. The recognition of this difference between past ages and the present enters into the very essence of the most important contemporary arguments. It is certain that the science of Political Economy, the only department of moral inquiry that has made any considerable progress, would fail to correspond with the facts of life if it were not true that Status Law had abandoned the largest part of the field which it once occupied, and had left men to settle rules of conduct for themselves with a liberty never allowed to them much before the advent of the United States. Legislators have all but given up their ability to keep pace with the activity of man in discovery, in invention, and in the manipulation of accumulated wealth-an ever-changing assemblage of contractual rules with which it seeks to contend. This despite observing that of the positive rules readily obeyed by men, the great majority are created by Contract, the minority by Status or Imperative Law. The inference to be obtained from Contract Law is that society could not possibly hold together without attaching a sacredness to promises and agreements and without which no sound understanding of legal history would be possible. The larger part of the collective existence of every community is consumed in transactions of buying and selling, of letting and hiring, of alliances between men for the purposes of business, of delegation of business from one man to another; no doubt this is the consideration which led the Romans, and more recent developing societies, to relieve those transactions from technical encumbrance, to abstain as much as possible from clogging the most efficient springs of social movement. Such Consensual Contracts constituted the stage in the history of law from which all modern conceptions of Contract took their start and were to be included in the *Jus Gentium* and finally in the Laws of Nature, both exclusively Roman.

The positive duty resulting from one man's reliance on the word of another is among the slowest conquests of advancing civilization. At first nothing is seen like the interposition of law to compel performance of a promise. But disregard of one iota of the performance of property and the accompanying ceremony was fatal to the obligation. Slowly the property aspect separated itself from simple transaction and becomes what the Romans deemed a Pact or Convention. The two main essentials were the signification by the promising party of his intention to do the acts or observe the forbearances which he promises to do or to observe. There is an accompanying signification by the promisee that he expects the promising party will fulfill the proffered promise. Contract was thus long regarded as an incomplete conveyance, artificially prolonged to give time to the debtor. His indebtedness was seen as an artifice and a distortion of the strict rule of exchange. Alternatively, the person who had duly consummated his part in the transaction must have stood in particular favor; nothing would seem more natural than for him to arm himself with stringent facilities for enforcing the completion of a proceeding which, of strict right, ought never to have been extended or deferred. Whether an agreement, Convention or Pact became a Contract depended on the question whether the law annexed an Obligation to it. The Obligation was the bond or chain with which the law joins together persons in consequence of their voluntary acts. Obligation signified both the right to have a debt paid as well as the duty of paying it. Romans kept the entire picture of the legal chain before it and regarded one end of it no more and no less than the other. Performance of either side imposed an ethical as well as a legal duty on the other. This was the first instance that moral considerations appeared as an ingredient in Contract-law. In the developed Roman law, the Convention, as soon as it was completed, was in almost all cases crowned with the Obligation, and so became a Contract. The chain was only undone by the full completion of the Contract.

....

The Law of Nature denoted the material universe, signifying the physical world, regarded as the result of some primordial element or law. In its simplest and most ancient sense, Nature was the manifestation of some single principle. Later the moral was added to the physical world in the Greek conception of Nature. They extended the term until it embraced not merely the visible creation, but the thoughts, observances and aspirations of mankind, all resolvable into some general and simple laws. Just as the material universe had evolved from its simple primitive form into its present heterogenous condition the human race could conform itself to simpler rules of conduct and a less tempestuous life. To live according to nature came to be considered as the end for which man was created, and which the best men were bound to compass. To live according to nature was to rise above the disorderly habits and gross indulgences of the vulgar, to follow higher laws of action which nothing but self-denial and self-command would enable the aspirant to observe. This being the sum of the famous Stoic philosophy, upon the subjugation of Greece the ideas made instant progress in Roman Republican society. It possessed natural fascination for the class which still adhered to the simple habits of the ancient Italian race, while contrasted with the later unbounded profligacy which was being diffused throughout the imperial city by the pillage of the world and by the example of its most depraved practices.

Equity in law refers to a body of rules existing above the civil law, founded on distinct principles and superseding the civil law in virtue of a superior sanctity inherent in those principles. The claim to authority is grounded, not on the prerogative of any person or body, not even on that of the magistrate who enunciates it, but on the special nature of its principles, to which all law ought to conform. The very conception of a set of principles, possessing intrinsic ethical superiority, invested with a higher authority than civil law and demanding application independently of the consent of any external body, belongs to a much more advanced stage of thought than that of anything previously conceived.

The character and history of the Equity of Roman law exercised profound influence on human thought, and through that seriously affected the destinies of mankind. In the *Institutional Treatise* published under the Emperor Justinian it was written that "all nations who are ruled by laws and customs, are governed partly by their own particular laws, and partly by those laws which are common to all mankind. The law which a people enact is called the Civil Law, but that which natural reason appoints for all mankind is called the Law of All Nations, because all use it." The widespread presence of foreigners on Roman soil explains the difference in usage; it exposed the difficulty of dealing with a multitude of persons who, not coming within the technical description of indigenous Romans, were nevertheless permanently located within Roman jurisdiction. It was probably half as a measure of police and half in furtherance of commerce that jurisdiction was first assumed in disputes to which the parties were either both foreigners or a native and a foreigner. This assumption brought with it the immediate necessity of discovering some principles on which the questions to be adjudicated upon could be settled. Roman lawyers refused to settle the cases by pure Civil Law, as this lowered their law to apply to the particular state from which the litigant came and gave the others the advantage of their own indigenous *Jus Civile*. The expedient resorted to was that of selecting the rules of law common to Rome and the different communities in which the immigrants were born. In other words, they set themselves to form a system answering to the Law of all Nations. When a particular usage was seen to be practiced by a large number of separate races to achieve a common object, though perhaps slightly different in actual subordinate form, it was set down as part of this *Jus Gentium*. Precedence was given to the element discerned as underlying and pervading the great variety of usage. By abstracting a common ingredient from the usages observed to prevail among the various tribes surrounding Rome, and, having been classed on account of its origin in the "law common to all nations" it was seen to fit into the conception of Natural Law. For instance, in the conveyance of property we speak of the common ingredient as being the essence of the transaction entered upon and stigmatize the remaining apparatus of ceremony which varied in different communities. Thus were elevated and respected rules and principles so universal. The *Jus Gentium* came to be considered a great though as yet imperfectly developed model to which all law ought as far as possible to conform.

The most striking principle of Natural Law is the conception of the fundamental equality of human beings, the effects of this statement which are far from being exhausted. The Roman jurisconsults of the Antonine era intended to affirm that, under the hypothetical Law of Nature, and in so far as positive law approximates to it, the arbitrary distinctions which the Roman Civil Law maintained between classes of person ceased to have a legal existence. The rule was of considerable importance to the Roman practitioner who must see to the fact that Roman jurisprudence conformed itself exactly to the code of Nature; there was no difference, in the contemplation of the legal tribunals, between citizen and foreigner, between freeman and slave, between Agnate (exclusively male descent, with the father's sole authority) and Cognate (through male and female descent). The peculiar Roman idea that Natural law coexisted with civil law and gradually absorbed it, had been lost sight of, and the words which conveyed a theory concerning the origin, composition and development of human institutions, were beginning to express the sense of a great standing wrong suffered by mankind. This idea transmitted from Rome to France to Jefferson to the Declaration of Independence is one of great importance to the political movements in Great Britain and the United States and which is far from having yet spent itself. Furthermore, the proposition that independent communities, however different in size and power, are all equal in the view of the law of nations, has at times contributed to the happiness of mankind, though it is constantly threatened by the political tendencies of each successive age.

An alliance of Roman lawyers with the Stoic philosophers lasted through many centuries. Ultimately, we have the golden age of Roman jurisprudence fixed by general consent at the era of the Antonine Caesars, the most famous disciples to whom that philosophy gave a rule of life. The belief gradually prevailed among the lawyers that the old *Jus Gentium* was in fact the lost code of Nature, and the assembly of the principles of the *Jus Gentium* was restoring a type from which the law had departed. Alexander Pope went as far as to claim that the State of Nature was the reign of God before the Fall, a system of simple and inflexible laws now being rediscovered. The inference was that it was the Praetor's duty to revive as far as might be the institutions by which Nature had governed men in their primitive state. The progress of the Romans in legal improvement was astonishingly rapid as soon as the stimulus of Natural Law was applied. The ideas of simplification and generalization had always been associated with the conception of Nature; simplicity, symmetry and intelligibility came to be regarded as the characteristics of a good legal system. The great juridical thinkers of the Antonine age produced a system to which few faults can be attributed except it perhaps aimed at a higher degree of elegance, certainty and precision, than human affairs will permit to the limits within which human laws seek to confine them.

Greek theories at once tempt lawmakers to advance while confining them to a particular course of progress. The influence of Roman Equity supplied the jurist with all his materials for generalization, with all his methods of interpretation, with his elucidations of first principles, and with that great mass of limiting rules which were rarely interfered with by the legislator, but which seriously controlled the application of every legislative act. A time always comes, however, when the moral principles originally adopted have been carried out to all their legitimate consequences, and the system founded on them becomes rigid, as unexpansive, and as liable to fall behind moral progress as the sternest code of rules avowedly legal. Such an epoch was reached at Rome in the reign of Alexander Severus (208-235); after which, though the whole Roman world was undergoing a moral revolution, the Equity of Rome almost ceased to expand.

No durable system of jurisprudence could be provided where a community never hesitated to relax the written rules of law in favor of the ideas of right and wrong which happened to be prevalent at the time. There could then be no framework to which the more advanced conceptions of subsequent ages could be fitted. It would amount at best to the philosophy marked with the imperfections of the civilization under which it grew up. The Romans had conceived that by careful observation of existing institutions parts of them could be singled out which either already exhibited, or could by judicious purification be made to exhibit, the vestiges of that reign of Nature they wished to affirm. One of the qualities of Roman national character was the capacity for applying and working out the law, at the cost of miscarriages of abstract justice, without at the same time losing the hope that law may be conformed to a higher ideal. The value and serviceableness of the conception of Natural Law arose from its keeping before it the mental vision of a type of perfect law, and from that inspiration the hope of an indefinite approximation to it, at the same time that it never denied the obligation of existing laws which had not yet been adjusted to the theory. Natural Law was never thought of as founded on untested principles; rather, the notion was that it underlay existing law and must be looked for through it. Its function was remedial, not revolutionary or anarchial. It is impossible to overrate the importance to a nation of having a distinct object to aim at in the pursuit of improvement. The happiness of mankind was assigned as the proper object of remedial legislation.

Legislation was one of the instrumentalities by which the adaptation of law to social wants was carried on, usually by an autocrat or by a parliamentary assembly which was the organ of the entire society. It differs from Equity in that its obligatory force is independent of its principles. No innovator wishes to be suspected of innovating, therefore the efficiency exhibited with which they effect the transformation of a system of laws while concealing the transformation. Legal Fiction designates any assumption which conceals the fact that the rule of law has undergone alteration, its letter remaining unchanged but its operation being modified. The legislature, whatever be the actual restraints imposed on it by a superseding law, acts to impose what obligations it pleases on the members of the community. There is nothing else but a fealty to the greater law to prevent it from legislating in wanton caprice. Legislation may happen to align with Equity in some cases but can only be compelled by the recognition and enforcement of the courts without the concurrence of the prince or parliamentary assembly.

Even the courts themselves become involved in expanding law. As soon as the decisions of case law became numerous enough to supply a basis for a substantive system of jurisprudence it was that precedence, rather than the superseding Code, to which judges seemed to refer. We do not admit that our courts legislate; we imply that they never should, yet the rulings of courts are coextensive with civil rules and the complicated interests of modern society. The legal language adjusts itself to the assumption that the Code is still being followed and its text remains unchanged. The authors of the new jurisprudence profess the most sedulous respect for the letter of the Code. They are merely explaining it, deciphering what was meant by the authors, bringing out its full meaning; yet, in the result, by piecing texts together, by adjusting the law to states of fact which actually presented themselves, by speculating on its possible application to others which might occur, by introducing principles of interpretation derived from the exegesis of other written documents which fell under their observation, they educed a vast variety of canons which had never been dreamed of by the compilers of the Code and which were in truth rarely or ever to be found there. All these treatises of the jurisconsults claim respect on the ground of their assumed conformity with the Code, but their comparative authority depended on the reputation of the particular jurisconsults who gave them to the world-see John Marshall. Any name of acknowledged greatness clothed a decision with a consecrating, binding force hardly less than that which belonged to enactments of the legislature, and such a collection constituted a new foundation on which a further body of jurisprudence might rest. There was nothing to prevent a judge from proceeding to adduce and consider an entire class of questions with which a particular feature of the original decision connected. As the end of the Roman Republic neared there were signs that this expansion of decisions, the uncontrolled multiplication of cases for adjudication, was assuming a form which must have been fatal to any further progress.

Praetorian Edict, or Statute Law, was the inevitable next step as the Republic transformed into the Empire. It was scarce with the former and voluminous with the latter. The enactments of emperors, clothed at first in the pretense of popular sanction, soon emanated undisguisedly from the imperial prerogative; they extended in increasing massiveness from the consolidation of Augustus' power to the publication of the Code of Justinian. The remaining history of Roman law involves these imperial constitutions and at the last the attempts to codify what had become an unwieldy body of jurisprudence. The strong will, and unusual opportunities of Justinian were needed to bring the Roman law to its existing shape, but the ground plan of the system had been sketched long before the imperial reforms were effected. Nature implied symmetrical order, first in the physical world, and next in the moral. The theory came in surrounded with all the prestige of philosophical authority and its association with an elder and more blissful condition of the race-the recovery of a lost perfection-the gradual return to a state from which the race has lapsed.

This tendency to look backward instead of forward for the goal of moral progress, to borrow from Greece the doctrine of a Natural state of man, anterior to the organization of a community by positive laws, produced on Roman jurisprudence effects the most serious and permanent. While there is nothing in ancient literature mandating that the progress of society is necessarily from worse to better, it is not easy to say what turn the history of thought, and therefore of the human race, would have taken, if the belief in Natural law had not become universal in the Greek world. We see, then, in the annals of Roman law, the combination of all the causes which contributed to its advancing and perfecting, an invariable sequence identical with necessary connection-the march of ideas from one great landmark of jurisprudence to another, from the Twelve Tables to the severance of the two Empires, a crumbling of one system and the formation of new institutions from the recombined materials, institutions some of which descended unimpaired to the modern world, while others, destroyed or corrupted with barbarism in the dark ages, had again to be recovered by mankind. Everywhere, in the final reconstruction by Justinian, symmetry, simplification and new principles usurped the old, and a new morality displaced the canons of conduct and reasons for acquiescence which were in unison with the ancient usages. The vast influence of the specific jurisprudence of Contract produced by the Romans upon the corresponding department of modern law did not make itself fully felt until the school of Bologna revived the legal science of twelfth-century Europe, following the recovery of a copy of the Corpus Juris Civilis of Justinian, the finding of which became the reason for the establishment of the first university in Europe and its first faculty of law.

There are two subjects of thought which are able to give employment to all the powers and capacities which the mind possesses. One of them is Metaphysical inquiry, which knows no limits so long as the mind is satisfied to work on itself; the other is Law, which is as extensive as the concerns of mankind. It happens that the Greek speaking provinces were devoted to one, the Latin speaking provinces to the other, of these studies. Rome and the West had an occupation in hand fully capable of compensating them for the absence of every other mental exercise, and the results achieved were not unworthy of the continuous and exclusive labor bestowed on producing them. Roman law had worked itself into Western thought not through the archaic system of the ancient city, nor the pruned and curtailed jurisprudence of the Byzantine Emperors; still less was it the mass of rules, nearly buried in a parasitical overgrowth of speculative legislative doctrine, which passes by the name of Modern Civil Law. When the new Eastern capital had been created at Constantinople, and the Empire subsequently divided into two-one Greek, one Latin-the divorce of the Western provinces from Greek theological speculation, and the West's exclusive devotion to jurisprudence, became more decided than ever.

The intellectual activity of the Western Romans had been *exclusively* expended on jurisprudence. They had been occupied in applying a peculiar set of principles to all the combinations in which the circumstances of life are capable of being arranged. For carrying it on they possessed a vocabulary as accurate as it was copious, a strict method of reasoning, a stock of general propositions on conduct more or less verified by experience, and a rigid moral philosophy. It was impossible that they should not select from the questions indicated by the Christian records those which had some affinity with the order of speculations to which they were accustomed, and that their manner of dealing with them should borrow something from their forensic habits. Anyone with a knowledge of Roman law may be trusted to say whence arose the frame of mind to which the problems of Western theology proved so congenial, and whence the description of reasoning employed in their solution.

Politics, Moral Philosophy and Theology found in Roman law was not only a vehicle of expression but the nexus in which some of their profoundest inquiries were nourished into maturity. The human mind has never grappled with any subject of thought unless it has been provided beforehand with a proper store of language and with an apparatus of appropriate logical methods. While vernacular Latin was degenerating into a barbarous dialect the only language which retained sufficient precision for philosophical purposes was the language of Roman law. As Roman jurisprudence supplied the only means of exactness in speech, still more emphatically did it furnish the only means of exactness, subtlety and depth in thought. The phraseology employed in metaphysical and theological inquiries was exclusively Greek and studied only in the Eastern half of the Empire. The earliest language of the Christian Church was Greek, and the problems to which it first addressed itself were those for which Greek philosophy in its later forms had prepared the way. Greek metaphysical literature contained the sole stock of words and ideas out of which the human mind could provide itself with the means of engaging in the most profound controversies. The Latin language and the meagre Latin philosophy were quite unequal to the undertaking. Latin Christianity accepted the creed of the East which its own narrow and barren vocabulary could hardly express in adequate terms. For many, though, of the educated classes in the West, the language of jurisprudence stood in the place of the poetry, history, philosophy and science of the East. It was not only the mental food of the ambitious and aspiring but the sole outlet of all intellectual activity. It is precisely because the influence of jurisprudence began to be powerful, that the foundation of Constantinople and the subsequent separation of the Western Empire from the Eastern, are critical epochs of philosophical history. What was it then, on two sides of the line which divided the Greek speaking East from the Latin-speaking West, in terms of the theological problems encountered there? Anyone who will observe in what characteristics the earliest Western theology and philosophy differ from the phases of thought which preceded them, may safely pronounce what was the new element which had begun to pervade and govern speculation. As the separation between East and West became wider the difference between the two theological systems is accounted for by the fact that, in passing from East to West, theological speculation had passed from a climate of Greek metaphysics to one of Roman law. It furnished a new body of words and ideas which then were from time to time forming on the subject of political obligation and the expression of moral truths. Like all great subjects of modern thought, the science of Moral Theology, was undoubtedly constructed by taking principles of conduct from the system of the Church, and by using the language and methods of jurisprudence for their expression and expansion.

The nature of Sin and its transmission by inheritance-the debt owed by man and its vicarious satisfaction-the necessity and sufficiency of the Atonement-above all the apparent antagonism between Free-will and Divine Providence-these were the points which the West began to debate as ardently as the East had discussed the articles of its creed.

The phraseology of Roman Contract law also began to be called upon to describe that reciprocity of rights and duties between sovereign and subjects. The consciousness of correlative rights possessed by the governed would have been entirely without the means of expression if the Roman law of Obligation had not supplied a language capable of shadowing forth an idea which was as yet imperfectly developed. The antagonisms between the privileges of rulers and their duties to their subjects have never been lost sight of since Western history began. The phraseology borrowed from the Law of Contract, which had been used in defense of the rights of subjects, crystallized into the theory of an actual original compact between the king and people, and was expanded into a comprehensive explanation of all the phenomena of society and law.

CHAPTER THREE-THE RIGHTS OF MAN

WILL DURANT
ARIEL DURANT

ISABEL PATERSON
THOMAS PAINE

RUSSELL KIRK
EDMUND BURKE

CLINTON ROSSITER SIR
HENRY SUMNER MAINE

FORREST MCDONALD

"Men's appetites are voracious; they are restrained by the collective and immemorial wisdom we call prejudice, tradition, and morality-reason alone can never chain them to their duty. Whenever the crust of prejudice and prescription is perforated at any point, flames shoot up from beneath, and terrible danger impends that the crack may widen, even to the annihilating of civilization. If men are discharged of reverence for ancient usage, they will treat this world as if it were their private property, to be consumed for their gratification, and thus will destroy in their lust for enjoyment the property of future generations, of their own contemporaries, and indeed their very own capital."

Russell Kirk, *The Conservative Mind*, 1953

"You defend the conservative principles on which our ancient system is founded, and the liberty and the individual responsibility attendant upon it; you defend especially the institution of property. One can hardly conceive life without these laws. Yet this I own, that this old world, beyond which we cannot see, appears to me to be almost worn out; the vast and venerable machine seems more out of gear every day; and though I cannot look forward, my faith in the continuance of the present is shaken...But it is no less the duty of honest people to stand up for the only system which they understand, and even to die for it if a better be not shown to them."

Alexis de Tocqueville, *Letter to Mrs. Grote,* July 24, 1850

"I have said on a former occasion...that I would employ a man to say it every day, that the people of this country, if they ever lose their liberties, will do it by sacrificing some great principle of government to temporary passion. There are certain great principles, if not held inviolate, at all seasons, our liberty is gone. If we give them up it is perfectly immaterial what is the character of our sovereign-whether he be King or President-we shall be slaves. It is not an elective government which will preserve us."

John Randolph

"When I contemplate the natural dignity of man; when I feel the honor and happiness of his character, I become irritated at the attempt to govern mankind by force and fraud, as if they were all knaves and fools, and can scarcely avoid disgust at those who are thus imposed upon."

Thomas Paine, *The Rights of Man,* 1791

John Locke's time (1632-1704) is a legitimate starting point for this portion of our inquiry, leading to an examination of the proper axioms of Law, by assembling bit by bit fragments of human behavior from which the "natural" man might be formulated. His *Second Treatise* remains a chief landmark of political thinking. To understand this work in its derivation, one needs to go back to the contrast between nature and convention established by the early Greek thinkers, and to the conception of a law of nature that grew out of this contrast, largely under Stoical influence, and became embodied in Roman law. Finally, one needs to trace through the centuries the process by which the Roman juristic conception finally became, in writers like Locke, the doctrine of the rights of man. The doctrine of natural rights, as maintained by Locke, looks forward to the American Revolution, and, as modified for the worst by Rousseau, to the French Revolution. Contrasted to Hobbes dim vision, Locke's state of nature is liberty, equality and reason. Locke's common good is taken to be identical with the protection of property.

If the artificial restrictions on society were just abolished man could then function more as he was designed to do. Americans had reached this continent by their own efforts in the teeth of Authority; they conquered enormous odds in taming the wilderness, incident to setting up local government. The central clue to the reform program of the philosopher Founders was their faith in Natural Law...all that was needed to unlock the millennium was a Euclid of the political sciences who would discover and formulate the natural principles of social harmony; it seemed a reasonable surmise that fundamental laws of human society and relation to government could be discovered by their combined genius. The principle of social harmony is liberty; the rights of the individual *are* the Natural Laws of man. For solitary man in search of spiritual peace, for society in search of permanent order, Natural Law has furnished means by which mankind may apprehend the moral universe. Life is possible to a human being only by virtue of his capacity for independent action. Liberty is truly part of Natural Law; man exists only by his rational volition and free will. Hence the rational and natural terms of human association are those of voluntary agreement, not command. Therefore, the proper organization of society must be that of free individuals. Only by the freedom of personal volition is man capable of pursuing his intellectual inquiries and making his inventions. Only the protection of private property makes personal volition possible. This was the genesis and genius of capitalism. And the equality of individuals is posited on the plain fact that the qualities and attributes of a human being are ultimately not subject to change at all, but one of the axioms of existence.

Our legal conceptions-using that term in its largest sense to include social and political institutions-are as much the product of historical development as biological organisms are the outcome of evolution. There is indeed a natural history of Law. Natural societies are comparatively free from law first because they are ruled by customs as rigid and inviolable as any that might be written. Custom is the time-hallowed mode of thought and action which provides a society with some measure of steadiness and order through all absence, changes and interruption of law. Custom gives the same stability to the group that heredity and instinct give to the animal, and habit to the man. It is the routine that keeps man sane, providing a path along which thoughts and action can move with unconscious ease; the mind otherwise would be perpetually hesitant and seek refuge elsewhere. A law of economy works in instinct and habit, in custom and convention; the most convenient mode of response to repeated stimuli or traditional situations is the automatic response.

Others had, in their analysis of legal sovereignty, postulated the commands of a supreme lawgiver by simply ignoring the fact that, in point of time, custom precedes legislation, and that even earlier law is a habit, and not a conscious exercise of the volition of the lawgiver or a legislator. The institutions, customs, arts and morals of a people represent the natural selection and elimination of its countless trial-and-error experiments, the accumulated and informulable wisdom of all its generations. Conventions are forms of behavior found expedient by a people; customs are conventions accepted by successive generations; morals are such customs as the group considers vital to its welfare and development; laws are the means by which society tries to compel adherence to such morals. In societies these customs or morals regulate every sphere of human existence and give stability and continuity to the social order. Through the slow magic of time customs, by long repetition, become second nature in the individual; if he violates them, he feels a certain fear, discomfort or shame; this is the origin of that conscience, or moral sense, which Darwin chose as the most distinctive difference between animals and men. The habits of obedience become the content of conscience, and soon every citizen is instilled with loyalty to right reason. In its higher development conscience is the feeling in the individual that he belongs to a community and owes it some measure of loyalty and consideration. Morality is this cooperation of the part with the whole, and of each community with some larger whole. Civilization, of course, would be impossible without it.

Prejudices, prescription and presumption are the instruments which the wisdom of the species employs to safeguard man against his own passions and appetites. Men must adapt this inherited mass of opinion to the exigencies of present times. The presumption must be that the innovator is wrong, that it will be wiser to continue an old practice rather than break radically with custom and risk poisoning the body social. The longer our prejudices have lasted, the more generally they have prevailed, the more we cherish them. The bulk of mankind have neither the leisure nor knowledge to reason right…will not honest instinct and wholesome prejudices guide them, much better than half-reasoning? Courage is required to make declarations in defense of prejudice. A prejudice is by no means necessarily an error; it may be an unquestioned truth, though it may remain a prejudice in those who, without examination, take it upon trust and entertain it by habit. Prejudice is not bigotry, though it may degenerate into that; prejudice is pre-judgment; the answer with which intuition and ancestral consensus of opinion supply a man when he lacks either time or knowledge to arrive at a decision predicated upon pure reason. It is an expedient. No man is prejudiced in favor of a thing, knowing it to be wrong. He is attached to it on the belief of its being right; and when he sees it is not so, the prejudice will be gone.

Prescription-the customary right which grows out of the conventions and compacts of many successive generations; presumption-inferences in accordance with the common experience of mankind-and prejudice-the half-intuitive knowledge that enables men to meet the problems of life without logic-chopping-these instruments enable men to live together in some degree of prosperity and amicability. Somewhere there must be control upon will and appetite; the less that there is within, the more there must be without. If one or the other of these checks fails to be in place only rationality remains for preventing man from relapsing into the primitive state which Hobbes described. But the mass of mankind hardly reasons at all-they can do no more than cheer the demagogue, enrich the charlatan and submit to the despot. Human reason can only assist in the adjustment of the old order to new things if it is employed in the spirit of reverence and used by men who are aware of their own fallibility. Yet most men form their opinions according to transitory circumstances and imperfect knowledge. Burke writes: "We are afraid to put men to live and trade each on his own private stock of reason; because we suspect that this stock in each man is small, and that individuals would do better to avail themselves of the general bank and capital of nations and the ages. Human beings participate in the accumulated experience of their innumerable ancestors; very little is totally forgotten. But only a small part of this knowledge is formalized in literature and deliberate instruction; the greater part remains embedded in custom, prejudice and common usage. Ignore this enormous bulk of practical knowledge, or tinker impudently with it, and man is left afloat in a sea of feelings and aspirations, with only the scanty stock of formal learning and the puny resources of individual reason to sustain him." A purely traditional humanism is always in danger of falling into a rut of pseudoclassic formalism. But the observance of prejudice and prescription does not condemn mankind to a perpetual treading in the footsteps of their ancestors. Men cannot be kept from social change-it is inevitable and designed for the larger conservation of society; properly guided, though, change is a process of renewal. But change must come from a need genuinely felt, not inspired by some Leftist abstraction. The difference between a slow, natural alteration and the infatuation of the hour must be discerned. The perceptive reformer combines an ability to adapt with a disposition to preserve.

Custom rises out of the people whereas law is forced upon them from above; law is a decree, but custom is the natural selection of those modes of action that have been found most effective in the experience of the group. Every habit was developed for some important purpose. Law replaces custom when the state disturbs the natural order of the family unit and the local community; it more fully replaced custom when writing appeared, and laws graduated from a code carried down in the memories of elders and priests into a system of legislation proclaimed in written form. The development of writing virtually created civilization by providing a means for the recording and transmission of knowledge, the accumulation of science, the growth of literature, and the spread of peace and order among peoples brought together by one language in a single state. This replacement, though, is never complete; in the determination and judgment of human conduct custom remains to the end the force behind the law and the last magistrate of men's lives. In such rough ways, through thousands of years, those traditions and habits of order and self-constraint were established which became part of the unconscious basis of civilization. The foundations of a civilized moral order are reverence for our forefathers and compliance with our prescriptive duties; history is the source of all worldly wisdom.

When to this natural basis of custom, a supernatural sanction was offered by religion, and the ways of one's ancestors was also the will of the gods, then custom became stronger than law, and subtracted substantially more from freedom of will. The Church looked with suspicion upon the advance of scientific rationalism because it might unveil to modern man the real secrets of his origins. Edmund Burke nevertheless recognized a divine order, the reality of a providential purpose and intelligent direction in the cosmos-the instinct for the perpetuation of the species, the compulsions of conscience; the intimations of immortality; the participation in some great continuity and essence are all evident in his writings. He had no sympathy with Polybius' suggestion that the ancients invented religion to save men from anarchy, or with Plato's willingness to create religious mythology out of whole cloth so that man will reverence the established order, in the illusion that it was ordained from the very beginning of things. According to Burke, the state was willed to us as the means whereby our natures could be perfected by our virtues. He could not conceive of a durable social order without the spirit of piety.

"The instincts which give rise to the process of nature are not of our making. But out of physical causes, unknown to us, perhaps unknowable, arise moral duties, which, as we are able to perfectly comprehend, we are indispensably bound to perform." The *is* becomes the *ought.* Burke is saying that the whole of Natural Law-earthly reality-is an expression of a moral order. Nature is not simply the sensation of the passing moment; it is eternal, though we evanescent men experience only a fragment of it. We have no right to imperil the happiness of posterity by impudently tinkering with the heritage of humanity. Men have no rights to what they please: their natural rights are only what may be derived directly from their human nature. Natural right is deduced from a mythical primeval condition of freedom described by Hobbes and Rousseau and a psychology chiefly from the thoughts of many others drawn together into the writings of Locke. To assure the reign of justice and to protect the just share of each man in the social partnership, government is established. The true natural rights of men are equal justice, security of labor and property, the amenities of civilized institutions, and the benefits of orderly society, none of which may be deprived or divested to our posterity. Without these rights government is usurpation. In nature men are obviously unequal-in mind, in body, in every material circumstance. Justice requires that every man receive according to the quality and quantity of his work though there is often in this competition a manifest inequality from the start. But deny the initial differences between men in favor of some egalitarian theory and one runs into the most palpable facts. Genuine justice demands that men should be judged, not by their intentions, but by their actual performance, no matter to what is attributed his superiority. One's view of work and of the rewards it deserves will necessarily determine one's attitude toward property. The laws of nature make no provision for sharing goods without regard for individual energies or merits, nor is political power naturally egalitarian. The barren monotony of any society stripped of diversity and individualism means a nation of slaves with a handful of masters. Social and political equality do not fall within the category of the real rights of man; on the contrary, aristocracy and hierarchy are the natural, the original framework of human life.

Edmund Burke again: "The rights of men, the natural rights of mankind, are indeed sacred things; and if any public measure is proved mischievously to affect them, the objection ought to be fatal to that measure. If these natural rights are further affirmed and declared by express covenants, if they are clearly defined and secured against power and Authority, by written instruments, they are in a still better condition: they partake not only of the sanctity of the principle so secured, but of the public wisdom itself, which secures an object of such importance. The things secured by these instruments may be very fitly called the chartered rights of man."

Burke's Platonic version of natural right is human custom attempting to conform with a divine blueprint. We know God's law only through our own laws that attempt to copy His. It was, of course, the old illusion that law has a supernatural origin superior to man, that it was a human groping after divine enactment. The principle of inner control that one needs impose upon the expansive desires is plainly a quality of will. The human will is hopelessly alienated from the divine will by the Fall. The gap between the two can only be traversed by a miracle of grace, a miracle that itself depends on the miracle of redemption. Since the Fall man's will is in helpless bondage to sin. He not only needs the mediation of Christ if his will is to be brought into harmony with the divine will, but also of the church and the sacraments and the elaborate priestly hierarchy that is required to administer them.

To think that divine law could not operate within the sanction of our human legislation would be presumptuous. As with the *Jus Gentium*, our imperfect statutes were only a striving toward an eternal order of justice, but there was no facile covenant, no utopian constitution written on a wall somewhere. We rise, slowly and feebly, out of the ancient imperfections of our nature, towards the light. Empirically, never does Nature say one thing and Wisdom say another. Human nature resides in man at his highest, not his simplest. Not natural man, but civilized man, was the object of Burke's solicitude. The purpose of civil society is "a conservation and secure enjoyment of our natural rights; to abolish or suspend these true rights in order to conform to some fanatic scheme for establishing some new fancied rights is a procedure as preposterous and cruel in argument as it is oppressive and cruel in its effect. As to the right of men to act anywhere according to their pleasure, without any moral tie, no such right exists."

It is never the object of conservatism to oppose all change, but rather to continue a school of politics, founded upon these concepts of veneration and prudence, to oppose the appetite for innovation, experiment and meddling; to counterpose complex forces to hem us in and condition all we do against the power to react against and modify the very environment that limits us. Radical innovations would cut us off from our past, destroying the bonds joining generation to generation, leaving us isolated from memory and from aspiration. Man is the only living species that can transmit and expand his store of knowledge from generation to generation; but such transmission requires a process of thought on the part of individual recipients. As witness, the breakdowns of civilization, the Dark Ages in the history of man's progress, when the accumulated knowledge of centuries vanished from the lives of men who were unable, unwilling or forbidden to think. Law is not manufactured-it grows; society cures its own maladies, effects its own adjustments, by a natural, self-healing process; the impertinent doctrinaire reformer almost certainly will obstruct this process without providing any passable arbitrary substitute.

Revolutionary radicals have such a commitment to change, and are so unwilling to brook delay, that they are prepared to work this change by subversion and violence. Their attitude toward the social process is simple and savage: they mean to disrupt the process as quickly and completely as possible in defiance of all rules. They are unaware of the logic of conservatism. Conservatism believes in preserving the great achievements of the past. It will be reactionary if that means acting against ignorant and reckless efforts to destroy precisely what is most precious in our great economic, political and cultural heritage, in the name of alleged progress. "Hasty innovation may be a devouring conflagration, rather than the torch of progress." (Kirk) A splendid storehouse of integrity and freedom has been bequeathed to us by our forefathers. In this day of confusion, of the extreme peril to liberty, our high duty is to see that this storehouse, like the Library at Alexandria, is not burned and robbed of its contents.

The older verities are closest to the origin of humankind. The essence of conservatism is the preservation of these ancient moral traditions. History eloquently makes clear the necessity and sources of order. Against those who claim that all values are relative, derived from will and desire, it shows their immutability over twenty-five centuries. To review the history of conservative ideas and examine them for validity in our own age, in the continuity of the American tradition, is another purpose of this study. Only through a reawakened moral imagination can order, justice and freedom be sustained through the coming difficult years. Liberty had risen through an elaborate process; its perpetuation depends upon retaining those habits of thought and action which guided the natural man in his slow and weary ascent to the state of civil social man. Habit and prejudice induce that conformity without which society cannot endure. Otherwise encouraging moral extravagance for the sake of novelty is as dangerous an experiment as man can undertake. Conservatism is an affirmation of normality in the variable concerns of society. There exist standards to which we may repair; man may achieve a tolerable degree of justice and freedom; a civil social order is possible. The mass of men must find renewed hope, true family links with the past, expectations for the future, duty as well as right, and resources that matter more than the mass amusements and vices in which the modern proletariat seeks to drown his mental faculties. The degeneration of the family and the plague of social boredom spreading in ever widening circles will bring a future more dreary than the round of life in the decaying Roman Empire.

Conservatism can be explained in intellectual, psychological, social and economic terms. It is conscious of the history, structure, ideals and traditions of society; of the real tendencies and implications of reform proposals, and the importance of maintaining a stable social order. Its principles are daily examined and found to be good. Its sense of history leads people to appreciate the long and painful process through which it developed onto something worth defending. Slow change is thus the means for society's preservation. A conservative sets severe conditions upon political alterations. Change must have preservation, and even restoration as its central object, be severely limited in scope and purpose, and worked out by slow and careful stages. A new constitution incorporates a good part of the old, and most successful reforms in the pattern of government are only recognitions of prescriptive changes that have already taken place. The essence of Conservatism is the feeling for the possibilities and limits of natural, organic change-change and reform that are sure-footed, discriminating and respectful of the past. The currents of change are channeled into the stream of progress by institutions and values that have stood the test of time. New laws must honor the traditions of the nation, meet the requirements of abstract justice, and be adjusted to the capacities of the citizenry.

"To discover the order which inheres in things rather than to impose an order upon them; to strengthen and perpetuate that order rather than to dispose things anew according to some formula which may be nothing more than a fashion; to legislate along the grain of human nature rather than against it; to pursue limited objectives with a watchful eye; to amend here, to prune there; in short, to preserve the method of nature in the conduct of the state"-this is Conservatism. (Burke)

Conservatives are full of harsh doubts about the goodness and equality of men, the wisdom and possibilities of reform, and the sagacity of the majority. They are deeply aware that constitutional republics are the only real alternative to totalitarianism. They refuse to contemplate Utopia, much less draw plans up for it. The many builders of Conservatism over the millennia have shared a common faith and purpose, sifting through history's prejudices, dogmas, theories and intuitions and creating a harmonious system of political principles exhibiting a high degree of unity and internal consistency. They hold definite opinions about man's nature, his capacity for self-government, his relations with other men, the kind of life he should lead, and the rights he may properly claim.

What Western system of ideas, common to England and the United States, has been transmitted to, and sustained men of conservative instincts in their resistance against radical theories and social transformation since the times of the Greeks and Romans? The soul of this Humanistic discipline is a study of the classics; they teach the meaning of Time and confirm in man his better judgement against the ephemeral and vulgarizing solicitations of the hour. Homer appealed to the assembly of gods for judgment upon a debased age. Sophocles, constant to normative truth in a century undone by sophistry, exhorted the Athenians to obey divine injunctions, superior to the edicts of man. Virgil, seeking to restore civilization after a generation of civil war, took for his themes the high old Roman virtue and the life-giving Roman piety. Dante, seeing the medieval order shattered by ignorance, selfishness and crime, described in his magnificent vision the antagonist realms of order and disorder. Machiavelli strove to retore the Italian State. Some Americans took their republicanism directly from these ancient sources. Among the more widely read Romans were Cicero, Livy, and Tacitus; among the Greeks, Demosthenes, Aristotle and Polybius. The most widely read ancient work was, undoubtedly, Plutarch's *Lives.* These men comprise part of the unnamed and immeasurable force lodged as a mystical purpose within the unfolding universe-not God, but knowledge-gained, kept and transmitted.

Writers of American political tracts conventionally signed their articles with pseudonyms such as Centinel, Cato, Brutus or Cassius, thereby identifying themselves with defenders of the late Roman Republic. Hamilton, Madison, and Jay signed their *Federalist Essays* as Publius, after the leader who established the Republican foundation of Rome. General Washington had Joseph Addison's play *Cato* performed at Valley Forge to boost the morale of the frozen troops. The writings of classical antiquity were especially "elegant and instructive," for in the histories of the ancient world would be found "a just hatred of tyranny and a zeal for freedom." (Quincy) Even being largely unfamiliar with the ancient sources Americans could nonetheless absorb republican sentiments and values without being fully aware of where they originally came from. Half of our political knowledge revolved around the mortality of those older republics. Mingled with their historical citations were repeated references to Natural Law writings of Enlightenment philosophers and the common-law writings of English jurists-both contributing to a more rational understanding of the nature of politics. No matter how eclectic were the Founder's historical and philosophical gleanings, to Eighteenth century Americans they represented the experience and reason of the Western world. The abstract process of development, the Laws or uniformities which applied equally to all peoples in all situations had been ransacked. They sought, as did the Romans and their *Jus Gentium*, constant and universal precepts about human and social behavior allowing them to discover those fundamentals applicable to every sort of government. They sought the "broadest Bottom, the Ground of Nature." (Lee) It was generalizations, scientific principles about the historical process that the age was after; men were engrossed in discovering the connectedness of things, particularly the relations between governmental institutions and society, and the principles that governed their changes through time. Society was organic and developmental rather than manufactured. The more thoroughly we understood our own political tradition, the more readily its whole resources were available to us, the less likely we should have been to embrace those false steps which waited for the ignorant and unwary. There is the illusion that in politics we can get on without a tradition of behavior, an illusion that the abridgement of a tradition is itself a sufficient guide to the future. Mutilate the roots of society and tradition, and the result must inevitably be the isolation of a generation from its heritage, the isolation of individuals from their fellow men, and the creation of the sprawling, faceless masses.

Robert Taft wrote: "In our Declaration of Independence, the Founding Fathers, with daring accuracy, planned and blueprinted the capture and subjugation of that elusive and often tyrannical thing called Government. Later, in the Constitution, they effectively seized the Government, securely tied it down, root, stem and branch. With the past history of the world spread out before them, these founders knew, as Washington said, that Government "is not reason, it is not eloquence, it is force. It is like fire, a dangerous servant and a fearful master. Never should it be left to irresponsible action." Before the revolutionary time, the uncontrolled and apparently uncontrollable fire of government *had* swept back and forth over the human race, burning man's freedom to a dry and painful crisp. "It shall not happen here," said the Founding Fathers-and so the fire of Government which they lighted in the Declaration was immediately restricted and confined behind the iron walls of narrow Constitutional limitations. Then and there, liberty was not merely proclaimed; it was practically defined and positively guaranteed to those who then and would subsequently be fortunate enough to be Americans. "Liberty", said the Founders, "lives only in a climate of strictly limited Government. Where the Government is unlimited, no citizen is free."

Speaking of the continuity which the tradition set forth by a principled constitution can provide, Edmund Burke wrote: "As the ends of such a partnership cannot be obtained but in many generations, it becomes a partnership not only between those who are living, but between those who are living, those who are dead, and those who are yet to be born. Each contract of each particular state is but a clause in the great primeval contract of eternal society, linking the lower with the higher nature, connecting the visible and invisible world, according to a fixed compact sanctioned by the inviolable oath which holds all physical and moral natures, each in their appointed place. A nation is not an idea only of local extent, and individual momentary aggregation; but it is an idea of continuity, which extends in time as well as in numbers and in space. And this is a choice not of one day, or one set of people, not a tumultuary and giddy choice; it is a deliberate election of ages and of generations; it is a constitution made by what is ten thousand times better than choice, it is made by the peculiar circumstances, occasions, tempers, dispositions, and moral, civil and social habitudes of the people who disclose themselves only in a long space of time."

Real harmony with the natural law is thus attained through adapting society to the model which eternal nature-physical and spiritual-sets before us. The exercise of any right must be circumscribed and modified to suit particular circumstances. Burke again: "Our political system is placed in a just correspondence and symmetry with the order of the world, and with the mode of existence decreed to a permanent body of transitory parts; wherein, by the disposition of stupendous wisdom, molding together the great mysterious incorporation of the human race, the whole, at one time, is never old, or middle-aged, or young, but in a condition of unchangeable constancy, moves on through the varied tenor of perpetual decay, fall, renovation and progression. Thus, by preserving the method of nature in the conduct of the state, in what we improve, we are never wholly new in what we retain, we are never wholly obsolete."

Spiritual continuity, much like a corporation that is always internally perishing and yet always renewing, the immense importance of keeping change within the framework of custom, and the recognition that society is an ongoing concern, helped England substantially abolish feudalism in the seventeenth century: all classes freely intermingled, all men were equal before the law, equal taxes prevailed; a free press, public debates, an eclipsed nobility, wealth rather than birth was installed as the path to aristocracy-all were phenomena unknown to medieval society. The old body was infused with young blood to preserve its life. Contract replaced Status.

Political tradition in any country develops as the result of a vast pattern of forces-ethnic, geographic, religious, sociological, economic, cultural and ideological. In America the unifying principle was a consuming belief in individual liberty. Such optimistic thought came easily to men living on the frontier-forests to be cut, soil to be plowed, rivers to be channeled and traveled upon, natural resources to be tapped. This was an environment inspiring to a new race more concerned with getting ahead than in maintaining the status quo. Change and progress *was* the American way of life. Following the Revolution Americans began their experiment of liberty with a society more open, an administration more constitutional, and minds more free than anything Europeans had known or would know for generations. It had no feudal past, no national church, no hereditary stratification of classes, no centralized and arbitrary government. The country inherited the freest society in the world, and this was bound, at least for a time, to influence their thinking on political matters.

Out of the past have come the values and institutions that have lifted man to civilization. The nature and capacities of man, the purposes and dangers of government, the origins and limits of change-we learn these things best by studying the past. Without the teachings of men and events, what other resources can we draw upon in the struggle for civilized survival? One can always read of the wickedness, folly, misery and failure embedded in the cruel delusions of Utopia and the tyrannies of force. Without principles, all reasoning in politics, as in everything else, would be only a confused jumble of particular facts and details, without the means of drawing out any sort of conclusions. Principle is right reason expressed in permanent form. One arrives at a principle through comprehension of nature and history, looked upon as manifestations of moral purpose. Principle becomes the director, the regulator and the standard of all the virtues. Men consent to live under mutually agreed upon principles to better their lives and those of the community.

In every man there is a sphere of personality and activity into which other men, whether private citizens or public officials, have no logical or moral claim to intrude. This sphere is protected by the Rights of Man. When a country's constitution places individual rights outside the reach of public authorities, the sphere of political power is severely delimited-and thus the citizens may, safely and properly, agree to abide by the decisions of a majority vote in this other, delimited sphere. The lives and property of dissenters or minorities are not at stake, are not subject to the vote of or endangered by a majority decision; no one holds power over their lives. But a nation that violates the rights of its own citizens can have no moral standing of its own. Individual rights are not subject to a public vote; a majority has no right to vote away the rights of the minority. "Man did not enter into society to become worse than he was before, nor to have fewer rights than he had before, but to have those rights better secured. His natural rights are the foundation of all his civil rights. Natural rights are those which appertain to man in right of his existence. Of this kind are all the intellectual rights, or rights of the mind, and also all those rights of acting as an individual for his own comfort and happiness, which are not injurious to the natural rights of others. Civil rights are those which appertain to man in right of his being a member of society, the enjoyment of which his individual power is not sufficiently competent. Of this kind are all those which relate to security and protection. The natural rights which he retains are all those in which the power to execute is as perfect in the individual as the right itself. The natural rights which are not retained are all those in which, though the right is perfect in the individual, the power to execute them is defective. He therefore deposits these rights in the common stock of society. Civil power is made up of the aggregate of that class of natural rights which are defective in point of power; but when collected to a focus, becomes competent to the purpose of everyone. Society grants him nothing. Every man is a proprietor in society and draws on his capital as a matter of right. The power produced from the aggregate of natural rights, imperfect in power in the individual, cannot be applied to invade the natural rights which are retained, in which the power to execute is as perfect as the right itself." (Thomas Paine, *The Rights of Man)*

If society is the environment in which abstract rights come to life, then government is the agency that defines and protects them. The rights that men in fact enjoy have developed through centuries of struggle to a point where they are recognized and enforced by Law. They are legal, constitutional and historical. Life, liberty and property form the irreducible minimum that must be honored. Property is as important to man's existence and improvement as any other right-conscience, association, expression and justice-and therefore must be championed without reserve. Property makes it possible for man to develop and grow to maturity and wisdom. It makes it possible for man to live freely, independent of any other persons or agencies, for food, shelter or material comforts. Property grants men a sphere in which he may ignore the state; a demarcation around the sphere of government activity; government cannot push into the area reserved to the individual, nor exercise their legitimate powers in an arbitrary manner. Property is essential to the existence of family, the natural unit of society. It provides the incentive for productive work which is essential for progress.

Behind our liberties, laws, customs, rules of conduct and Constitution stand eternal principles of right and justice. No free government or the blessing of liberty can be preserved to any people but by a firm adherence to justice, moderation, temperance, frugality and virtue, and by frequent recurrence to these fundamental principles. This ineluctably leads to calls for the restoration of the constitutional government of the United States. It is the foundational underpinning of our national life. Our constitutional system has proved to be the most effective protection for human liberty ever devised by the brain for the purpose of man. Ordinary law must conform to the higher law or be utterly void; for extra-constitutional acts, there is no Authority even where not restrained by an express prohibition. For as there are unchangeable principles of right and morality, without which society would be impossible, and men would be but wild beasts preying upon each other (Hobbes State of Nature), so there are fundamental principles upon the existence of which all constitutional government is founded, and without which government would be an intolerable and hateful tyranny. Respect for the old ways and permanent values is the prerequisite for true progress.

The Progressive erosion of this underpinning now threatens to topple the whole superstructure of American freedom. If America falls, all of that which goes by the name of civilization will be suffocated in the ruins. Liberty was the foundation of our government, the reason for our growth, the basis of our happiness, and the hope of the future. The greatest threat to liberty today is internal, from the constant growth of government, specifically the constantly increasing power and expansion of the federal government. The price of continued liberty, including a free economic system, is the reduction of federal spending and taxes, the repudiation of arbitrary powers in the Executive and Congress, and the stand against the statutory extension of power and law by the creation and growth of the bureaucracy. The traditional suspicion of government exercising concentrated, arbitrary power is well-founded. Not once, anywhere in history, has that model proved the answer to the wish for justice and order.

To be a conservative in the United States has for so long been considered identical with being backward. Thoughtful Americans concerned with the rapidity with which totalitarian theories have spread through the country should re-acquaint themselves (below) with the founding principles. These tracts open men's eyes to the splendor of our moral heritage-the permanent things of human existence. They teach us a way of life, one tried in experience and springing from our condition-resisting the destruction of the old patterns of life and the damage being done to the footings of the social order. Short cuts to Utopia are the road to ruin. We are not called upon to immediately scrap or transform some malfunctioning part of the order, but to get it into the hands of better men and rebuild it to the specifications or our Founders. The conservation of America's moral worth, its regeneration, a conservatism of prosperity and hope, and a free and benevolent Republic should be the core of any program of national renewal.

These principles alone can transform a confused mass into as purposeful conservative movement.

CHAPTER FOUR-THE STATES DEBATE

NATURAL LAW AND VIRTUE

ROSE WILDER LANE
GORDON WOOD

SIR HENRY SUMNER MAINE
ISABEL PATERSON

CLINTON ROSSITER
RALPH KETCHAM

RUSSEL KIRK

"In free governments and equal representations, the levy of taxes, or other state transactions, do not imply compulsion; for how can that be compulsion, which reason has suggested, his delegate advised, and his self-permitted?"

Anonymous, 1783 Rudiments of Law and Government, Deduced from the Law of Nature

"Men become concerned about government because they participate daily in the affairs of their tithings and towns, not only by paying taxes but by performing public duties and by personally making laws. When these tasks are taken out of the people's hands and given to superior bodies to perform, men fall into a political stupor, and have never, to this day, thoroughly awakened, to a sense of the necessity there is, to watch over both legislative and executive departments in the state. If they have now and then opened their eyes, it is only to survey, with silent indignation, a state from whence they despair of being able to recover themselves."

(Demophilus, Genuine Principles)

"The people of Britain, through long ages of civil war, extorted from their rulers-not acknowledgements, but grants, of right. With this concession they were content to stop. They received their freedom as a donation from the Sovereign; they held title to their liberty, like their title to lands; in their moral and political chronology the great charter of Runnymede was the beginning of the world. But instead of solving civil society into its first elements in search of their rights, they looked only to conquest as the origin of their liberties and claimed their rights but as a donation from their Kings. This faltering assertion of freedom neglected to trace civil government to its foundations in the moral and physical nature of man."

John Quincy Adams, *Independence Day Speech,* 1826

The passage of political development is especially well known to us through the accidents which have preserved to us a portion of the records of two famous societies, the Athenian Republic, the cradle of philosophy, art and science, and the Roman Republic, giver of Law and destined through conquest to embrace a great part of the world. The opinion that Democracy was irresistible and inevitable, and probably perpetual, would have in earlier times appeared a wild paradox. There had been more than 2000 years of tolerably well ascertained political history. Monarchies and some aristocracies had shown themselves extremely tenacious of life. But the democracies which had risen and perished, or had fallen to extreme insignificance, seemed to show that this form of government was a rare occurrence in political history, and was characterized by an extreme fragility. At worst Democracy meant the end of feudal society and at best it signified the ascendancy of the middle classes. Nothing is more remarkable than the small amount of respect for it professed by actual observers, who had the opportunity and the capacity for forming a judgment on it. The founders of Athenian political philosophy found themselves in the presence of Democracy, in its pristine vigor, and thought it a bad form of government. The Roman Empire, the Italian tyrannies, the English Tudor Monarchy, the French centralized Kingship, the Napoleonic despotism, were all hailed with acclamation, most of it perfectly sincere, either because anarchy had been subdued, or because petty local and domestic oppressions were kept under, or because new energy was infused into national policy. From the reign of Augustus Caesar to the establishment of the United States it was Democracy, as a rule, that was on the decline. The French Revolution and Terror completely stopped any further progress. But it was only as the political history of the American Union developed itself that we were able to detect in wide popular government the same infirmities that characterized the kingly governments, of which they are inverted reproductions. Under the shelter of one government or the other, all sorts of selfish interests breed and multiply, seizing on weaknesses and pretending to be its servant, agent and delegate. Democracy differs from autocratic Authority only in essence. It has exactly the same conditions to satisfy; it has the same functions to discharge; the tests of success in the performance of the necessary and natural duties of government are precisely the same in both cases.

The Founders, as educated men, had studied the many attempts to establish Authority; each had in their libraries thousands of years of human experience with every form of Government to review and think about. They believed if we were to resist tyranny "they ought to be well versed in the various governments of ancient and modern states, search into the spirit of the British Constitution; read the histories of ancient ages, contemplate the great examples of Greece and Rome; set before us the conduct of our own British ancestors, who have defended for us the inherent rights of mankind against foreign and domestic tyrants and usurpers." (Adams) If a man called himself a Republican, he was thinking of the Athenian or Roman Republic, one for a while possessing a certain sense of democracy, the other from first to last an aristocracy. It is of no small importance that a nation should possess a class of public men of undoubted competence and experience, who have a large stake in the prosperity of the country, who possess a great position independent of politics, who represent the traditions and continuity of political life, and may be trusted to administer affairs with complete personal integrity and honor. Out of their reading of the classics and of the contemporary histories of the ancient world, all set within the framework of Enlightenment science, the Americans put together a conception of the ideal republican society, filled with great and manly virtues that they would have to have if they would sustain any new republic, where every man was master of his own soul and destiny.

The classical world had been the main source of inspiration and knowledge for enlightened politicians at least since Machiavelli, and never more so than to the classical republicans and their heirs of the seventeenth and eighteenth centuries. Classicism helped shape their values and their ideals of behavior. The Americans interest in the ancient republics was crucial to their attempt to understand the moral and social basis of politics. The American view of antiquity was highly selective, focusing on decline and decadence; the names of the once-renowned ancient republics were full of instruction for those attempting to build a new republican world. Those vices which ruined the illustrious republics of Greece, and the mighty commonwealth of Rome, and which were just then ruining Great Britain, must eventually overturn every state, where their deleterious influence is suffered to prevail. The history of antiquity thus became a kind of laboratory in which autopsies of the dead republics would lead to a science of social illness and health matching the science of the natural world. It was not the force of arms which made the ancient republics great, or which ultimately destroyed them. It was rather the character and spirit of the people. The traits of character most praised were restraint, fortitude, dignity and independence. Frugality, industry, temperance and simplicity-the rustic traits of rural yeomen-were the stuff that made a society strong. Republics died not from invasions from without but from decay from within.

Rome's preeminence in the ancient world and its influence on Western culture was the result of the literary legacy Rome had passed on to the modern world, a body of writing that was obsessed with the same questions about degeneracy that fascinated the eighteenth century. Rural life was celebrated not for its wild or natural beauty but for its simplicity and repose, which Horace, Virgil and Ovid showed virtuous men could retire to after a lifetime of devotion to duty and country. More pessimistic Romans such as Cicero, Sallust, Tacitus and Plutarch contrasted the growing corruption and disorder they saw about them with an imagined earlier republican world of ordered simplicity and arcadian virtue and sought to explain the transformation. It was if these writers, in their literature of republican nostalgia were speaking directly to the revolutionary concerns of the eighteenth century, scrutinizing not only actions but motives.

By 'reading and reasoning' on politics the Founders had learned 'how to define the rights of nature-how to search into, to distinguish, and to comprehend, the principles of physical, moral, religious and civil liberty,' how, in short, to discover and resist the forces of tyranny before they could be applied. "Justly it may be said, the present is an age of philosophy, and America is the empire of reason." (Randolph) From the outset the colonists attempted to turn their decade-long controversy with England into a vast exercise in the deciphering and applying of the philosophy of the age. By drawing on the evidence of antiquity and their own English past as transmitted to them through the radical Whig tradition the colonists sought to formulate a science of politics and of history that would explain what was happening to England and themselves. Americans knew their rights and the limits of power and aimed to act before it was felt. This one thing gave the Founders pause: their *fear* of Democracy. They had no faith in The People and no notion of consulting or obeying public opinion. The Constitution was not their ideal; it was an effort at compromise, a desperate hope. The men who devised this new Government were not enthusiastic. They had no dreams of any Utopia. You can see their realism in the words that they wrote. They did not regard adult human beings as helpless children. They knew that all men, by their nature, are free. Weakening the government, hampering its use of force in human affairs, was the only way to permit individuals to use their natural freedom. The divisions and prohibitions contained in the structure of American Constitutional Government made it the weakest that could possibly exist at that time. They prevented monarchy. They went on to prevent democracy.

At this time French philosophers were writing about the Mechanistic Universe-its wheels revolving forever, never changing, nothing new being created-it simply is; that's all. It has been created; now it is controlled. What controls it? The answer is Natural Law. Men do not make the principles of astronomy or mathematics, nor give properties to the circle or the triangle, they discover these facts. The French were crazy about Science and made it their new God. A false Civilization had gotten control of man, causing all human miseries and crimes. Civilization depended upon Religion, and Science, the new hope of mankind, was making war on Religion. Science would win the war, destroy Religion and wipe out corrupt Civilization with all its evils. Science would then reveal Natural Law. This would establish the Age of Reason. All of this intellectual world was far above the heads of most Americans. In America they read the Bible. In Genesis they read the hypothesis of creation, and the evolutionary theory of life's development on earth. They read the unsparing analysis of human motives and human nature. They read the words of Abraham and Moses and Gideon and Christ, saying that every individual is self-controlling and responsible; these words checked with the fact they knew from experience. So when the British Government tried to control them, they ignored it. When the King tried to control trade, they went right on trading. Cutting it off would have meant widespread ruin in the British colonies. This made criminals of every colonist.

The Founders did not talk, following the French, about Science and the Age of Reason. They knew men. They were realists. The men fighting the war had no Latin or Greek, they knew nothing about all the previous efforts to make democracy work, yet they were shouting for it. Since the opening phase of the Revolution the inherited system of government by gentlemen chosen by a restricted electorate had been under severe assault from the disenfranchised and disinherited. The drive of the plain people and their leaders to democratize the limited Republic of the Fathers initially concentrated on state constitutions while the Articles of Confederation remained nominally untouched. The discussion of political ideas that accompanied and followed the American Revolution was seminal to the effort in 1787-88 to draft and ratify a new constitution for the United States. The colonies-turned-states were a laboratory of proposals and revised forms of union and confederated government. There were years of vigorous, creative political thinking which produced hundreds of pamphlets, sermons and newspaper articles on the questions at hand.

The original sacrifice of individual interests to the greater good of the whole was alone enough to make the Revolution one of the great Utopian movements of history, where the common good would be the only objective of government, a vision, however, divorced from and contrary to the purposes and reality of the final Constitution. That the great body of people could have an interest separate from their country, or individuals thereof, was not to be imagined. By allowing the people to elect their magistracy, republicanism would work to blend the interests of the people and their "rulers" and thus put down every animosity among the people. In the kind of state where their governors shall proceed from the midst of them the people could be surer that their interests would exclusively be promoted. The common interest was not simply the sum or consensus of the particular interests that make up a community. It is rather an entity in itself, prior to and distinct from the various private interests of groups and individuals. At that period it was still believed that the State, that Authority had a legitimate interest and will of its own. No one denied that the community was filled with different, often clashing combinations of interests. But these interests and parties were regarded as aberrations in the body politic and should not be dignified by their incorporation into the political theory being formulated. Party differences should never be admitted into the institutions of government. The representatives of the people would not act as spokesmen for private interests but be disinterested men who could have no interest of their own to seek and thus would work only to achieve the public good. Because of the persistence of social incoherence and change in the eighteenth century, Americans creating a new society could not then conceive of the state in any other terms than organic unity. Rousseau's *general will* had seemingly won the day. The contracts, balancing mechanisms and individual rights so much talked about in 1776 were generally regarded as defenses designed to protect a united people against their rulers and not yet as devices intended to set off parts of the people against the majority. The solution to the problems of American politics seemed to rest not so much in emphasizing the private rights of individuals against the general will as it did in stressing the public rights of the collective people against the privileged interests of their rulers. A tyranny by the people was theoretically impossible, because the power they held *was* liberty, whose abuse could only be licentiousness or anarchy. Thus in 1776 individual rights possessed little of their modern theoretical relevance when set against the will of the people. Even John Adams thought a democratic despotism was a contradiction in terms. Who could be more free than the People who representatively exercise supreme power over themselves?

Under the pressures of the intensifying controversy the American's conception of their place in history was suggested in their writings and deduced from their understanding of the nature of social development. The Americans began piecing together the immense significance of what they were involved in, ultimately creating one of the most coherent and powerful revolutionary ideologies the Western World has seen. The theory of government that the Americans clarified in their reading and discussion possessed a compelling simplicity: politics was nothing more than a perpetual battle between the passions of the rulers, whether one or a few, and the united interests of the people. Every state differed in religion, laws, customs and manners. Every man followed his own interest as he understood it, similar enough though in the essentials of society and government to be connected for the purposes of politics. The remedy was thought to be the transference of political power to the entire community. It was impossible that they should abuse it, for the interest they would try to promote was the interest of all, and the interest of all was the proper end and object of all legislation. Frequent and short periods for Congress, returning immediately to private life to experience the consequences of their actions was the answer. Congress could presumably never enact legislation contrary to the interests of the whole people. Applying the rule to the whole of a political community, we ought to have a perfect system of government. But in what sense can a multitude exercise volition? Taking it in connection with the fact that the masses include too much ignorance to be capable of understanding their interest, it furnished, for some, the main principle *against* Democracy.

Let us assume an election which extracts a vote from every eligible elector. It is, then, that the average opinion of a great multitude has been obtained, and this average becomes the basis and standard of all government and law. There is hardly any experience of the way in which such a system would work, except in the eyes of those who believe that history began with their own birth. The strangest of vulgar ideas is that a wide suffrage could or would promote axioms of progress, new ideas, new discoveries and inventions, or new arts. The realization of universal suffrage in its consequences has always been the end of the beginning of representative government. Parliamentary government which is mainly directed by the educated and propertied classes is an essentially different thing from parliamentary government resting on a purely democratic basis. In all the instances where a conservative government is returned it is on the basis of a restricted suffrage. Suffrage may only be extended to lower classes where the powers of the representative body are greatly limited. The most certain effects of wide suffrage would be the extensive destruction of existing institutions. For to what end, towards what ideal state, is the process of stamping upon Law the average opinion of an entire community directed? The principles of legislation at which they point would probably put an end to all social and political activities and arrest anything which has ever been associated with Republicanism. To what social results does the Progressive overthrow of existing institutions promise to conduct mankind? It merely prepares us for the Great Reset.

It is possible, by agitation and exhortation, to produce in the mind of the average citizen, a vague impression that he desires a particular change. They mix up the theory that the masses are capable of volition, with the fact that it is capable of adopting the opinions of one man or of a limited number of men, and of founding direction to its instruments upon them. Phrases like the "will of the people," "public opinion," and the "sovereign pleasure of the nation," mean that a great number of people, on a great number of questions, can come to an identical conclusion, and found an identical determination on it. But this is manifestly true only of the simplest questions; a slight addition of difficulty at once diminishes the chance of agreement. On the more complex questions of politics, which are calculated in themselves to task to the utmost all the powers of the strongest minds, but are in fact vaguely stated, and dealt with for the most part in the most haphazard manner by the most experienced statesmen, the common determination of a multitude is a chimerical assumption; and, indeed, if it were really possible to extract an opinion upon them from a great mass of men, and to shape the administrative and legislative acts of a State upon this opinion as a sovereign command, it is probable that the most ruinous blunders would be committed, and all social progress would be arrested.

Fisher Ames, the forgotten Founder, set the tone: "Democracy fails on both legitimate objects of government: the protection of property and the tranquility of society. Even Federalism was based on a fallacious premise: "the supposed existence of sufficient political virtue and the permanency and authority of the public morals." Of all the terrors of democracy, the worst is its destruction of moral habits. Popular reason does not always know how to act right, nor does it always act right, when it knows. "The agents that move politics, are the popular passions; and those are ever, from the very nature of things, under the command of the disturbers of society…Few can reason, all can feel; and such arguments are gained, as soon as they are proposed. Nor can constitutions, however artfully designed, suffice to restrain men who have embraced the doctrines of complete equality and an inalienable popular right to power. *The key to political decency lies in private morality.* (Author's italics) Every student of history is aware of the significance of this particular symptom lurking in a democracy, when it is found wanting. Corruption is not intimidated by a parchment charter. When the old respect for hierarchy and prescriptive title are swallowed up, only naked force counts, and a constitution may be torn to scraps in an instant. To mitigate a tyranny is all that is left for our hopes." The political smashers are always at work, and their dupes are constantly multiplying. Yet there is little corresponding activity in applying the proper tests to all this spurious manufacture. No greater service can be rendered to his country by men of ability than to analyze and correct the assumptions which pass from mind to mind among the masses, inspiring a doubt of their truth and genuineness.

John Adams: "With Democracy, the day always comes, when a multitude of people, none who have more than half a breakfast, or expects to have more than half a dinner, will choose the legislature. There will be nothing to restrain the poor from despoiling the productive. The Constitution is all sail and no anchor. Once entered upon this downward progress, either civilization or liberty must perish. You will have created Huns and Vandals within the country by the corruption of its own institutions."

Alexander Hamilton never hid his own contempt for the common people, speaking repeatedly of "the folly and wickedness of Mankind" and "the ordinary depravity of human nature." In his *Speech on the Compromise of the Constitution,* June 21, 1788, Hamilton declaimed: "It has been observed that a pure democracy, if it were practicable, would be the most perfect government. Experience has proved, that no position in politics is more false than this. The ancient democracies, in which the people themselves deliberated, never possessed one feature of good government. Their very character was tyranny; their figure deformity. When they assembled, the field of debate presented an ungovernable mob, not only incapable of deliberation, but prepared for every enormity. In these assemblies the enemies of the people brought forward their plans of ambition systematically. They were opposed by their enemies of another party; and it became a matter of contingency, whether the people subjected themselves to be led blindly by one tyrant or by another."

Democracy hopes to find the equivalent of standards and leadership in the appeal to a numerical majority. A large number of individuals falsely believe that the majority is another Authority that has a right to control them. The majority chooses a man or men to run the Government. But Government cannot control anyone; it can only hinder, restrict, or stop anyone's use of their energy. Because a majority supports the ruler, nothing checks the use of force against the minority. So the rulers of a democracy soon become tyrants. And that is the death of the democracy. Demos, the People, was a fantasy imagined by the ancient Greeks, in their search for an Authority that they imagined controlled men. Democratic Athenians believed that justice was the will of a majority, on the theory that fifty-one men are right and forty-nine are wrong. The notion that wisdom resides in a popular majority at any particular moment should be the most completely exploded of all fallacies.

In practice any attempt to establish democracy is an attempt to make a majority of persons in a group act as the ruler of that group. Goethe wrote: "There is nothing more odious than the majority; for it consists of a few powerful leaders, a certain number of accommodating scoundrels and subservient weaklings, and a mass of men who trudge after them without in the least knowing their own minds…everything that frees a man's soul, but does not give him command over himself, is evil." And every attempt to establish democracy has failed. It failed in Athens twenty-five centuries ago. It failed in France when the majority elected Napolean. It failed in Germany when a plurality elected Hitler. Just as a man can evade the responsibility of dealing with reality, so a society can evade reality and establish a system ruled by arbitrary dictates, by the majority at any given moment, led by the current demagogue, achieving nothing save the rule of brute force and progressive self-destruction. Nothing that society does is right solely because society chose to do it. When Madison wrote that "democracies have ever been found incompatible with personal security and the rights of property," all Americans knew that he was saying that majority-rule has always been the enemy of human rights, and that he was stating the reason why this Republic was not a democracy. Madison knew the historic fact that in a democracy there is nothing to check the inducements to sacrifice the weaker party. There is no protection for liberty.

Majority rule, even with delegated representatives, means that the majority may vote away the rights of a minority-and dispose of their lives, liberty and property, until such time, as they may form a bigger gang, and do the same to the first group. It means the majority may do anything it wishes; that anything it does is right and practical, because it is omnipotent. Political freedom requires much more than the wishes of a majority. It requires an enormously complex knowledge of political theory and how to implement it in practice. It took centuries of intellectual and philosophical development to achieve political freedom. It was a long struggle, stretching from Aristotle to Cicero to John Locke to the Founding Fathers. The system finally established was not based on unlimited majority rule, but on the opposite: individual rights, which were not to be alienated by majority vote or government action. The individual was not left at the mercy of his neighbors or the politicians: the Constitutional system of checks and balances was devised to protect him from both. The honest and serious students of American history will recall that our Founding Fathers managed to write both the Declaration of Independence and the Constitution without using the term "democracy." No part of any one of the existing state constitutions contained any reference to the word. Such men as Adams, Madison, Hamilton, and Jefferson, who were the most influential in the institution and formation or our government refer to 'democracy' only as an epithet, to distinguish it sharply from the Republican form of our American Constitutional system. In scorning democracy eighteenth century theorists had in mind Aristotle's picture of a heedless, emotional, manipulated populace. This warning was the great American achievement and is what we should be teaching the world.

The antecedents of a body of institutions like this, and its mode of growth are found in the *Federalist* papers, published in 1787-1788 by Hamilton, Madison and Jay. The purpose was to explain the new Constitution, then awaiting ratification, and to dispel misconstructions of it which were already in circulation. They show us the route by which the strongest minds among the American statesmen of that period had traveled to the conclusions embodied in the Constitution, or the arguments by which they had become reconciled to them. There was also a body of Anti-Federalist papers, revealing the dissenting opinions of such statesmen as Patrick Henry and John DeWitt, who saw in the

Constitution threats to rights and liberties so recently won from England. Henry stated that "the preservation of our liberty depends on the single chance of men being virtuous enough to make laws to punish themselves." The problem that he and many other Anti-Federalists saw was the lack of responsibility, the lack of means to hold men answerable to something higher, implying the possibility of their punishment.

About the *Federalist*, Guizot said that in the application of the elementary principles of government to practical administration, it was the greatest work known. "The acuteness of understanding would do honor to the most illustrious statesmen; a work on the principles of free government comparable in instruction and intrinsic value to those of Aristotle, Cicero, Machiavelli, Montesquieu, Locke or Burke. It is equally admirable in the depth of its wisdom, the comprehensiveness of its views, the sagacity of its reflections, and the freshness, simplicity and eloquence with which its truths are uttered." (Chancellor Kent) The writers attach especial importance to all of Montesquieu's opinions. But far the most important experience to which they appealed was that of their own country-the earliest link had been supplied by the first Continental Congress. The miscarriages in particulars and disappointments in actual execution, of the Articles of Confederation, gave rise to a storehouse of instances and warnings to the writers who undertook to remove its vices in the new Constitution. It was written in the infancy of constitutions, when the inefficiencies of requisitions were unknown, no commercial discord had arisen among any states, no rebellion had appeared in Massachusetts, foreign debts had not become urgent, and the havoc of paper money had not been foreseen. These were the subsequent defects that the Founders sought to remedy. This new constitutional link had to be formed from local materials; there were none for making a hereditary King or Second Chamber; yet the means to discharge the functions of this now separated portion of the British Empire must somehow be found. The American constitution was the fruit of signal sagacity and prescience applied to this necessity.

The signers of the Declaration had undertaken not only to win a war against impossible odds, but to create an entirely new kind of government. Without unity, without money, without an organized army, without any social order or any Ruling Authority, surrounded on all sides by the Spanish and the British, America won the war. Eternal vigilance would be the price of the liberty won. Only the ordinary, unknown individual could defend freedom on earth, for not by any use of force can men in Government maintain any man's use of his natural human rights. In one century an entirely new world was created, a dynamic world, constantly changing under the drive of a terrific, incalculable energy. What permits this? Nothing but the existence of conditions which permit that energy to operate naturally, under its own natural control. Then what are the conditions that permit human energy to work effectively to satisfy human needs and desires? The unhindered use of natural rights-free thought, free speech, free action and freehold property-created the modern world. Nothing else makes it possible for men to create new things, and improve them, and keep on improving them.

With independence it became obvious that the Continental Congress, not really a governmental body and created out of the exigency of events, needed some more solid basis; the congressional delegates immediately began working on an agreement that would permanently connect the new states by means of the Articles of Confederation. Similar to the Roman search for *jus gentium* the colonists continually sought to define those "fundamental principles, those true, certain and universal principles, those Sacred Laws of Justice," from the English constitution. The isolating of these fundamentals from the rest of the constitution was what marked their peculiar conception of government, but it was not an isolation easily achieved. The thread of the argument led from an admiration for the perfection of the British constitution, to the idea that it was but a jumble of contradictions, and incongruous with the laws of Nature. Bred up in the erroneous notion of the freedom and excellence of the English constitution the states unthinkingly adopted many of its faults. The Americans had initially uncritically imitated the English constitution, attempting to balance different bodies, as if, said Turgot, "the same equilibrium of powers which has been thought necessary to balance the enormous preponderance of royalty, could be of any use in republics, formed upon the equality of all citizens." The people could hardly have two different wills at the same time on the same subject.

It became the responsibility of the Founders to closely investigate the origin of power and deduce from unvarying laws the designs of the British monarchy and make clear to their fellow subjects what had happened. They knew it would be no small task to awaken the people to the dangers confronting their liberties. Men were born to be deluded, "to believe whatever is taught, and bear all that is imposed." Insignificant, piecemeal changes, none of which seemed decisive or unbearable at the time, spread over the country in such a manner as to touch individuals but slightly. America's political history was, and remains today, an object lesson in the power of the seemingly insignificant. Every one of Parliament's acts of usurpation was like a small spark which had suddenly blazed out into an irresistible flame. "From what slight beginnings the most extensive consequences have flowed." While political leaders used some British concepts and precedents, they also fashioned anew for a new nation in a New World. New institutions and new ideas of government were needed, then, to replace the rejected British models and form a new polity.

In the 1760' English constitutionality was identified with legality and continually assumed that English rights, government, laws, and constitution were all of a piece, all bound together and "fixed in judgment, righteousness and truth," permeated by common principles of equity and justice and by a common respect for the "natural, essential, inherent, and inseparable rights of the people, rights that no man or body of men, not excepting Parliament, can take away." Edmund Burke wrote: "Parliament was not a congress of ambassadors from different and hostile interests, which interests each must maintain, as an agent and advocate, against other agents and advocates; but Parliament is a deliberative assembly of one nation, with one interest, that of the whole, where, not local purposes, not local prejudices ought to guide, but the general good, resulting from the general reason of the whole."

What was never conceived were that there were principles and rights so fundamental that they had to be differentiated and separated from the institutions of government and the ordinary statutes of government. It was deemed impossible for the absolute and unaccountable power of Parliament to act against the constitution or the rights of the colonists since it was from that very constitution that the political and civil rights of the colonists were derived. But the Crown and Parliament must be restrained from arbitrary violations of the fundamental principles and rights embedded in the ancient common law and the constitution by the inner workings of the institutions of government; if not, then somehow these principles and rights must be protected and guaranteed by lifting them out of government. "Something must exist in a free state, which no part of it can be authorized to destroy, otherwise the idea of a constitution cannot subsist. (Hume) The liberties of the people were only statutes of Parliament, but they were undoubtedly of a nature more sacred than those which established a turnpike road." It seems inconceivable that the liberties of the people should depend upon nothing more permanent or established than the vague, rapacious, or self-interested inclination of a majority of Parliament, open to the insidious attacks of weak and designing parties. And yet the Founders' English ancestors had made no provision for limiting the power of the people's representatives, because they never imagined they could ever possess an interest distinct from that of his constituent, or that pecuniary advantage could outweigh the public good in his breast.

All previous nations had been compelled to accept their constitutions from some conqueror, or some supreme lawgiver, or had found themselves entrapped by a form of government molded by accident, caprice or violence. Americans were the first people who had the opportunity of deliberating upon and choosing the form of government under which they would live. The building of a permanent foundation for freedom was the essence of the Revolution. Americans had very little beyond their reading of the classics, British ideology and practical experience from which to fashion a new nation. But the political language of Great Britain had long since lost its relevance for Americans, and they recognized it. A century and one-half of physical separation and relatively isolated development had nurtured what in many ways were two distinctive societies. "The mysterious doctrine of undefinable privileges, transcendent power and political omnipotence ascribed to the British parliament, may do very well in a government where all authority is founded in usurpation, but ought certainly to be forever banished from a country that would preserve the freedom of a commonwealth." (T.T. Tucker) "The British constitution was established only on precedents, or compulsory concessions, upon a compromise of differences between two or more contending parties, each according to the means it possesses, extorting from the others every concession that can possibly be obtained, without the smallest regard to justice or the common rights of mankind. Whatever stability there was in the English government was a kind of truce, a government of contention, in which the opposite parties had been for a length of time by chance so balanced as not yet to have destroyed each other. The King, Lords and Commons were limited in an uncertain way with respect to each other, but the three together were without any check in the constitution, and none could be properly called the representatives of the people. Acts of Parliament, though law, were not declaratory of the ancient principles of *traditional* law." As Jefferson said, "their purpose was to make law where they found none, and to submit us at one stroke to a whole system no particle of which has its foundation in the Common Law."

Common law was that system of law introduced by the Saxon upon their settlement in England and altered from time to time by proper legislative authority to the date of the Magna Carta, which terminated the period of the Common Law, and began that of Statute Law. Such a distinction between unwritten and written law came to correspond in American thought with the distinction between legal and constitutional. "The only remedy for the people was rising in a tumultuous opposition or civil war." The controversy with Britain tended to obscure American factional politics, cementing for a time in one common cause those various interests which were otherwise to later break into parties and ruin each other.

The separation from Great Britain had left Americans with an uncertain national identity, an intriguing republican idealism, and an intricate array of unresolved tensions and practical problems. Between 1776 and 1787 Americans undertook to create a new republic. They had to articulate and establish, perhaps with a revised understanding of human nature itself, the basic principles and axioms of free government. Beginning with New Hampshire every state drafted at least one constitution in the intervening decade. They added considerable practical experience in forming new laws; they tried many novel proposals for the legislative, executive and judicial departments, all of which contributed to the idea that Americans could govern themselves.

The Massachusetts General Court declared "that the fundamental basis of all laws is the law of God and right reason, and that if anything hath been otherwise established, it was an error, and not a law…, however it may bear the form of a law." Law was not the enacted will of a legislature but more in the nature of a judgment declaratory of the moral principles of the Law. The presumption was that a law had to be intrinsically just and reasonable in order to indeed be Law. Such a belief in the morality of law had been a central part of the American's legal history in the New World. Their law had existed in such a confused and chaotic state that the only criterion for its authority had seemed to be its intrinsic justice.

It was the very simplicity of American jurisprudence, trying to adapt itself to the complex subtleties of English legal practice, statutes and court precedents, that created the ambiguities and complexities of colonial law. With no printed indigenous decisions there could be little reliance on local precedents other than those in memory, while citing English authorities seemed to expand rather than restrict judicial discretion. The use of some writs and not others, the corrupting and blending of forms of action, the avoidance, insufficient and inaccurate pleadings lying at the heart of common law jurisprudence helped to create an atmosphere of permissiveness and uncertainty which a clever lawyer could exploit. These legal complexities were responsible for the colonist's central concern for reason and equity in their law, where the right reason of the common law, as accumulated and passed on in the law reports and minds of the English judges, had constructed and controlled the declarations of what was properly and equitably the law in every particular case. Parliament was the sovereign lawmaker in the country whose power, however arbitrary and unreasonable, was uncontrollable. It could even create new law whose binding force came not from its intrinsic justice and conformity to the principles of the common law, but from its embodiment of the will of the social constituents of the nation or simply from its sovereign authority. Alternatively, the binding force of common law came not from enactment but from long and immemorial usage preserved in the law books and court decisions from earliest times. But Law was more than a judgment, more than simply the acts of a court that could be interpreted, adjusted or voided by other, superior, courts when required by the principles of reason and equity that supposedly adhered in all Law. Numerous precedents served no other purpose than to increase the influence of lawyers, who could cull through and select them to answer every purpose. "What people in their senses would make the judges, who are fallible men, depositaries of the law; when the easy, reasonable method of printing, at once secures its perpetuity, and divulges it to those who ought in justice to be made acquainted with it?" (Moses Mather) Society needed but a few laws, and these simple, clear, sensible and easy in their application to the actions of men. Jefferson said of his efforts at reformation in Virginia "that it was at last possible for the whole legal system to be reviewed, adapted to our republican form of government, and corrected in all its parts, with a single eye to reason, and for the good of those for whose government it was framed."

"Man's essential rights are guaranteed not by pieces of paper but by the laws of God and nature as well as by the common law and the constitution of the country. If an act of Parliament should annihilate all those charters it could not in any way shake one of the essential, natural, civil or religious rights of the colonists." (James Otis) Such rights and liberties, said John Dickinson in 1766, were not annexed to us by parchment and seals. They are created in us by the decrees of Providence, which establish the laws of our nature. They are born with us, exist with us, and cannot be taken from us by any human power, without taking our lives. In short, they are founded on the immutable maxims of reason and justice. "Legal rights are those rights which we are entitled to by the eternal laws of right reason." (Philip Livingstone) Putting them on parchment did not create them; it only affirmed their natural existence. An Englishman's rights existed in the maxims of the common law and nature, whatever Parliament might or might not say. The attempt by codification to explode all law from precedent only made the attaining of simplicity and equity more difficult. Allowing judicial discretion to set law aside made the judiciary paramount to the legislature, which was never intended either. Law was what the principles of right reason declared to be law, the codification of which could hardly be hardly inclusive.

With the questioning of legislative enactment as the only foundation of law, other criteria were more easily emphasized. It seemed increasingly clear that sound policy and strict justice were inseparably connected; and that nothing ever was politically right that was morally wrong. As Trenchard and Gordon had written in *Cato's Letters,* the essence of law, of right and wrong, did not depend upon words and clauses, inserted in a code or statute book, much less upon the conclusions and explications of lawyers; but upon reason and the nature of things, antecedent to all laws. The result was a growing discussion in pamphlets and the press of the morality and equity that presumably made Law what it was. Will and Law were not synonymous in free governments. The imaginary omnipotence of the legislatures, that whatever is ordained must be law, must be restrained within the bounds of reason and justice. Any acts without such a grounding were null and void, being mere corruptions and not laws. Equity jurisdiction, once so much feared, now seemed increasingly necessary to act upon such parts of Natural Law, as had not been rendered sufficiently clear and plain. Law had to be in accord with common right and natural equity in order to have judicial force.

"The powers of legislation, in every possible instance, are derived from the people at large, are altogether fiduciary, and subordinate to the association by which they are formed." (James Varnum) When the people entered into civil society, the charter or constitution, being conclusive evidence of a compact with the people, surrendered some of their natural rights to government. The representatives of the people were not really the people, but only the servants of the people with a limited, delegated authority to act on their behalf. The aggregate of this surrender of power forms that of the government, including the power to make laws. But the legislature cannot interfere with the retained rights of the people, and it was the duty of the judiciary to measure the laws of the legislature against the constitution and those retained rights. Americans had no intention of enabling the representatives of the people to substitute their will to that of their constituents." (Hamilton) The judges were in a sense as much agents of the people as the legislators; neither could overlap the bounds of their appointment. The judiciary's special task was to reject all acts of the legislature that were contrary to the trust reposed in them by the people. Where the will of the legislature, as declared in its statutes, stands in opposition to that of the people, declared in the constitution, the judges must side with the fundamental law rather than with those which are not.

Amidst the confusion and disorder of colonial law, lawyers and judges really had no other basis but reason and equity for clarifying their thinking and making deviations in their jurisprudence from that of the English. The haphazard and piecemeal introduction of common law into the colonies and the American's adoption of only those laws "which from a similarity of genius and local situation suited this country" strengthened their idea that the authority of law came not from its being old or being English, "but as being founded in the nature and fitness of things." But could a reliance on reason and equity be maintained without the judicial discretion to diverge from English usages, which colonists wished to end? At the Revolution most of the state constitutions provided for the retention of as much of the English statute and common law as was applicable to the local circumstance-until it should be altered by future legislative acts-thus perpetuating the problem while still providing a remedy. What would eventually evolve was a proper system of laws adapted to each particular state and circumstances. Most established legislative supremacy based on these principles of consent in their new constitutions. Those elected often appointed the executive, some judges and other officials. Other states, notably Massachusetts and New York, elected their governor directly by the qualified voters. Bills of Rights were drafted and debated in every state. By 1787 the theory of self-government had been widely debated; virtually every conceivable device for implementing it had been suggested if not tried. The early state constitutions possessed many defects. But in one thing they were all perfect; all left the undistorted, unfiltered and uncorrupted will of the people in the power of altering and amending them, whenever they pleased.

....

Religion had always been the strongest promoter of virtue, the most important ally of a well-constituted republic. Although many Americans in 1776 had blended the evangelical and legal schemes in an uneasy combination, the events of the 1780's were forcing a separation between those who clung to moral reform and the regeneration of men's hearts as the remedy for viciousness, and those who looked to mechanical devices and institutional contrivances as the only lasting solution for America's ills. Since at least the seventeenth century enlightened intellectuals had been fascinated with the attempt to replace the fear of the hereafter as the basis for morality with a more natural scientific psychology. Men must be convinced that their fullest satisfaction would come from the subordination of their individual loves to the greater good of the whole. "Public good is not a term opposed to the good of individuals; on the contrary, it is for the good of every individual collected. The public good is a common bank in which every individual has his respective share; whatever damage that sustains the individual unavoidably partakes of that calamity." (Lovejoy) The jarring interests of individuals regarding themselves only, and indifferent to the welfare of others, with the assistance of the selfish passions, would end in the ruin and subversion of the state. Popularly based government could not be supported without virtue. The best government and the wisest laws would be ineffective among a corrupt, degenerate people. Until "ambition, pride, avarice and all that dark train of passions which usually attend on them were absent from the American soul," many still doubted the outcome. (Charles Inglis) This concept of public spirit-an expected Jeffersonian alteration in the very behavior of the people-laid the foundation of the Constitution not over, but within the subjects. The willingness of the people to surrender all, even their lives, for the good of the state, though, was concretely the philosophy of Rousseau.

Since the individual conduct of those who compose a community must have an intimate and extensive connection with all our public measures, it is from the nature and tendency of that conduct that our public character must receive its complexion. The self-sacrifice and disinterested patriotism of the early war had given way to greed and profiteering at the expense of the army and the public good. The fluctuation in the value of money was making every kind of commerce and trade precarious. Virtue was being debased by the "visible declension of religion, the rapid progress of licentious manners, and open profanity." Luxury was destroying the simplicity of manners, native manliness of soul, and equality of station, which is the spring and peculiar excellence of a free government. Instead of industry, frugality and economy-luxury, dissipation and extravagance were encouraged. Americans had been warned. No virtue, no Commonwealth.

Americans could not rid themselves of the compelling and frightening analogy with the collapse of the ancient worlds of Athens and Rome. Every page of its history shows some instances of the degeneracy of Roman virtue, and the impossibility of a nation's continuing free after its virtue was gone. "Spartan constitutions and Roman manners, peculiar to her declining state, never will accord." Apparently, unlike the early Plebian demand for the Twelve Tables, the revolution from the infection of the mother country had not been in time after all. "In emancipating ourselves from British tyranny, we expected to escape from that torrent of corruption which deluges their land, preys upon the labor and industry of its best citizens and reduces them to little better than slaves. But the expectation was in vain. The child was already going the way of the parent, dissipated and corrupted even as it got on its feet. Americans were "a luxurious, voluptuous indolent expensive people without economy or industry." Such a people could not possess the proper character for republican government. America was not to be another Sparta or Roman Republic after all. "Shall we alone expect an exemption from the fate of mankind? Too much has been expected from the virtue and good sense of the people." (John Jay) "Americans do not exhibit the virtue necessary to support a republican government." "No government under heaven can prevent a people from ruin, or keep their commerce from declining, when they were exhausting their valuable resources in paying for superfluities and running themselves in debt for articles of folly and dissipation. As long as men are morally corrupt, we may contend about forms of government, but no establishment will enrich a people, who wantonly spend beyond their income." (Benjamin Austin) Republicanism could not work unless the foundations of the state were laid as deep as Lycurgus had driven them. Farmers coveted more land as much as merchants were greedy for cash. "Was this not sufficient evidence that the people of this country are not long to be governed in a democratic form?" (Jeremy Belknap)

"We have changed our forms of government, but it remains yet to effect a revolution in our principles, opinions, and manners so as to accommodate them to the forms of government we have adopted. We assumed these forms in a hurry, before we were prepared for them. (Benjamin Rush) Let us have patience. All will end well." In a statement which could serve as a mission statement for the Progressive Party of today, he said: It is possible, to convert men into republican machines. They must be instructed that their lives are not their own. The republican pupil must be taught that he does not belong to himself, but that he is public property." The Founder's radicalism was grounded in the best, most enlightened knowledge of the eighteenth century-from Rousseau-and it was this grounding that gave the Republican ideology much of its persuasive force.

If laws and a constitution must be adapted to the manners of the People, did Americans have the industry, frugality, economy and virtue that was necessary to constitute it? The concept of the Revolution was also intended to be an antidote to moral decay. Success was dependent on the repentance and reformation of the principles and practices of the people. Independence became not only political but moral. Richard Henry Lee, the strongest mind among the Antifederalists, believed the moral regeneration of America's character, rather than legalistic manipulation of constitutions, was the proper remedy for American problems. "I fear it is more in vicious manners, than mistakes in form, that we must seek for the causes of the present discontent." (Letter from Lee to Mason, 1787) Revolution, republicanism and regeneration all blended together in American thinking. There was, the eighteenth century believed, a reciprocating relationship between the structure of the government and the spirit of the people. Republicanism was not only a response to the character of the American people but could be an instrument of reform as well. Men become good citizens or the contrary, noble or base, according to the impression that they have received from the government that they are under. New habitual principles, the constant authoritative guardians of virtue, could be created and nurtured by republican laws, and that, along with the power of the mind, these could give ideas and motives a new direction. By the repeated exertion of reason, by recalling the lost images of virtue: contemplating them, and using them as motives of action, till they overcome those of vice again and again until, after repeated struggles, they at last acquire habitual superiority. The erecting of a Republican government was not only a natural political adjustment to the social reality of the New World, but also the instrument for reestablishing and preserving the virtue Americans thought they were losing prior to the Revolution. The Revolution, with all its evocation of patriotism, would cleanse the American soul of its impurities.

To the republican patriots of 1776 the commonweal was all-encompassing; ideally republicanism obliterated the partial consideration of individuals. Early on, latent Puritanism tended to be a check on individual excess, but the dilemma became one of finding the means of controlling the amassing and expenditure of men's wealth without doing violence to their freedom. Americans were allowed prosperity but denied luxury. To solve this conflict, one patriot wrote, "all systems of education, all laws, all the efforts of patriotism ought to be directed." (William Smith) Like Puritanism, republicanism was essentially anti-capitalistic, a final attempt to come to terms with the emergent individualistic society that more than threatened to destroy the at least superficial communion and benevolence of earlier times. Right from the beginning of the Revolution there were Americans who doubted the ability of any people to surrender their individual interests for the good of the whole. The scrambling of the people to satisfy their private wants and aspirations became a vindication of their doubts. Men could not be expected, for some nebulous public good, to quit the line which interest had marked out for him. "It is inconsistent with the principles of liberty to prevent a man from the free disposal of his property on such terms as he may think fit." (Robert Morris)

CHAPTER FIVE-THE STATES DEBATE REPRESENTATION

ROSE WILDER LANE
GORDON WOOD

SIR HENRY SUMNER MAINE
ISABEL PATERSON

CLINTON ROSSITER
RALPH KETCHAM

"The celebrated Montesquieu, in his *Spirit of Laws,* says 'that in a democracy there can be no exercise of sovereignty, but by the suffrages of the people, which are their will: it is as important to regulate in a republic in what manner, by whom, and concerning what suffrages are to be given, as it is in a monarchy to know who is the prince, and after what manner he ought to govern."

Centinel

"I will submit to your recollection, whether liberty has been destroyed most often by the licentiousness of the people, or by the tyranny of the rulers? I imagine, Sir, you will find the balance on the side of tyranny. Happy you will be if you miss the fate of those nations, who, omitting to resist their oppressors, or negligently suffering their liberty to be wrested from them, have groaned under intolerable despotism. Most of the human race are now in this deplorable condition. And those nations who have gone in search of grandeur, power and splendor, have also fallen a sacrifice, and been victims of their own folly: When they acquired those visionary blessings, they lost their freedom. My great objection to this government is, that it does not have the means of defending our rights, or of waging war against tyrants."

Patrick Henry, *Speech before the Virginia Ratifying Convention,* 1788

The newly formed state legislatures were the heirs to most of the prerogative powers taken away from the colonial governors. The real importance of the legislatures came from their being the constitutional repository of the democratic element of the government. They were, in fact, the government. Out of the impossibility of convening the whole people arose the invention of representation. No political conception was more important to Americans in the entire Revolutionary era than representation. It should in miniature have been an exact portrait of the people at large:

"Experience has taught mankind that legislation by representation is the most eligible, and the only practicable mode in which the people of any country can exercise that right. It is a matter of the highest importance, then, in forming the representation, that it be so constituted as to be capable of understanding the true interests, the views and wishes of the society for which it acts, and is disposed to pursue the good and happiness of the people as its ultimate end. The great art is to frame a constitution so that those to whom the power is committed shall be subject to the same feelings, and aim at the same objects as the people do, who transfer to them their authority. One of the most capital errors in the system, is that of extending the powers of the federal government to objects to which it is not adequate, which it cannot exercise without endangering public liberty, and which it is not necessary they should possess, in order to preserve the union and manage our national concerns." "Brutus," November 29, 1787, *(IV)*

"There can be no free government where the people are not possessed of the power of making laws by which they are governed, either in their own persons, or by others substituted in their stead. Before the institution of legislating by deputies, the whole free part of the community usually met for that purpose;

when this became impossible, by the increase of numbers the community was divided into districts, from each was sent such a number of deputies as was a complete representation of the various numbers and orders of citizens within them. The more complete the representation, the better one's interests will be preserved, and the greater the opportunity you will have to participate in government. It further appears that when a person authorizes another to do a piece of business for him, he should retain the power to displace him, when he does not conduct that business accordingly." "Brutus," November 29, 1787, (*IV*)

"This is natural, and exactly corresponds with the conduct of individuals towards those in whose hands they entrust important concerns. If the person confided in, be a neighbor with whom he is intimately acquainted, whose talents he knows, are sufficient to manage the business with which he is charged, his honesty and fidelity unsuspected, and his friendship and zeal for the service of the principal unquestionable, he will commit his affairs into his hands with unreserved confidence, and feel himself secure. They should be satisfied that those who represent them are men of integrity, who will pursue the good of the community with fidelity, and will not be turned aside from their duty by private interest, or corrupted by undue influence; and that they will have such a zeal for the good of those whom they represent, as to excite them to be diligent in their service. It is impossible, though, for the people of the United States to have sufficient knowledge of their representatives, when the numbers are so few, to acquire any rational satisfaction on any of these points. If the person employed be a stranger, whom he has never seen, and whose character for ability or fidelity he cannot fully learn-whose talents and regard for the public good they are unacquainted-if he is constrained to choose him, because it was not in his power to procure one more agreeable to his wishes, he will trust him with caution, and be suspicious of all his conduct. They will not be considered by the people as part of themselves, but as a body distinct from them, and having separate interests to pursue. The consequence will be that a perpetual jealousy will exist in the minds of the people against them, their conduct will be narrowly watched, their measures scrutinized, and their laws opposed, evaded, or only reluctantly obeyed. The execution of the laws in a free government must be founded in the good opinion of and confidence in the former; without that, force will be required to compel obedience to the laws, and would likely as well be employed by the latter to wrest from the people their constitutional liberties. "Brutus," November 29, 1787, (*IV*)

It was a mistrust of the representational system that gave meaning to the notion of actual representation; instead of having the ability to petition the government, there was an expanded use of instructions by constituents directly to their delegates in the legislature. The petitioning and instructing of representatives were rapidly becoming symbols of two quite different attitudes toward representation. Petitioning implied that the representative was a superior so completely possessed of the full authority of all the people that he must be solicited, never commanded, by his electors and must speak only for the general good and not merely for the interests of his local constituents. Instructing implied that the delegate represented no one but the people who elected him and that he was simply a mistrusted agent of his electors, bound to follow their directions. Representatives were to speak the sense of the people in every case when expressly declared or when they by other means can discover it. A representative who acts against the explicit recommendation of his constituents would be in a breach of trust and deservedly forfeit their regard and all pretensions to their future confidence. For what nation in their senses ever sent their ambassadors to another without limiting them by instructions?

Political power is of two kinds, one principal and superior, the other derived and inferior. The principal supreme power is possessed by the people at large, the derived and inferior power by the servants which they employ. Those who believed in binding instructions erroneously imagined the legislature to be nothing more than agents or trustees. But this is precisely what many Americans believed their representatives to be. “From the nature of the government by representation, the deputies must be subject to the will of their principals, or the plain consequence must follow, that a few men would be greater than the whole community and might act in opposition to the declared sense of all their constituents.” (Samuel Chase) The people only could be the constitutional judges of legislative or public oppressions, best exercised through their issuing of instructions. If sovereignty had to reside somewhere in the state, then many Americans concluded that it must reside only in the people at large. There is an original, underived, and incommunicable authority and supremacy in the collective body of the people, to whom all delegated power must submit, and from whom there is no appeal. The legislatures could never be sovereign; no set of men, representatives or not, could set themselves up against the general voice of the people. But “if the collective sense of a state is the basis of law, and that sense can be known officially nowhere but in an assembly of all the people or their representatives, there can be no power residing in the State at large, which does not reside in the legislature. Unless the legislature is the supreme power, and invested with all the authority of the State, its acts are not laws, obligatory upon the whole state.” The principle of sovereignty requires that if the legislature has an unlimited power to do right for the state, then it must also have an unlimited power to do wrong. Strong government could as much serve the people when controlled by them as it could injure them when it is hostile to them. There was no other choice. At the same time no sufficient reason can be assigned why the representatives of a country should not be restricted in their power. It ought to be a maxim that authority extends not into doing wrong. At the heart of America’s troubles lay this misconception of the nature of representation and the subsequent resorts to rein in the delegated power.

Americans had not grasped the science of politics after all. After lopping off the monarchial part of the English constitution, and forming first principles, they imagined they had arrived at perfection, and that freedom was established on the broadest and most solid basis that could possibly consist with any social institution. They were ignorant of the forms and combinations of power in republics and refused to copy some things in the British government which *did* work. The freedom of a community is reduced in proportion to the power conferred to a small number of its members, and such reduction of freedom is a necessary evil in an extensive country, where all the people cannot meet at one place to transact their public concerns. Under such circumstances it was essential for the people to acquaint themselves with the character and conduct of those who represent them at a distance. Their constituents were virtually present, acting for themselves, by the votes and suffrages of their representatives. Whenever the elected deputies deviated from the fundamental principles of government they acted in their private capacity, and not as a substitute for the people. It seemed obvious, then, that the voice of the representatives was not always consonant with the voice of the people. Because of the abuse of representative authority, the people were increasingly urged to take back into their own hands the power they had delegated. They still reserved the right of making and judging all of their laws themselves. A majority of the people at large would have the right to reverse and annul every act and contract made by the legislature, weakening the binding character of law, and leading to anarchy and confusion by dissolving and rendering neutral every civil compact. The legislatures were being bullied, becoming simply the instruments and victims of parties and private combinations, manipulated by narrow minded, designing men, issuing binding instructions to the representatives. But since the power of making rules or laws to govern or protect the society is the essence of sovereignty, the legislatures of the states had become the sovereign powers in America. There thus could be no power in the states existing outside of the legislatures, because this sovereignty can never be a subordinate power, or be amenable to any other power. But there needs to be a quicker way of changing the course of an administration than waiting for the next election. There was no real accountability. Sovereignty must in its nature be absolute and uncontrollable by any civil authority: a subordinate sovereignty is nonsense. In America there can be no supreme power but what the people themselves hold. It is in them even when the constitution is formed, and the government is in operation, the supreme power still remains. (Wilson) The powers of the people were thus never alienated or surrendered to a legislature. The representatives can never eclipse the people-at-large. "A portion of their authority they indeed delegate; but they delegate that portion in whatever manner, in whatever measure, for whatever time, to whatever persons, and on whatever conditions they choose to fix. Such a delegation was necessarily fragmentary and provisional; it may extend to some things and not to others or be vested for some purposes and not for others." (James Sullivan) Only a proper understanding of this principle of the sovereignty of the people could make federalism intelligible. The very government itself is a creature formed by themselves and may, whenever they think it necessary, be at any time new modelled. (John Stevens)

Benjamin Rush summed up the arguments: "The people of America have misunderstood the meaning of the word sovereignty. It is often said that the sovereign and all other power is seated in the people. It should be 'all power is derived from the people.' They possess it only on the days of their elections. After this, it is the property of their rulers, nor can they exercise it or resume it, unless it is abused." In the transition from monarchy to republic the people must not only retain the right of delegating, but of resuming power, at stated periods, if they will be free. If not, then the Revolution had been meaningless. If there was no bound on the legislature, we were no longer in a free country but governed by an oligarchical tyranny. For a people to be so enslaved, either to their rulers, or even their own laws, as not to be able to exercise their essential right of sovereignty for their own safety and welfare, was as inconsistent with civil liberty, as if they were enslaved to any foreign power. (Moses Hemenway) Because of the breakdown of the mutuality of interests between the people and their delegates it was becoming entirely comprehensible to regard the electoral process as the only foundation and measure of representation. All elected officials were in some way representatives of the people, equally deriving their power from the same source, and therefore dependent on the people, and equally accountable to them for their political conduct. It was not unlike the very divinities that men have set up that often impress one as being in considerable measure their pooled self-esteem. What a man takes to be his idealism is merely some windy inflation of his ego, when it lacks support in the facts of human experience. Metaphysical conceit leads to various theories of unlimited sovereignty, theories which, according to John Adams, are "equally arbitrary, cruel, bloody and in every respect, diabolical." They can be shown to be hard to reconcile with a proper respect for personal liberty.

Opponents conceded that the people were the source of all political power, but the people could express this power only through periodic elections, not through binding instructions to their representatives. The people retained elective powers, but the deliberative powers of lawmaking belonged to the sovereign, elected legislature. Once they choose representatives to make laws, they were bound by the laws so made. There would be no remedy, if the business conducted was not done agreeable to one's opinion and sentiments, but to elect a different representative to do one's business in the future. It would be wrong to refuse obedience to the laws made by our representatives, as it would be to break laws made by ourselves. While something was a law it ought to be obeyed. A right to instruct the sovereignty of the legislatures places the deliberative powers in the people and brings everything back to that chaos which existed before the compact. And what do those who are continually declaiming about the people even mean? No part of the government, even their representatives, seemed capable of embodying them. The republican emphasis on talent and merit in place of connections and favor now seemed challenged, becoming identified simply with the ability to garner votes, thus enabling the most unfit men to shove themselves into stations of influence, where they soon gave way to the unrestrained inclination of their bad habits. Republicanism was supposed to unleash men's ambitions to serve the state. But what was praiseworthy ambition and what was spurious? An emulation to excel in virtue is laudable, it gives vigor to every political nerve, advances the meritorious, and produces the most happy effects in a community; but a desire of excelling in power, grandeur and popularity, tends to the certain ruin of a society. Who was to distinguish? Who was to judge the people's good? Who else but the people? But were they any more capable than the crown had been? The authority of the legislatures had become wholly undefined and unlimited, so that neither the people knew the extent of their privileges nor the legislatures the bounds of their power. Small districts, annual elections, rotation in office, versions of referendum and recall were among the other devices tried to tie representatives to the will of the electors.

Americans were soon telling themselves that their early constitutions were hasty productions, formed on the spur of exigency, and ill adapted to the nature, manners and circumstances of society. Within even a few months states were beginning to entertain doubts about the capacity of their people to maintain popular governments. They had supposed perfect equality, and equal distribution of property, wisdom, and virtue, among the inhabitants of each state. If the American character was not capable of sustaining the popular nature of the Revolutionary constitutions, then the structure of those governments must be changed. The ink was barely dry on the early state constitutions of 1776 before defects were appearing and reforms being proposed. The violent convulsions of a revolution, of themselves, would obviously unsettle any government. Some time must intervene before new ideas are well received, new forms established, and the machine of government brought back to a regular motion. Defects appeared which only time could bring to view; many things required amendment, and some must undergo a total alteration.

What had been initially a problem of guarding against an excess of power in the rulers had become the question of the defect in obedience in the subjects. It was said that only the institutions of government arranged in a certain manner could manage an unvirtuous people. If men's souls could not be redeemed from a corrupt and vicious spirit of avarice, then governments must be adjusted to this sinfulness. The American dilemma was to make such an arrangement of political power as ensures the existence and security of the government, even in the absence of political virtue. The task was daunting: establish a republican government even though the people were apparently not capable of sustaining it. The liberty of the people in the traditional mixed government must therefore be lessened and the power of the monarchial and aristocratical elements must be strengthened. Power had to be taken from the houses of representatives and given to the senates and governors. The demand was for the licentiousness of the people to be offset by an increase of magisterial power, of energy in administration, providing for a better execution of the laws necessary for the preservation of justice and internal tranquility. (Ben Franklin) Wherever there were pressures to strengthen the magisterial elements at the expense of the legislature without doing violence to the popular principles of the Revolution, men developed new lines of thought to justify and explain the constitutional changes they proposed. Because these developments grew out of what was firmly established and acceptable, because they seemed to be extensions rather than repudiations of what Americans of 1776 believed, and because they were inextricable parts of a broad intellectual front that was emerging in those years after Independence, few sensed any deviation or newness in what they were doing.

It seemed now unquestionable that the executive and a senate should participate in legislation through some sort of revisionary power or limited veto as a check to precipitate, unjust and unconstitutional laws. The people's liberty was the essential barrier against arbitrary power. But there must also be a constitutional check upon the power to oppress. Unless we are to submit to that power, we will make all of our laws useless, our Constitution and Government precarious. Democracy, unless incorporated in a mixed polity, was a vituperative term that could be used to discredit the new republic.

In the effort to oblige government to control itself theorists made use of the essentially different orders of traditional society-kings, lords, commons from the British, or the first, second and third estates of the French, to achieve an equilibrium. Each preserved a balanced freedom by giving the orders of society a means of self-defense. The British system worked because the king, nobility and commons were formally and permanently separate while each had an effective legislative voice. But in the United States, without a hereditary monarch or nobility, or other privileged elements distinct from the commons, how would checks and balances work? The integrity of the American system depended on the forms of a mixed government-monarchy (Executive), aristocracy (Senate) and democracy (House of Representatives)-standing fast on the imagined spectrum of power, on the differentiation by their means of election and thereby the differentiation of interests that they represented. But experience shows that none of the simple forms of government can by themselves remain stable. Left alone, each ran into perversion in the eager search by the rulers, whether one, the few or the many, for more power.

How could America isolate the different principles in the legislative branches? "There is a diversity of interest in every country between property and persons, the few and the many. Both being essential objects of government, the most that either can claim, is such a structure of it as will leave a reasonable security for the other. And the most obvious provision of this double character seems to be that of confining to the holders of property, the object deemed least secure in popular governments, the principal right of suffrage for one of the two legislative branches." (John Adams) To the House of Representatives, who ostensibly would guard the purse strings of the people, must be added a strong Senate, which would embody "the wisdom and foresight of persons, who have a long acquaintance with the history and manners of mankind, where the contemplative and well informed of the community could revise and correct the well-intentioned but often careless measures of the people and where the power of the ruler and the integrity of the people could be balanced by the wisdom of the wise and learned." (John Adams) The Senate would be a moderating, restraining, and retarding body, rather than an impelling one; its members are of the class naturally favoring the side of habit and tradition, and conservative in questions pertaining to property. But if both houses of the legislature were elected by the people, what then was the advantage of constituting two houses? What real balance could there be when ultimately, as republican theory required, all legitimate power came from one entity, the people? Could the separation of powers among levels and branches of government all resting on consent provide checks like those arising from the distinct orders of a hierarchical society? Unless the law givers are a compound of distinct interests and principles they will have but one spirit and can therefore neither check nor aid each other. Being chosen by the same electors, at the same time, and out of the same subjects, the choice falls of course on men of the same description. Yet if the theory of mixed government were to be meaningful the two houses could not embody the same interests, could not contain the same types of men with similar education and social standing. The two houses could never wrangle or deadlock, both drawing their power from the same source. They could not have opposite interests which were the causes of frequent clashes. But a homogeneity of interests between the two houses was precisely the deficiency of American mixed governments-what, otherwise, was the purpose of the second house? If a single Assembly chose to disregard constitutional controls, to whom was there to apply for relief? The lower house was to represent the people and the upper house the property of the state. But the right kind of person was not being elected to the Senate. (Jefferson, Notes on Virginia) If the Senate was to be a useful check on the House of Representatives it had to be constructed of a different, better and wiser, sort of people with longer and firmer tenure. The design of the Senate was not just to check the legislative assembly, but to provide a means for the collection of wisdom and experience in that branch. As it was the people in the states were electing the same kinds of persons to both houses, creating a homogeneity of interest between the two branches, and destroying the purpose for instituting a mixed polity. Election of the Senate by the House was impracticable, as that would make the latter dependent on the former. Neither were the people as a whole qualified. Wisdom and integrity were hard to measure, property was not. As the people were unable to perceive the truly talented among them they were thus compelled to endorse property as the best possible source of distinction in the legislatures. In property Americans saw a criterion by which their senatorial branch could be more rigidly distinguished. A property requirement for electors was proposed. Then the same requirement was proposed for the Senators themselves. It was not that all men of property were men of learning and wisdom; but that among the wealthy were the largest number of men possessed of education and stability of character. Yet by focusing on property as the criterion Americans were being pushed toward a basic shift in their assumptions about the nature of the society; this in turn had a disturbing significance for their ideology of republicanism. Instead of being a mere distinction it was fast becoming an interest in its own right, to be especially represented in the legislature. This isolation of property as a distinct ingredient of the society, that must be separately embodied in the government, marked an extraordinary change in American thinking, reflective of a general reappreciation of the nature of American society that took place in the 1780's. Such a conception of the community had radically altered the 1776 assumptions about the nature of republicanism. A division between persons and property was a clear violation of equality and homogeneity. "To allow privileges and immunities to men of differing fortunes is to allow different ranks and different interests among us, which is the subversion of a free system." (Madison)

One answer was to try to build into the mechanism of government enough variations on election, powers, term of office and complication of function to *create* separate interests and perspectives. Even though an upper and a lower house might each derive from the same people enough differences could be established, enough different definitions of authority might be found in order to have an equilibrium of power. Somehow the counterbalancing by opposing forces would result in the overall good. (Madison, contradicting himself) But could mere complication of government, together with devices to refine the expression of majority will, without departing fundamentally from the principle of consent, protect rights both from potential tyrants and from popular passions, from tyranny and from mob rule? If the administrators of government are actuated by views of private interest and ambition, how is the welfare and happiness of the community to be the result of such jarring adverse interests? If you complicate the plan by various orders, the people will be perplexed and divided in their sentiments about the sources of abuse or misconduct. Some will impute it to the senate, others to the house of representatives. (Centinel)

In all civilized societies, distinctions are various and unavoidable. There are rich and poor, creditors and debtors, a landed interest, a monied interest, a mercantile interest, a manufacturing interest, together with numerous subdivisions of these economic categories, along with interests based on different religious and political opinions. All of this heterogeneity was responsible for the instability in the states. From the moment when Americans realized that their separate states were not to be homogenous units, they sought to adjust their thoughts and their institutions to the diversity. The essential struggle of politics was not between the magistracy and the people, but between social groups comprised of the people themselves. As early as the seventies men talked of the struggle between the few and the many, and in some states, came to see this struggle embodied in two houses of the legislature, each representing distinct concerns: one, the propertied and the rich and the other the ordinary person. Since persons and property were both essential objects of government both should be embodied in and protected by the structure of the government. This could most obviously be done through the bicameral system and giving the right of suffrage for one of the two branches to property. Similarly, setting apart the aristocratic interest would allow it to be better controlled. The influence of the rich was to be greatly feared and must therefore be kept within their proper sphere. The danger of the legislature's betraying its trust would be mitigated by dividing that trust between different bodies of men who might watch and check each other.

Property, following Locke, were not simply material possessions but the entire attributes of a man's personality, the dominion which gave him his political character. While the standing of all property holders was considered to be essentially identical, within that group, by the 1780's, the various sub-groups and parties-creditors and debtors, farmers and manufacturers, merchants and professionals-were also seen to have discordant interests. In republics they may all of them be easily and directly traced to the rights of persons and property. (Benjamin Lincoln) These differing interests exist in all governments at their time of inception, but grow, increase their strength, and ripen with age, ending in dissolution. To prevent such a dissolution the rich must be specially protected in the constitution; indeed, men of property are entitled to a greater share in political authority than those who are destitute of it. Government is essentially a machine for taxing, and it is therefore right that those who paid taxes should have a decisive voice, and that those who chiefly paid should chiefly control. No danger in representative government was deemed greater than that it should degenerate into a system of veiled confiscation-one class voting the taxes while another class was compelled to pay. Property holders had a fixed, permanent, inalienable interest in the country; they represented in the highest degree that healthy continuity of habit and policy which is most essential to the well-being of nations.

For the Americans it was necessary to represent with the same completeness and proportion the various and often conflicting class interests, so that the wants of each class might be attended to and the grievances of each class might be heard and redressed. By segregating the interests of the rich in a separate house of the legislature they could forestall them from securing power they otherwise could not constitutionally obtain. Hamilton thought only of class interests-the few and the many, the rich and well-born against the mass of the people, the educated versus the more common man. All must be given power so that each may defend itself against the other. The country needed to be rescued from too much democracy. A democratic assembly is to be checked by a democratic senate, and both by a democratic chief magistrate. Nothing but a permanent body-a senate for life-could check the imprudence of a democracy. But there were no aristocratic orders, no separate social interests like that of the English peers, which could only be represented by themselves. In a government where citizens having an equality of power consider the power of property to be repugnant, the idea of such an inequality of power must be abandoned. By challenging the right of an elite to represent them the common people had brought into question the traditional hierarchical and organic nature of society. What gave such an argument force was the earlier belief that a republic, wholly based as it was on the suffrage of the people, had to possess a population homogeneous in its customs and concerns. Otherwise, the unitary public good, the collective welfare of the people that made a republic what it was, would be lost in the clashing of opposite interests and dissimilar in their nature. (George Clinton)

By separating the two cardinal objects of government-the rights of persons and the rights of property-rights that most Americans in 1776 had assumed would be more and more identical, and assigning each to a single house of the legislature, the Americans solved the problem of populating a bicameral legislature, but in doing so they had perverted the classic meaning of mixed government, which had placed honor and wisdom, not wealth and property, in the Senatorial branch, and had explicitly violated the homogeneity of interests on which republicanism was based. Because republicanism depended so thoroughly on a unity of interests in the society, some Americans questioned the propriety of accommodating republican principles with either kind of upper house. The denial of bicameralism and the move towards direct democracy was the most radical political impulse of the American Revolution. "In the mixed constitution the different parts, by unnaturally opposing and destroying each other, prove the whole character to be absurd." (T. Paine) The origin and essence of the power of government is in the people. Why not keep that power in our own hands? Executives and Senates contributed nothing towards the freedom of the state." Hamilton, contradicting *himself,* added "Compound governments, though they may be harmless in the beginning, will introduce distinct interests, and these interests will clash, throw the state into convulsions, and produce a change or dissolution. A complex legislature would only cause delay and dilatoriness." If the whole body of the people were to govern directly, error and confusion and instability must be expected, but not in a representative democracy, where the people's power is vested in their elected delegates, in a single chamber.

The republican aversion to artificial distinctions was being broadened into a general denunciation of all differences, whether economic, social, intellectual or professional. For the constitutionalists equality became the great ideological weapon to be used not only against would-be social superiors but against any sort of privilege that stood apart from the equal rights of the people. A genuine republic holds out this equality to its citizens; and it is this, which gives it the preeminence over monarchies and aristocracies; in this consists its excellence. The unequal or partial distribution of public benefits within a state creates distinctions of interest, influence and power which leads to the very worst species of government. Party strife becomes bitter; not the people against the rulers; they were instead parties among the people themselves, each aiming at its own aggrandizement. Such divisions among the people were obvious indications of selfishness and infirmity in the society. Parties, unless they were cramped in embryo, would grow and eventually tear the state apart. By incorporating social distinctions into the government, and thereby recognizing distinct interests apart from the general welfare of the people, no equitable form of administration was possible. Acting on what they knew of history and the English government the founders went beyond the common interest which a government is capable of promoting. The economic interests which tear apart every known democracy should have been excluded from legislative debate. The functioning of a market, and the division of labor, unknown until that same year of 1776, put forward in a book by Adam Smith, was the proper outlet for contending interests of that sort.

Wherever and whenever the fear of aristocracy and disparate interests was intense, stemming from the potential and ruinous inconsistency between the single interest of republican equality and a bicameral legislature of clashing interests, the nature and function of the senates were compelled to change. Republicans' entire justification for an upper house had come to rest on the view that the Constitution and the people's liberty could be preserved only if the legislative power were divided between the two branches, who might mutually restrain and inform each other. In time the Constitutionalists had to concede their opponent's premise and agreed with the need for a check on the possible dangerous usurpations of a single legislature. But what kind of check? A clause of the constitution, the right of the whole people to peruse and discuss all bills before they became law, became for the radicals a justification for their omission of an upper house, while their opponents wished the check to be in the hands of a Council, or Senate. Such supposed discussion among the people would never truly express the sense of the people. Because their opinions could never be gathered in this absurd way, the people must out of necessity elect delegates to express their will. Therefore, would not an upper house composed of members elected from each county be properly the representatives? Again, though, since the senates had been composed of the self-same elements as the lower houses, they were ineffectual checks to the thrusts of the common people. If bicameralism could not work, then some other constitutional solution would have to be found.

Since it was the power of the houses of representatives in particular that had to be checked the constitutional reformers urged that the upper branches of the legislature be made more stable, if they were to withstand the occasional impetuosities of the more numerous branch. This meant longer terms for senators and some distinct means of qualification which would supply the defect of knowledge and experience incident to the other branch. (Madison) Members of the two branches of the legislature and the governor would be qualified by an ascending scale of age, property holding and residence. Only steadiness in the senate and a tenured executive could now be seen to maintain the system of public affairs in a respectable manner.

Where the justification of an upper house no longer had any relation to the incorporation of an aristocracy, whether of talent or wealth, the argument became that the two houses were designed only to prevent impetuous action, both branches endeavoring to justify their conduct in the judgment of their constituents. Their interests would be identical since they flowed from the same source. In order to justify the existence of an upper house the Republicans had been compelled by the exigencies of Pennsylvania politics to disavow completely the traditional social foundation of mixed government. Additionally, in Maryland, the lower house argued that both houses were bound by the instructions of the people. On a diversity of sentiment between us and the senate, the delegates told the people, you alone are to decide, and to you only can there be any appeal. Senators there replied that once the appeal is made from the dictates of their judgment to the voice of numbers, that freedom of discussion and decision which the constitution intended for the upper house would be taken away. This remarkable action was to raise the most significant constitutional debate of the entire confederation period.

Petitions from troubled Maryland citizens called for clarification. "It cannot be questioned that both branches of our legislature are the representatives and trustees of the people, and from that political relation the representative must always speak and execute the sense of the constituent whenever it was collected and communicated to him." Picturing the people as partaking equally in both branches of the legislature not only destroyed the conventional theory of mixed government but it necessarily involved a major adjustment in the conception of representation; for it was now somehow possible for the people, simply through the electoral process, to have two different agents speaking for them at the same time. The genuine principles of republicanism were necessarily leading others to disavow any suggestion of a different social basis for the upper houses, though differently recruited, and with their organization and tenure emphasizing stability and continuity. Their existence, though, was justified publicly almost solely in terms of a division of mistrusted legislative power. This concept would in time fundamentally alter American's understanding of politics. The arguments exposed the incongruity of a traditional upper house in the America of the 1780's and set the stage for the forthcoming federal constitutional convention.

Was a mixed form of government incompatible with republicanism? Would it inevitably prevent Americans from becoming an egalitarian and virtuous society? The revelation of the social assumptions implicit in the theory of mixed government was creating doubts and disturbing second thoughts. The addition of governors and upper chambers in the legislatures would only be setting up distinctions and creating separate and jarring interests into the government of society, which should possess but one common interest. Only a single house legislature could make the interest of the legislator and the common interest perfectly coincident. An apparent inconsistency between the theory of balanced government and the ideology of republicanism confused American defenders of the senates and at once brought into question the supposed egalitarian image of the authors. The Revolutionary resentment against the aristocracy and the social equality of republicanism soon became a serious intellectual obstacle in the explanation of the need for an upper house designed to embody a distinct social and intellectual group. This demanded an even newer explanation of the position of the senate. The House of Representatives should be the true picture of the people, possessing a knowledge of their circumstances and their wants, sympathizing in all their distresses, and disposed to seek their true interest. It would be hardly a match, though, for the President and a Senate which would, contrarily, be a compound of the monarchy and the aristocracy, representing other interests.

Most American believers in the theory of mixed government anticipated senates composed only of an aristocracy of talent-the wisest and best men of the community, men of proven merit, arising temporarily out of the community-selected by the people to fill the upper house of the legislature. They had seen no incompatibility between a senate possessing interests different from those of the representatives of the people in the lower house. Jefferson and others believed that the senate had to embody principles distinct from those of the house if the balance or mixture was to be viable and the elusive good of republicanism were to be found and properly promoted. Wisdom and sufficient independence in the senators would correct the honest and well-meaning blunderings of the people's representatives in the lower houses and find what was really good for society.

The difference between a hereditary, aristocratic upper chamber and one composed of the natural elite was difficult to put into words that would satisfy a people who seemed particularly sensitive about equality. Benjamin Rush of Pennsylvania thought it out best. The English House of Lords derived its power from the Crown, not from the people, and possessed privileges which did not belong to the House of Commons. No wonder those Lords consulted their own interests in preference to those of the people. In America, there were no artificial distinctions of noblemen and commoners, but superior degrees of ability and energy *had* produced inequalities of property among Americans, and these introduced natural distinctions of rank. In fact, an upper house *was* necessary in order to isolate the rich and enable the middling people to collect their whole strength against the influence of wealth. A single unchecked assembly could become a frightening arbitrary power, unwilling to share with their constituents the burdens which they had imposed upon them. In Pennsylvania the anti-constitutionalists, or Republicans, as they came to call themselves, began a campaign to overturn the new Pennsylvania Constitution, arguing particularly against the single-house legislature. They were determined to undermine the new government in any way possible. By abstention and obstruction, the established social leaders immobilized a government that could not function without their participation, and thus with self-fulfilling prophecy they realized their own dire predictions of its unworkability. A simple republic was impossible in America because of the great distinction of persons, and differences in their estates or property. A second chamber, formed of wise senators, would be men better educated in the general and particular history of mankind. A second chamber was also necessary to prevent a small number of educated men from overawing the ordinary representatives of a single one. The Pennsylvania radicals, while advocating for a single legislature, had written into their constitution all sorts of curbs on its power. Why then all these arguments in favor of restraints on their Assembly? Was this not a recognition that a single legislature naturally tended to disregard the checks placed upon it and move toward despotism? Was there not justification for another, more formidable and more effective check? Was there not a need for an upper house, a double representation of the people?

But a bicameral legislature in a simple democracy was a contradiction. The homogeneity of interests stressed by the Republicans was identified by others as the principal fault in America's system. A senate chosen by the same people who chose the House meant similar interests, with no distinctions, and defeated the purpose of a bicameral legislature; it would be simply another superfluous representative body, a repetition of the lower house. A Senate chosen by the House would be by definition less representative of the people than the House itself. Advocates for a single chamber, though, could not bring themselves to admit the expediency of a senate with a negative power. And they could not admit that a single chamber might produce legislation at odds with some or all of the people who chose them, or that there might not always be enough virtue in men to do what was best for the larger community; moreover, they could not admit that an elected representative might not follow the constitution at all. States were relentlessly carried into finding a new conception of their upper houses. To bring their abiding belief in the intrinsic equitableness of all law into harmony with their commitment to legislative supremacy, without doing violence to either, became the task of the 1780's. The concept of the constitution as fundamental law was not by itself a sufficient check on legislative will, unless it possessed some other sanction than the people's right of resistance. It was even suggested that after a certain passage of time a Council of Censors, an institution modeled on the Spartan Ephori and the Roman Censors, be elected to survey the laws made in the interim and prevent the regularly elected delegates from becoming the people's masters, by inquiring if any inroads were made infringing on the constitution and having the power to remove them.

The structure of government could be established on an enduring base, without pinning men down under the foundation. Regional areas were delimited to which the instruments of political action were attached, without confining any person by law to any given area or confiding the powers of wielding such instruments to persons by hereditary rule or making such power unlimited. The instruments were properly defined as agencies. They pertained to the several states, and this effect was secured by the method of appointment to the Senate. Senators were to be chosen by the legislative bodies of the states; their office was attached to the state, being derived from the state; unlike the Roman provincial governors who were appointed by the central authority. This made the thrust against the center, instead of from the center; it therefore countered the weight of the superstructure. And since the Senator had no political function within the state he represented, the office had no intrinsic tendency toward separatism. The stresses were double equalized. The several states also preserved their political integrity by keeping to themselves the primary authority to qualify voters in Federal elections. Citizens of one state retained the rights of citizenship in all other states, giving unity to the whole without prejudice to the regional bases.

Madison, in *Federalist* #46, writes "The federal and state governments are in fact but different agents and trustees of the people, constituted with different powers and designed for different purposes…The ultimate authority, wherever the derivative be found, resides in the people alone, and that it will not depend merely on the comparative ambition or address of the different governments whether either, or which of them will be able to enlarge its sphere of jurisdiction at the expense of the other."

As the state had to be a regional area with its representatives, to preserve its basic function, so was it necessary for citizens to have a direct vote for the mass inertia veto; hence the two legislative chambers, the Senate for the States and the House of Representatives for the citizens as individuals. The House, elected frequently by the direct vote of the citizens, was enabled to express their property rights, given the ultimate veto of negation, by being entrusted with the initiative in laying taxation and spending. All spending was to be granted only in denominated sums for allotted purposes; any such grant must be used up in time and granted again were it to be renewed. If no grant was made the veto of inertia was in force. It was only necessary to let the bill expire. The executive was given no specific means of initiating domestic legislation, and only a provisional or delaying veto.

To prevent the larger, wealthier or more populous states from throwing their weight against the smaller states, their representation in the Senate, as states, was made equal. To prevent the smaller or poorer states from ganging up and fleecing the more opulent ones the popular representation was made proportional to the number of citizens, verified by census every ten years. The states were forbidden to issue bills of credit or make anything but gold and silver legal tender. Thus, the flow of production could not be cut or tapped by the political agency of any state. The Federal government was given no power to issue paper currency. Though it has done so, the authority is not in the Constitution, while it is expressly stated that powers not delegated to the Federal authority are reserved from it. Madison is seen to predict future problems when he writes in *Federalist* #47, "The accumulation of all powers, legislative, executive, and judiciary, in the same hands, whether of one, a few, or many, and whether hereditary, self-appointed or elective, may justly be pronounced the very definition of tyranny. Were the federal Constitution really chargeable with this accumulation of power, or with a mixture of powers, having a dangerous tendency to such an accumulation, no further arguments would be necessary to inspire a universal reprobation of the system."

Madison continues in *Federalist* #48, "Unless these departments be so far connected and blended as to give to each a constitutional control over the others, the degree of separation which the maxim requires, as essential to a free government, can never in practice be duly maintained. It is agreed on all sides that the powers properly belonging to one of the departments ought not to be directly and completely administered by either of the other departments. It is equally evident that none of them ought to possess, directly or indirectly, an overruling influence over the others in the administration of their respective powers. It will not be denied that power is of an encroaching nature and that it ought to be effectually restrained from passing the limits assigned to it. After discriminating therefore in theory, the several classes of power, as they may in their nature be legislative, executive, or judiciary, the next and most difficult task is to provide some practical security for each, against the invasion of the others. *What this security ought to be is the great problem to be solved."* (Author's italics)

"In a representative republic, where the executive magistracy is carefully limited, both in the extent and the duration of its power; and where the legislative power is exercised by an assembly, which is inspired by a supposed influence over the people with an intrepid confidence in its own strength; which is sufficiently numerous to feel all the passions which actuate a multitude, yet not so numerous as to be incapable of pursuing the objects of its passions by means which reason prescribes; it is against the enterprising ambition of this department that the people ought to indulge all their jealousy and exhaust all their precautions."

"The constitutional powers of the legislative department, being at once more extensive, and less susceptible of precise limits, it can, with the greater facility, mask, under complicated and indirect measures, the encroachments which it makes on the co-ordinate departments...nor is this all; as the legislative department alone has access to the pockets of the people, and has in some constitutions full discretion, and in all a prevailing influence, over the pecuniary rewards of those who fill the other departments, a dependence is thus created in the latter, which gives a greater facility to the encroachments of the former. The conclusion which I am warranted in drawing from these observations is that a mere demarcation on parchment of the constitutional limits of the several departments is not a sufficient guard against those encroachments which lead to a tyrannical concentration of all the power of government in the same hands."

Madison adds, in *Federalist* #50, "Is it to be imagined that a legislative assembly, consisting of a hundred or two hundred members, eagerly bent on some favorite object, and breaking through the restraints of the Constitution in pursuit of it, would be arrested in their career by considerations drawn from a censorial revision of their conduct at the future distance of ten, fifteen, or twenty years? In the next place, the abuses would often have completed their mischievous effects before the remedial provision would be applied. And in the last place, where this might not be the case, they would be of long standing, would have taken deep root, and would not easily be extirpated."

Madison offers a solution in *Federalist* #51, "The great security against a gradual concentration of the several powers in the same department consists in giving to those who administer each department the necessary constitutional means and personal motives to resist encroachment on the others…it may be a reflection on human nature that such devices should be necessary to control the abuses of government. But what is government itself but the greatest of all reflections on human nature? If men were angels, no government would be necessary."

Every government assembly has at times something of the character of a mob. Men acting in crowds and in public, amid the passions of conflict and debate, are strangely different from when they are considering a serious question in calm seclusion. They know that a considerable part of the constituencies to which they must ultimately appeal is composed of fluctuating masses of very ignorant men, easily swayed by appeals to class interests or class animosities, and for the most part entirely unable of disentangling a difficult question, of judging distant and obscure consequences, of realizing conditions of thought and life widely different from their own, estimating political measures according to their true proportionate value, and weighing nicely balanced arguments in a judicial spirit. The confusion becomes greater when legislatures subordinate general political interests to the furtherance of particular, local interests and opinions, and when political skill consists mainly of combining these factions in a single division.

"It is not to be expected that a legislature will be found in any country that will not have some of its members, who will pursue their private ends, and for which they will sacrifice the public good. Men of this character are, generally, artful and designing, and frequently possess brilliant talents and abilities; they commonly act in concert, and agree to share the spoils of their country among them; they will keep their object ever in view, and follow it with constancy. Those who are acquainted with the manner of conducting business in public assemblies know how prevalent art and address are in carrying a measure, even over men of the best intentions, and of good understanding." "Brutus," November 27, 1787, *(IV)*

"The policy of supplying, by opposite and rival interests, the defect of better motives, might be traced through the whole system of human affairs, private as well as public. We see it particularly displayed in all the subordinate distributions of power, where the constant aim is to divide and arrange the several offices in such a manner as that each may be a check on the other-that the private interest of every individual may be a sentinel over the public rights."

Hamilton in *Federalist* #62, commenting on the separation of interests and powers: "Were these arrangements maintained, "no law or resolution can now be passed without the concurrence, first, of a majority of the people, and then of a majority of the States…It doubles the security to the people by requiring the concurrence of two distinct bodies in schemes of usurpation or perfidy, where the ambition or corruption of one would otherwise be sufficient…I will barely remark that as the improbability of sinister combinations will be in proportion to the dissimilarity in the genius of the two bodies, it must be politic to distinguish them from each other by every circumstance which will consist with a due harmony in all proper measures and with the genuine principles of Republican government."

Hamilton, *Federalist* #62, continued: "The necessity of a Senate is not less indicated by the propensity of all single and numerous assemblies to yield to the impulse of sudden and violent passions, and to be seduced by factious leaders into intemperate and pernicious resolutions…a body which is to correct this infirmity ought to itself to be free from it, and consequently ought to be less numerous. It ought, moreover, to possess great firmness, and consequently ought to hold its authority by a tenure of considerable duration…the mutability in the public councils arising from a rapid succession of new members, however qualified they may be, points out, in the strongest manner, the necessity of some stable institution in the government."

Hamilton, from *Federalist* #63, concludes: "It adds no small weight to all these considerations to recollect that history informs us of no long-lived Republic which had not a senate. Sparta, Rome and Carthage are, in fact, the only states to whom that character can be applied. These examples, though unfit to compare to the genius of America, are, notwithstanding, when compared with the fugitive and turbulent existence of other ancient republics, very instructive proof of the necessity of some institution that will blend stability with liberty."

Hamilton, *Federalist* #71, on having the Senate ready to stop the precipitant actions of the House: "But their good sense would despise the adulator who should pretend that they always *reason right* about the *means* of promoting the Public Good. They know from experience that they sometimes err; and the wonder is that they so seldom err as they do, beset as they continually are by the wiles of parasites and sycophants, by the snares of the ambitious, the avaricious, the desperate, by the artifices of men who possess their confidence more than they deserve it, and of those who seek to possess rather than to deserve it. When occasions present themselves in which the interests of the people are at variance with their inclinations, it is the duty of the persons whom they have appointed to be the guardians of those interests to withstand the temporary delusions in order to give them time and opportunity for more cool and sedate reflection. Instances might be cited in which a conduct of this kind has saved the people from very fatal consequences of their own mistakes, and has procured lasting monuments of their gratitude, to the men who had courage and magnanimity enough to serve them at the peril of their displeasure."

There is certainly no proposition in politics more certain than that the attempt to govern a great heterogenous empire simply by a single assembly must ultimately prove disastrous, and the necessity of a second chamber, to exercise a controlling, modifying, retarding and steadying influence has acquired the position of an axiom. It is a matter of vital importance that there should be a delaying power, capable of obstructing measures until they have been distinctly sanctioned by the electorate, until they have come to represent the reasoned and deliberate opinion of the constituencies. The mere consciousness that there is another and a revising assembly, whose assent is indispensable to legislation, has a moderating influence on majorities which is difficult to overvalue. The tyranny of majorities is that, which in the conditions of modern life, is most to be feared, and against which it should be the chief object of a wise statesman to provide.

There is no escaping from the fact that all such Second Chambers such as a Senate are founded on a denial or a doubt of the proposition that the voice of the people is the voice of God or even of Wisdom. This is not to assert that the decisions of popularly elected representatives are always or generally wrong. But it is impossible to be sure that they are always right. And the more the difficulties of government are probed, and the more carefully the influences acting upon it are examined, the stronger grows the doubt of the infallibility of such legislatures. What is expected from a Second Chamber is not a rival infallibility but an additional security. What is wanted from an Upper House is the security of its concurrence, after full examination of the measure to be decided.

"But it was not possible to give to each department an equal power of self-defense. In Republican government, the legislative authority necessarily predominates. The remedy for this inconvenience is to divide the legislature into different branches; and to render them, by different modes of election and different principles of action, as little connected with each other as the nature of their common functions and their common dependence on the society will admit…and an absolute negative on the legislature appears, at first view, to be the natural defense with which the executive magistrate should be armed." (Madison)

Hamilton follows up in *Federalist* #60, "There is sufficient diversity in the state of property, in the genius, manners, and habits of the people of the different parts of the Union to occasion a material diversity of disposition in their representatives towards the different ranks and conditions in society…The House of Representatives to be elected immediately by the people, the Senate by the State legislatures, the President by electors chosen for that purpose by the people, there would be little probability of a common interest to cement these different branches in a predilection for any particular class of electors…to be exercised in a discrimination between the different departments of industry, or between the different kinds of property, or between the different degrees of property." The effort to place the President and his veto power outside the play of party spirit, to make him independent of democratic faction, signally failed. It was hoped that he might be elected by the independent votes of a small body of worthy citizens who were not deeply part of party politics. Soon this process appeared insufficiently democratic, and the change was made to choose the President by direct suffrage, their sole duty being to elect the candidate selected by the party machine.

ROSE WILDER LANE
GORDON WOOD

SIR HENRY SUMNER MAINE
ISABEL PATERSON

CLINTON ROSSITER
RUSSELL KIRK

"Mr. Chairman, the wisest thing this body could do, would be to return to the people from whom they came, re infecta. I am willing to lend my aid to any small and moderate reforms which I can be made to believe that our government requires. But far better would it be that they were never made, and that our Constitution remained unchangeable like that of Lycurgus, than that we should break it upon the main pillars of the edifice…It has been better said, that the lust of innovation-for it is a lust-that is the proper term for an unlawful desire-this rerum Novarum lubido-has been the death of all Republics…recollect that change is not always improvement. Remember that you have to reconcile to new institutions the whole mass of those who are contented with what they have, and seek no change-and besides these, all the disappointed of the other class."

John Randolph, in front of the 1829-30 Virginia Ratifying Convention

"Men have been too careless in the delegation of their governmental power; and not only disposed of it in an improper manner, but suffered it to continue so long in the same hands, that the deputies have at length become the possessors, and instead of public servants, are in fact the masters of the public."

(Demophilus, Genuine Principles)

"At the very moment when nations are plunged into unfathomable abysses of disgrace and disaster, they have suddenly emerged. They have begun a new course and opened a new reckoning; and even in the depths of their calamity, and on the very ruins of their country, have laid the foundations of a towering and durable greatness."

Edmund Burke

"My contribution is an attempt to conserve the spiritual, intellectual and political tradition of our civilization. If we are to rescue the modern mind, we must do it soon. If we are to make the coming era something beyond one of stagnant repression, we need to move with decision. The issue will be decided by the minority who still possess the gift of reason. It may well be that we are trampled into the mire, despite all that we can do. But Cato conquered. By opposing what seems inevitable, often we find that its force is not irresistible."

Russell Kirk, 1952

"All that democracy means, is an equal participation in rights as is practicable; and to pretend that social equality is a condition of popular institutions, is to assume that the latter are destructive of civilization, for, as nothing is more self-evident than the impossibility of raising all men to the highest standard of tastes and refinement, the alternative would be to reduce the entire community to the lowest."

James Fenimore Cooper

"The case for universal suffrage and political equality does not rest on any superstition that all men, by acquiring the vote, become equally wise or equally intelligent. It rests, historically and philosophically, on the belief that if any section of the community is deprived of the ability to vote, then its interests are liable to be neglected, and a nexus of grievances is likely to be created which will fester in the body politic."

David Thompson

The investigations termed pre-historic are really aimed at enlarging the domain of history, by collecting materials for it beyond the point at which it began to be embodied in writing. They proceed by the examination of the modes of life and social usages of men in a semi-civilized condition, and they start from the assumption that civilized races were once in that state. In the earliest and barbarous state of society, men existed in a condition of Status; individual personality manifested itself only in rudimentary form; property was the possession of the group; subsistence, gratification of hopes, marriage, and life itself wholly dependent upon the patriarch, community or the King. Progress consisted of a release from this bondage; and in the future civilized people would exist in a condition of Contract, possessing several property, and be able to develop fully their individual talents.

During centuries past, in Europe, various liberties had been wrested or bought from Authority; but such concessions had always been phrased as grants from the monarchy, not a right but a privilege. When the sum of those became considerable, the Society of Contract could at least be imagined, and it was projected to the New World. In the New World it become fact. At length the time was ripe to affirm it as a political concept, without reservations. The terms were found: all men are endowed by their Creator with an inalienable right to life, liberty and the pursuit of happiness. Freedom was a pre-condition; it was indivisible. But for the concept of freedom, the appropriate form of government remained to be devised. Though it was not exactly clear why a measure of government was unavoidable, the necessity was felt.

It is impossible to imagine a sounder grasp of statecraft than the Magna Carta revealed, given the existing circumstances. Nothing better could have been devised at the time. It was rightly looked to for five centuries as a beacon and a landmark of English liberty. Its principles and some of its practical measures remain in effect to some degree permanently, in spite of interruptions, as indispensable axioms for future reference. The secular form of government evolved; the authority of the king soon existed only in conjunction with Parliament and within the scope of the Law. As with Rome, the world accepted the British empire because it opened world channels of energy for commerce in general and for a revolution in the Law. Though repressive government was still imposed in places, on the whole England's invisible exports were Law and free trade. Practically speaking, while England ruled the seas any man of any nation could go anywhere, taking his goods and money with him, in safety. As in the case of Rome, when the repressive element of England's mixed economy grew to become her dominant policy and turned her to statism, her empire fell apart. It was not military force that held it together. Capitalism wins and holds markets by free competition. All of mankind's history is the practical demonstration of the same basic principle-the degree of human prosperity, achievement and progress is a direct function and corollary of the degree of political freedom, whether in ancient Greece, the Renaissance, or the nineteenth century. No one needs to look further than the differences that existed in East and West Germany, East and West Berlin, when the Germanys were divided. No political philosopher can evade the existence of that contrast, leaving its causes unidentified, and its lessons unlearned. Remember that Russia, with some of the best agricultural land on the planet, is unable to feed its population and has had to import grain.

The barons who forced King John's hand on the Magna Carta were the pillars of the state resting on regional bases. The problem which confronted the founders of the United States was how to maintain regional bases for a political structure without such an aristocracy. The American revolutionaries had declared the axiom of the rights of the individual, the Society of Contract, as the reason and justification for their independence. An indigenous aristocracy would nullify their intention. Such vestige as remained, in the form of entail, was accordingly abolished. The original goal of the Founders was to restore the old order rather than build a new one; to consolidate, then expand by cautious stages, the large measure of liberty and prosperity that was part of their established way of life, the legacy of their connection with England. It had been a good order badly administered. The goal of the earliest founders was paradoxically to make the British Constitution work in the American wilderness, chiefly by preserving the social, economic and political leadership of gentlemen pledged to serve the public while they served themselves.

Leonard Labaree wrote: "It was not they primarily who gave this nation its distinctive and special character, who introduced here the ideas as of economic opportunity, religious liberty and political freedom which we like to think are fundamental doctrines of the American faith...But it was the conservatives, more than any others, who were responsible for the perpetuation in a raw, new country of much that was the best in the cultural heritage from the Old World...Without them the physical separation from Europe, the frontier, and the new environment generally might well have led to the destruction of much that we hold important today." The patriot Founding Fathers were especially anxious to keep a tight rein on the rebellion and to oppose whatever schemes of the vulgar mob that might hurry the colonies into a scene of anarchy. Their idea of revolution was separation from England and little more. Cadwallader Colden wrote: "It seems evident to me that it is most prudent in us to keep as near as possible to that plan which our mother country has for so many ages experienced to be best, and which has been preserved at such vast expense of blood and treasure."

That personal liberty and private rights to property were beyond the reach of the king and could be taken from the individual only as provided by the law of the land-this principle was deeply rooted in the English common law, had been confirmed by Magna Carta in the thirteenth century, by parliamentary enactment in the fourteenth, and reconfirmed by Parliament as recently as 1773. Liberty and property were a complex and subtle combination of many rights, powers and duties, distributed among individuals, society and the state. Among the most important property rights at that time were grazing (appendant and appurtenant), wood gathering (estover), hunting, passage (trespass) and the use of water (riparian), all pertaining to the private ownership of land. The tension between public and private property rights was continuous, ever subject to a gradual drift in favor of one at the expense of the other. Property holding was an unalienable natural right that was morally and historically antecedent to government. The method of conserving it in the present owner, and of transmitting it from man to man, was entirely derived from society. Madison, in Federalist # 10, wrote "The diversity in the faculties of men, from which the rights of property originate, is not less an insuperable obstacle to a uniformity of interest. The protection of these faculties is the first object of government. From the protection of different and unequal faculties of acquiring property, the possession of different degrees and kinds of property immediately results; and from the influences of these on the sentiments and views of the respective proprietors ensues a division of the society into different interests and parties."

"But the most common and durable source of factions *has* been the various and unequal distribution of property. Those who hold and those who are without property have ever formed distinct interests in society. Those who are creditors, and those who are debtors, fall under a like discrimination. Many lesser interests, grow up of necessity in civilized nations, and divide them into different classes, actuated by different sentiments and views. The regulation of these various and interfering interests forms the principal task of modern legislation and involves the spirit of party and faction in the necessary and ordinary operations of government."

"When a majority is included in a faction, the form of popular government enables it to sacrifice to its ruling passion or interest both the public good and the rights of other citizens. A common passion or interest will, in almost every case, be felt by a majority of the whole; a communication and concert results from the form of government itself; and there is nothing to check the inducements to sacrifice the weaker party or an obnoxious individual. Hence it is that such democracies have ever been spectacles of turbulence and contention; have ever been found incompatible with personal security or the rights of property; and have in general been as short in their lives as they have been violent in their deaths. To secure those against the danger of faction, and at the same time to preserve the spirit and the form of popular government, is then the great object to which our inquiries are directed. It is alone by which this government can be rescued from the opprobrium under which it labors and allow it to be recommended by the esteem and adoption of mankind."

Private property and Contract make possible the variety of personality, the wealth, the leisure and the fertility of invention that sustain civilization. "The prudent statesman, feeling that there is a link between Contract and the nobility of culture, will shrink from tampering with so powerful an instrument of civilization. Immediate advantages in seeming expediency or popular approbation must not be allowed to outweigh this enduring necessity for respecting the system of Contract. Contract is one of the more efficient means of moral education, teaching through the necessity of exact performance how much depends upon fidelity." (Madison)

Liberty, like property, was not a single right, but a congeries of rights, derived from civil society and ultimately from the sovereign. Common sense taught that man needed the protection that the sovereign provided against one's fellow man; history taught that man needed protection from the sovereign as well. Freedom of petition and speech and trial by jury came with the English Bill of Rights enacted in 1689. Writs of habeas corpus were extracted under Magna Carta, counsel for the accused, testimony by the defendant, and having witnesses testify were finally affirmed under Queen Anne; the right to face one's accuser, security against unwarranted searches and seizures, and the exception from being tried twice for the same offense came to be established in England and America by the late eighteenth century.

The American Revolution had no leader. Only unknown individuals can create and maintain conditions in which men can act freely, conditions in which human energy can operate to improve the human world. Hundreds of thousands of men and women who lived and died and interacted, unknown to anyone but their neighbors, and are now completely forgotten, began the current attempt to create conditions in which human beings could use their natural freedom. A great many-one by one-must stop believing in pagan gods and know the real nature of human energy before that energy can operate effectively to make the world fit for human beings to live in. Nothing in history is more valuable than an individual who knows that men are free. The first Americans did not need a leader. They had learned what reality was from experience. They came up against the actual human situation on earth, stuck metaphorically and actually, between an empty sea and a howling wilderness, both totally indifferent to their fate. They soon learned that nothing but human energy, attacking this earth, could keep a man alive. They could not afford the illusion that anyone or anything outside himself controlled them or would provide for them. If they did not save themselves, no one would. For some their lives had always consisted of working for others. In the New World not a single job existed. Men had to attack the earth with their bare hands in order to survive.

Individuals began the Revolution as early as 1660. They began it in every colony. They fought against Government's pretended control for a hundred and twenty years. When at last this rebellion compelled the British Government to use the only power that any Government has-force-British troops moved into Boston to restore order. Americans stood up and fought the British Regulars. Those men did not consent to a control which they knew did not exist. Not acting on any orders, those men defied a world empire. They were unknown men, individuals, the only force that can ever defend freedom. How and when men chose between the conformity and submission that looked like safety, and the fight that looked hopeless, no one can know. At some point they made a direct application of the doctrines they daily heard-that it was their duty and privilege to assert their own rights to their own circumstances.

"Two different views may be taken [says Sir James Stephen] of the relation between rulers and their subjects. If the ruler is regarded as the superior of the subjects, as being by the nature of his position presumably wise and good, the rightful ruler and guide of the whole population, care must be given not to cast any censure of his mistakes in a way designed to diminish his authority. If, though, the ruler is regarded as the agent and servant, and the subject the actual master, who is only obliged to delegate his power to the so-called ruler because, being a multitude, he cannot use it himself, it must be evident that this sentiment be reversed. Every member of the public who censures the ruler for the time being exercises in his own person the right which belongs to the whole of which he forms a part. He is finding fault with his own servant."

Americans saw how absurd it was to believe that a government can give anyone liberty. The true belief was the statement that men are naturally free. In every colony a few men had thought through to "the foundation of civil government in the moral and physical nature of man." Any authority that is exercised over any other man must be granted to them by that man. The adoption of some kind of written constitution would safeguard men from fundamental changes by the caprice of a single assembly. Time and space did not permit all men to meet in one place; they must meet in many places and each group would send someone to represent the individuals in that group. They were used to delegating to one man their natural right of free speech and free contract. After many trials, most of the delegates met. A year and three months after the farmers fought at Lexington, more than a year after Bunker Hill, six months after the sound doctrine and unanswerable reasoning in Thomas Paine's *Common Sense* had gathered all the men's voices into one roar for independence, a group of gentlemen met in Philadelphia. The King's troops were advancing down the Hudson, the King's fleet was approaching New York. These men were safe if they stood with the King; every man there had a large estate, a substantial business or professional position; he need only do nothing, and he would surely keep his money, his superior class-status, and his life. The penalty for signing the Declaration was death, not only for them, but for their families and dependents. Each man pledged "their lives, their fortunes and their sacred honor." "We hold these truths to be self-evident, that all men are created equal, and endowed by their Creator with certain unalienable rights, that among these are Life, Liberty, and the pursuit of Happiness."

....

The uneven trend of constitutional thought in the Revolutionary era was a consequence of the varied political and social realities pushing and pulling commonly held ideas into new shapes and forms. Unity of thought by 1776 saw a constitution as something fundamental, something other than ordinary law. Yet American state legislatures still acted as the principal interpreters of the fundamental laws they sat under, and upon any occasion, violated the constitutions to serve some purpose. The constitution was merely the collection of the laws of the state. The problem for Americans was therefore to refine and make effective the distinction between fundamental and statutory law, making clear the precise nature of a constitution. It was clear to Jefferson that no assembly elected by the people for the purposes of passing ordinary legislation could have the power to alter or amend the constitution itself. What was established by the constitution could not be altered by the General Assembly. The legislature, however representative and however instructed, simply had no business meddling with the constitution. There were certain established rights which no Assembly could touch.

"The authority of the convention is to form a constitution; the authority of future assemblies will be to legislate according to the principles and forms prescribed in that constitution; if experience should show that alterations, amendments or additions are necessary, the constitution will point out the mode by which such things shall be done, and not leave it to the discretionary power of those future governments. A government on the principles on which constitutional governments arising out of society are established cannot have the right of altering itself. If it had, it would be arbitrary. It might make itself what it pleased; wherever such a right is set up, there is no constitution. If the practice was once admitted, it would grow into a principle, and be made a precedent for any future alterations the government might wish to establish." Paine)

Under pressure of debate with England in the 1760's and seventies Americans had molded the basic form of their ideas of a constitution would assume; yet the implications of the new ideas were only drawn in the years of actual constitution-making. The idea of a constitution revealed and clarified by 1776 was not only explored and expanded in subsequent years but the metaphors and analogies that underlay the American's constitutional conceptions were radically altered as well-all contributing by the late 1780's to an often loosely grasped but decisively new interpretation of the character of constitutional restraints on political power-one that has come to characterize the very distinctiveness of American political thought. So enthralled were Americans with the idea of a constitution as a written, superior law set above the entire government against which all other law is to be measured that it is difficult now to appreciate a contrary conception.

Sam Adams wrote "that in all free States the Constitution is fixed; and as the supreme Legislature derives its power and Authority from the Constitution, it cannot leap the Bounds of it without destroying its own foundation. If the people were to be truly free they must fix on certain regulations, which if we please we may call a constitution, as the standing measure of the proceedings of government. With this kind of clarification, the basic principles were being taken out of the complex array of institutions, laws and rights that made up the English constitution. So that not a single point may be subject to the least ambiguity, it was important that these principles-the fundamental Pillars of the Constitution should be comprised in one act or instrument. Power could only be limited by some certain terms of agreement. Expressly written documents were the best security against the danger of an indefinite dependence upon an undetermined power. The Magna Carta had been very explicit.

A constitution and a form of government are frequently confounded together, and spoken of as synonymous things, whereas they are not only different but are established for different purposes. Magna Carta and the English Bill of Rights were only restrictions on assumed powers. A constitution in America had become a charter of power granted by liberty rather than a charter of liberty granted by power. The English had no constitution, for the people had given up all their power to the legislature, allowing whatever it enacted to be both legal and constitutional. There was no constitution which said to the legislative powers, "Thus far shalt thou go, and no farther." A constitution in its proper form intends a system of principles established to secure the people in the possession and enjoyment of their rights and privileges, against the encroachments of the governing body, including even the legislature. Constitutions were compelled by a pervading suspicion of all governmental authority set above the people, including even their elected representatives. The search for a remedy-a way to control and restrict the representatives in their power-dominated the politics and constitutionalism of the Confederation period. Yet the devices to limit legislative omnipotence being discovered or implemented in these years-the idea of a written constitution as fundamental law, the resort to special constituting bodies, and the actualization of representation through the growing use of instructions and local residence requirements-were all products of the very breakdown of confidence between people and representatives and the atmosphere of suspicion and jealousy so much condemned.

"Binding instructions to representatives rests on the belief that the constituents, with none or very imperfect information, are better judges of the propriety of a law, and of the general good, than the most judicious men are after attending to the best official information from every quarter, and after a full discussion of the subject in an assembly, where clashing interests conspire to detect error and suggest improvements." They imply a decision of a question before it is heard, subverting the reason of the representative and the very principles of republican government. The public good that made republicanism viable would never be promoted, and the local views and attachments which now embarrass government would never be eliminated."

But the idea of disinterested representation, free of localism and binding instructions, attending to the common interests of the whole State, was too bound up in the idea of the homogeneity of the people to be easily abandoned. The foundation for this concept was weak in experience; what, indeed was the common good when no man entered society except to promote his own ends, and not the good of others? The use of binding instructions and the growing sense that the representative was merely a limited agent or spokesman for the local interests of his constituents, in the decade after Independence, ate away the authority of the representative and distorted, even destroyed, the traditional character of representation. Evidently the people could never embody their sovereignty and ultimate power to make law in their representatives without the extra-legal devices remaining with the constituents as a control. Delegates might be sent to a convention with powers, under certain restrictions, to frame a constitution. Delegates were sent to the General Assembly with powers, under certain restrictions prescribed by a previously established compact, to make salutary laws. If either body should exceed the powers vested in them, their act is no longer the act of their constituents. The power of the people outside of the government was always absolute and untrammeled; that of their various delegates in the government could never be. (Thomas Tudor Tucker)

The colonists were familiar with previous written documents as barriers to encroaching power. "Anxious to preserve and transmit their liberties unimpaired to posterity" the English people had repeatedly "caused them to be reduced to writing, and in the most solemn manner to be recognized, ratified and confirmed," first by King John, and in a great variety of other instances, by bills of rights and acts of settlement. These were recognitions of, not the source of their liberties. This was the most prominent, although not the only contractual image of the day-that of a mutual bargain between two parties drawn from the legal and mercantile world of Contract, but also a political agreement between ruler and people in which protection and allegiance became the considerations. This was a way to reduce to a certainty the rights and privileges we were entitled to, and to point out and circumscribe the prerogatives of the government. It assumed a mutuality of interests and good will between citizens and government that the colonists doubted to exist. The prerogatives of the magistracy become as much its right as the privileges reserved by the people were theirs. The compact, like any legal bargain thereby bound the people to respect these prerogatives and to "yield all due obedience to their civil rulers, as long as the terms of the Contract were in effect. The rulers on their part were obliged to secure the people in their rights and promote only the public good. When the magistracy perverted the proper end of government for its own selfish ends it then broke the contract and released the people from their duty of obedience, throwing both parties back into a state of nature. The contractual notion explained the right of people to throw off oppressive rulers who had broken the agreement. But pressure was being put on the contractual metaphor that had been designed to explain the people's obedience to the prerogatives of the rulers. When Americans began conceiving of their written constitution as something more than a Magna Carta granting them rights, and more as a set of principles circumscribing all parts of government, the constitution's characterization as a charter or reciprocal agreement between rulers and people lost its meaning. To suppose that any government can be a party in a compact with the whole people is to suppose it to have a prior existence. (Thomas Paine) "Government has of itself no rights; they are altogether duties."

There was another contractual analogy, the idea of a social compact, the conception John Locke had developed in his *Second Treatise on Civil Government;* not a contract between magistrates and people, rulers and ruled, but an agreement between isolated individuals in a state of nature to combine in a society-a social compact which by its very character was anterior to the formation of government. The Lockean notion of a social contract was little drawn upon in their dispute with Great Britain, for it had little relevance in explaining either the nature of their colonial charters or their relationship to the empire. The Declaration of Independence destroyed the political relations and connections, even the constitutions of the colonies and threw the people back into the state of nature. After 1776, under the changing exigencies of their state politics, Americans needed some new contractual analogy to explain their evolving relationships among themselves and with the government. Only such a Lockean contract seemed to make sense of their rapidly developing idea of a constitution as a fundamental law designed by the people to be separate from and controlling of all the institutions of government. It would describe the portions of power with which the people invest the legislative and executive bodies, and the portions which they retain for themselves. It was the particular business of the constitution to mark out just how much power they shall give up. Shay's Rebellion in 1786 was the climactic episode of all the imaginings of political philosophers for centuries, when the dissolution of government and a return to the state of nature became an everyday fact of life, being lived out in the hills of New England.

Under the pressure of events in the 1760's and seventies Americans were determined to provide for the protection of their fundamental rights and moved toward a definition of a constitution as something distinct from and superior to the entire government including even the legislative representatives of the people. The distinction between the fundamental law of the constitution and ordinary statutory law was strong enough in 1776 for states to begin to put their constitutions beyond the reach of mere legislative acts. “This is the time when we must have recourse to original principles; when no longer fettered by human institutions we obey the unchangeable laws of nature.” States resolved to form conventions outside of the legislatures; their proceedings had to be in the form of resolves or recommendations. The precarious legal position of these conventions persuaded many to institute colonial governments even before independence was actually proclaimed. As justifiable by expediency, nature or history as the American’s Revolutionary conventions and congresses were, still they were no substitute for properly constituted representations of the people in regular legislatures. Yet the conventions became something more than a legally deficient legislature; they became a constitution making body that was considered to be something very different from and even superior to the ordinary legislature. When a society was thrown into a state of nature by revolution it had the inherent right to put itself under any form of government it chooses. No legislative assembly seemed capable of satisfying the demands and grievances of large numbers of Americans. It was this dissatisfaction and the suspicion engendered, as much the idea of fundamental law, that explained the prominence of conventions existing outside of normal representative legislatures, and later legitimized what the actual Constitutional Convention attained. So prevalent did the usurpation of governmental functions by conventions and associations become that some Americans feared that the whole society would shortly be overrun with committees. They best served to embarrass the State Assemblies and split the members into parties.

Legislative bodies of men have no power to destroy or create the authority they sit by, otherwise every legislative body would have the power of suppressing a constitution at will; it is an act that can be done to them but cannot be done by them. As long as the constitution remained “nothing more than an act of the General Assembly made by a former Legislature,” it will be found impracticable without a greater solemnity being made use of, to prevent a future one from new modelling our government to that shape, which the majority present shall be of opinion will best answer their own private purpose. A constitution must be formed by a convention of the delegates of the people, appointed for that express purpose. Only then would it be unalterable in any respect by any power besides the power which first framed it. Its members were to be invested with powers to form the plan of government only, and not to execute it after it is framed; for nothing can be a greater violation of reason and natural rights, than for men to give authority to themselves. Conventions proved to be the most distinctive institutional contribution that Americans made to Western politics, enabling constitutions to rest on an authority different from the legislatures. Americans were fundamentally unsettling the traditional understanding of how the people in a republic were to participate in government. A series of small changes were preparing Americans for a revolution in their conceptions of Law, constitutionalism and politics. The laws of the state legislatures in the 1780's seemed to be the acts of mistrusted individuals that were in the nature of temporary recommendations to the people, standing only so far as the vote of the community did not oppose. With resorts to conventions and other extra-legal devices one could deny that the will of the people could be properly known from the acts of their legislatures, and thus the representation of the people could never be full and inclusive.

These new ideas about politics were not the products of extended reasoned analysis but were rather numerous responses of different Americans to a swiftly changing reality, of men involved in endless polemics compelled to contort and draw out from the prevailing assumptions the latent logic few had foreseen. They were bits and pieces thrown up by the necessities of argument and condition without broad design or significance, yet to crystallize into a new conception of politics. So piecemeal was the Americans' formulation of this system, so diverse and scattered in authorship, and so much a response to the pressures of democratic politics was their creation, that the originality and theoretical consistency and completeness of their constitutional thinking was obscured by the later consequences. America no longer seemed governed by the one, the few, the many, or even by all together. The classical categories of government were of little help in untangling the knotted lines of American political thinking. Alexander Hanson tried to clarify: "When the legitimate power is in the people at large it is truly the government of the people, or a direct democracy. However, when society enters into a solemn compact, prescribing modes of election by the people, whereby a select body or two, shall be forever kept up, to legislate for the people, this is government by representation."

Because the Revolution represented a utopian effort to reform the character of American society and to establish truly free government, men in the 1780's could believe that the effort was failing. High expectations led to disillusionment. "Unless a proper education of the rising electorate could be effected, and a new way of thinking and new principles introduced among the people, there would be little hope of the present republican governments being of any duration." (Benjamin Rush) Equality was not creating harmony and contentment after all. In fact, equality had become the very cause of the evils it was designed to eliminate. Although the Revolution had placed government almost wholly in the hands of the people, the people were still suspicious and jealous, the offspring of envy and disappointed ambition. Every man wanted to be a judge, a justice, a sheriff, a deputy, or something else which would bring him a little money, or what is better, a little authority. All the evils which the Revolution was designed to eliminate were instead being aggravated. "It is the favorite maxim of despotic power that mankind are not made to govern themselves. The experience of ages too highly favors the truth of the maxim; and what renders the reflection still more melancholy is, that the people themselves have, in almost every instance, been the ready instruments of their own ruin." It had become all too evident that in "times of public confusion, and in the demolition of ancient institutions, that blustering, haughty, licentious, self-seeking men" were gaining the ear of the people, exploiting the republican ideology and disrupting the social fabric. (Fisher Ames)

The economic and social instability engendered by the Revolution was finding political expression in the state legislatures at the very time they were larger, more representative, and more powerful than ever before in American history. The laws had become so profuse and complicated that the very means appointed to preserve order had become the source of irregularity and confusion. A serious shattering of older ways of examining politics and a fundamental questioning of majority rule threatened to shake the foundations of their republican experiments. It was extremely difficult for Americans to grasp what was happening with dizzying speed and fit it in their accepted paradigm of politics. No more appropriate term than crisis could have been used. Writings from previous historical periods were ransacked in a continuing search to understand what was increasingly being called political pathology. Counterintuitively, the distresses of the period did not arise because the people-at-large had been abandoned by their legislatures, but because their transient and indigested sentiments were too implicitly adopted. This brought into question the fundamental principle of republican government, that the majority who rule in such governments are the safest guardians both of the public good and private rights. Madison told Jefferson; "Wherever the real power of government lies there is the danger of oppression. Governmental power, when it attains a certain degree of energy and independence, goes on to expand itself. In our governments the real power lies in the majority of the community, and the invasion of private rights is chiefly to be apprehended, not from acts of government contrary to the sense of its constituents, but from acts in which the government is the mere instrument of the major number of the constituents." Licentiousness, therefore, leads only to a new kind of popular despotism. In 1776 Americans had assumed that their society was unique-so egalitarian that the rights of persons and the rights of property coincided-so different that a provision for the rights of person, following Locke, was supposed to include of itself those of property.

Every human function was being drawn into the vortex of the maw of government. This legislative arrogation acquired too great a sanction with the people. They had been taught to consider an application to the legislature as a shorter and a more certain mode of obtaining relief from hardships and losses, than the usual process of law, or doing it themselves. State legislatures had strengthened their controls, accentuating their medieval court-like character, regressing from Contract to Status law. The law books were filled with legislation for individuals and with resolves redressing minor grievances. The American political experience was actually changing the meaning of the word 'grievances.' Formerly this referred to excessive and oppressive proceedings of the executive power, and courts of justice, which, arising from the undue influence of the crown, could not be remedied without the interposition of the people's representatives. In America, however, grievances had become simply the hardships which will always arise from the operation of the general laws, or even the misdeeds of particular officers, or private men, for which there is an easy and legal remedy, or sometimes inconveniences growing out of the negligence of the sufferer himself. "The legislature swallowing up all the other powers might be multiplied without end." (Madison) "We daily see laws repealed or suspended, before any trial can have been made of their merits, or even before a knowledge of them can have reached the remote districts within which they were to operate." Debtor relief legislation was founded not upon the principles of justice, but upon the right of the sword, because no other reason can be given why the act was passed other than the legislature had the power and the will to enact it. Public faith and private confidence were being destroyed by paper money and ex post facto legislation. "Who would lend money, if an omnipotent state legislature can set aside contracts ratified by the sanction of law?

"The pulling down of government tends to produce a settled and habitual contempt of authority by the people." (David Ramsey) All the mobbing, the conventioneering, all the actions of popular legislatures, seemed to indicate that the people were fast running into anarchy and licentiousness. It was too much government, not the lack of it, that seemed so frightening. The confiscation of property, the paper money schemes, suspension of the means for recovering debts, were not the decrees of a tyrannical and irresponsible magistracy, but laws enacted by state legislatures which were probably as equally and fairly representative of the people as any legislatures in history. Legislatures inevitably substitute power for right and destroy free government. "Have the people, or those to whom they have delegated legislative power, the right to suspend, or render void by decrees, the established standing laws, by which the payment of debts were secured? Acts which took property and denied men's rights without equivalent compensation, whatever the legality of the procedure by which they were passed, could not have the force of law." (Hamilton)

American ideas of what constituted governmental power and what constituted popular liberty were constantly in flux, continually adapting and adjusting to ever-shifting political and social circumstances. All the developments in political thought taking place in the decade after 1776, as states wrote their new constitutions-changes in the character of representation, in the nature of the senate and the magistracy, in the conception of a constitution and the institution of a convention, in the growing discrepancy between people in extra-legal institutions and their delegates in the legislatures-all these were furthered and used by those who in the early eighties sought to amend those same state charters. The Assembly could be attacked without in any way impugning the authority of the people at large, so much was the discrepancy between the people and their representatives emerging in American thought. "Wherever the Assembly assumes the exercise of powers not granted them, they act arbitrarily and without authority." (Burgh) In the 1780's the American's inveterate suspicion and jealousy of political power, once concentrated almost exclusively on the Crown and its agents, was transferred to the various state legislatures. As the supposedly representative legislatures drifted away from the people, men more and more spoke of the legislators' being just other kinds of rulers, liable to the same temptations and abuses other rulers throughout history had shown-all of which made comprehensible the intensifying desire to make the representatives more dependent on the opinion of their constituents and the increasing invocations of the collective body of the people set against the legislatures.

....

....

As vigorously as the constitutional reforms of the states were urged and adopted in the 1780's they never seemed sufficient. Only by shifting the arena of reform to the federal level could the evils of American politics be remedied. The war was dragging on and the value of paper money issued to finance it was sinking fast. The attempts of the states to prevent the depreciation of their currency by legal-tender laws, price-fixing, and anti-monopoly legislation only aggravated discontent among business interests. It was not the debility of the Confederation, which was immense, that provided the main impulse for the Federalist movement of 1787; it was more the problems of politics within the separate states themselves, that eventually made constitutional reform of the central government possible. Urging the people to obey the laws of their state governments as a cure for the anarchial excesses of the period was backfiring. Obedience to iniquitous laws was no solution to the evils of the day. The continental-minded of the early eighties now found their efforts to invigorate the national government reinforced with the support of hitherto suspicious state-minded men. It was no longer a matter of cementing the union, prosecuting the war, or of satisfying the demands of creditors; the ability of America to sustain any sort of republican government seemed to be at question. As long as these were the issues, support for revision was erratic and fearful. But once men grasped that reform of the national government was the best means of remedying the evils caused by state governments, then revision assumed an impetus and importance that it had not had a few years earlier. The desire for reform of the states came together with that of national reform to create a new and powerful force. The public mind was prepared for general reform. The federal Constitution would be the culmination of a decade's efforts by Americans to readjust their constitutional structures to fit what Hamilton called the "commercial character of America" and what Jay called "manners and circumstances" that were "not strictly democratical." The calling of the Philadelphia convention in 1787 was the climax of the process of rethinking that had begun with the reformation of the state constitutions in the late seventies and early eighties, a final step taken from the fullest conviction that there was not a better way which could be adopted to solve the crisis of public affairs. The federal Convention would frame a constitution that would decide forever the fate of republican government. (Madison) But what Madison had in mind was not, as the Anti-Federalists perceived, a mere revision and amendment of our first Confederation, but a completely new system for the future government of the United States. All saw the need for some material change, but few expected what they got-a virtual revolution in American politics, promising a serious weakening, if not a destruction of the power of the states. This was bred from despair and from the sense of impending failure of the earlier revolution. "We have, probably, had too good an opinion of human nature in forming our confederation." (Washington)

Because the proposals for constitutional reform attempted to reverse the excessive democratic tendencies of the early constitutions, lessening the power of the representatives in the legislatures, and strengthening the more restrictive powers, they were bitterly resisted, on the ground that such reform were antagonistic to the spirit of 1776 and all that the revolution was politically about. To enhance the rulers' power and to diminish the power of the houses of representatives was precisely what British officials had attempted on the eve of the Revolution. It seemed to many that the proposed reforms were but insidious devices to return to the aristocratic and monarchial tones of the former colonial governments.

The move towards some sort of reform of the Articles became for the Federalists a means toward a much larger end. To them the ideals of human rights and rule by the people required not suspicion of government but the *use* of it. They were confident that human ingenuity could devise mechanisms that would at once protect liberty, allow effective government, and rest on the consent of the people. It was possible both to give sufficient powers to the House of Representatives and to the President, and to guard against the abuse of those powers. It was only prudent to erect barriers against tendencies toward greed, passion, and selfish ambition in any human government, but it was also important to benefit from wise and good rule. The federalists saw the possibilities of agricultural and commercial growth with the national government as a guide and partner, compatible with the Revolutionary ideals of freedom and self-government. They believed the new Constitution would provide an effective resolution of these intricacies.

The antifederalists had a positive idealism of their own, a republican vision they thought far closer to the purpose of the American Revolution than the political and commercial ambitions of the federalists. The antifederalists looked to the classical idealization of the small, pastoral republic where virtuous, self-reliant citizens managed their own affairs and shunned the power and glory of empire. To them, victory in the Revolution meant not so much the chance to become a wealthy world power, but rather the opportunity to achieve a genuinely republican polity, far from the greed, lust for power, and tyranny that had generally characterized human society. Was it possible to found society on other bases and with other aspirations that would nourish the virtue and happiness of all the people? Could they break the self-fulfilling cycle where selfish people needed to be controlled by checks and balances, which in turn required and encouraged more and more self-seeking by the people? To the antifederalists this meant retaining as much as possible the vitality of local government where rulers and ruled could see, know, and understand each other. They cherished the Revolutionary emphasis on local councils, and the Articles of Confederation, where the central government rested entirely on the states. Only with such intimacy could the trust, goodwill and deliberation essential to wise and virtuous public life be a reality. Anything else, even though resting on the consent of the people, would not really be self-government.

But to Madison, by 1787, it seemed that the "individual independence of the states was utterly irreconcilable with the idea of an aggregate sovereignty." There was no doubt in Madison's mind that a new federal government should be clearly paramount to the state governments. Without a federal veto of all state legislation the whole purpose of the constitutional revision of 1787 would be defeated. States would continue to evade or ignore federal authority. What was needed was some dispassionate and disinterested umpire that would control disputes between the passions and interests in the State. At the same time it would itself be sufficiently restrained from the pursuit of interests adverse to society. Efficiency in government would be set against the turbulence and follies of democracy. If such changes were to be made it would require something more than simple amendment of the Articles. A new government had to be founded on different principles and have a different operation from the Articles because its purpose was truly radical. The Federalists of the late eighties wanted much more; their focus was not so much on the politics of Congress as it was on the politics of the states. To the Federalists the move for a new central government became the ultimate act of the entire revolutionary era; it was both an attempt to salvage the Revolution in the face of imminent failure and a reactionary effort to restrain its excesses. Only a new continental republic that cut through the structure of the states to the people themselves, and yet was not dependent on the character of that people, could save America's experiment in republicanism. In some way this new republican government had to accommodate itself to the manners and habits of a people which experience in the past few years had demonstrated were incapable of supporting exactly such a government. The Federalists hoped to create an entirely new and original sort of republican government-a republic which did not require a virtuous people for its sustenance. If they could not reform the character of American society then they would somehow influence its operation and moderate the effects of its viciousness. More than anything else the Federalist's obsession with disorder in American society and politics accounts for the revolutionary nature of the proposals offered by men like Madison and Hamilton in 1787.

CHAPTER SEVEN-THE NATIONAL DEBATE

RALPH KETCHAM
GORDON WOOD

ISABEL PATERSON
ROSE WILDER LANE

"You must determine that the Constitution of your Commonwealth, especially calculated for your territory, and is made conformable to your genius, your habits, the mode of holding your estates, and your particular interests, shall be reduced in its powers to those of a city corporation. The skeleton of it might remain, but its vital principle shall be transferred to the new

Government. Nay, you must go still further, and agree to invest the new Congress with powers, which you have yet thought proper to withhold from your present Government. All these and more, which are contained in the proceedings of the Federal Convention, may be highly proper and necessary. In this overturn of all individual governments, in this new-fashioned set of ideas, and in this total dereliction of those sentiments which animated us in 1775, the political salvation of the United States may be very deeply interested, but BE CAUTIOUS."

John DeWitt, 1787, *Essay II*

"Consider what you are about to do before you part with this government. Take longer time in reckoning things. Revolutions like this have happened in almost every country in Europe. Similar examples are to be found in ancient Greece and Rome. Instances of the people losing their liberty by their own carelessness and the ambition of a few... When power is given to this government to suppress sedition and licentiousness, or for any other purpose, the language it assumes is clear, express and unequivocal; but when this Constitution speaks of rights, there is an ambiguity. Sir, a fatal ambiguity."

Patrick Henry, *Speech to the Virginia Ratifying Convention,* 1788

"Whither is the spirit of America gone? Whither is the genius of America fled? If there was any danger I would recur to the American spirit to defend us-that spirit which has enabled us to surmount the greatest difficulties. To that illustrious spirit I address my most fervent prayer, to prevent our adopting a system destructive to liberty."

Patrick Henry, *Speech to the Virginia Ratifying Convention,* 1788

"The Honorable Gentleman who presides, told us, that to prevent abuses in our Government, we will assemble in Convention, recall our delegated powers, and punish our servants for abusing the trust reposed in them. Oh, Sir, we should have fine times indeed, if to punish tyrants, it were only sufficient to assemble the people. You will find all the strength of this country in the hands of your enemies. Your arms wherewith you could defend yourselves are gone; did you ever read of any revolution in any nation, brought about by the punishment of those in power, inflicted by those who had no power at all? All power would be in their possession: you cannot force them to receive their punishment. Can the annals of mankind exhibit one single example, where rulers overcharged with power, willingly let go the oppressed, though solicited and requested most earnestly?"

Patrick Henry, *Speech to the Virginia Ratifying Convention,* 1788

THE SOCIAL QUESTION

Many models found in the states had shown through experience their excellencies and deficiencies. Out of this formation and reformation of the state constitutions during the previous decade the Federalists found the intellectual materials for the explanation for their new system. Because new ideas had grown often imperceptibly out of the familiar, the arguments the Federalists used in 1787-88 never really seemed disruptive or discontinuous. A century and a half of political experience had been telescoped into the rapid intellectual changes that had taken place in the three decades of the Revolutionary era. The Federalist achievement lay in their ability to bring together into a comprehensive whole, diffuse and often rudimentary lines of thought, to make intelligible and consistent the tangles and confusions of previous American ideas.

The Founders knew history and the nature of republican government; they had inquired into the causes which prevented its success. And they concluded that past experience was no real measure of the expediency or duration of republicanism. The Founders felt that what had happened to previous republics could not happen in America, due to the peculiar circumstances and resources available from which a new one could be established.

Their adoption of Republicanism was to be matched and ultimately sustained by a basic transformation of the social structure. Henceforth their society would be governed by the principle of equality, one which was adverse to every species of subordination besides which arises from the difference in capacity, disposition and virtue-the equality of opportunity in a meritocracy. No one could command the suffrages of the people unless by his superior capacity. In their republican system only talent would matter. A social movement founded on merit would prevent the perpetuation of privilege and the consequent stifling of talent. Such an association with other men and the state would end the envy of those who had not developed the necessary personal attributes of success. Men would readily accede to such distinctions as emerged as long as they were fairly earned. Heretofore colonial assemblies had been composed of plain, illiterate husbandmen, whose views seldom extended farther than the maintenance of highways and other local interests of the particular counties which they represented. The apprehension was that men without character and men without fortune would be asked to pass judgment on issues beyond their abilities. In addition, this type of man was changeable and liable to error, possibly leading to disaster for the state. "To conduct the affairs of a community in a safe and successful way, requires all the wisdom of the most learned and experienced members of the state, as well as the vigilance and particular attention of the peculiar deputies of the whole people." The body of the people no doubt possessed common sense, honesty and virtue; yet "few of them are much read in history, laws, or politics, even of their own, not to mention other states, from whose rises, revolutions and declensions the great landmarks of legislations and government are taken." (John Adams)

The state assemblies were filled with narrow minded politicians who constantly mistook the particular circle in which they moved for the general voice of society. The great objects of the nation had been constantly sacrificed to those of the local views, and even the general interest of the States had been sacrificed to those of the counties, lost in the scramble for private advantages and personal favors. Such developments had occurred precisely because the best people had lost control of politics. The great danger to republicanism was not magisterial tyranny or aristocratic dominance but faction, dissension, and the consequent subjection of the minority to the caprice and arbitrary decisions of the majority, who instead of consulting the interest of the whole community collectively, attend to partial and local advantages. (Madison to Jefferson) It was this factious majoritarianism, a frightening conception for republican government, grounded as it was on majority rule, that was at the center of the Federalist perception of the political problem. The measure of a free government had become its ability to control factions, especially those of an interested and overbearing majority.

The answer the Federalists gave to these questions reveals the social bias underlying both their fears of the unrestrained state legislatures and their expectations for their federal remedy. The Federalists were not as much opposed to the governmental power of the states as to the character of the people who were wielding it. Much of the quarrel with the viciousness, instability and injustice of the various state governments was at bottom social. Government will partake of the qualities of those whose authority is prevalent. Men of sense and property had lost much of their influence by the popular spirit of the war. The real happiness and well-being of society had been deranged by men of no genius or abilities who had tried to run the machine of government. It was the large number of obscure, ignorant and unruly men, persons of vicious principles and loose morals, occupying the state legislatures, and not the structure of the governments, that was the real cause of so much that was complained of. (John Dickinson) The direct democracy that large representative bodies effect most resemble a mob, as likely filled with fools and knaves as wise and honest men. The people are as nearly unfit to choose legislators, or any of the more important public officers, as they are in general to fill the offices themselves. (Jonathan Jackson)

The Federalist image of the Constitution as a sort of philosopher's stone was appropriate. Patrick Henry acutely perceived what they were driving at: "The Constitution, reflects in the most degrading and mortifying manner on the virtue, integrity and wisdom of the state legislatures; it presupposes the chosen few who go to Congress will have more upright hearts and more enlightened minds than those who are the members of the individual legislatures." The powers of the new central government were not as threatening as the powers of the state governments precisely because they anticipated that somehow the new government would be staffed largely by the worthy, the natural social aristocracy of the country. The secret of good government was to put good men into the administration; vicious or idle men will ever make a bad government, let its principles be ever so good. (Pelatiah Webster) Only if the respected and worthy lent their natural intellectual abilities and their natural social influence to political authority could governmental order be maintained. (Hamilton) The only kind of aristocracy possible in America would be an aristocracy of experience, and of the best understandings, a natural aristocracy that had to dominate public authority in order to prevent America from degenerating into democratic licentiousness, into a government where the people would be directed by no rule but their own will and caprice, or the interested wishes of a very few persons, who affect to speak for the sentiments of the people. (Jonathan Jackson)

The greatest dangers to republicanism, then, were flowing not from any distinctive minority in the community but from the widespread participation of the people in the government. It seemed evident that if the public good was to be truly perceived and promoted then the American people must abandon their reliance on their representative state legislatures and place their confidence in the high mindedness of the natural leaders of society, which ideally everyone had the opportunity of becoming. Since the Federalists presumed that only such a self-conscious elite could transcend the many narrow and contradictory interests inevitable in any society, however small, the measure of a good government became its capacity for ensuring the predominance of these kinds of natural leaders who knew better than the people as a whole what was good for the society.

The central problem facing America was to bring this natural aristocracy back into government and to convey authority to those and those only, who by nature, education, and good dispositions, were qualified for government. (Jackson) It was this problem that the federal Constitution was designed to solve. The result would be that the administration, the political counsels, and the judicial decisions of the national government will be more wise, systematical and judicious than those of the individual states. But how can a constitution ensure the choice of such men? A constitution that leaves the entire choice with the people? No constitution could guarantee that only the natural aristocracy would be elected to office. How could the federal one accomplish what the state constitutions could not? How could it ensure that only the respectable and worthy would hold power? Through the artificial contrivance of the Constitution the Federalists meant to restore and to prolong the traditional kind of elitist influence in politics that social developments were undermining. The Constitution was an aristocratic document designed to check the democratic tendencies of the period.

In *Federalist #35* Hamilton suggested that what justified elite rule, together with the notion of virtual representation, and the idea of homogeneity and unity of the people's interest, was the sense that all parts of the society were of a piece, that all ranks and degrees were organically connected through a great chain in such a way that those on top were necessarily involved in the welfare of those below them. The narrow limits of the state were necessary to maintain this social homogeneity and to prevent factionalism. In such an organic republic the interest of the majority would be that of the minority also, the decisions could only turn on mere opinion concerning the good of the whole of which the major voice would be the safest criterion. Within a small sphere this voice could be most easily collected and the public affairs most accurately managed. The result was a confidence in the efficacy of institutional devices such as a constitution for solving social and political problems. Through the proper arrangement of new institutional structures, the Federalists aimed to turn the political and social developments that were weakening the place of the "better sort of people" in government back upon themselves and to make these developments the very source of the perpetuation of the natural aristocracy's dominance of politics. They offered the country an elitist theory of democracy, which saved the Revolution and popular government from their excesses and attempted to again rest the political experiments of the country on the capacity of mankind for self-government. In the context of eighteenth-century political thought, the Constitution represented a reinforcement of energy at the expense of liberty, strengthening the ruler's power at the expense of the people's participation in the government. In order to have "a power in the legislature sufficient to check every pernicious measure it was necessary to divide the powers of legislation between the two bodies of men, whose debates shall be separate and not dependent on each other." (Noah Webster) Bicameralism was defended as simply another means of restraining and separating political power.

The Antifederalists opposed this view, of course, because their ideology of the Revolution was filled with suspicions of power, especially distant, centralized power. The Antifederalists came to oppose the new national government for the same reason the Federalists favored it: because its very structure and detachment from the people would work to exclude any kind of actual and local interest representation and prevent those who were not rich, well born, or prominent from exercising political authority. Their intense distrust of the resultant corruption, greed and lust for power was directed at those who ruled from on high and without restraint. Tyranny would be rampant, as always, when those who exercised power felt little connection with the people. (John DeWitt) If the Revolution had been a transfer of power from the few to the many, the federal Constitution was a transfer of power from the many to the few. (Richard Henry Lee) The Antifederalist response claimed that the Constitution was a continental exertion of the well-born of America to obtain that domination which they have not been able to accomplish in their respective states. It was obviously calculated to increase the influence, power and wealth of those who had it already. The complaints against the separate governments, even by the friends of the new plan, remarked the Antifederalist James Winthrop, are not that they have power enough, but that they are disposed to make a bad use of what power they have. Surely, the Federalists were reasoning badly, when they propose to set up a government possessed of much more extensive powers and subject to much smaller checks than the existing state governments possessed and were subject to. How would private rights be more secure under the guardianship of the general government than under the state governments, since they are both founded on the republican principle which refers the ultimate decision to the will of the majority? What, indeed, was different about the new federal Constitution that would enable it to mitigate the effects of tyrannical majorities? What would keep the new federal government from succumbing to the same pressures that had beset the state governments? Why should the representatives be trusted any more than rulers or governors in the past had been? Will not the members of the new Congress have the same passions which other rulers had? If any tyranny or oppression should arise, how are those who perpetrated such oppression to be tried and punished? By a tribunal consisting of the very men who assist in such tyranny? Can any tribunal be found, in any community, who will give judgement against their own actions? (Joseph Taylor) Since there was no actual responsibility, no real representation of the people's interests, the House was no more to be trusted than were the President and the Senate. It is the people that give power and can take it back. What shall restrain them? There could be no real difference between the Congress and the state legislatures. Are they not both the servants of the people? Why should we not fear so much greater dangers from our representatives in the federal government than from those of the state? -Where every branch is formed on the same principle-preserving throughout the representative- responsible character?

“Liberty is the power of governing yourselves. If you adopt this Constitution, you give it into the hands of a set of men who live one thousand miles distant from you, secure in their ten-mile square. Congress will be vested with more extensive powers than ever Great Britain exercised; too great to entrust with any class of men, let their talents or virtues be ever so conspicuous. After we have given them all our money, established them in a federal town, given them the power of coining money and raising a standing army, and to establish arbitrary government, what resources have the people left? (James Lincoln) “The ten miles square (Washington, DC) would be the asylum of the base, idle, avaricious and ambitious, and the government will possess a language and manners different from yours.” “Cato”, November 27,1787

“The extensive powers given to Congress would make the federal rulers masters and not servants. There is little doubt that the Constitution was intended to be a creation of power, which meant a corresponding reduction in the kinds of liberty which enervate a necessary government.” The plan, according to Lee, was “designed totally to change, in time, our condition as a people.” Contrary to the Federalist opinion, the Antifederalists lack of faith was not in the people themselves but only in the organizations and institutions that presumed to speak for the people. They were localists, fearful of distant governmental, even representational, authority. It was impossible that the powers in the state constitution and those in the general government can exist and operate together. “Those two concurrent powers cannot exist long together,” warned George Mason, “the one will destroy the other.” The state governments will soon dwindle into insignificance and be despised by the people themselves. There was really nothing new or unprecedented in this latest attempt at usurpation.

The histories of the Greek and Roman republics, the maturing ideology of natural rights, and the substantial experience of local self-government in the New World seemed to offer a more alluring prospect. If the basic decency in human nature, most evident among ordinary people at the local level amid family, church, and school, along with other nourishing institutions, could impinge directly and continuously on government, then perhaps it too could be kept virtuous and worthy of confidence. Then, instead of endless suspicion of and guarding against the evil and corruption of government, it might be possible to trust it and use it for the public benefit. The result might be a society where honest, hard-working people could enjoy the fruits of their labor, where institutions encouraged and rested on virtue rather than greed, where officials were servants of the people rather than oppressors, and where peace and prosperity came from vigilant self-confidence rather than from conquest and dominion. (Patrick Henry) Mild, grassroots, small scale governments were in sharp contrast to the splendid edifice and overweening ambition implicit in the new Constitution heralded by Publius and its other proponents. The first left citizens free to live their own lives and to cultivate the virtue vital to republicanism, while the second soon entailed taxes and drafts and offices and wars damaging to human dignity and thus fatal to self-government.

At the heart of the proposed political transformation was the Federalist's conception of the flow and structure of authority. "The purpose was to establish a very strong government in order to prostrate all the state legislatures and form a general system out of the whole." (William Grayson) Edmund Randolph's Virginia plan was "to create a strong consolidated union in which the idea of states should be nearly annihilated." Local authorities would be allowed to exist only "so far as they can be subordinately useful." (Madison) "There is no instance in which the laws say that the state should be bound in one case, and at liberty to judge whether it will obey or disobey in another. Federal liberty is to the states, what civil liberty is to private individuals. States are not more unwilling to purchase it by the necessary concession of their political sovereignty, than the savage is to purchase civil liberty by the surrender of his personal sovereignty, which he enjoys in a state of nature. (Wilson) A discretion must be left on one side or another. We must either subject the states to the danger of being injured by the power of the national government or the latter to the danger of being injured by the states. Will it not be most safely lodged on the side of the National government?"

Antifederalists had no doubt that it was precisely an absorption of all the states under one unified government that the Constitution intended. States, said Patrick Henry, are the characteristics and soul of a confederation. If the states be not the agents of this compact, it must be one great, consolidated, national government, with state governments being eliminated. If there could be only one supreme legislative power in every state it would be the larger, more powerful one that prevailed. Were the laws of the states to be suspended in the most urgent cases until they can be sent seven or eight hundred miles, and undergo the deliberations of a body who may be incapable of judging? Is the national legislature to sit continuously in order to revise the laws of the states? The Antifederalists said that so extensive a territory as that of the United States, including such a variety of climates, productions, interests; and so great differences of manners, habits and customs could never be a single republican state. Southerners and Northerners were different peoples with different cultures, and therefore would never constitute a single organic society with a similarity of interests. The differentiating influence of the environment was such that men in various ranks and classes now seemed to be broken apart from one another, unconnected, and often incompatible. A single republic, reduced to the same standards of morals, of habits, and laws, was itself an absurdity, and contrary to the whole experience of mankind. Nothing would support the government in such a case as that but the force of Authority. Different interests, different climates, different habits would require different laws and regulations. For a single legislature to control the whole country it would be necessary to cramp and to mold the various groups of the population. A single legislature could not represent so many different interests for the purposes of legislation and taxation.

Madison and other Federalists turned around the assumptions about republicanism in regard to the size of the state in which it could best operate. Religion and exhortation had proved effective in restraining rash and overbearing majorities in small republics. By instead giving them a larger extent no one common interest or passion will be likely to unite a majority of the whole number in an unjust pursuit. Although an impassioned and factious majority could not be formed in the new federal government, the public good was still its goal, and should be promoted. The advantage of the new national republic lay in the substitution of representatives whose enlightened views and virtuous sentiments render them superior to local prejudices and to schemes of injustice, in men who possess the most attractive merit and the most established characters, men free to pursue the true interest of the country, free of local prejudices and sinister designs. If elected officials were concerned only with the interest of those who elected them, then their outlook was most easily broadened by enlarging their electorate.

The quarrel between Federalists and Antifederalists was essentially that of aristocracy versus democracy. The men of the most exalted rank in life were by their very conspicuousness irreparably cut off from the great body of the people and hence could never share in their concerns. If the natural elite, whether their distinctions were ascribed or acquired, were not in any organic way connected to the "feelings, circumstances, and interests of the people, and were incapable of feeling their wants, then it followed that only ordinary men in middling circumstances, untempted by the attractions of a cosmopolitan world and thus more temperate, of better morals, and less ambitious, than the great, could be trusted to speak for the great body of people. The Antifederalists were saying that the people of America were not homogeneous entities each with a basic similarity of interest for which an empathic elite could speak. Society was not an organic hierarchy composed of ranks and degrees indissolubly linked one to another; rather it was a heterogeneous mixture of merchants, planters, mechanics and gentry. In such a society, men from one class or group could never be acquainted with the situation and wants of those in another class or group. If men were truly to represent the people in their government, it was not enough for them to be for the people; they had to be actually of the people. In a truly self-governing society there would be such dialogue, empathy and even intimacy that the very distinction between ruler and ruled would disappear. Such a close link between the people and officials would embody the idea of liberty being both the security of rights and effective voice in public affairs. Melancton Smith envisioned a government of popular confidence and respect, vital at the local levels where the virtues of ordinary people could prevail.

The Antifederalists were directly challenging the conventional belief that only a few were best equipped, through learning and experience, to represent and to govern the society, as well as denying the assumption of organic social homogeneity on which republicanism rested. But the emphasis on local autonomy and a desire for actual representation turned the supposed homogeneity of the people into an infinite number of jarring, disunited factions. As long as deputies thought of themselves as spokesmen for the special interests in their constituencies, so far from being the representatives of the people as a whole, they were only an assembly of private men, securing their own interest to the ruin of the Commonwealth. They were undermining the social basis of republicanism and shattering that unity and harmony of political authority which Revolutionary leaders had considered essential to the maintenance of order. The Federalists, though, could not resist defending those beliefs in elitism that lay at the heart of their conception of politics and of their constitutional program. All the Federalist desires to establish a strong and respectable nation in the world, all of their plans to create a flourishing commercial economy, all of what they wanted out of the new central government seemed dependent upon the perquisite maintenance of aristocratic politics. In the Federalist mind the struggle over the Constitution was not one between kinds of wealth or property, or one between commercial or noncommercial elements of the population, but rather represented a broad social division between those who believed in the right of natural aristocracy to speak for the people and those who did not.

If upward mobility were to be meaningful then some sort of distinctions *were* necessary. No American could justifiably oppose a man commencing in life without any other stock but industry and economy. Could the Antifederalists actually intend to mark out those most noted for their virtue and talents as the most improper persons for the public confidence, ending any hope for a meritocracy? This could only lead to a government by the unjust, the selfish and the unsocial, where all the vices, the infirmities and the passions of the people would be represented. "Can it be thought that an enlightened people believe the science of government is best leveled to the meanest capacity? (Robert Livingston) That experience, application and education are unnecessary to those who are to frame laws for the government of the state?" Anti-federalism represented a war being levied on the virtue, property and distinction in the community. The real object of all their zeal in opposing the system, said Madison, was to maintain the supremacy of the state legislatures, with all that meant in the printing of money and the violation of contracts. To their opponents, Antifederalists were blustering demagogues trying to push their way into office, those who owe the most and have the least to pay, those whose dependence and expectations are upon changes in government and distracted men in order to cancel their debts. Men respectable neither for their property, their virtue nor their abilities, without reading, experience or principle, were taking a lead in public affairs that they had never quite had before, courting the suffrages of people by tantalizing them with improper indulgences. A set of unprincipled men, who sacrifice everything to their popularity and private views, seem to have acquired too much influence in the Assemblies. Most revolutionary leaders clung tightly to the concept of a ruling elite, presumably based on merit-a natural aristocracy embodied in the eighteenth century ideal of an educated and cultivated gentleman. It was obvious that social and political standing must coincide. The first and greatest service a government can render to morals seems to be the maintenance of a social organization in which the path of duty and the path of interest as much as possible coincide; in which honesty, industry, providence and public spirit naturally reap their rewards, and the opposite vices their punishment. No worse habit can be implanted in a nation than that of looking for prosperity in politics rather than industry; forming contracts and incurring debt with the belief that a turn of the political wheel may make it possible to cancel them.

An aristocracy, derived from merit and that influence, with a character for superior wisdom, and known services to the commonwealth, has to produce veneration, confidence and esteem among a people, who have felt the benefits. That the people were represented better by one of the natural aristocracy whose situation leads to extensive inquiry and information, than by one whose observation does not travel beyond the circle of his neighbors and acquaintances, was the defining element of the Federalist philosophy. Being an aristocrat was much more subtle than the mere possession of wealth; it was a deeper social feeling, a sense of being established, of possessing the attributes of education and family that allowed one to move easily among those who considered themselves to be respectable and cultivated.

SOVEREIGNTY

The coming of independence dissolved the claims of rights by virtue of their being Englishmen as well as direct grants from the Crown in their royal charters. While Americans already enjoyed a complex and interrelated variety of property rights derived from the disavowed British sources, all claims to common law and the British constitution now became theoretically irrelevant. Declaring independence threw them temporarily back into a state of nature wherein all previously existing law was nullified. In 1776 sovereignty devolved among the people. Grants of fundamental rights could thenceforth originate only in compacts among them. Americans wanted to believe that their rights were founded, not on mere will or caprice, but upon some broader legitimizing principle. There were tensions among the several theories of rights and their implications tended in different directions. Choosing Natural Law was to go outside the forms and norms of English law and tend toward independence. The Declaration in effect asserted that the colonies were in a state of nature, government having been dissolved. That is precisely why the radicals embraced it. Independence was unequivocally justified by an appeal to "the Laws of Nature and to Nature's God." The rights of Americans arose from the same source.

The change from the old European basis of government was made by positing that men are born free, that since they began with no government, they must therefore institute government by voluntary agreement, and thus government must be their agent, not their superior. Since volition is a function of the individual, the individual has the precedent right. Government has no existence as a separate entity, and no intrinsic authority; it could not be justly empowered to act excepting as individuals infringed on another's rights, when it should enforce prescribed penalties. Generally, it would stand in the relation of a witness to Contract, holding a forfeit for the parties. As such, the least practicable measure of government must be the best. Anything beyond the minimum must be oppression. The immediate task, then, was to determine the mode of minimum government, by examinations and comparison of historic examples, checking intentions and devices against performance. The source of secular authority having been postulated as residing in the individual, the object then was to prevent that authority being usurped by its agent. The decision entirely brought into question the legitimacy of existing relationships, including the undermining of the liberty and property rights of those who remained loyal to the Crown. Independence implied Republicanism, and that ineluctably implied a set of attitudes toward liberty that were foreign to those which Americans had been accustomed. One factor was clearly understood-the function of private property as an inalienable right of the individual.

Federalists saw the constitution not as a compact between rulers and ruled. In other countries, where the origin of government is obscure, and its formation different from ours, government may be deemed a contract between the rulers and the people. But our government is founded on nobler principles. The people are known to have originated it themselves. Those in power are the servants and the agents, and the people, without their consent, may new-model their government whenever they think proper. Governmental power in America was not pre-existing; the people did not have to contract to gain their liberties. The people divest themselves of nothing; the government and powers which the Congress can administer are the mere result of a compact made by the people with each other, for the common defense and the general welfare. Most of the governments of the world had been dictated by a conqueror, or sprung out of confusion, where a popular leader restores order at the expense of liberty and proceeds to become a tyrant over the people. From the very beginning such governments had necessarily bred hostility between the interest and ambition of the ruler and the good of the people. The two parties are thus in a state of perpetual warfare. (Edmund Pendleton) But the misapprehensions of the dangers, drawn from observations of other governments, did not apply to the United States. The guards against an encroaching Crown and an aristocratic House of Lords were not relevant for the American republic.

Madison, in *Federalist* #37-38 comments on the difficulties the Funders *did* encounter: "The experience of ages, with the continued and combined labors of the most enlightened legislators and jurists, have been equally unsuccessful in delineating the several objects and limits of different codes of laws and different tribunals of justice, as between the states and the federal governments. ...Besides the obscurity arising from the complexity of objects and the imperfection of the human faculties, the medium through which the conceptions of men are conveyed to each other adds a fresh embarrassment. The use of words is to express ideas. Perspicuity, therefore, requires not only that the ideas should be distinctly formed, but that they should be expressed by words distinctly and exclusively appropriate to them. Hence it must happen that however accurately objects may be discriminated in themselves, and however accurately the discrimination may be considered, the definition of them may be rendered inaccurate by the inaccuracy of the terms in which it is delivered...these lessons admonish us of the hazards and difficulties incident to such experiments, and of the great imprudence of unnecessarily multiplying them...The first question that offers itself is whether the general form and aspect of the government be strictly Republican. It is evident that no other form would be reconcilable with the genius of the people of America; with the fundamental principles of the Revolution; or with the honorable determination which animates every votary of freedom to rest all of our political experiments on the capacity of mankind for self-government."

During the intervening years between the Declaration and the Constitution, in newspapers, pamphlets, town meetings, and legislative debates, the political assumptions of 1776 had been extended, molded and perverted in ways that no one had clearly anticipated. Under the severest kind of political and polemical pressures old words had assumed new meanings, and old institutions had taken on new significance. In these debates Federalists were never free to use whatever ideas they wished. They could not push and pull thought into any shape they desired. They could employ only those ideas that were available and consistent with what Americans had learned about politics.

Federalist claims to be the champions of democracy were believed because so many piecemeal changes in thought had occurred in the decade since independence that the whole intellectual world of 1776 had become unraveled. Under the pressure of debate the scattered strands of Antifederalist thought were picked up and brought together by the Federalists and woven into a new explanation of politics, of whose beauty and symmetry they themselves only gradually became aware. Antifederalists were left without any effective intellectual opposition to the Constitution because the weapons they chose were mostly in their opponent's hands. In effect Federalists appropriated and exploited the language that more rightfully belonged to their opponents. The government was founded on the broadest of bottoms-the whole of the people of the United States were to be trebly represented in it in three different modes of representation. With this understanding of the delegation of authority firmly in the Federalist grasp the Antifederalist arguments for more democracy and bills of rights could be turned back on them. The Federalists thought they had discovered a constitutional antidote for the ancient diseases of republican government-an antidote that did not destroy its vices, but rather accepted, endorsed and even relied on them. The result was the beginning of a hiatus in American politics between ideology and motives that was never again closed. By using the most popular and democratic rhetoric available to explain and justify their aristocratic system, the Federalists helped to foreclose the development of an American intellectual tradition in which differing ideas of politics would be genuinely related to differing social interests. The real social antagonisms of American politics were obscured. A distinct American political theory was created but at the cost of impoverishing later American political thought.

None of the arguments about joint jurisdictions or coequal sovereignties refuted the Antifederalist doctrine of one supreme and indivisible sovereignty. Federalists initially tried to refine, to evade, and even to deny the doctrine. James Wilson finally dealt with it most effectively: the supreme power did not rest with the state governments, it resides in the people. They have not parted with it; they have only dispensed such portions of power as were conceived necessary for the public welfare. Sovereignty always stays with the people. They can delegate it in such proportions, to such bodies, on such terms, and under such limitations, as they think proper. Only this makes it possible to comprehend how the people may take from the subordinate governments powers with which they have hitherto trusted them and place these powers in the general government. They can distribute one portion of power to the more contracted circle called state government; they can furnish another proportion to the government of the United States. Therefore, neither the state legislatures nor the Congress would be sovereign. Each would be limited to its own particular objects. Their power under this system emanates from the people. Only the people could decide how much power their various governments should have. A state legislature could never lose its sovereignty because they never truly possessed it. Relocating sovereignty in the people seemed to make sense of the entire system.

"A general convention for mere commercial purposes was moved for-the authors of this measure saw that the people's attention was turned solely to the amendment of the federal system; and that, had the idea of a total change been started, probably no state would have appointed members to the convention. The idea of destroying, ultimately, the state governments, and forming one consolidated system, could not have been admitted-a convention, therefore, merely for vesting in Congress power to regulate trade was proposed. Not a word was said about destroying the old constitution and making a new one; the states still unsuspecting, and not aware that they were passing the Rubicon, appointed members to the new convention, for the sole and express purpose of revising and amending the confederation." *Letters From a Federal Farmer,* 1787)

The very idea of calling a national convention to change the Articles attested to the advantage of avoiding the states. There was political and constitutional importance in founding the new structure directly on the people; the states individually would never agree on reform. It had become clear that by 1787 the state legislatures were no longer competent to change their constitutions. The Articles themselves required unanimous consent of the state legislatures for amendment. By appealing directly to the people, the federal compact could be altered by a majority of them, in like manner as the constitution of particular states may be altered by a majority of people there. By resorting to the people, all difficulties were got over. They could alter constitutions as they please. (Madison) All the considerations which recommended this Convention in preference to Congress for proposing the reform were also in favor of state conventions in preference to the legislatures for examining and adopting it. If the Constitution were to be a truly fundamental law against which ordinary, statutory law could be declared by judges to be null and void, then it must be ratified in the most unexceptional form, and by the supreme authority of the people themselves. The arguments for enhanced judicial authority and discretion would have made little headway if it had not been for the fundamental changes in American attitudes towards politics and Law taking place in these years. The growing mistrust of legislative assemblies and the new ideas rising out of the conception of the sovereignty of the people were weakening legislative enactment as the basis for law. Legislatures seemed to be only another kind of magistracy, promulgating decrees to which the collective people, standing outside the entire government, had never really given their full and unqualified assent. Yet the same opponents were at a loss of what expedient to substitute. While the state constitution makers were early on absorbed in the problems of gubernatorial curtailment and establishing legislative supremacy the judiciary had been virtually ignored. Courts were initially tentative and cautious in declaring the nullity of a law passed in its forms by the legislative power, particularly a law enacted over a governor's veto by a two-thirds majority. Such a declaration of law as unconstitutional and invalid seemed inconsistent with free popular government. To declare a law void ran counter to the theory of legislative sovereignty and to the American's fear of judicial discretion. But once reaction to legislative supremacy had set in, once legislative interference in judicial matters had intensified, a new appreciation for the role of the judiciary in American politics began to emerge. The evils of legislative meddling were heightened when one party was lobbying the assembly for one thing, and the opposite party for another. In such instances the assembly could not help but interfere by an exertion of legislative power, rather than leave the contending parties to apply to the proper tribunals for a decision of their differences. Hamilton said that no one could be deprived of their rights without the due process of law, terms which were applicable only to the proceedings of the courts. They should never be referred to an act of the legislature. Thus, all acts of the legislature were liable to scrutiny by the Supreme Judiciary, the people's servants for this purpose; those that undermine the fundamental laws, or impugn the principles of the constitution, are to be judicially set aside as void, and of no effect.

The proposed Constitution, the Federalists could now point out to their opponents, provided for more of a government of the people than the present Continental Congress ever would. This was the broad basis on which our independence could be placed. On the same certain and solid foundation the entire system was erected. The people could meet in convention and wholly recall their delegated powers. Then, possessing all power, form a government, such as they think will secure happiness. Through the conventions the people vest some of their supreme power in the general government, some in the state governments, but the fee simple continues, resides and remains with the body of the people.

The people hold all powers in their hands, and delegate them cautiously, for short periods, to their servants, who are accountable for the smallest maladministration. All government power, whatever its nature or function, was something of a delegation by the people, essentially indistinguishable in its character. Since the people obviously cannot exercise the powers of government personally, they must trust to agents. By the Constitution all members of the government were delegated part of the people's power to manage, not for themselves and as their own, but as agents and overseers for the people to whom they are continually responsible. The federal and state governments, wrote Madison, are in fact but different agents and trustees of the people, constituted with different powers, and designed for different purposes. The power given to the Congress by the Constitution was not granted by the people in a wholesale fashion to some detached and alien legislature but is parceled out in a partial and tentative way to responsible and limited servants.

The power of their argument won the day. "Strange it is, remarked James Sullivan, that the critics of the Constitution "should suppose it unjustifiable for the people to alter, amend or even entirely abolish, what they themselves have established." Who but the people can delegate powers? Who but the people have a right to form a government? All power, said the Federalists, is in the people, and not in the state governments. Antifederalists soon found themselves in the embarrassing position of seeming to deny the voice of the people. Every attempt by the Antifederalists to oppose calling the ratifying conventions was met with Federalist charges that they were trying to take away from the people the power of judging and determining for themselves. Their language amounted to this: "we are better judges of what suits the people than they are-we are acquainted with government-we think this a bad form and will not even submit it to the people."

....

T.T. Tucker summed up the clearest conception of a constitution so far, in his pamphlet *Conciliatory Hints, Attempting by a Fair State of Matters, to Remove Party Prejudice:* "The constitution should be the avowed act of the people at large. It should be the first and fundamental law of the State, and should prescribe the limits of all delegated power. It should be declared to be paramount to all acts of the Legislature, and irrepealable and unalterable by any authority but the express consent of a majority of the citizens collected by such regular mode as therein provided. The Constitution was fundamental Law, as well as law in writing, created specially by the people; a law limiting the powers of the legislature, and with every exercise of those powers, must necessarily be compared. When faced with a decision between the fundamental, unrepealable law made by the people, and an act inconsistent with the Constitution, founded on an authority not given by the people, and to which, therefore, the people owe no obedience, judges simply determine which law is superior. The exercise of this power was unavoidable, for the Constitution was not an imaginary thing, but a written document to which all may have recourse, and to which, therefore, the judges cannot willfully blind themselves."

Once the Philadelphia Convention had decided to establish a real legislature in place of a congress of independent states, the division of the national legislature was agreed to without debate. The House was to be the depository of the democratic principle of the government, and thus was to be elected directly by the people. The upper house of the Senate was expected to be a body with more system, more wisdom than the popular branch, that will check the Democracy of the lower. Its members would be older and fewer in number, and somehow refined through a filtration process of election to ensure that the wisest and most experienced in the society were selected. The precise nature of this process was, though, not at all yet clear to the delegates. Electing them in the same manner as the lower House destroyed the "dissimilarity in the genius of the two bodies" that, as Madison had written in Federalist #62, "lay at the heart of the bicameral principle."

The problem of sovereignty was the most powerful obstacle to the acceptance of the new Constitution that the opponents could have erected. Sovereignty was the single most important abstraction of politics in the entire Revolutionary era. Every new institution and new idea had to be reconciled with the persuasive assumption that there could be but one final, indivisible, and incontestable supreme authority to which all other authorities were subordinate, and from which there could be no appeal. Following Blackstone's *Commentaries,* this power also admits no restrictions; it pervades the whole mass of the community; regulates and adjusts all subordination; enacts laws or repeals them; erects or annuls judicatures; extends contracts or privileges. Federalists found the doctrine of popular sovereignty unassailable and made it a major weapon in their argument.

But did the new system propose a consolidation or a confederation of the states? Antifederalists could only see all important powers collecting in one center, where a few men will possess them almost at discretion, where the exercise of government would be left to the operation of causes, which, in their nature, are variable and uncertain. "In short, consolidation pervades the whole constitution. It begins with an annunciation that such was the intention. The main pillars of the fabric correspond with it, and the concluding paragraph is a confirmation of it. The preamble begins with the words, "We the people of the United States," which is the style of a compact between individuals entering into a state of society, and not that of a confederation of states." (Centinel) "Perhaps nothing could have been better conceived to facilitate the abolition of the state governments than the constitution of the judicial. They will be able to extend the limits of the general government gradually, and by insensible degrees. In this situation the general legislature might pass one law after another, broadening the general and abridging the state jurisdictions, and to sanction the proceedings would have a course of decisions of the judicial to whom the constitution has committed the power of explaining the construction." "Brutus," March 20, 1788 *(XV)*

"The judicial are not only to decide questions arising upon the meaning of the constitution in law, but also in equity. By this they are empowered to explain the constitution according to the reasoning spirit of it, without being confined to the words or letter. 'From this method of interpreting laws,' says Blackstone, by the reason of them, arises what we call equity; which is thus defined by Grotius, ‘the correction of that, wherein the law, by reason of its universality, is deficient; for since in laws all cases cannot be foreseen or expressed, it is necessary, that when the decrees of the laws cannot be applied to particular cases, there should somewhere be a power vested of defining those circumstances, which had they been foreseen the legislator would have expressed. That equity, thus depending essentially upon each individual case, there can be no established rules and fixed principles of equity laid down, without destroying its very essence, and reducing it to positive law.’ They will give the sense of every article of the constitution, that may from time to time come before them. And in their decisions, they will not confine themselves to any fixed or established rules, but will determine, according to what appears to them, the reason and spirit of the constitution. The opinions of the Supreme Court, whatever they may be, will have the force of law; because there is no superior power provided in the constitution, that can correct their errors, or control their adjudications. From this court there is no appeal. The legislature themselves cannot set aside a judgment of this court, because they are authorized by the constitution to decide in the last resort. The legislature must be controlled by the constitution, and not the constitution by them…the judicial power will operate to effect, in the most certain, but yet silent and imperceptible manner, what is evidently the tendency of the constitution-an entire subversion of the legislative, executive and judicial powers of the individual states. Every adjudication of the Supreme Court, on any question that may arise upon the nature and extent of the general government, will affect the limits of state jurisdiction. In proportion as the former enlarge the exercise of their powers, will that of the latter be restricted. “The legislative power vested in Congress is so unlimited in its nature, may be so comprehensive and boundless in its exercise, that this alone would be amply sufficient to annihilate the state governments, and swallow them up in the grand vortex of general empire.” (Centinel)

"In determining questions the court must and will assume certain principles from which they will reason in forming their decisions. These principles, when they become fixed, by a course of decisions, will be adopted by their legislature, and will be the rule by which they will explain their own powers. They cannot execute a law which in the court's judgment, opposes the constitution. The legislature, therefore, will not go over the limits by which the courts may adjudge they are confined. There is little room to doubt, though, that they will come up to those bounds, as often as occasion and opportunity may offer, and they may judge it proper to do it. They will not readily pass laws which they know the courts will not execute and so the judgment of the judicial, on the constitution, will become the rule to guide the legislature in the construction of their powers. "Brutus," *(XII)*

"That the judicial power of the United States will lean strongly in favor of the general government, and will give such an explanation to the constitution, as well as favor an extension of its jurisdiction, is very evident from a variety of considerations. The constitution itself strongly countenances such a mode of construction. Most of the articles which convey powers of any considerable importance, are conceived in general and indefinite terms, which are either equivocal, ambiguous, or which require long definitions to unfold the extent of their meaning. "Brutus" January 31,1788 *(XI)*

"The necessary and proper clause will be an excellent auxiliary to assist the courts to discover the spirit and reason of the constitution, and when applied to any and every of the other clauses granting power, will similarly operate in extracting the spirit from them. Enough has been said to show that the courts have sufficient ground in the exercise of this power to determine that the legislature have no bounds set to them by this constitution, by any supposed right the legislatures of the respective states may have, to regulate their local concerns. Where the constitution gives them concurrent jurisdiction, the laws of the state must be repealed, restricted, or so construed, as to give full effect to the laws of the union on the same subject. It is easy to see that in proportion as the general government acquires power and jurisdiction, by the liberal construction which the judges give the constitution, will those of the states lose its rights, until they become trifling and unimportant." "Brutus," *(XII)*

The necessary and proper clause, while it confers no specific power on the legislature, implies that the constitution is not to receive an explanation strictly, according to its letter, but that more power is implied than expressed. And this clause, if it is to be considered as explanatory of the extent of the powers given, is to be understood as declaring, that in construing any of the articles conveying power, the spirit, intent and design of the clause should be attended to, as well as the words in their common acceptation. The constitution gives sufficient color for adopting an equitable construction, if we consider the great end and design it professedly has in view- "to form a more perfect union, establish justice, insure domestic tranquility, provide for the common defense, promote the general welfare, and secure the blessings of liberty to ourselves and posterity." If the end of the government is to be learned from these words, which are clearly designed to declare it, it obviously has in view every object which is embraced by any government. It would appear by a consideration of all of them separately, as it does by taking them together, that if the spirit of this system is to be known from its declared ends and design in the preamble, its spirit is to subvert and abolish all the powers of the state governments. This idea suggests that the court will be countenanced in giving the articles a broad sense, as will effectually promote the ends the constitution had in view; having this power, they will strongly incline to extend the powers of the general government, to the diminution, and finally to the destruction, of that of the respective states. If this equitable mode of construction is given to all of the enumerated powers of the constitution, then nothing can stand before it. The most natural and grammatical construction authorizes Congress to do anything which in their judgment will provide for the general welfare, and this amounts to the same thing as general and unlimited powers of legislation in all cases. Furthermore, this will operate strongly upon the courts to give such a meaning to the constitution in all cases where it can possibly be done, as will enlarge the sphere of their own authority. The dignity and importance of the judges will increase in proportion to the extent and magnitude of the powers they exercise." "Brutus," February 7, 1788, *(XI & XII)*

A BILL OF RIGHTS

Once the Antifederalists grasped the consolidating aspects of the new Constitution, particularly with its supreme law, the general welfare and the necessary and proper clauses, they rose in defense of a declaration of rights to "serve as a barrier between the general government and the respective states and their citizens." "A government could be founded only by reserving to the people such of their essential rights, as are not necessary to part with." The experience of all ages had confirmed that rulers were always eager to enlarge their powers and abridge the public liberty. Most of the state constitutions, the Antifederalists emphasized, were prefaced by bills of rights or were interwoven with certain express reservations of rights.

The absence of a bill of rights was a major drawback to the acceptance of the Constitution. "A bill of rights is what the people are entitled to against every government on earth, and what no government should refuse, or rest on inference alone." (Jefferson) Any constitution needs a plain, strong and accurate criterion by which the people might at once determine when, and in what instance their rights were violated; it is a preliminary, without which, this plan ought not to be adopted." (John Smilie) The Antifederalists were jealous of each ambiguity in law or government, or the smallest circumstance that might have a tendency to curtail the republican system. As the Revolution had demonstrated, all natural and common law rights not specified and codified, not set down in documents, "that were clear and unequivocal," were hopelessly insecure. Any system which appoints a legislature without any reservation of the rights of individuals surrenders all power in every branch of legislation to the government. (James Winthrop) Unless some criterion is established by which it could be easily and constitutionally ascertained how far our governors may proceed, and by which it might appear when they transgress their jurisdiction, the principles of the Declaration endorsing the people's right of resistance were mere sound without substance. (John Smilie) A constitution to the Antifederalists represented a concession of power, on the part of the people to their rulers, a bargain between two hostile interests, between power and liberty. Patrick Henry kept coming back to this idea that "government is a compact between the rulers and the people, a contract by which liberty ought not to be given up without knowing the terms. Is it (the Constitution) worthy of that manly fortitude that ought to characterize republicans? You are not to inquire how your trade may be increased, nor how you are to become a great and powerful people, but how your liberties can be secure; for liberty ought to be the direct end of your government. Liberty, the greatest of all earthly blessings-give us that precious jewel, and you may take everything else…suspect everyone who approaches that jewel. Guard it with jealous attention. Nothing will preserve it but downright force; whenever you give up that force, you are inevitably ruined." The verbal assurances of disinterested representatives have led to the catastrophe we now face. Antifederalist distrust did not arise so much from the nature of the institutions as from the characters or conduct of those who will compose the Congress. In framing a system for the ages, we should not lose sight of the changes the ages will produce. (Madison) Time and social maturation will accentuate distinctions in the society; the gap between a rich minority and a poor majority would widen.

"That a constitution for the United States does not require a Bill of Rights, when it is considered, when a constitution for an individual state would, I cannot conceive. Miserable indeed would be the situation of those individual states who have not prefixed to their Constitutions a Bill of Rights, if the people, when they established the powers of legislation under their separate governments, invested their Representatives with every right and authority which they did not, in explicit terms, reserve; and therefor every question, respecting the jurisdiction of the Assembly, if the frame of government is silent, is efficient and complete. In other words, those powers which the people by their Constitutions expressly give them, they enjoy by positive grant, and those remaining ones, which they never meant to give them, and which the Constitution says nothing about, they enjoy by tacit implication, so that by one means or another, they become possessed of the whole." (John DeWitt)

Federalists believed the advocacy of a bill of rights masked a basic desire to dilute the power of the national government in favor of the states. They were determined to resist all efforts at amendment. Too precise an enumeration of rights would imply that every right not included in the exception might be impaired by the government without usurpation. "No power was given to Congress to infringe on any one of the natural rights of the people by this Constitution; and, should they attempt it without constitutional authority, the act would be a nullity and could not be enforced." (Theophilus Parsons) "If the United States goes beyond their powers, if they make a law which the Constitution does not authorize, it is void, and the judicial power, who, to secure their impartiality, are to be made independent, will declare it to be void." (Oliver Ellsworth) "There was no more positive and unequivocal declaration of the principle underlying the Constitution than the view that the powers granted are the gift of the people and may be resumed by them when perverted to their oppression, and every power not granted thereby remains with them, at their will." (Madison)

Since the English kings had claimed all power and jurisdiction, bills of rights like the Magna Carta had been considered by them as grants to the people. A bill of rights was used to limit the king's prerogative; he could trample on the liberties of the people in every case where not previously restrained. Similarly in the state legislatures of 1776 the people invested their representatives with every right and authority which they did not in explicit terms reserve. In the federal Constitution every power that was not expressly delegated to the general government was ostensibly reserved in the people's hands. Given that the federal government resulted from a partial delegation only of the people's supreme power, a declaration reserving specific rights belonging to the people was superfluous. All rights not given away to the general government would still be retained. To list the people's rights might imply that those not enumerated were in fact delegated. If codification did not create but only declared what was the already existing Law and the rights of the people, then it followed that the rights and principles of the constitution did not actually have to be specified and written down in order to be in force. Federalists realized that the new national constitution was based on a fundamentally different principle from that of the earlier state constitution, that, indeed, the very nature of the Constitution obviated the need for a bill of rights. "Bills of rights, according to Hamilton, have no application to constitutions, professedly founded upon the power of the people, and executed by their immediate representatives and servants. Here, in strictness, the people surrender nothing, and as they retain everything, they have no need of particular reservations." Unable to grasp the significance the Federalists were attributing to the sovereignty of the people, the Antifederalists were irate. In a world of arbitrary legislative power where law could be "de jure" as well as "de facto" unjust, reliance on the intrinsic justness of the law itself seemed patently and frighteningly insufficient. To deduce our rights from the principles of equity, justice and the Constitution, is very well; but equity and justice are no defense against power. (James Cannon, *An Historical Essay on the English Constitution*) Constitutional rights must be protected and defended or they will be lost forever. They must be established on a foundation never more to be shaken, that is they must be specified and written down in immutable documents. William Henry Drayton: "In republics, the very nature of the constitution requires the judges to follow the letter of the law. Let the rule of right be not a matter of controversy, but that of fact alone, through codification and strict judicial observance so that the people did not become slaves to the magistrates. Such codification assumed that equity and the fair principles of Law could be precisely defined and adapted to every man's information. The insatiable thirst for unconditional control over our fellow creatures, and the facility of sounds to convey essentially different ideas, produced the first Bill of Rights ever prefixed to a frame of national government. The people, although fully sensible that they reserved every bit of power they did not expressly grant away, yet afraid that the words made use of, to express those rights so granted might convey more than they originally intended, they chose at the same moment to express in different language those rights which the agreement did not include, and which they never designed to part with, endeavoring thereby to prevent any cause for future altercation and the intrusion into society of that doctrine of tacit implication which has been the favorite theme of every tyrant from the origin of all governments to the present day." (John DeWitt)

Denying the need for bills of rights, unalterable forms of government, perpetual constitutions, and special conventions with powers not given to the representative legislatures, and by indicting the conception of actual representation, Noah Webster called into question one of the fundamental maxims of American politics, which is, that the sovereign power resides in the people. Written constitutions and bills of rights could *never* be effective guarantees of freedom. "Government takes its form and structure from the genius and habits of the people; and if on paper a form is not accommodated to those habits, it will assume a new form, in spite of all the formal sanctions of the supreme authority of a State. A bill of rights, and a perpetual constitution on parchment guaranteeing those rights, was a useless form of words, because opposed to the temper of the people." Americans had become too enamored with such artificial devices. "Unless the advocates for unalterable constitutions of government, can prevent all changes in the wants, the inclinations, the habits and the circumstances of people, they will find it difficult, even with all their declarations of unalterable rights, to prevent changes in the government. A paper-declaration is a very feeble barrier against the force of national habits, and inclinations."

"The jealousy of the people in this country has no proper object against which a paper constitution can arm them-it is therefore directed against themselves, or against an invasion which they imagine may happen in future ages." The Americans' efforts to fix a form of government in perpetuity supposed a perfect wisdom and probity in the framers, which indeed is both arrogant and impudent. The very attempt to make perpetual constitutions is the assumption of a right to control the opinions of future generations and to legislate for those over whom we have no authority." But why should the Americans be so jealous of future legislatures and at the same time be so confident of the infallibility of present conventions?

It was necessary 'that certain great first principles be settled and established, determining and bounding the power and prerogatives of the ruler, ascertaining and securing the rights and liberties of the subjects, as the foundation of the government, which in all civil states is called the constitution, on the certainty and permanency of which, the rights of both the ruled and ruler depend. The great rights which men never ought to lose should be guaranteed, not granted, by the constitution. (Hamilton, again contradicting himself) Bills of Rights provided a proper and clear line, drawn between the powers necessary to be conferred by the Constitution to their Delegates, and what ought to prudently remain in their hands. Heretofore bills of rights had been designed to delineate the people's rights against the Crown, not against Parliament, which presumably represented the people. Americans would spend the following years in expanding such prohibitions and attempting to make them more effective. "If we suffer our representatives to assume powers never committed to their trust unnoticed once, we may not be surprised to have it done a second time." (Benjamin Gale)

TAXATION

The American Revolution was not intended as an innovating upheaval, but a conservative attempt at restoring colonial prerogatives. Accustomed from their beginnings to self-government, the colonials felt that by inheritance they possessed the rights of Englishmen and by prescription certain rights peculiar to themselves. When a designing king and a distant parliament presumed to extend over America powers of taxation and administration never before exercised, the colonies rose to vindicate their freedom. Men essentially conservative found themselves triumphant rebels and were compelled to reconcile their traditional ideas with the necessities of independence. Federalists appealed to the lessons of history, the legacy of British liberties, and the guarantees of previous constitutions. The levelling agrarian republicanism sought to abolish entail, primogeniture, church establishments and all vestiges of aristocracy; it opposed a strong, centralized government, public debt, and a standing army. Federalists tended to be the party of the cities, with their commercial and manufacturing interests, and creditors. Shay's Rebellion (1787), in Massachusetts, and later (1790) the Whiskey Rebellion, in western Pennsylvania, gave the Federalists notice of the power and aspirations of their opponents, and their dislike of taxes, inspiring in Hamilton a desperate resolution to oppose local radicalism by means of a consolidation of power in a national government.

In *Federalist* #23 Hamilton wrote that the taxing powers of government ought to exist without limitation, "because it is impossible to foresee or to define the extent and variety of national exigencies, and the correspondent extent and variety of the means which may be necessary to satisfy them... Every view we may take of the subject, as candid inquirers after truth, will serve to convince us that it is both unwise and dangerous to deny the federal government an unconfined authority in respect to all those objects which are entrusted to its management."

“The adversaries of the plan promulgated by the convention…ought not to have wandered into inflammatory declamations and unmeaning cavils about the extent of the powers; the POWERS are not too extensive for the OBJECTS of federal administration…for the absurdity must continually stare us in the face of confiding to a government the direction of the most essential national interests, without daring to trust it to the authorities which are indispensable to their proper and efficient management.”

Hamilton, in *Federalist* #31, continues his argument: “In disquisitions of every kind there are certain primary truths, or first principles, upon which all subsequent reasonings must depend. These contain an internal evidence which, antecedent to all reflection or combination, commands the assent of the mind. Of this nature are the maxims of geometry that things equal to the same are equal to each other; that two straight lines cannot enclose a space; and that all right angles are equal to each other. Of the same nature are these other maxims in ethics and politics, that there cannot be an effect without a cause; that the means ought to be proportioned to the end; that every power ought to be commensurate with its object; that there ought to be no limitation of a power destined to effect a purpose which is itself incapable of limitation.”

“While geometric principles are susceptible of demonstration, in the sciences of morals and politics men are found far less tractable…Caution and investigation are a necessary armor against error and imposition…Though it cannot be pretended that the principles of moral and political knowledge have the same degree of certainty with those of mathematics, we may attribute to the passions and prejudices of the reasoner, rather than the subject, their opposition…A government ought to contain in itself every power requisite to the full accomplishment of the objects committed to its care, and to the complete execution of the trusts for which it is responsible, free from every other control but a regard to the public good and to the sense of the people. I repeat here what I have observed in substance in another place, that all observations founded upon the danger of usurpation ought to be referred to the composition and structure of the government, not to the nature or extent of its powers."

In *Federalist* #33 Hamilton continues to be disingenuous, as he was both with the discussion over the Bill of Rights and the need for an aristocracy, trying to make clear his point while trying to allay fears: "If the federal government should overpass the just bounds of its authority and make tyrannical use of its powers, the people, whose creature it is, must appeal to the standard they have formed, and take such measures to redress the injury done to the Constitution as the exigency may suggest and prudence justify…But it is said that the laws of the Union are to be the *supreme law* of the land… A LAW, by the very meaning of the term, includes supremacy. It is a rule which those to whom it is prescribed are bound to observe. If individuals enter into a state of society the laws of that society must be the supreme regulator of their conduct. If a number of political societies enter into a larger one, the laws which the latter may enact, pursuant to the powers entrusted to it by the constitution, must necessarily be supreme over those societies and the individuals of whom they are composed. But it will not follow from this doctrine that acts of the larger society which are *not pursuant* to its constitutional powers, but which are invasions of the residuary authorities of the smaller societies, will become the supreme law of the land. *But no information is given on how the lesser power is to hold the party of force accountable."* (Authors italics)

The Antifederalist response: "The legislature has authority to contract debts at their discretion; they are the sole judges to determine what is for the general welfare; this power therefore is neither more nor less than a power to lay and collect taxes at their pleasure; not only is the power to lay taxes unlimited, as to the amount they may require, but it is perfect and absolute to raise them in any mode they please. It is proper here to remark, that the authority to lay and collect taxes is the most important of any power that can be granted; it connects with it almost all other powers, or at least will in process of time draw all others after it; it is the great means of protection, security and defense in a good government, and the great engine of oppression and tyranny in a bad one." "Brutus," October 18, 1787, *(I)*

"To provide for the general welfare is an abstract proposition, which mankind differ in the explanation of, as much as they do on any political or moral proposition that can be proposed; the most opposite measures may be pursued by different parties, and both may profess, that they have in view the general welfare; and both sides may be honest in their profession, or both may have sinister views. Those who advocate for this new constitution declare they are influenced by a regard to the general welfare; those who oppose it, declare they are moved by the same principle. But nothing is more certain than this: that to adopt this constitution, and not to adopt it, cannot both of them be promotive of the general welfare." "Brutus," October 18, 1787, *(VI)*

"A power to make all laws, which shall be necessary and proper, for carrying into execution, all powers vested by the constitution in the government of the United States, or any department or officer thereof, is a great and uncontrollable power, very comprehensive and definite, and may, for ought I know, be exercised in such a manner as entirely to abolish the state legislatures. If they may do it, it is pretty certain that they will, for it will be found that the limited power retained by the states will be a clog upon the wheels of the consolidated government; the latter will be naturally inclined to move it out of the way." "Brutus," October 18, 1787, *(I)*

"The powers of the general legislature extend to every case that is of the least importance-there is nothing valuable to human nature, nothing dear to free men, but what is within its power. It has authority to make laws which will affect the lives, liberty and property of every man in the United States; nor can the constitution or laws of any state, in any way prevent or impede the full and complete execution of every power given." "Brutus", October 18, 1787, *(I)*

"The general legislature will thus be empowered to lay any tax they choose, to annex any penalties they please to the breach of their revenue laws, and to appoint as many officers as they may think proper to collect the taxes. They will have plenary power to collect them in any way which to them may appear eligible. The courts of law, which they will be authorized to institute, will have cognizance of every case arising under the revenue laws, and the officers of these courts will execute their judgments. A power that has such latitude, which reaches every person in the community in every conceivable circumstance, and lays hold of every species of property they possess, and which has no bounds set to it, but the discretion of those who exercise it; such a power must necessarily, from its very nature, swallow up all the power of the state governments. There is no way of avoiding this destruction, unless the people rise up, and with a strong hand, resist and prevent the execution of unconstitutional laws. The fear of this will, it is presumed, restrain the general government, for some time, within proper bounds, but it will not be many years before they will have a revenue, and force, at their command, which will place them above any apprehensions on the score." "Brutus," October 18, 1787, *(VI)*

"Many instances can be produced in which the people have voluntarily increased the powers of their rulers; but few, if any, in which rulers have willingly abridged their authority. This is sufficient reason to induce you to be careful, in the first instance, how you deposit the powers of government. Should the thirteen United States be reduced to one great republic, governed by one legislature, or should they continue thirteen confederated republics, under direction and control of a supreme federal head for certain defined national purposes only? This enquiry is important, because, although the government reported by the convention does not go to a perfect and entire consolidation, yet it approaches so near to it, that it must, if executed, certainly and infallibly terminate in it." "Brutus", October 18, 1787, *(I)*

"If the constitution be a wise one, calculated to preserve the invaluable blessings of liberty, to secure the inestimable rights of mankind, and promote human happiness for millions yet unborn; generations to come will rise up and call you blessed. You may rejoice in the prospects of this vast extended continent becoming filled with freemen, who will assert the dignity of human nature. The mind will expand in knowledge and virtue, and the golden age will be, in some measure, realized. But if, on the other hand, this form of government contains principles that will lead to the subversion of liberty-if it tends to establish a despotism, then, if you adopt it, this only remaining asylum for liberty will be shut up, and posterity will execrate your memory." "Brutus," October 18, 1787 *(I)*

"The confidence which the people have in their rulers, in a free republic, arises from their knowing them, from their being responsible to them for their conduct, and from the power they have of displacing them when they misbehave; but in a republic of the extent of this continent, the people in general would be acquainted with very few of their rulers; the people at large would know little of their proceedings, and it would be extremely difficult to change them. The consequence will be, they will have no confidence in their legislature, suspect them of ambitious views, be jealous of every measure they adopt, and will not support the laws they pass." "Brutus," October 18, 1787, *(I)*

FINAL ARGUMENTS FROM THE ANTIFEDERALISTS

The following are excerpts from speeches before the Virginia state ratifying convention by Patrick Henry. Others included are newspaper articles by "Centinel," "Brutus," "Cato," "John DeWitt" and the "Federal Farmer." No further comment is necessary.

“The American spirit has fled from hence. Shall we imitate the example of those nations who have gone from a simple to a splendid Government? Are those nations more worthy of our imitation? What can make an adequate satisfaction to them for the loss they suffered in attaining such a Government for the loss of their liberty? If we admit this Consolidated Government it will be because we like a great splendid one. Some way or another, we must be a great and mighty empire, we must have an army and a navy. When the American spirit was in its youth, the language of America was different: Liberty, Sir, was then the primary object. We are descended from a people whose Government was founded on liberty; we drew that spirit from our British ancestors; by that spirit we have triumphed over every difficulty. But now, Sir, the American spirit, assisted by the ropes and chains of consolidation, is about to convert this country to a powerful and mighty empire. If you make the citizens of this country agree to become the subjects of one great consolidated empire of America, your Government will not have sufficient energy to keep them together. Such a Government is incompatible with the genius of republicanism. There will be no checks, no real balances, in this Government. But Sir, we are not feared by foreigners, we do not make nations tremble. Would this, Sir, constitute happiness, or secure liberty?

Consider our situation, Sir: Go to the poor man, ask him what he does; he will inform you, that he enjoys the fruits of his labor, under his own fig tree, with his wife and children around him, in peace and security. Go to every other member of society, you will find the same tranquil ease and content; you will find no alarms or disturbances. Why then tell us of dangers to terrify us into an adoption of this new Government? We shall be found to be surrounded by no real dangers. We have the animating fortitude and persevering alacrity of republican men, to carry through misfortunes and calamities And yet who knows the dangers that this new system may produce; they are out of sight of the common people; they cannot foresee latent consequences. I dread the operation of it on the middling and lower class of people; it is for them I fear the adoption of this system."

Patrick Henry, *Speech to the Virginia Ratifying Convention,* June 5, 1788

"Sir, I am made of such incredulous materials that assertions and declarations, do not satisfy me. I must be convinced, Sir. I shall retain my infidelity on that subject, till I see our liberties secured in a manner perfectly satisfactory to my understanding."

"Where are the checks in this Government? Your strongholds will be in the hands of your enemies; it is on a supposition that our American Governors shall be honest, that all the good qualities of this Government are founded. But its defective, and imperfect construction, puts it in their power to perpetrate the worst of mischiefs, should they be bad men. Show me that age and country where the rights and liberties of the people were placed on the sole chance of their rulers being good men, without a consequent loss of liberty? I say that the loss of that dearest privilege has ever followed with absolute certainty, every such mad attempt."

"I say, they may ruin you; for where, Sir, is the responsibility? The yeas and nays will show you nothing, unless they be fools as well as knaves. For after having wickedly trampled on the rights of the people, they would act like fools indeed, were they to publish and divulge their iniquity, where they have it equally in their power to suppress and conceal it. Where is the responsibility-that leading principle in the British Government? They may go without punishment for the grossest maladministration. They may go without punishment though they commit the most outrageous violation on our immunities. That paper may tell me they will be punished. I ask, by what law? They must make the law-for there is no existing law to do it. What-will they make a law to punish themselves? The preservation of our liberty depends on the single chance of men being virtuous enough to make laws to punish themselves. In the country from where we are descended, they have real, not imaginary responsibility-for there, maladministration has cost their heads, to some of the most saucy geniuses that ever were."

Patrick Henry, *Speech to the Virginia Ratifying Convention,* June 7, 1788

"Before the existence of express political compacts it was reasonably implied that the magistrate should govern with wisdom and justice, but mere implication was too feeble to restrain the unbridled ambition of a bad man, or afford security against negligence, cruelty or any other defect of mind. It is alleged that the opinions and manners of the people of America are capable to resist and prevent an extension of prerogative or oppression; but you must recollect that opinion and manners are mutable, and may not always be a permanent obstruction against the encroachments of government; that the progress of a commercial society begets luxury, the parent of inequality, the foe to virtue, and the enemy to restraint; and that ambition aided by flattery, will teach magistrates, where limits are not explicitly fixed, to have separate and distinct interests from the people. Therefore, a general presumption that rulers will govern well is not sufficient security. You are about to precipitate yourselves into a sea of uncertainty, and adopt a system so vague, and which has discarded so many of your valuable rights. If this be the case you rest on a weak basis; Americans are like other men in similar situations, when the manners and opinions of the community are changed by outside causes, and your political compact inexplicit, your posterity will find this great power connected with ambition, luxury, and flattery, will as readily produce a Caesar, Caligula, Nero, and Domitian in America, as the same causes did in the Roman Empire. You are then under a sacred obligation to provide for the safety of your posterity, and would you now basely desert their interests, when by a small share of prudence, you may transmit to them a beautiful political patrimony, that will prevent the necessity of their travelling through seas of blood to obtain that, which your wisdom might have secured?

“Cato,” November 27, 1787

“A constitution is a compact of the people with their rulers; if the rulers break the compact the people have the right and ought to remove them and do themselves justice; but in order to enable them to do this with the greater facility, those whom the people choose at stated periods should have the power in the last resort to determine the sense of the compact; if they determine contrary to the understanding of the people, an appeal will lie to the people at the period when the rulers are to be elected, and they will have it in their power to remedy the evil; but when this power is lodged in the hands of men independent of the people, and of their representatives, and who are not, constitutionally accountable for their opinions, no way is left to control them but with a high hand and an outstretched arm.”

“Brutus,” March 20, 1788 *(XV)*

"All contracts are to be construed according to the meaning of the parties at the time of making them. By which is meant, that mutual communications shall take place, and each shall explain to the other their ideas of the contract before them. If any unfair practices are made use of, if its real tendency is concealed by either party, or any advantage taken in the execution of it, it is in itself fraudulent and may be avoided. In government, the form is the mode in which the people choose to direct their affairs, and the magistrates are but the trustees to put that mode in force. That government, originally consented to, which is in practice, what it purports to be in theory, is a government of choice; from its appearance in theory, however it may be in letter a government of choice, it can never be in spirit. Of this latter kind appear to me to be the proceedings of the Federal Convention. They are presented as a Frame of Government purely Republican, and perfectly consistent with the individual governments in the union. It is declared to be constructed for national purposes only, and not calculated to interfere with domestic concerns. You are told that the rights of the people are very amply secured, and when the wheels are put in motion it will wear a milder aspect than its present one. Whereas the contrary of all this doctrine appears to be true. Your consent is requested, because it is essential to the introduction of it; after having received confirmation, your complaints may increase the whistling of the wind, and they will be equally regarded." "John DeWitt," November 5, 1787

"Go, and establish this Government, which is unanimously confessed imperfect, yet incapable of alteration. Entrust it to men, subject to the same unbounded passions and infirmities as yourselves, possessed with an insatiable thirst for power, and many of them, carrying in them vices, tho' tinsel'd and concealed, yet, in themselves, not less dangerous than those more naked and exposed. Prepare an apology for the blood and treasure, profusely spent to obtain those rights which you now so timely part with. Conceal yourselves from the ridicule of your enemies and bring your New England spirits to a level with the contempt of mankind."

"John DeWitt," November 5, 1787

"If the people of America will submit to a constitution that will vest in the hands of any body of men a right to deprive them by law of the privilege of a fair election, they will submit to almost anything. Reasoning with them will be in vain, they must be left until they are brought to reflection by feeling oppression-they will then have to wrest from their oppressors, by a strong hand, that which they now possess, and which they may retain if they will exercise but a moderate share of prudence and firmness."

"Brutus," November 27, 1787

THE RESULT

The Founders were determined to create a diffused, limited, balanced form of government in which men like themselves-principled and propertied-would fill the leading positions. They worked against the democratic sentiment of the moment for a unicameral legislature, plural executive, annual election of all officers, manhood suffrage, exhaustive bill of rights, easy method of amendment; they produced a distinctly different Constitution, with separation of powers, an imposing array of checks and balances, including a strong President with a veto, a bicameral legislature, including a Senate intended to slow down legislation, staggered elections for President and Congress, aimed at preventing sudden reversals in public policy, a severely limited procedure for amendments, requiring the approval of a super-majority of Congress and the States, and a key clause forbidding the states to pass any law impairing the obligation of contracts. The mechanical friction resulting from the checks and balances, the diffusion of power, of American government, was a small price to pay for insurance against reckless experiment and oppressive centralization.

The Founding Fathers identified the nature and needs of a free society and devised the means to translate it into practice. A complex legal system, based on objectively valid principles, was required to make and keep a society free-a system that does not depend on the motives, the moral character and the intentions of any given official, a system that leaves no loophole for corruption or tyranny. The American Constitution, with its system of checks and balances, was just such an achievement. The system worked to lengthen the delays built into the constitutional process. The Constitution was written by men who believed in free government, with a mechanism of majority rule only to decide elections, strained and balanced by a variety of ingenious parliamentary devices. Written laws, the separation of powers, federalism, bicameralism, the Presidential veto, judicial review, the delaying roles in the machinery of Congress-these arrangements are the diffusion and restraint of popular power in the manner of representative, limited, divided government. It was designed to check and frustrate the ill-considered plans of men while yet permitting them to govern in a responsible and popular way.

While flawed, it was the first to give the means of limiting and restricting the power of government. The government holds a monopoly on the legal use of physical force. Its actions have to be rigidly defined, delimited and circumscribed with the Law as its only motive power. If a society is to be free its government has to be controlled. A private individual may do anything except that which is legally forbidden; a government official may do nothing except what is legally permitted. The nature of the laws proper to a free society and the source of its government's authority are both to be derived from its founding principles: to "secure these [individual] rights, governments are instituted among men, deriving their just powers from the consent of the governed." Since the protection of individual rights is the only proper purpose of government it is also the only proper subject of legislation. The government is not the ruler, but the agent of the citizens. This is the American concept of a government of laws and not of men. Hamilton, in Federalist #15 writes: "Why has government been instituted at all? Because the passions of men will not conform to the dictates of reason and justice without restraint. Has it been found that bodies of men act with more rectitude or greater disinterestedness than individuals? The contrary of this has been inferred by all accurate observers of the conduct of mankind; and the inference is founded upon obvious reasons. Regard to reputation has a less active influence when the infamy of a bad action is to be divided among a number than when it is to fall singly upon one. A spirit of faction, which is apt to mingle its poison in the deliberations of all bodies of men, will often hurry the persons of whom they are composed into improprieties and excesses for which they would blush in a private capacity…they will consider the conformity of the thing proposed or required to their immediate interests or aims… which can hardly fail to mislead the decision."

The American Constitution was framed by men, represented by Washington and Adams, by Gouverneur Morris, Madison and Hamilton, who had the strongest sense of the dangers of democracy, who inspired the *Federalist* arguments and the Federalist Party, and was utterly opposed to the school of

Rousseau. It did not prevent America from becoming a democracy, but it framed a form of government under which the power of government was broken and divided, restricted to a much smaller sphere, and attended with far less disastrous results than other such attempts. Hamilton, probably the greatest political thinker America produced, was, in the essentials of his political thought, quite as conservative as Burke, but he never concealed his preference for monarchial institutions. Democratic government, he thought, must end in despotism and be in the meantime destructive to public morality and to the security of private property. Such, in essence, was the purpose of any proper government: to make existence possible to men, by protecting the benefits of society and combatting the evils which they cause to one another. What is essential is the principle to be implemented: the purpose of law and government is the protection of individual rights. The Constitution is a limitation on the government, not on private individuals, not a charter for government power but a charter of the citizens' protection against the government. Instead, today there is a moral and political inversion, where the government is free to do anything which it pleases, while the citizens may act only with permission. Given that mankind has faced this situation through most of its history it is remarkable that even a semblance of civilization remains. One begins to clearly see the nature of the political principles that have to be accepted and re-instated in the battle for man's intellectual Renaissance.

The American Constitutional provisions, thought beforehand to make Democracy tolerable, included carefully defining the public powers, fixing the mode in which they are to be exercised, and taking the amplest security that none of the more important arrangements shall be altered without every guarantee of caution and every opportunity for deliberation. The Revolution protected every American's exercise of his natural freedom: due process, the right to a jury trial, the right to petition the government, the right to bear arms, the right to own property. The right to own property was a legal right, absolutely essential to an individual's exercise of his natural rights. Without legal protection no one could safely exercise any of them. Every one of these was necessary to protect an individual's use of his natural liberty. Other key topics resulting in extended discussion were the provisions for representation, the forbidding of hereditary elements in government, as well as positive prohibitions against titles of nobility, the absence of property qualifications for federal suffrage and office holding, the provision for the adding of new states on an equal footing with the original, and the prohibition for religious tests for office holding.

Congress was debarred by the Constitution from making any law prohibiting the free exercise of religion or abridging the freedom of speech and of the press, or the right of assembly, or the right of petition. No person could be deprived of life, liberty or property without due process of law. The main articles of liberty were guaranteed, and property so fenced around by constitutional provisions that confiscatory legislation became almost impossible. No private property could be taken without just compensation. Taxes were to be apportioned among the states according to population, not the partial and highly graduated taxation falling on the few, and voted for by the many, that we have today. Bills of attainder or ex post facto laws were not permitted

Constitutions are an expression of a nation's historical experience. In America, royalty and aristocracy never existed, so therefore ours was framed to suit a nation in which the commons were the only order in the state. Republicanism was the best government for America, and the true conservative would struggle to maintain the Republic in its purity, strictly obeying its laws, cleaving fast to the Constitution. No human institution is immutable; constitutions must be mended and healed now and then; but the social reformer does not create: he develops, he restores to health, but he knows he cannot hack a new constitution out of raw humanity. Madison, in *Federalist* #14, suggests the same: "they have not suffered a blind veneration for antiquity, for custom, or for names, to overrule the suggestions of their own good sense, the knowledge of their own situation, and the lessons of their own experience." In *Federalist*

#37-38 he continues the theme: "it has been shown in the course of these papers that the existing [Articles of] Confederation is founded on principles which are fallacious; that we must consequently change this first foundation, and with it the superstructure resting upon it. It has been shown that other confederacies-Greece and Rome-which could be consulted as precedents have been vitiated by the same erroneous principles and can therefore furnish no other light than that of beacons, which give warning of the course to be shunned, without pointing out that which ought to be pursued. The most that the convention could do in such a situation was to avoid the errors suggested by the past experience of other countries, as well as of our own; and to provide a convenient mode of rectifying their own errors, as future experience may unfold them."

"Among the difficulties encountered by the convention, a very important one must have lain in combining the requisite stability and energy in government with the inviable attention due to liberty and to the republican form...Stability in government is essential to national character and to the advantages annexed to it, as well as to that repose and confidence in the minds of the people, which are among the chief blessings of a civil society. Energy in government is essential to that security against external and internal danger and to the prompt and salutary execution of the laws...On comparing, however, these valuable ingredients with the vital principles of liberty, we must perceive at once the difficulty of mingling them together in their due proportions. The genius of Republican liberty seems to demand on one side not only that all power should be derived from the people, but that those entrusted with it should also be kept dependent." Madison goes even further in *Federalist* #41: "In every political institution, a power to advance the public happiness involves a discretion which may be misapplied and abused...In all cases where power is to be conferred, the point first to be decided is whether such a power be necessary to the public good; in the case of an affirmative decision, to guard as effectually as possible against a perversion of the power to the public detriment."

Whatever prevents the concentration of power is preservative of freedom and traditional life. Decentralization keeps from the hands of the majority, which would like to be a despot, the chief instruments of tyranny. So long as power could be denied to pure numbers, so long as great fields of human activity were exempt from the influence of government, so long as the Constitution limited the scope of legislation-so long as these things endured, democratic despotism was kept at bay. If democracy were persuaded to accept as a habit such limitations upon its sovereignty, to approve them from reason and from prejudice, freedom might have continued to exist in the same world with equality. The surest, and indeed only, check lay in the customs, the collective habits of the people. The great utility of tradition, prescription and institutions is to sustain liberty during those periods when the human mind is otherwise occupied. It can be referred back to-this is the knowledge that we have collected and found to be sound and useful. Everything an American values depends upon his keeping clear in his mind the revolutionary basis of the Republic. This revolutionary basis is the recognition of the fact that human rights are natural rights, born in every human being with his life, and inseparable from his life; not rights and freedoms that can be granted or revoked by any power on earth. "A people entering into society surrender such a part of their natural rights as shall be necessary for the existence of that society. They are so precious in themselves that they would never be parted with, did not the preservation of the remainder require it. They are entrusted in the hands of those who are very willing to receive them, who are naturally fond of exercising them, and whose passions are always striving to make a bad use of them. They are conveyed by a written compact, expressing those which shall be given up, and the mode in which those reserved shall be secured. The compact itself is a recital upon paper of that proportion of the subject's natural rights, intended to be parted with, for the benefit of adverting to it in case of dispute. (John DeWitt) Language is so easy of explanation, and so difficult is it by words to convey exact ideas, that the party to be governed cannot be too explicit. The line cannot be drawn with too much precision and accuracy. The necessity of this increases in proportion to the greatness of the sacrifice and the numbers who make it"

This knowledge attacks the very foundations of the Old World. This is the knowledge that the Old World's defenders are determined to destroy. True American Government is not an Authority; it has no control over individuals and no responsibility for their affairs. True American Government is a permission which free individuals grant to certain men to use force in certain necessary, strictly known and limited ways; a permission which can always be withdrawn. The true revolutionary course which must be followed toward a free world is a cautious, experimental process of further decreasing the uses of force which individuals permit to Government; of increasing the prohibitions on Government's action, and thus progressively decreasing the use of brute force in human affairs. Responsibility for whatever men in American Government do is the individual citizen's responsibility. The American who leaves Government to the politicians, permitting or urging the men of his party, when they are in office, to increase their power and use it upon other Americans for his benefit, and howling when men of the other party are doing the same against him, is evading his responsibility. In trying to make any other person responsible for his welfare, he must transfer his control of himself to that other man, for control and responsibility cannot be separated. In demanding that men in Government be responsible for his welfare, a citizen is demanding control of his affairs by men whose only power is the use of force. A man is able to use his self-controlling energy more effectively toward its natural aim of improving living conditions, precisely to the extent that no use of force restrains him. Majorities will protect themselves; minorities, especially the individual, have no protection, save the sacredness and supremacy of the Law.

Royal charters had been grants of freedoms, from Government to its subjects. But Americans knew, and the Declaration stated, that there is no such superior Authority. It is the men in government who can do nothing without permission from the individuals whom they govern. This meant turning all past Old World experience upside down. There was no precedent in known history, for a government that was not a controlling Authority. Men knew old Government pretended to use Authority, and actually used force, to prevent individual action. The job in America was first to get the delegates to secure their freedoms and then to get the citizens back home to agree to the delegate's actions. Americans grudgingly and suspiciously accepted this new form of Government, but only on the condition that it was prohibited from using its force as it had always been used previously. These prohibitions are called the Bill of Rights. It is a statement of the uses of force which American citizens do not permit to men in American Government. It is the difference between the American Revolutionary Government and every other Government, ever, on earth. If Americans forget that Government is not permitted to restrain or coerce any peaceful individual without his free consent, if Americans ever regard their use of their natural liberty as granted to them by the men in Washington, then their exercise of human rights is at an end. The curbing of Government is the only defense against the tyranny that has reigned over men for all their history. It is the protection of every American's life. The counter-revolution that now threatens must be defended against in the mind of every American.

The Enlightenment's John Locke and the Founding Fathers expressed the thought that the legitimate authority of government depends on observing limitations on its just powers. Constitutionalism is a compound of ideas, attitudes and patterns of behavior elaborating the principle that the authority of government is limited by a body of fundamental law. It subjects the officials who exercise government power to the limitations of that higher law. These derived from a dynamic political and historical process, from Greece forward, rather than from a static body of thought laid down in the eighteenth century. Constitutionalism proclaims the desirability of the rule of law as opposed to the rule of the arbitrary judgment or mere fiat of public officials. The central element of the concept of constitutionalism is that in political society government officials are not free to do anything they please in any manner they choose; they are bound to observe both the limitations on power and the procedures which are set out in the supreme law of the country. Constitutionalism establishes the intellectual and institutional framework for the government but similarly supplies the rhetorical currency with which political transactions are carried on. It also refers to the historical struggle for recognition of the people's right to consent, along with other rights, freedoms and privileges. The main idea is that government can and should be limited in its powers and that its legitimate authority exists wholly in observing these limitations. A constitution prescribes both the source and limits of government power derived from fundamental law. It defines what grants and guides the legitimate exercise of government authority. Rules were to be recognized and enforced by the courts. Its effect is a limited government under a higher law. Progressives have utter contempt for the strict construction of the Constitution by conservative judges who restrict the power of the national government to act against perceived social evils. The real evil was states' rights and limited government.

The old system of Constitutionalism was supported and consolidated by a tone of political feeling which has so completely passed away that it is somewhat difficult to realize the power which it once possessed-the strong indisposition to ideological change, as distinguished from simple administrative reform. The system of the Constitution had grown up in accordance with the wants of the nation; it was a highly complex and delicate machine, fulfilling many different purposes and acting in many obscure and far-reaching ways; a disposition to pull it to pieces in the interests of some new theory or speculation would inevitably lead to the destruction of representative government. American statesmen clearly saw how useless it would be to reproduce all English institutions in a country where they had little historical or traditional basis. The United States did not contain the materials for founding a constitutional monarchy or a powerful aristocracy; it was necessary to adopt other means, but the ends that were aimed at were much the same. To divide and restrict power; to secure property; to check the appetite for hurried change; to guard individual liberty against the tyranny of the multitude; to infuse into American political life a spirit of continuity and of sober and moderate freedom-these were the ends which the Founding Fathers set before themselves, and which they in a large measure attained. They restricted by a clearly defined and written Constitution the powers of the representative body, placing the security of property, the sanctity of Contract and the chief forms of personal and religious liberty beyond the powers of a mere parliamentary majority to infringe. They established a Supreme Court with the right of interpreting authoritatively the Constitution and declaring Acts of Congress which exceeded their powers to be null and void; they made such large majorities necessary for the enactment of any change that these changes became impossible, except where there was an overwhelming consensus of public opinion in their favor.

Here, man is born free, and comes into his political inheritance at maturity. By this concept all rights belong to the individual. Society consists of individuals in voluntary association. In the Society of Status, nobody has any rights. The individual is not recognized; a man is defined by his relation to the group. The presumed moral value of Status is that it gives everyone security, a place in society from which he cannot be ousted, and which, conversely, he may not leave. Contract becomes dominant only when the theory of Status is explicitly repudiated by limitation of the scope of government. The Roman Republic was remarkable for its almost even apportionment of Contract and Status. Politically, it included more of the Contract basis than any previous or contemporary state; much more than Greek democracies, since it limited the scope of political power. In the Empire, the administration of law by a central authority, and the prerogative ceded to the emperor, tended toward Status. The citizen ceased to participate actively in political thought. Men do not quite understand what they have no part in making or doing. With the law handed down, men from the subject nations were unlikely to learn self-government. Using the materials available, in accordance with architectural and mechanical principles, the Founders solved the problem on which the Roman Empire had failed. The Constitution is laid out in broad general principles and encourages the interest of the citizens. The separate elements embody relations and are thus capable of infinitely complex application. But the intrinsic balanced design must always have been maintained. Once the foundations were removed, and the keystone withdrawn, the whole must necessarily fall, smashing the entire mechanism. A greater volume of energy does not and cannot alter the necessary structural relations involved. The belief that it does is the fatal delusion of the Progressive Movement beginning with Woodrow Wilson. Increased volume of energy has been made the pretext for destroying the principles of government, when they should rather have been strengthened.

The American Constitution, by its treason clause, which includes the statement that there can be no treason in peacetime, ended the idea of the "corruption of blood" found in Status society. With the principle's resurgence in Communist Russia, this gave that government an invisible and unspecified power over an accused man by means of threats to his family. A man of integrity might face death for himself calmly but be forced into acts to protect his family from the prospect of torture and penury. In the United States, though, a convict's property passes unimpeded to his legal heir, and they may not be punished for mere kinship. The principle effectively nullifies the claims for reparations by the 1619 Project. But with the return of collectivism the Left's legal imputation of collective guilt inevitably returned also.

All these provisions in the Bill of Rights and the Constitution are of the utmost importance in relation to the energy of the country; the facts which they express account for the unparalleled expansion of the United States both territorially and even more for the extraordinary extension of the field of physical science and invention. In a hundred and fifty years, men suddenly corrected and enlarged their knowledge of scientific principles which had taken many thousands of years to discover at all; and devised means of application which made possible a concurrent increase of population and a rise in the standard of well-being beyond the dreams of humanity in the past. Nothing of the sort had happened in the world before the Saracens; history reveals nothing comparable to the United States as a nation, since.

What happened was that the dynamo of the energy used in productive human association was located. It is in the individual. It was withdrawn from political interference by a formal reservation of power, along with the means and material by which it can organize the great world circuit of trade. The dynamo is the mind, the creative intelligence, which our Bill of Rights and the treason clause assert to be free of political control. The material means on which intelligence projects, by initiative, is private property. Nothing else will serve. The citizens, by the institution of private property, were given resistance against all the agencies of government. Private property is the standing ground of the citizen; there is no other. Hence, the Left's hatred for it.

....

Democracy is not an end but a means. To seek out the uncertain voice of Democracy is as hazardous as interpreting the ambiguous Greek oracles. "The oracles were consulted, and whatever they were made to say, became the law; and this sort of government lasted as long as this sort of superstition lasted." (Paine) Democracy must be taught a modesty about its own functions-the principal safeguard for popular government is an exact and august conservatism. Democracy in America manifested a modest success chiefly due to the conservatism of the Federal Constitution. Two assemblies, recognizing the rights of individuals and the several states, the necessity for limiting the power of positive legislation, capping the system with the dignified check of the Supreme Court, made possible by John Marshall's Chief Justiceship-these were instruments of government unparalleled as conservative props for ordered liberty.

The Federal judiciary was to be appointed for life in order to preserve its independence and to also keep a check on the legislative and executive branches. The jurisdiction of the Supreme Court is specified as covering only cases "arising under the Constitution, and the laws of the United States, and treaties made under their authority," while "this Constitution, and the laws of the United States which shall be made in pursuance thereof, shall be the supreme law of the land." No sophistry can evade the proposition that the supreme law must govern the verdict; that is what supreme means. But after arguing for a hundred years against this proper and indispensable principle, and function of judicial review, the Left invented a singularly vicious hypothetical perversion of it. Justice Frankfurter expressed it, writing of "the dangers and difficulties inherent in the power to review legislation. For it is a subtle business to decide, not whether legislation is wise, but whether legislators were reasonable in believing it to be wise." But judicial review is not concerned with deciding whether legislation is wise or legislators reasonable in believing it to be wise. Judicial review is confined to finding whether or not a given law contravenes the Constitution, the supreme law; as it does if the legislature exceeded the Constitutional power in passing the law in question, as it has no authority except what is expressly delegated to it in the Constitution.

Hamilton, *Federalist* #78, "There is no position which depends on clearer principles than that every act of delegated authority, contrary to the tenor of the commission under which it is exercised, is void. No legislative act, therefore, contrary to the Constitution, can be valid. To deny this would be to affirm that the deputy is greater than his principal; that the servant is above his master; that the representatives of the people are superior to the people themselves; that men acting by virtue of powers may not only do what their powers do not authorize, but what they forbid."

"If it be said that the legislative body are themselves the constitutional judges of their own powers, and that the construction they put upon them is conclusive upon other departments, it may be answered that this cannot be the natural presumption, where it is not to be collected from any particular provisions in the Constitution. It is not otherwise to be supposed that the Constitution could intend to enable the representatives of the people to substitute their will to that of their constituents. A constitution is, in fact, and must be regarded as fundamental law designed to keep the legislature within the limits assigned to their authority; the Constitution ought to be preferred to the statute, the intention of the people to the intention of their agents."

Only man's legal rights, clearly stated in writing, protects the individual from the arbitrary use of force by the men in government. "The internal effects of a mutable policy are still more calamitous. It poisons the blessings of liberty itself. It will be of little avail to the people that the laws are made by men of their own choice if the laws be so voluminous that they cannot be read, or so incoherent that they cannot be understood; if they be repealed or revised before they are promulgated, or undergo such incessant changes that no man, who knows what the law is today, can guess what it will be tomorrow. Law is defined to be a rule of action. But how can that be a rule, which is little known, and less fixed?" Madison, *Federalist* #37

Legally restricting Government's action to its smallest possible minimum reduces the use of force in human affairs. Precisely by restricting Government, American Constitutional law permits Americans to act more freely than any other people on earth. The Constitution restricts the Government. Voting can restrict it further where voters have the opportunity to elect men who will repeal bad laws and make their Constitution stronger. When the Declaration was written, a way of thinking about individuals appeared which completely reversed all the old ideas. The individual would be master of his own fate. Kings were just ordinary mortals. Government would be the servant and not the master of men. With the establishment of the Republic of the United States of America, a great landmark in history was achieved. Beforehand, nations were formed by chance and circumstance and doubtful experiment. As often as a democracy might be tried, it must shortly collapse into despotism. This is the first nation founded on reasoned political principles, proceeding from the axiom that man's birthright is freedom. As long as those principles were maintained, it succeeded beyond all precedent. A new federal republic can still be reconstituted on the same principles and bases.

In the face of the preponderance of wealth and respectability in support of the Constitution what remains extraordinary was the political strength of the Antifederalists. That large numbers of Americans could actually reject a plan of government created by a body composed of the finest intellects on the continent, backed by the character of Washington and nearly the whole of the rest of the natural aristocracy of the country, was remarkable. The Antifederalists, thought, in opposing, that the goal of the American Revolution was to end the ancient equation of power where arrogant, oppressive and depraved rulers on one side produce subservience and a gradual erosion of the self-respect, capacities and virtue of the people on the other side. The result was an increasing corruption and degeneracy in both rulers and ruled. Unless this cycle could be broken, independence would mean little more than the exchange of one tyranny for another. The aspirations of the federalists for commercial growth, westward expansion, increased national power, and effective world diplomacy were in some ways attractive and worthy, but they also fitted an ominous, familiar pattern of "great, splendid, consolidated government and Universal Empire" (Henry) that the Revolution had been fought to eradicate. Many Antifederalists were unwilling to abandon their ideal and the hope that the New World might be a different and better place to live. There could be a society where virtuous, hard-working, honest men and women lived simply in their own communities, enjoyed their families and their neighbors, were devoted to the common welfare, and had such churches, schools, trade associations, and local governments as they needed to sustain their values and purposes. The later successes of Jefferson, with their antifederalist overtones, attest to the vigor and influence of its principles even under the document opposed so vehemently in 1787-1788. Antifederalist arguments, along with the writings of Publius in the Federalist, are both to be viewed as belonging to the philosophy of the Constitution.

Constitutionalism is the guardian of our heritage and the most noble of all experiments in human liberty. Our community should rise naturally out of the American way of life. For its realization of these moral relations and structural embodiment of them, the Constitution of the United States has justly been described as the greatest political document ever struck off by the mind of man. The individual could exercise self-government under Law, free of the universe to pursue knowledge by reason. Whoever is fortunate enough to be an American citizen came into the greatest inheritance man has ever enjoyed. He has had the benefit of every heroic and intellectual effort men have ever made, realized at last. After twenty-five hundred years the resources of science were released for productive application. If Americans turn back now, submitting again to slavery, it would be a betrayal so base that the human race might better perish. The opportunity is equally great to justify the faith which animated that long travail and bequeathed them such a noble and happy heritage.

No kind of conservatism is possible in America unless political democracy first is made secure and just. Any society, if it is to remain civilized, must submit to moral discipline-the general subjection of appetite to reason-permanent institutions, and the beneficent claims of property. Every individual is naturally self-governing; but because men must combine their energies in order to live, they need to stop those men who wish to injure others-that is the necessity for Government. Government has the monopoly in the use of force by general consent. The problem is to devise some method by which a majority of citizens could peacefully give, or deny, their consent to the men in Government. But here is the danger. Democracy has been tried again and again. It always destroys personal safety, and ownership of property, and it quickly creates a tyrant, who oppresses the people until they revolt in civil war. The Greeks could not solve the problem. The Early Romans of the Republic could not solve it. No one has ever been able to solve it. The Founding Fathers tried to solve it by not only dividing and checking Government's use of force, but also by dividing and checking the majority. The House, with spending power, represented the people's veto, while the Senate, originally selected through the states, was to represent their interests. The President was to represent the Republic. Votes would take place at different times for different constituencies. Constitutional law gave taxpayers a quick recall of the men who assessed and spent their taxes. This was representative government.

The results, however, were clear twenty-five hundred years ago in Greece. Democracy does not work. It cannot work because every man is free. He cannot transfer his inalienable life and liberty to anyone or anything outside himself. When he tries to do this, he tries to obey an Authority that does not exist. It makes no difference what he imagines this Authority to be-Ra or Zeus or Jupiter, Economic Necessity or the General Will, or the Voice of the People; the stubborn fact is that there is no Authority, of any kind, that controls individuals. They control themselves. The premise of democracy is supposed to be natural equality. Neither the Greeks nor Rousseau were able to validate their hypotheses for democracy because its inner logic, and proper application, would not admit human equality, or any other principle of human association, where there are no rights or moral questions outside of the reach of majority vote. But the American axiom asserted political equality as a corollary of the inalienable right of every man to liberty. Democracy was untenable because it must ultimately deny that right and lapse into despotism, as it has always done, and is doing now. It does so abstractly, by its own logical contradiction; and in practice because logic is a statement of sequence. It is not liberty and equality that are opposites, but liberty and democracy. Democracy is a collective term; it describes the aggregate as a whole and assumes that the right and authority reside in the whole, derived from the adult condition of the individuals comprised. It must be supposed that at an unknown moment by an unknown sanction and for no reason whatever such right and authority was irrevocably transferred from the individual to a group which was nothing but a numerical sum. Thus, democracy is pure process, and even the process is fictitious, for groups have no rights, and exist only as a mathematical and non-moral order. In practice democracy must abandon its own pretended entity of the collective whole, and rely upon majority, and in some cases only a plurality, in which case one minority commands several others which if added together are greater in number. The distinction is that between a principle and a process; the confusion arises from an unwarrantable identification of a negative proposition with a positive. It is falsely assumed that when the claim of the few to command the many is refuted, the converse claim of the many to command the individual is proved. If one man has no right to command all other men-nor then does any number of men have the right to command even one other man. The practical defect of democracy corresponds to the moral defect. Right as a concept is necessarily opposed to force; otherwise, the word is meaningless.

Nonetheless Democracy became the national religion. The progress from Status to Contract was the work of aristocratic minds; the retrogression from Contract back to Status would be the achievement of democratic complacency. By far the largest part of modern law is nothing more than a sedimentary formation left by the Roman legal reforms. Behind the curtain of Democracy lies private property, the achievement of Contract, which is now menaced with socialism, or the return to primitive Status. If this reaction be consummated, civilization will sink proportionately to the barbarism that is described by Status.

If the works and thoughts of the men who founded the United States are examined, it is evident that they had a highly developed structural sense, a remarkable feeling for and an understanding of form, proportion and perspective. They thought in terms of mathematics and architecture as naturally as in words. A cornerstone of government cannot be fixed on a mound of sand. There must be something solid, self-contained and immovable. A political organization consists of both structure and mechanism, giving a fixed base to which agencies of action are attached. Failure to discern this has led to the disasters of history. With feudalism, requiring an immovable base meant binding men to the land, crushing living bodies with the weight of the structure. In the Roman Empire it was impossible to continue direct representation of the people's veto power, but it was later utilized through the Church's power of excommunication and interdiction. The same function has been rightly expressed in modern government by placing with the representatives elected by the people on short tenure the power of the purse and the public finances. The effective veto was thus exercised by negation. When unlimited monies are voted automatically in un-apportioned lump sums, it is obvious that the function of the stabilizing element is no longer included in government; the connection has broken somewhere and as such the citizens have no representation at all. The inherent veto power must now express itself, indicating imminent danger, with economic inertia and dysfunction. The crowning folly of government is to suppress the signals.

The ideas of the house of Adams, carried by Henry Adams to their twentieth century philosophical culmination, obtained their political summary in the writings of Brooks Adams: "Democracy is an infinite mass of conflicting minds and interests which become resolved into nothingness and loses its collective intellectual vigor in proportion to the perfection of its expansion." The Left's New America can only be accompanied by the effacement of the political system created by Washington, Jefferson, Madison, Adams and Hamilton. What the country needs is a philosophical revolution in the name of our first Founding Father-Aristotle. This means a reassertion of the supremacy of reason, with its consequences: individualism, freedom, progress, civilization, all leading to laissez-faire capitalism. According to Aristotle, a government, if it is to endure, must reflect the ethos or body of moral habits and beliefs in the governed. Another way of saying that a country gets the government it deserves.

Tocqueville and Burke believed that Providence paves the way for enormous changes in the world, and that to oppose such changes when their direction is manifest amounts to impiety. But neither were willing to sacrifice democracy's virtues upon the altar of democracy's lusts. A democracy preys upon itself, and presently exists only corrupt and hideous-still, perhaps, preserving its essential characteristic of equality, but devoid of those aspirations toward liberty and progress. Political egalitarianism must end in anarchy or tyranny. Tocqueville thought it likely not a simple collapse of order, nor usurpation by a single individual, but a tyranny of mediocrity, a standardization of mind and spirit and condition enforced by the central government-the collectivist discipline. This is the planners' society, exerted from the top downward, dominated by a bureaucratic elite. Most advocates of a planned economy are hardly able to understand Tocqueville's loathing for this kind of existence. The omnicompetent, paternalistic state, guiding all the affairs of mankind, satisfying all individual's wants, scarcely conceives of wants that are not material. That men are kept in perpetual childhood-that, in spirit, they never become full human beings-seems no great a loss to a generation of thinkers accustomed to compulsory schooling, compulsory insurance, compulsory military service, and compulsory taxation of money earned by others. A world of uniform compulsion is death to variety, and the life of the mind, and freedom.

A CODA FOR JOHN ADAMS

"Once the people give way, their deceivers, betrayers, and destroyers press upon them so fast, that there is no resisting afterwards. The nature of the encroachment upon the American constitution is such, as to grow every day. Like a cancer, it eats faster and faster every hour. The revenue creates pensioners, and the pensioners urge for more revenue. The people grow less steady, spirited, and virtuous, the seekers more numerous and corrupt, and every day increases the circles of their dependents and expectants, until virtue, integrity, public spirit, simplicity, and frugality become the objects of ridicule and scorn, and vanity, luxury, foppery, selfishness, meanness, and downright venality swallow up the whole society."

John Adams, *Thoughts on Government, Volume IV,* 1819

GORDON WOOD

In 1765 John Adams wrote with Enlightenment enthusiasm that America was designed by Providence for the Theater, on which Man was to make his true figure, on which science, Virtue, Liberty, Happiness and Glory were to exist in Peace. He thought that any distress that might arise "would inspire us with many virtues which we have not, and correct many errors, follies, and vices which threaten to disturb, dishonor and destroy us." He knew full well the dependence of republicanism on the character of the people. The cause by 1776 seemed doubtful, not for lack of power or wisdom, but for that very lack of virtue. Adams was carrying in his own mind all the promise and all the anxiety engendered by the Revolution. He counted on the regenerative effects of republican government and on the emergence of politicians who could mold the character of the people, extinguishing their follies and vices and inspiring their virtues and abilities. He clung to the capacity of education to curb the violent passions of men. In his most famous passage, he wrote "If pure virtue, the only foundation of a free constitution, cannot be inspired into our people, in a greater measure than they have it now, they may change their rulers and the forms of government, but they will not obtain a lasting Liberty. They will only exchange tyrants and tyrannies." The reliance he placed on the ameliorative power of republicanism, the optimism he had for the refinement of the American character was soon gone. By the 1780's he saw that "Americans had never merited the Character of very exalted Virtue and it was foolish to have expected that they should have grown much better." He saw and expressed more vividly that if the new Republic was to rely simply on the virtue of the people then they were destined, like every previous republic, for eventual destruction. There was no special providence for Americans and their nature was the same with that of others. Ambition, avarice and envy, not virtue and benevolence, were the stuff of American society.

Adams never tired of investigating politics and saw with more speed and insight than most the mistaken assumptions about the character of the people on which the Americans of 1776 had rested their Revolution. His *Defense of the Constitutions of Government of the United States* was an attempt to translate what he had learned about society and politics into basic principles of social and political science that were applicable to all peoples of all times. Adams clung tightly to the truth of enlightened politics as he had learned: government bore an intimate relation to society and unless the two were reconciled no state could long remain secure.

Those who argued that Americans were especially egalitarian were blind to reality. "Was there a nation, whose individuals were all equal, in natural and acquired qualities, in virtues, talents and riches? Every people, contended Adams, possessed inequalities "which no human legislator can eradicate. They were rooted in nature, in wealth, in birth, or in merit. Because of greater industry or a greater legacy, some were richer than others. Some were better born than others, inheriting from their families position and prestige in the community. Some were wiser and more talented, more bold than others, displaying courage or learning in a way as to command respect. All such distinctions produced inequality in the society; all were common to every people, and can never be altered by any, because they are founded in the constitution of nature." The inevitability of these distinctions lay at the heart of Adam's vision of society. All life was a scramble for them, for wealth and power, for social eminence, that would be passed on to one's descendants. "We may call this effort childish and silly, but we cannot alter the nature of man." Only a handful of men made it to the top in this struggle for superiority, and unfortunately there was little guarantee that these few would be men of talent and virtue. The republican hope that only real merit should govern the world was laudable, but hollow. How shall the men of character be discovered? Who shall be the judge? The republican reliance on elections had hardly worked out. The voters had repeatedly been deceived by those of pretended merit. Men disguised their lack of talent with any artifice, any hypocrisy that could convince others that they were worthy to rule. Once on top the few would only seek to stabilize and aggrandize their position by oppressing those below them. Those on the bottom of society, driven by those more ambitious, would only seek to replace and to ruin the social leaders they hated and envied. "To better their condition, to advance their fortunes, without limits, is the object of their constant desire, the employment of all their thoughts by day and by night." They want to share in that pleasure "which they presume those enjoy, who are already powerful, celebrated and rich. Adams concluded that the inevitable social division between men, a division neither rigid nor secure, grounded in irrationalities was a division from which America, however republican, however egalitarian, could never escape. Americans would inevitably seek to set themselves off from one another, yet their republicanism gave them no sanction for such distinctions. America would become a ceaseless scramble for place and prestige, a society without peace, contentment or happiness.

What could keep this restless society from tearing itself to pieces? Nature had “wrought these passions into the texture and essence of the soul, and man could never destroy them.” To regulate them and not to eradicate them, then must be the policy. Education no longer seemed to Adams capable of disciplining the emotions of men, of compelling the people to submerge their individual desires into a love for the whole. No nation could so educate their people. “Millions will be brought up, whom no principles, no sentiments, derived from education, can restrain them from trampling on the laws.” It was impossible to reconcile the “diversity of sentiments, contradictory principles, inconsistent interests and opposite passions of America by declarations against discord and wishes for unanimity. Neither education, religion, superstition, nor oaths could control human appetites. “Nothing but Force, and power and strength can restrain them,” a bitter Adams told Jefferson.

“Only by isolating the natural aristocracy together in a separate house would the state have the benefit of their wisdom, without fear of their passions.” The only way to control and use the aristocracy properly was to ostracize it in a separate house of the legislature. The many were just as dangerous to liberty and the public good as the few. Unchecked, the people would not only turn on the aristocracy, robbing them and ruining them without hesitation, but they would also despoil and plunder among themselves. All history, said Adams, offered irrefutable proof that the people, unrestrained, “have been as unjust, tyrannical, brutal, barbarous, and cruel, as any king or senate possessed of uncontrollable power.” The passions of the people must also be institutionalized in order to counter the wiles and greed of aristocracy. Their House of Representatives thus became the bulwark against the exploitation of the many by the few.

Adams, like most in 1776, had assumed that politics was essentially a struggle between the ruler or chief magistrate and the people, in which the aristocracy sitting in an upper house would act as mediator. Later the basic struggle became one between the people and the aristocracy in which the executive assumed the function of balancer. Where earlier Adams had conceived of the aristocracy as constituting the ablest and wisest men of the state, different from the people but by no means opposed to the people's welfare, he now saw the aristocratic interest set in opposition to the people's or democratic interest. Between these antagonistic social elements stood the executive as an independent social entity obliged to share in the lawmaking of the state. The perfect constitution, said Adams, "was the tripartite balance, the political trinity in unity, trinity of legislative and unity of executive power." Only orders of men, watching and balancing each other, could preserve the constitution. It was not a jumbling of diverse passions that Adams pictured. In his mind the interests of society could be reduced to the few and the many, those who attained superiority and those who aspired to it. The legislature must provide separate chambers for those on the top and those on the bottom of the society, for the aristocracy and for the people; an organizing, segregating and balancing of the social elements, mediated by an independent executive who shared in the law making with a qualified, partial veto, designed to produce a revision of a law. "If there is one certain truth to be collected from the history of all ages, argued Adams, it was "that the people's rights and liberties, and the democratical mixture in a constitution, can never be preserved without a strong executive, possessed of a negative on all legislation, the irrational and oppressive measures of either branch of the legislature, and so mediating between the clashing passions of the democracy and the aristocracy. The executive was the mainstay of the entire mechanism, the indispensable balancer, the essence of government "that kept the social forces in equilibrium."

For Adams this balancing of the forces inevitable in every society was the Enlightenment fulfilled. Only by "combining the great divisions of society in one system, only by forming an equal, independent mixture of the three classic kinds of government, monarchy, aristocracy and democracy, could order in any state be achieved." It was this remedy of a mixed constitution, this constitutional overlay on the ferocious social scramble he described, that makes Adam's political theory so contrary to the central thrust of constitutional thought by 1787. He never quite realized what polemics were doing to American's understanding of politics and to the assumptions underlying the theory of a mixed polity. Though he immediately saw the similarity of the internal structure of the new Constitution to his own proposals for balance he remained unaware of the originality of the newly emergent American thought concerning the concept of sovereignty and the allocation of powers. Adam's advocacy of a two-house legislature with an independent executive sharing in the lawmaking power coincided with the Federalist remedy for the constitutional problems of the 1780's and so obscured the obsolescence of his reasoning behind the scheme. John Stevens of New Jersey was particularly bothered by Adams' obsession with aristocracy. If Adams' arguments were correct, America's grand experiment in republicanism was not unique after all, and "we have hitherto been only in pursuit of a phantom." The American Republic was different and was not a mere copy of the English constitution. It was, in fact, a democratic form of government.

A second representative branch was to be added: these two separate houses form mutual checks upon each other. As a further means of curbing legislative inconstancy and usurpation, other checks were to be placed in the executive and the judiciary, which should be made as independent as possible from the legislature. "The several component powers of government should be so distributed that no one man, or body of men, should possess a larger share thereof than what is absolutely necessary for the administration of government." (Stevens) The balance of powers was not designed to embody and confine the major constituents of the society, but was intended only to separate, diffuse and check the mistrusted political authority wholly delegated by the people.

For men like Madison and Stevens the parts of government had lost their social roots, becoming more or less equal agents of the people. Power, not society, was divided. The institutions for Stevens and Adams were identical, but the rationale was quite different. Adams accepted the axiom of the Revolution that all political authority stemmed from the people; yet he remained so wrapped up in the traditional categories of political theory that he could not grasp what his countrymen had done to the relationship between the people and the government.

Sam Adams further described the change: the people exert their sovereignty continually, by electing their representatives and senators; "they delegate the exercise of the powers of government to particular persons, who, after short intervals, resign their powers to the people, and they will re-elect them, or appoint others, as they think fit." John Adams conception that the people only shared in the supreme power of government went back to the concept of a government of adversarial clashing interests. John Adams could not understand that by 1787 the executive and the Senate had become as representative of the people as the House itself. To Adams the mere presence of an executive and a senate inevitably made the government something other than a democracy.

John Adams had been the Minister to England at the same time as Jefferson was in Paris. Many saw his book as an encomium on the British Constitution rather than a defense of American systems. Instead of explaining the principles of the American Constitution, Adams seemed to be "insidiously attempting to overturn our constitution, or at least sow the seeds of discontent." Papers called it "one of the most deep wrought systems of political deception that was ever penned by the ingenuity of man." *The Defense,* Adams said to Benjamin Franklin in 1787, "contains my confession of political faith, and if it is heresy, I shall, I suppose, be cast out of communion. But it is the only sense in which I am or ever was a Republican." "Popularity, he told James Warren, was never my mistress, nor was I ever, or shall I ever be a popular man. This book will make me unpopular."

In a letter to Adams Roger Sherman tried to correct Adams' thinking: "As both branches of Congress are eligible from the citizens at large, and wealth is not a requisite qualification, both will commonly be composed of members of similar circumstances in life." There could be no real struggle then between the several branches of the government; all were equal agents of the people, 'directed to one end, the advancement of the public good." Adams separately replied "Have not our parties behaved like all parties beforehand? Is not the history of Hancock and Bowdoin, the history of the Medici and Albizi?" Adams even praised hereditary institutions as not only possessing "admirable wisdom and exemplary Virtue in a certain stage of society in a great nation, but also as the hope of our posterity, to which Americans must eventually resort as an asylum against discord, seditions and civil war, and that at no very distant period of time." He saw himself as a Promethean figure, cast aside and punished for his knowledge, while his fellow Americans went on bawling about a republicanism they didn't understand.

In 1814 John Taylor launched a final assault on Adams' writings, pointing out the intellectual chasm that separated Adams and his countrymen. The Revolution had finally freed men from the numerical analysis of politics-the classification of governments into the one, the few, the many- into monarchy, aristocracy, and democracy-which had inhibited political thinking since antiquity. New principles had been discovered, a new way of looking at politics which moved more rapidly in twenty years toward an understanding of political science than the world had in twenty centuries. Yet Adams was unaccountably oblivious of these breakthroughs in political thinking. He did not appear to understand the new basis of the American states and still insisted on the old societal classifications. Adams still considered the people an order, electing only one branch of the legislature, the democracy standing alongside and checking the other two orders of monarchy and aristocracy. But the American government, said Taylor, no longer had anything to do with these ancient categories of politics. The American Constitution did not consider society as made of orders encompassed by the government, but as made of individuals existing outside all government, distributing pieces of power into different hands. Inequalities and distinctions would inevitably exist, but in America, they were so numerous and fluctuating that they could never be gathered together and confined in the upper house of the legislature.

While Adams was carrying on about virtue and honor Taylor was showing how republican government could be sustained with the members of a society possessed of neither quality. "If virtue, as a basis of government, be understood to mean, not that the principles of government, but the individuals composing the nation must be virtuous, then the republic would be founded in the evanescent qualities of individuals and thus doomed to destruction. American government had demonstrated that the principles of a society may be virtuous though the individuals composing it are vicious." (Taylor) Since Adams never comprehended any of the new principles included in the constitution and made the error of confounding the division of power with his balance of orders, his work was in no way a defense of the American constitution. Once a society was divided into three hostile interests in the manner Adams had proposed, there remained no outside body, no national will, that could bring the government to account or alter the form of the constitution. The entire conception of mixed government rose out of the ancient belief that the power of a government was unlimited and therefore must be split into three balancing and interacting parts in order to preserve liberty. The American Revolution had set a new policy, the people retaining whatever power had not been parceled out to their agents. We had constructed a unique system of politics, one founded on the self-interest of its members.

If the ancient notion of Contract was to be preserved in American thinking, then it must be a Lockean contract, one formed by the individuals of the society with each other, instead of a mutual agreement between rulers and ruled. This image of a social contract formed by hostile and isolated individuals in a state of nature was now the only contractual metaphor that comprehended American social reality. Since an American Constitution could no longer be regarded as a contract extracted from rulers, representing distinct and unified interests, considerations like protection and allegiance lost their relevance. Obedience to the government in America followed from no such traditional consideration. The flow of authority was reversed, and consent, which had not been the basis of authority before, now became the sole obligatory principle of human government and human laws. (Nathaniel Chapman)

"The American government is transacted by representation expressed in different ways. Each derive their whole power from the people, are accountable to them for the use and exercise they make of it, and may be replaced by the election of others. (Samuel Williams) Liberty and security no longer come from participation in one antagonistic part of the government, but from the responsibility and dependence of each part of the government upon the people." Americans had destroyed the ancient conception of mixed government and found new explanations that rested on the principle of representation. America was a democracy as far as the supreme power was ostensibly "inherent in the people and is either exercised by themselves or by their representatives." (James Wilson)

Wilson optimistically stated that a government where the supreme power remains with the people at large is capable of being formed, arranged, proportioned and organized in such a manner, as to exclude the inconveniences, and to secure the advantages of the three different forms of government. Though its outward form resembled a conventional mixed government all authority was derived from the people's representation, and all aspects represented only the people's interests. Americans had retained the forms of the Aristotelian schemes of government while divesting the various parts of their social constituents. Sovereignty having been settled, the focus became the distribution of this power into executive, judiciary and legislative, and a subdivision of the latter into two branches. The portioning of political power, the creation of a plurality of discrete governmental elements, distinct in office yet connected in operation, all detached from yet responsible to and controlled by the people, checking and balancing each other, preventing any one power from asserting itself too far, was the aim.

The departments so constituted were not a balance of social elements but rather a balance of governmental functions without social connections, all monitored by the people; a balanced government that worked, though the materials of which it was constructed were the same. It is contrived so that its several constituent parts may by their mutual relations, be the means of keeping each other in their proper places. (Madison, Federalist #51) The departments of government, though drawn directly from the same fountain of authority, would be elected through channels having no communication with each other. In the compound Republic of America, the power surrendered by the people is first divided between two distinct governments, and then the portion allotted to each subdivided among distinct and separate departments." (Madison) "The portioning of power in America would be amplified by the extent of country and number of people comprehended under the same government, so that the society itself will be broken into so many parts, interests and classes of citizens, that the rights of individuals, or of the minority, will be in little danger from interested combinations of the majority."

It was such an atomization of authority, such a parceling of power, creating such a multiplicity and a scattering of designs and passions, so many checks, that no combination of parts could hold, no group of evil interests could long cohere. Yet out of the clashing and checking of this diversity Madison believed the public good, the true perfection of the whole, would somehow arise. The impulses and passions would so counteract each other, so neutralize their potencies, that the reason adhering in the natural aristocracy would be able to assert itself and dominate.

The stability of government no longer relied upon its embodiment of the basic social forces of the state. It now depended on the prevention of the various social interests from incorporating themselves *too* firmly in the government. Without the distinctions of titles, families, or nobility they acknowledged and reverenced only those distinctions which nature had made, in a diversity of talents, abilities and virtues. There were no family interests, connections, or estates large enough to oppress them. There was no wealth in the hands of a few, sufficient to corrupt them. "They all feel that nature made them equal in respect to their rights; or rather that nature has given them a common and equal right to liberty, to property, and to safety; to justice, government, laws, religion and freedom. They all see that nature has made them very unequal in respect to their original powers, capacities and talents. They became united in claiming and in preserving the equality, which nature has assigned them; and in availing themselves of the benefits, which are designed and may be derived from the inequality, which nature has also established." (Joel Barlow) This marked the beginning of what might be called the romantic view of politics.

How could Adams reply? For him the analysis of antiquity was still the eternal, unchangeable truth. For too long and with too much candor he had tried to tell his fellow Americans some truths about themselves that American values and American ideology would not admit. He refused to pervert the meaning of language and could not deny or disguise the oligarchic nature of American politics. He correctly saw that no society could ever be truly egalitarian, and the design of government must come to terms with this fact of social and political life. He steadily and perversely moved in a direction that eventually left him isolated from the main line of American intellectual development.

The Enlightenment and Adam's interpretation of these eighteenth-century ideas had sought to understand politics, as it had all of life, by capturing in an integrated, ordered, changeless plan the totality and complexity of the world-an ideal that the concept of the mixed constitution and the proportioned social hierarchy on which it rested perfectly expressed. It was a static equilibrium among synthetic orders with no motion among the miscellaneous parts that made up society. By destroying this ideal Americans placed a new emphasis on the piecemeal and the concrete in politics at the expense of order and completeness. The Constitution marked the end of the Enlightenment idea that the endless variety and perplexity of society could be reduced to a simple harmonious system. Once the people were thought to be composed of various interests in opposition to one another, all sense of a graduated chain in the social hierarchy became irrelevant, symbolized by the increasing emphasis on the Lockean image of a social contract. The people were not tied together by their unity of interest but rather an agglomeration of hostile individuals coming together for their mutual benefit to construct a society. This broke the connectedness of interest among them and put them at war with one another.

Political struggles would be among the people themselves, among all the various groups and individuals seeking to create inequality out of their equality by gaining control of a government divested of its former identity with the society. It was this disembodiment of government from society that made possible the conception of modern politics and the justification of competing parties among the people. Jealousy and opposition must naturally exist while there exists a difference in the minds, interests and sentiments of mankind. (William Hornby) "The people could be better protected not by attempting to perfect a legislature out of some combination of assemblies but by forming a government in such a manner that its frailties may continually be corrected by its interest. The lesser alternative is simply the delegating and controlling of all governmental power in such a way that no one, legislators or executive, could abuse it."

The new interpretation was tending to blur the once distinct theory of balanced government among social orders with the doctrine of separation of governmental departments. The proper balance was no longer between monarchial, aristocratic and democratic elements in a mixed polity, but one of the separation of powers of the executive, legislative and judicial functions. The assumption behind this was that power in the hands of legislators was no different than power in the hands of governors, senators and judges. In Jefferson's words, "the powers of government should be so divided and balanced among several bodies of magistracy, as that no one could transcend their legal limits, without being effectually checked and restrained by the others." Separation of powers had previously been used to justify the isolation of the legislature and the judiciary from what was believed to be the corrupting influence of executive power. The governor's power of appointment was clipped, and magisterial and administrative officials were prohibited from sitting in the legislatures. This principle was magnified and expanded; it reiterated that the separation of powers had become the major justification for all the constitutional reforms, so much so that the principle soon became the dominant cry of the American political system.

"If government powers were truly to promote the happiness of the people, its several powers-legislative, executive and judicial-must be so divided and guarded as to prevent those given to one from being engrossed by the other; and if properly separated, the persons who officiate in the several departments become sentinels on behalf of the people to guard against every possible usurpation." (Jefferson) The first object was to separate the legislative from the executive functions. Where they are united in the same persons, there is wanting a natural check, which is the principal security against the enacting of arbitrary laws. The second was to remove the power of the executive to appoint officials, which, through an almost pyramidal geometric progression, leads to the bureaucracy feeding off of, and living under the shadow and protection of their superiors, who had appointed *them* in due course. The entire structure was held together by the strongest of links and permeated the whole society. The great chain of political self-interest was formed by the creation of the bureaucracy, an unelected body supported by taxpayers, who, through administrative and regulative law, coerce the public in ways that Congress would be unable or unwilling to do. Men belonging to the bureaucracy are enthralled with their place in the ruling hierarchy and lose their concern for the good of the country.

The separation of this governmental power, rather than simply the participation of the people in a part of government, became the best defense of liberty. The liberty that was now emphasized was personal or private, the protection of individual rights against all governmental encroachments, particularly by the legislature, the body beforehand traditionally seen as the people's exclusive repository and their surest defense. Men now began to see the interests of society and the rights of individuals as distinct, and to regard public and private liberty as antagonistic rather than complimentary. Government was to protect citizens in their personal liberty and their property against the public will, including a fluctuating majority. (James Iredell) "Unless individuals and minorities were protected against the power of majorities no government could be truly free." (Madison) Legislation would not be the transcending of the different interests but the reconciling of them. Despite his hope, the public good could only be the "general combined interest of all the state put together, as it were, upon an average."

But the collected wisdom of the ages *had* been interwoven into this form of government. A mere separation from England would have been of little matter had it not been accompanied by a revolution in the principles and practices of more recent governments. Important and perceptible alterations *had* taken place in the situation of men and things. With their new plan Americans *had* placed the science of politics on a footing with the other great scientific discoveries of the Enlightenment. Representation-that was the key conception in unlocking an understanding of the American political system. The American Republican polity was representation ingrafted upon democracy, ingrafted upon a constitution, creating a system of government capable of embracing and confederating all the various interests and every extent of territory and population. For Madison a Republic had become a species of government to be classed alongside aristocracy or democracy, a distinctive form of government.

The right of representing is conferred by the act of electing and was the pivot on which the whole American system moved. The National Senate would be derived from the people, through the dual election of the State Senates, representing no particular order of men. It was to be only a weight in the power of legislative deliberation, not a weight of property, of privileges or of interests. All governmental officials were agents of the people, not fundamentally different from the people's nominal representatives in the lower House. The various parts of the government were functionally but not substantively different. The executive and judicial powers are now drawn from the same source, are now animated by the same principles and are now directed to the same ends, with the legislative authority. The entire government had become the limited agency of the sovereign people. (James Wilson) The House of Representatives, now no more trusted than other parts of the government, also seemed to be no more representative of the people. They had lost their exclusive role of embodying the average citizen in the government. The people participated in all branches. They remained as the absolute and perpetual sovereign, distributing bits and pieces of power to their various agents. (Hamilton, Federalist #71)

The emphasis on public virtue existing throughout the society lost some of its thrust; men could argue now that virtue and patriotism never was nor will be, till men's natures are changed, a fixed, permanent principle and support of government. Americans had no other object beyond their own individual happiness. Jefferson told Madison that it was ridiculous for a man to surrender himself to the state. "This would be slavery, and not that liberty which the bill of rights has made inviolable, and for the preservation of that which our government has been changed. Freedom would be destroyed by the establishment of the opinion that the state has a perpetual right to the services of all its members." Local attachments would always exist, self-interest was all there ever was. But under the new system a self-interested man must ally himself with the people's interest in order to gain the benefits of knowledge and trade with society.

"But it must be assumed that the people will at least have sufficient virtue and intelligence to select men of virtue and wisdom, or no theoretical checks, no form of government, can render us secure." (Madison) Undoubtedly virtue in the people had been an essential substitute for the lack of good laws and the indispensable remedy for the traditional defects of most democratic governments. Either the Constitution or the people had to retain their virtue; in the end neither has. While virtue was advantageous for any kind of government it was absolutely necessary to the existence of a republic. The people are not only the source of authority, but the exercise of it is in a great measure lodged in their hands. Corruption therefore must be immediately felt, and if not immediately prevented, would prove fatal in the end. The checks and controls, introduced into the very form of government, intended to be the higher corrective for the lower self, have eroded and not proven effective. The need to simplify the government, and the need for a virtuous people, remains as high as it was in 1787.

America would remain free not because of any quality in its citizens of spartan self-sacrifice to some nebulous public good, but rather because of the concern of each individual for his own interest and freedom. Such a grounding of government in self-interest and consent, at the same time the newly forming ideas of economics put forward by Adam Smith were becoming known, was a fortuitous occurrence. All previous peoples had been compelled to suffer with the same forms of government-unplanned and unsuitable from the first-despite extensive changes in the nature of societies. Governments had never been able to adjust continually to the operations of human nature. There was usually an incongruity between the form of government and the character of society that ended in a violent eruption, in a forceful effort to bring the government into accord with the new social temperament of the people. It was impossible to form any human institution which should accommodate itself to every situation in progress. But this new government put the science of politics on a footing with the other sciences, by opening it to improvements from experience, and the discoveries of future ages. The American Constitution contained a healing principle allowing it the means of its own improvement. A plan of reformation was incorporated into the constitution, enabling the people to periodically and peacefully return to its first principles, as Machiavelli and Randolph had urged. The illimitable progress of mankind promised by the Enlightenment could at last be coincident with the history of a single nation. For the Americans the endless cycles of destructive governments could finally be broken. Americans for the first time demonstrated how a people could diagnose the ills of society and work out a peaceful process of cure. They had broken through the conceptions of political theory that had imprisoned men's minds for centuries and reconstructed the framework for a new Republican polity.

"A constitution is a declaration of particular powers by the people to their representatives, for particular purposes. It may be considered as a great power of attorney, under which no power can be exercised but what is expressly given. (James Iredell) "A constitution is not a thing in name only; it is the body of elements, to which you can refer, and quote article by article; and which contains everything that relates to the complete organization of a civil government, and the principles on which it shall act, and by which it shall be bound." A constitution is thus a "thing antecedent to government, and a government is only the creature of the constitution." (Thomas Paine) "Only by conceiving of a constitution as a written delimitation of the grant of power made by the people to the government was the important distinction between a constitution established by the people and unalterable by the government, and a law established by the government, and alterable by that government, rendered truly comprehensible." (Wilson)

John Adams and Thomas Jefferson died within hours of each other on July 4, 1826. After each served as President, followed by years of estrangement, Adams' last words were "Thomas Jefferson still survives."

CHAPTER EIGHT-ALEXANDER HAMILTON AND MODERN MONETARY THEORY

FORREST MCDONALD
CLINTON ROSSITER

RUSSELL KIRK
JAMES TRUSLOW ADAMS

GORDON S. WOOD

"The statesman, who should attempt to direct people in what manner they ought to employ their capital, would assume an authority which could not safely be trusted, not only to no single person, but to no council or senate whatever, and which would nowhere be so dangerous as in the hands of a man who had folly and presumption enough to fancy himself fit to exercise it."

Adam Smith, *Wealth of Nations*

"I have no faith in the parchment, sir, I have no faith in the abracadabra of the constitution. There never was one under the sun, in which by an unwise exercise of powers of government, the people may not be driven to resistance by force…if under the power to regulate trade, you draw the last drop of blood from our veins; if you draw the last shilling from our pockets, what are the checks of the constitution to us? Like the animal whose fleece forms so material a part of this bill, shall we quietly lay down and be sheared?"

John Randolph

"What can avail your specious imaginary balances, your rope-dancing, chain rattling, ridiculous ideal checks and contrivances?"

Patrick Henry

"For why declare that things shall not be done which there is no power to do?"

Alexander Hamilton, *Federalist* #84

Two men-Alexander Hamilton and Thomas Jefferson-represented the fundamental principles of political philosophy of the two sides in the Washington administration. While on Washington's wartime staff, Alexander Hamilton had become frustrated with the decentralized nature of the Continental Congress, particularly its dependence upon the states for voluntary financial support that was not always forthcoming. Under the Articles, Congress had no power to collect taxes or demand money from the states. This lack of reliable funding made it hard for the army to obtain provisions and pay the soldiers. Hamilton argued that Congress needed the ability to make laws that superseded those of the individual states. It was once thought that the power of Congress was amply sufficient to secure the end of their institution. The error was now seen by everyone. While Congress met in Princeton Hamilton drafted a call to revise the Articles of Confederation. He made a resolution calling for a constitutional convention, proposing many of the features that might bring about a stronger federal government. The members most tenacious of Republicanism, though, were as loud as any in declaiming against the vices of democracy. The ongoing progress of the public mind led Hamilton to anticipate the time when a government could be formed which "united public strength with individual security." The hope was that men who were properly educated, encouraged, informed and checked could govern themselves wisely and well. The Federalist was grimly confident of the feasibility of liberty.

As to the question of whether the Constitutional Convention even had the authority, to write an entirely new document, rather than revise the Articles as requested, Hamilton wrote that "the states sent us here to provide for the exigencies of the Union. To rely on and propose any plan not adequate to these exigencies, merely because it was not clearly within our powers, would be to sacrifice the means to the end. It may be said that the States cannot ratify a plan not within the purview of the Articles of Confederation, providing for alterations and amendments. Isn't the great question that of the provision we will make for the happiness of our country?" Furthermore, he was convinced that no amendment of the Confederation which left the states in possession of their sovereignty could possibly answer the purpose. Neither was John Randolph scrupulous on the point of power. "When the salvation of the Republic was at stake, it would be treason to our trust, not to propose what we found necessary." A national government alone, properly constituted, would answer the purpose; he begged it to be considered that the present is the last moment for establishing one. We owed it to the country to do in this emergency whatever we deem essential to its happiness. The unauthorized growth of government had begun. Paterson of New Jersey, among others, tried to oppose, saying logically and appropriately that if the "confederacy was radically wrong, let us return to our states, and obtain larger powers, not assume them of ourselves. I came here not to speak my own sentiments, but the sentiments of those who sent me. Our object is not such a government as may be best in itself, but such a one as our constituents have authorized us to prepare, and as they will approve." "We are razing the foundations of the building, when we need only repair the roof." (Oliver Ellsworth) "It is natural for men, who wish to hasten the adoption of a measure, to tell us, now is the crisis-now is the critical moment which must be seized, or all will be lost: and to shut the door against free enquiry, whenever conscious the thing presented has defects in it, which time and investigation will probably discover. This has been the custom of tyrants and their dependents in all ages." *Letters from a Federal Farmer,* 1787) "Now is unquestionably the proper time to examine it, and see if it really is what, upon paper, it appears to be. If with your eyes open, you deliberately accept it, however different it may prove in practice from what it appears in theory, you will have nobody to blame but yourselves; and, what is infinitely worse, you will be wholly without a remedy." "John DeWitt" November 5, 1787)

....

The general principles of politics that the colonists sought to discover and apply were not merely abstractions that had to be created anew out of nature and reason. Some were in fact already embodied in the historic English constitution-those which were esteemed by the enlightened of the world precisely because of their agreeableness to the laws of nature. By balancing within the confines of Parliament the ancient contending interests of English society, and by mixing within a single government the several categories of politics that had been known to the Western world for centuries, the English, it seemed, had concretely achieved what political philosophers from antiquity on had only dreamed of. It united public strength with individual security. Hamilton favored the British monarchial system, which he considered the best in the world, but which the United States had just freed itself of by revolution. Hamilton based his idea of the Executive on the English model. The hereditary interest of the king was so interwoven with that of the nation, and his personal emolument so great, that he was placed above the danger of being corrupted from abroad; he at the same time was both sufficiently independent and sufficiently controlled, to answer the purpose of the institution to be formed. Hamilton favored Washington for this role. Hamilton comments on the election of the executive in *Federalist #s 68-76*: Optimism that men of virtue would be in the government affirms that the electoral college "affords a moral certainty that the office of the President will seldom fall to the lot of any man who is not in an eminent degree endowed with the requisite qualifications." In fact, he speaks of "a constant probability of seeing the station filled by characters pre-eminent for ability and virtue, or at least respectable."

He insisted that his plan was within the proper sphere of both Republicanism and federalism rather than a reformulation of monarchy and nationalism: "In every community, where industry is encouraged, there will be a division of it into the few and the many. Hence, separate interests will arise. There will be debtors and creditors, and give all power to the many, they will oppress the few. Give all power to the few, and they will oppress the many. Both, therefore, ought to have the power, that each may defend itself against the other. Gentlemen differ in their opinions concerning the necessary checks, from the different estimates they form of the human passions. To the proper adjustment of it the British owe the excellence of their Constitution." He maintained that good government required long terms in office. For us, "they suppose seven years a sufficient period to give the Senate an adequate firmness, from not duly considering the amazing violence and turbulence of the democratic spirit. When a great object of government is pursued, which seizes the popular passions, they spread like wildfire and become irresistible." On the other hand, he termed the House of Lords a "most noble" institution. Having nothing to hope for by a change, and a sufficient interest, by means of their property, in being faithful to the national interest, they form a permanent barrier against every pernicious innovation, whether attempted on the part of the Crown or of the Commons. No temporary Senate will have firmness enough to answer the purpose. But the Jeffersonians believed that where frequent elections end, tyranny begins.

Hamilton believed that the great generality of men were incapable of self-government, due to ignorance, selfishness, and the absence of self-control. Being a practical man, without the idealistic dreams of moral reform held by Jefferson, the inferences he drew were obvious. He believed that the vices of the rich would be less dangerous for a governing class than would the vices of the poor. In a democracy he could foresee only eventual anarchy, with liberty for no one. He thought that power should be kept, as far as possible, in the hands of those who by their position in society showed they had ability to govern and property interests to protect. He was not interested in Jefferson's idea of popular education and of gradually lifting the entire mass of possible electors to a position where they might be more capable of self-government. In his ideas he had a unique opportunity to imprint them upon the country, as a member of the Constitutional Convention, as the leading advocate for its adoption through the *Federalist* papers, and as the chief cabinet officer in the first years of establishing the new government. In both the scheme of government and its practical operation the common people as much as possible must be excluded, compatible with their newly won expectations of power. The only liberty for the people themselves would be that permitted by the strength of the governors, not a doctrinaire liberty which inhered by any natural process in the governed themselves. Nonetheless, he realized that in some way a favorable public opinion of the government would have to be organized.

Hamilton and the Federalists believed that the virtues of successful industrialists-self-reliance, autonomy, innovation and entrepreneurship-were the bedrock on which the political system should be modeled. The commercial classes were talented, industrious and prosperous men who could be trusted to wield federal political power. For the Federalists, the development of manufacturing was of primary importance to federal policy because it would serve as a breeding ground for new generations of leaders. Commerce, Hamilton thought, would produce a body of wealthy men whose interests would coincide with those of the national commonwealth while providing moral, political and intellectual leadership for the nation. The strongest element in human nature would have to be enlisted on his behalf. That element Hamilton believed to be self-interest, manifested most strongly in matters concerning money. From the start he undertook to push through measures which would not only enlist the moneyed interest of the country on the side of government but would enlarge both the extent and numbers of such interest. His part as statesman would be to tie up the success of all who had money with the success of the government, to tie them so closely as to make the success of the government an inevitable element in their personal success. Hamilton's distinctive lack of an agricultural policy, in favor of his commercial plan, alienated him from some of his political contemporaries in the South-for an independent farmer might be a rebellious subject. A man who had money in government bonds or whose business was dependent upon a tariff would conversely be a loyal citizen. This idea, in the stark simplicity of its psychology and logic, seems rather remote from the ideals of the Declaration of Independence; it must be admitted, nevertheless, to have been enormously successful in practice ever since.

The government had issued millions in fiat money, called Continentals, that had sunk to a few pennies on the dollar in the inflation it inevitably caused. The phrase "not worth a Continental" would be part of the American lexicon for a century to come. Hamilton, brilliant, and deeply read in economic theory and politics, understood how useful an instrument a national debt could be in asserting national power. Britain had founded the Bank of England in 1694 and its government bonds traded freely in the marketplace. It was thus able to borrow at a much lower cost than France and repeatedly defeat its much larger and presumably more powerful rivals in the endless wars that perforated the 18th century. Hamilton suggested assuming the old state debts and replacing them with new government bonds. This was regionally controversial, because some Southern states, notably Virginia, Maryland, North Carolina and Georgia, had already paid off their revolutionary debts, while states in New England had not. Hamilton thought that the tariffs, the surest source of funds to pay the debt and now exclusively a federal revenue, should be tied to the federal debt. Making the state debt holders now federal debt holders would give them a stake in the success of the union. But tariffs raised the prices that Southerners had to pay for imported goods, for which they exchanged their agricultural products. Only when Hamilton made a deal with Madison and Jefferson to steer the Nation's capital away from New York to the shores of the Potomac did the state funding proposal pass Congress.

To conduct the Revolution, the Continental Congress also had to borrow heavily from the French government, and from Dutch bankers, but stopped paying both principal and interest on the loans in 1786. Led by Washington the Revolution had been won and a Constitution agreed upon. Now the country had to win respect at home and abroad, and the Republic had to be put on a firm political and financial footing. The Constitution required the new government to assume the debts of the old one incurred under the Articles of Confederation. The nation's books were a mess. "Whence, then, is the national revenue to be drawn? From commerce and exports-fit objects of *moderate* taxation." In January of 1790 Hamilton presented Congress with his *Report on the Public Credit* which included a plan for addressing the country's then-staggering 40-million-dollar debt. Income from federal tariffs and excise taxes amounted to just 4.4 million (The excise tax on whiskey sparked the rebellion of 1791-94 in Western Pennsylvania. Whiskey was easier and cheaper to transport across the mountains than grain. Taxes eliminated its profitability per gallon in comparison with the eastern producers, who produced larger amounts and paid a flat fee. In addition, prices were higher in the East.) Westerners believed Hamilton deliberately designed the tax to ruin them and promote big business in the East. It was also proposed that Hamilton intentionally pursued a course of action that would provoke the kind of violence that would justify federal military suppression. He wished to crush popular resistance to direct taxation for the purpose of promoting national unity and enriching the creditor class at the expense of common taxpayers. The excise law was used more as *an exercise of social discipline* (Author's italics) than as a source of revenue. "He (Hamilton) sees the Union dissolving, or already dissolved-he sees evil operating in the states which must soon cure the people of their fondness for democracies." (As President, Jefferson's Republican Party repealed the tax).

Hamilton suggested that the United States look at debt not as a problem but as an asset. He recommended paying only interest on the debt and deferring principal payment until far in the future. Incorporating the wartime debt of the states, raising the total to nearly 80 million, supported the creation of a unified national debt and discouraged state taxation efforts. It could be a powerful cement for the union. "States, like individuals, who observe their engagements (pay off their debts), are respected and trusted, while the reverse is the fate of those who pursue an opposite conduct. This reflection derived additional strength from the nature of the debt of the United States. It was the price of liberty. The faith of America has been repeatedly pledged for it, and with solemnities, that gives peculiar force to the obligation." In turn this would increase the size of the national credit market Hamilton hoped to create. "The necessity for borrowing in particular emergencies cannot be doubted…it is equally evident that, to be able to borrow on good terms, it is essential that the credit of the nation should be well established." The plan would also help establish America's international credit rating and hinder individual states from becoming too powerful in the new nation. Jefferson cautioned, saying that "it is a wise rule and should be fundamental in a government disposed to cherish its credit, and at the same time restrict the use of it within the limit of its faculties, never to borrow a dollar without laying as tax in the same instant for paying the interest annually, and the principal within a given term." In 1792 he complained to Washington that "I would wish the debt paid tomorrow; he (Hamilton) wishes it never be paid, but always to be a thing with which to corrupt and manage the legislature." It also appeared to be an attempt to secure the hegemony of Northern financial interests, to which Hamilton was connected through his marriage. The fact that the beneficiaries of his innovative economic policies were concentrated in the northeast, threatened to stimulate further divisive geographic differences in the new Republic. Some, like Fisher Ames of Massachusetts, came to Hamilton's defense: "The science of finance is new in America, and perhaps the reports' critics don't understand quite what they're asking for." Hamilton proposed two additional reports: one calling for a national bank and one urging the imposition of tariffs to protect American trade from foreign competition and encourage the growth of industry in this country. In February a deal went through for temporary loans from the Bank of New York (Hamilton was a founder) and the Bank of America-the only two banks in the country at that time.

The United States needed its own Bank, according to Hamilton's plan, modeled after that of England, to create an active economy. Basic to his ideas was that the *general welfare* required the encouragement of manufacturers, and that the federal government was obligated to direct the economy to that end. James Madison argued that the enumerated powers of the Constitution did not include the authority to create a Bank. In a speech he declared that "the ways and means ought always to face the public engagements; that our appropriations should always go hand in hand with our promises." After all, the Preamble to the Constitution put the purpose of the government to "secure the blessings of liberty to ourselves *and* our posterity. Jefferson concurred, in his letter to Washington, adding that the bank represented a vast constitutional overreach. He thought the debt a monstrous fraud upon later generations. He wrote that the necessary and proper clause didn't license merely convenient but *indispensable* means. If government goes down the Hamiltonian Road, Jefferson argued, it takes "possession of a boundless field of power, no longer susceptible of any definition"-exactly the arbitrary, monarchial power we fought a revolution to overthrow.

Hamilton countered Jefferson, saying that there was a natural relationship between a bank and several enumerated powers of the government. He argued that "a sovereign government has the right to employ all the means requisite and fairly applicable to the attainment of the ends" for which it was established. The bank would operate as an instrument to expedite the processing of tariff receipts, collection of taxes and regulation of commerce, closely allying government and business. Hamilton hoped to bind the men of wealth and influence, who had acquired most of the domestically held bonds, to the national government. Above all, Hamilton argued that to deny the power of government to add ingredients to its plan, following the necessary and proper clause, would be to refine away all its power. "This restrictive interpretation of the word necessary is also contrary to this sound maxim of construction; namely, that the powers contained in a constitution of government, especially those which concern the general administration of the affairs of the country, its finances, trade, defense, etc., ought to be construed liberally in advancement of the public good. This rule does not depend on the particular form of government, or on the particular demarcation of the boundaries of its powers, but on the nature and objects of government...An adherence to the letter of its powers would at once arrest the motions of government." (Hamilton, *Letter to Robert Morris,* 1780) "After all our doubts, our suspicions, and speculations on the subject of government, we must return at last to the important truth, that when we have formed a Constitution upon free principles, when we have given a proper balance to the different branches of administration, and fixed representation upon pure and equal principles, we may with safety furnish it with all the powers necessary to answer in the most ample manner the purposes of government. The great desiderata are a free representation and mutual checks. When these are obtained, all our apprehensions of the extent of powers are unjust and imaginary." (Hamilton, S*peech to the Senate,* June 27, 1788) Hamilton thus began the mantra of the Left wishing to be trusted, and judged by their good intentions, not by their adherence to the Law.

"Whatever may be the limits or modifications of the powers of the Union, it is easy to imagine an endless train of possible dangers; and by indulging an excess of jealousy and timidity, we may bring ourselves to a state of absolute skepticism and irresolution. I repeat here…that all observations founded upon the danger of usurpation ought to be referred to the composition and structure of the government, not to the nature or extent of its powers. Upon this ground, it will not be difficult to obviate the objections which have been made to an *indefinite* power of taxation in the United States." Hamilton, *The Federalist,* #9

The letters that Jefferson, Madison and Attorney General Edmund Randolph sent to Washington, encouraging his veto of Hamilton's bill to create a National Bank, were considered and rejected. Washington signed the bill. Even he, though, warned lawmakers, that "no pecuniary consideration is more urgent, than the regular redemption and discharge of the public debt: on none can delay be more injurious, or an economy of time more valuable." Within a few years United States bonds were selling above par in European markets because they were considered so safe. This helped move the country away from Jefferson's agrarian dream and toward the commercial Republic Hamilton hoped it would become. The American economy had traditionally rested upon large scale agricultural exports-tobacco, rice, indigo and cotton-to pay for the import of British manufactured goods. Rather than accept this, Hamilton wanted the United States to adopt a mercantilist economic policy. This would protect American manufacturers through direct government subsidies and tariffs. The protectionist policy would help fledgling American producers to compete with European imports. This effectively brought capital markets into existence for the first time, and by 1792 the Philadelphia and New

York Stock Exchanges were in session. Hamilton saw that a stable debt issue could serve as money, a medium of exchange that would give greater means for enterprise, extending trade, manufacture and agriculture. But the government could just as easily prioritize boondoggles as it might sound investments; disentangling wise ones from dead ends takes careful analysis and an understanding of what works and what doesn't.

Hamilton had little sympathy for state autonomy or the fear of excessive central authority. In his *Defense of the Constitutionality of the Bank*, he argued that Congress could choose any means not explicitly prohibited by the Constitution to achieve a constitutional end-even if the means to this end-even to achieve the common good-were deemed unconstitutional. Thus continued in earnest the discussion of constitutional, strict construction versus unconstitutional, loose construction and the meaning of the terms necessary and proper, and enumerated or expressed versus implied as they apply to the powers of the Constitution, begun in the ratification debates. The earlier mentioned Supreme Court case *McCulloch versus Maryland* later (1819) granted the federal government broad freedom to select the best means to execute its constitutionally enumerated powers-the doctrine of implied powers-and said that the Federal government was supreme over the states, and states' ability to interfere with the Federal government was limited. This was a direct result of Hamilton's earlier influence.

Ames again wrote that "the men of sense and property in the North wish to keep the government in force enough to govern." Washington ultimately signed the bill creating a bank, but the argument had formed another invisible, ominous division further separating members of Congress along North-South lines. One result of the struggle over Hamilton's program was the emergence of national political parties. Like Washington, Hamilton deplored parties, equating them with disorder and instability. He nevertheless became the leader of the Federalist Party, the political organization dedicated to the support of his policies. Challenging him was the Republican Party, organized by Madison and Jefferson. The Federalists favored close ties to England while Republicans preferred to strengthen the old ties to France which had helped win the war.

Not surprisingly, Jefferson disagreed with elements of Hamilton's *Defense*. High protective tariffs protected and promoted the growth of US manufacturing against cheap imports. They also provided most of the federal government's revenue. The South, though, saw them as a system penalizing agriculture with higher prices for manufactured goods and encouraged reciprocal tariffs levied by other countries against Southern products, especially tobacco and cotton. Jefferson had of course read, in *Cato's Letters,* by Trenchard and Gordan, accounts of the South Sea bubble of 1720 in England, which caused widespread loss, debt and poverty. The English king and his ministers were implicated in a series of financial manipulations aided by the power of government. The event inspired American revolutionary thinking and informed the Founding Fathers' determination to set up a limited government wherein the power for mischief would be checked. Jefferson predicted that politicians would manipulate bank shareholders, and that members of Congress who held shares, would vote for the best interests of the bank over those of the nation.

Jefferson: "A departure from principle becomes precedent for a second; that second for a third; and so on, till the bulk of society is reduced to mere automatons of misery, to have no sensibilities left but for sinning and suffering…and the forehorse of this frightful team is public debt. Taxation follows that, and in its train wretchedness and oppression." A departure from sound principle in legislation is nearly always advocated on the ground that it is entirely exceptional, strictly limited in its application, certain to do no practical harm, and intended to secure some particular benefit. Once admitted, it soon becomes a starting-point or logical premise, an axiom, and is pushed into new fields and to new consequences. Frequent government interventions attempt to normalize themselves in the minds of citizens and accustoms people to authoritarianism. It is important to consider whether the proposed intervention of the Government lies apart from the proper sphere of politics, and whether it may become a source or engine of politics. Can the things which the State is asked to assist of a kind that might flourish without its aid? Only if it can be shown that the State management of some great enterprise can be conducted with efficiency, and at the same time made to pay its expenses; if it can be shown that, by the excellent credit of the State a useful enterprise can effect some useful change or call into being some useful enterprise without loss to the State or to its credit; a large portion of the objections to this intervention will have been removed. This never happens, and so the objections to the vast extension of State regulations and subsidies are many. It is almost certain that, when this system is largely adopted, it will not remain within the limits just described. It will advance with an accelerated rapidity; every concession becomes a precedent or basis for another step, till the habit is fully formed of looking on all occasions for State assistance or restriction, until a weight of taxation and debt has been accumulated from which the first advocates of the movement would have shrunk with horror. (Paine) Washington, despite his authorization of the Bank, initially echoed Jefferson: "Avoid occasions of expense…and avoid likewise the accumulation of debt not only by their shunning but by vigorous exertions to discharge the debts, not throwing upon posterity the burden which we ourselves ought to bear." Franklin contributed to the argument: "When you run in debt, you give to another power over your liberty."

Following Washington's approval of the National Bank, Hamilton's next task was to nurture a diversified economy that featured manufacturing. "Every new scene, which is opened to the busy nature of man to rouse and exert itself, is the addition of a new energy to the general stock of effort. The bowels as well as the surface of the earth are ransacked for articles which were before neglected. Animals, Plants and Minerals acquire a utility and value, which were before unexplored. Prosperity grows, invention and ingenuity flourish, dependence and vulnerability to foreign powers shrinks." The object was not just the production of more goods and services, but in human fulfillment in thinking them up and creating them. So, "while more ample and varied fields of enterprise" will certainly increase the wealth of the nation, it will also allow all "the diversity of talents and dispositions which discriminate men from each other" to develop to their fullest excellence. In a society with limited opportunity "minds of the strongest and most active powers for their proper objects…labor without effect, if confined to uncongenial pursuits."

Echoing Adam Smith, Hamilton wrote: "To cherish and stimulate the activity of the human mind, even with things not immediately advantageous, sometimes become so, by their tendency to provoke exertion. The spirit of enterprise, useful and prolific, must necessarily be contracted or expanded in proportion to the simplicity or variety of the occupations and productions, which are to be found in a Society. The spirit must be less in a nation of mere cultivators, than in a nation of cultivators and merchants; less in a nation of cultivators and merchants, than one in a nation of cultivators, artificers and merchants. When all the different kinds of industry obtain in a community, each individual can find his proper element, and call into activity the whole vigor of his nature. To cherish and stimulate the activity of the human mind, by multiplying the objects of enterprise, is not among the least considerable expedients, by which the wealth of a nation may be promoted."

Hamilton's system was designed to use financial means for achieving political, economic and social ends. The establishment of public credit was necessary for the nation's honor and useful in creating a strong and stable government but was only a step towards erecting his system of political economy. Money and liquid capital had always been in short supply in America, and it would take forever to accumulate by frugality what Hamilton considered to be an adequate store. But paper money has a special aspect. Like a bond, a banknote is just a promise, resting on the credit of the issuer, and credit is mere belief. "Opinion is the soul of it, and this is affected by appearances, as well as realities." Hamilton took a leap of faith, believing that the country had a vast latent productive capacity and raw developable land that just needed to be unlocked with capital to start gushing wealth. The Bank's ability to put its capital to work, incessantly circulating it in notes at interest, so that it never lies idle, is to "all the purposes of trade and industry an absolute increase of capital. By "contributing to enlarging the mass of industrious and commercial enterprise, banks become nurseries of national wealth." By giving loans to the creditworthy, banks "enable honest and industrious men, of small or perhaps no capital to undertake and prosecute business with advantage to themselves and to the community." As a self-made man he hoped to give others the same opportunity.

Under the fractional reserve plan has to lie a foundation of hard reality: some specie is really there; loans go to people whose character and business plan the bank finds, after careful inspection, solid enough to pay back the money. A private bank will take care not to print more money than its capital could support or that the economy could productively employ, since otherwise people would cash in superfluous banknotes for specie, depleting the bank's reserves. But politicians are less prudent. "The stamping of paper is an operation so much easier than the laying of taxes," that in an emergency, government would too readily roll the presses, producing inflation and ruining the bank's credit. Stupid, yes. "But what government ever consulted its true interest in opposition to the temptations of momentary exigencies?" Henceforward, money to lend would not have as its source past production and savings but the expectation of future earnings and profits. To channel it properly would be the last step in Hamilton's overall system, a comprehensive program of inducements and deterrents designed to expand the manufacturing that the country was already engaged in and to promote the development of other industries that it needed for which it was well adapted.

Subsequent to Hamilton's reports to Congress, the national government began to shape the country's future direction and identity. Hamilton had developed his ideas to secure America's legacy from the War and chart the nation's course toward greater power and prestige. He championed mercantilism, protectionism, economic interventionism, corporate welfare, central banking, excise, property taxation, and government debt. These are part neither of conservatism nor capitalism. Mercantilism viewed using business in the service of government. The public debt was an integral part of his statist scheming. Government debt has always been a means of disguising the true costs of government to the public by forcing future generations to pay for spending that only benefits the current population. It allows the politicians to promise something now yet deferring the tax bill to others not even born.

Hamilton: "The whole force of the attachment of the people is to the states. Sovereignty is immediately before the eyes of the people; its protection is immediately enjoyed by them. From its hand distributive justice, and all those acts which familiarize and endear a government to a people, are dispensed to them. Almost all of the weight of the honors and emoluments which produce an attachment to the government are weighted on the side of the states and must continue as long as the states continue to exist as at present. Only by a complete sovereignty in the General Government will the strong principles and passions turn on its side. Conversely, if states are to deliberate on requisitions of Congress, they will deliberate on the mode, the object and the amount; they will grant or not grant as they approve or disapprove of it. The delinquency of one will invite and countenance it in others. They must, and will fail in their duty, and the union itself will be dissolved."

"If we are in earnest about giving the Union energy and duration, we must abandon the vain project of legislating upon the states in their collective capacities: we must extend the laws of the Federal Government to the individual citizens of America, making the national government supreme at the expense of the state governments." The country had to decide "whether societies of men are really capable or not, of establishing good government from reflection and choice, or whether they are forever destined for their political constitutions, on accident and force."

Hamilton's intention *was* to reduce the states to an inferior position. "The general power, whatever be its form, if it preserves itself, must swallow up the state powers. Otherwise, it will be swallowed up by them." Subordinate authorities would be necessary but must be mere district tribunals-corporations for local purposes. His ideas, which he voiced on the floor of the Convention, were irrelevant in that democratic environment and were certainly not those of an American conservative. The basic assumption was that the way to achieve sound government is to make the rulers of the economy the rulers of men; that the way to achieve a sound economy is for government to support these men and their plans with vigorous legislation; that the power of government may be used boldly and profitably by men of financial and industrial property; that it must not be used by the enemies of this class, lest all society suffer; and that a nation may embark on a course of unlimited industrial progress without straining its political institutions or upsetting its social stability. "The aim of every political constitution is, or ought to be, first to obtain for rulers, men who possess the most wisdom to discern, and most virtue to pursue, the common good of the society; and in the next place, to take the most effectual precautions for keeping them virtuous whilst they continue to hold the public trust." (Hamilton, *The Federalist,* # 9) But no man was so indifferent to the established order, so full of schemes for its alteration, dazzled by aristocracy, casual about centralized power, and biased towards economics.

Hamilton's economic vision of investment, industry and expanded commerce had no place for agriculture based on slavery. While he abhorred the practice, on one hand he swallowed his sentiments as he attempted to be accepted by the colonial elite; he nevertheless strove to reorient the American economy away from the peculiar institution. The tensions engendered in the debate over the Bank and Hamilton's financial system became the mainspring of American history from the 1820 Missouri Compromise until the Civil War. To his rivals, Hamilton's programs were a counter revolution against liberty and limited government.

Jefferson and Madison interpreted the Constitution differently, not as a charter of but as the final barricade to national government power-along with state and local autonomy-rather than the first tool that it could use to find and wield. The American identity resided in the connections that people had with farming and the land, and those layers of government closest to them. These, then were the tenets of the new Jeffersonian Republican Party. The reports of Hamilton had crystallized divergent views among the political parties, regions, and ways of life. Hamilton's argument was that manufacturing complemented agriculture by increasing the demand for its products. Jefferson, contrarily, saw women and children being dragged into filthy workplaces, in crowded and corrupt cities, to work the machines requiring the increase in labor. Hamilton's tax raising activism led to the demise of the Federalist Party and the success of the Republicans. The anti-tax mentality following the Whiskey Rebellion helped elect Jefferson President in 1800.

But let us hear from the same Alexander Hamilton, worshipped by today's big government Left, and loathed by present-day conservatives, who warned us against an unlimited use of the taxing and borrowing facilities. He counseled against high taxes to pay off the debt: "Taxes are never welcome to a community. They seldom fail to excite uneasy sensations more or less extensive; hence a too strong propensity in the government to anticipate and mortgage the resources of posterity (bonds), rather than encounter the inconveniences of a present increase of taxes." (Hamilton, March 16, 1792, *Report of the Secretary*) Hamilton, the proponent of an active and powerful government, cautioned the country in his report: "persuaded as the Secretary is, that the proper funding of the present debt, will render it a national blessing, if it is not excessive. Yet he is so far from according to the position, in the latitude in which it is sometimes laid down, that 'public debts are public benefits,' a position inviting to prodigality, and liable to dangerous abuse, that he ardently wishes to see it incorporated, as a fundamental maxim, in the system of credit of the United States, that the creation of debt should always be accompanied with the means of its extinguishment. This he regards as the true secret for rendering the public credit immortal. And he presumes, *that it is difficult to conceive a situation, in which there may not be adherence to the maxim."* (Author's italics) Hamilton, January 14, 1790 Given his predilection for big government, he disingenuously adds that "sound policy condemns the practice of accumulating debts. As the vicissitudes of Nations beget a perpetual tendency to the accumulation of debt, there ought to be in every government a perpetual, anxious and unceasing effort to reduce that, which at any time exists, as fast as shall be practicable consistently with integrity and good faith. Nothing can more interest the National Credit and prosperity, than a constant and systematic attention to husband (manage prudently) all the means previously possessed for extinguishing the present debt, and to avoid, as much as possible, the incurring of any new debt." Hamilton, March 16, 1792

By this he meant that if interest on the debt were paid regularly then the country would begin to earn a positive financial reputation: "In framing government for posterity as well as ourselves, we ought, in those provisions which are designed to be permanent, to calculate, not on temporary, but on permanent causes of expense. Credit supposes specific and permanent funds for the punctual payment of interest, with a moral certainty of a final redemption of the principal. *Establish that a government may decline a provision for its debts, though able to make it, and you overthrow all public morality, you unhinge all the principles that must preserve the limits of free constitutions."* (Author's italics) "But though a funded debt is not in the first instance, an absolute increase of capital, or an augmentation of real wealth; yet by serving as a new power in the operation of industry, it has within certain bounds a tendency to increase the real wealth of a community, in like manner as money borrowed by a thrifty farmer to be laid out in the improvement of his farm may, in the end, add to his stock of real riches. But there are respectable individuals, who from a just aversion to an accumulation of public debt, are unwilling to concede to it any kind of utility, who can discern no good to alleviate the ill with which they suppose it is pregnant, who cannot be persuaded that it ought in any sense be viewed as an increase in capital lest it should be inferred, that the more debt the more capital, the greater the burthens the greater the blessings of the community." Hamilton, Dec. 5, 1791

"Neither will it follow, that an accumulation of debt is desirable, because a certain degree of it operates as capital. There may be a plethora in the political, as in the natural body; there may be a state of things in which no such artificial capital is necessary. The debt too may be swelled to such a size, as that the greatest part of it may cease to be useful as capital, serving only to pamper the dissipation of idle and dissolute individuals: as that the sums required to pay the interest upon it may become oppressive, and beyond the means, which a government can employ, consistently with its tranquility, to raise them, as that the resources of taxation, to face the debt, may have been strained too far to admit of extensions adequate to exigencies, which regard the public safety." Hamilton, Dec 5, 1791

"It is of the greatest consequence that the debt should, with the consent of the creditors, be remolded into such a shape as will bring the expenditure of the nation *to a level with its income*. Author's italics) Till this be accomplished the finances of the United States will never wear a proper countenance. Arrears of interest, continually accruing, will be as continual a monument, either of inability or of ill faith, and will not cease to have an evil influence on public credit." Was Hamilton sincere with his seemingly conservative writings and speeches, or simply trying to allay the democratic critics of his plans with assurances that he meant what he said, and no further?

Hamilton's hostility to democracy stemmed from his support of the rights of private property, which he held sacred. His concern for property was a means to an end; upon it he planned to build a strong central government, one capable of limiting internal disorder and assuring tranquility. The quelling of the Whiskey Rebellion demonstrated that the new national government had the will and ability to suppress violent resistance to its laws and sped up the division of politics into parties. He argued that liberty and the security of property were inseparable, and that the government should honor the bonds previously issued, as that formed the Contract basis of public and private morality. Hamilton had a contempt and distrust for the masses of people in the country, as do Democrats today, for anyone in middle America: "Men are reasoning rather than reasonable animals, for the most part governed by their passions...the same state of the passions which fits the multitude, who have not a sufficient stock of reason and knowledge to guide them, for opposition to tyranny and oppression, very naturally leads them to a contempt and disregard of all authority. When the minds of these are loosened from their attachment to ancient establishments and courses, they seem to grow giddy and are apt more or less to run into anarchy…In such tempestuous times, it requires the greatest skill in the political pilots to keep men steady and within proper bounds, on which account I am always more or less alarmed at everything which is done of mere will and pleasure, *without any proper authority*." (Author's italics) *Hamilton Letter to John Jay, December, 1775*

Hamilton's terms of thought were national wealth, power, law, order, and stability. He rarely thought in terms of the improvement and the happiness of the individual citizens. He did not have the vision, which so possessed Jefferson and the Antifederalists, of a possible new order in which the common man might be happier, wiser and better off than before. What Jefferson feared and Hamilton dared hope for has come to pass, with the states having become for the most part merely administrative units for the federal government. Hamilton: "This balance between the National and State governments ought to be dealt with particular attention, as it is of utmost importance. It forms a double security to the people. If one encroaches on their rights, they will find a powerful protection in the other. Indeed, they will both be prevented from overpassing their constitutional limits by a certain rivalry, which will ever subsist between them." It never happened.

Hamilton was a realist. Americans had never been able to govern themselves in larger units than parishes or towns, or at the most, individual colonies. In every instance in which they attempted concerted action the meanness, the jealousy, the parsimoniousness of their narrowly provincial minds had wrecked their purpose. In the condition of the Congress there was every indication that such would again be the case. Hamilton was not a philosopher, nor was he in any great degree an original thinker. On the other hand, in the practical application of his political faith to the problems confronting the new country, no one surpassed him, and no man of his time left a deeper impress upon the form of the nation than he. Nor did any of the Founders leave a more influential body of expressed doctrine than did he in his papers comprised in the *Federalist*. Hamilton's one idea was to build a strong ship of state, while Jefferson was thinking in terms of the welfare of the crew. We needed both men then. We have to compose their apparently conflicting philosophies into a more harmonious whole which the clash of interests, and lack of sustained thought, have yet allowed us to consummate.

Even with the example of Jacobin France right before him, it seems hardly to have occurred to Hamilton's mind that force in a government may be applied to purposes other than the maintenance of a conservative order. Even with political economy he ignored the possibility that the industrialized nation he projected might conjure up not only conservative industrialists, but also radical factory workers, the latter infinitely more numerous and more inimical to Hamilton's old-fashioned idea of class and order than all the agrarians out of Jefferson's Virginia. He was almost naïve, rarely speculating upon what might result from mixing his prejudices with American industrial vigor. His vision of the coming America was of another, stronger, richer eighteenth-century England. As England was a single state, its sovereignty indivisible and its parliament omnicompetent, so should America be. He sought the principle of strength and stability in the organization of government, and vigor in its operation. To the difficulties in the way of his dream-the territorial extent, historical origin and local prerogative-he was almost oblivious. In addition, the forces of history, habit and interest combined to make most men loyal to their familiar, tangible state governments rather than to an abstraction called the United States. A bastard from the Leeward Islands, Hamilton had none of the attachments of ancestry and nativity that caused the other Founders to love their states with a passion beside which nationalism was a feeble infatuation. This tended to initially conceal from him the obdurate resolution latent in several state governments which would make his job more difficult. He thought his whole nationalizing program-the federal courts, Congress, the tariff, the Bank-would bring the states around. He succeeded, but only by provoking a civil war which dissipated the eighteenth-century aristocracy that really was Hamilton's aspiration.

Hamilton sought a mercantilist balance of trade for the nation as the leading aim of his policy. The influence of government might be properly exerted to encourage and enrich particular classes and occupations; the natural consequence of this would be an ultimate benefit to the country in general. Without Hamilton, industrial growth would have been slower but no less sure, perhaps with mitigated consequences. Hamilton, though, was fascinated by the idea of a planned economy, but gave few hints as to how this mercantilist America was to be managed. Given his contempt for the ordinary man, he perhaps thought that through political manipulation and national consolidation the rich and well-born could prevail. The powers which Hamilton was so ready to bestow upon the State were eventually diverted to opposite ends when the urban population that his policies stimulated became the source of an even newer radicalism. Randolph and after him Calhoun denounced the coming industrial era, more hideous in their eyes than the old colonial condition.

....

Modern Monetary Theory (MMT) synthesizes ideas from the book *The State Theory of Money* by Georg F. Knapp, written in 1905. His concept of Chartalism defined money as being the creation of government that derives its value only by its status as legal tender. Chartalism argues that money is valuable in use because governments require you to pay taxes in that currency. Chartalist fiat money has no intrinsic use value outside of that which the government gives it; its use as a medium of exchange generally coincides with the sphere of influence of the government that issues it and compels its employment. Knapp thus said that money is a creature of the law, rather than a commodity. The previous, prevailing view of money was that it had evolved from systems of barter, to become a medium of exchange, because it represented a durable commodity-gold and silver-which had its own use value and intrinsic worth; the value of the currency was tied to the value of the commodity. Not coincidentally, Knapp's *State Theory of Money* was introduced about the same time as the federal government began its attempt to direct economic activity more to its liking, that is, away from free market capitalism, and towards the use of debt to finance programs otherwise not affordable.

MMT challenges conventional beliefs about how the government interacts with the economy, the nature of money, the use of taxes, and the significance of budget deficits. These concepts, proponents say, are a hangover from the gold standard era and are no longer accurate, useful or necessary. MMT says that governments that spend, tax and borrow in a fiat currency that they fully control are not operationally restricted by revenues when it comes to funding federal programs. Such governments need not rely on taxes or borrowing for spending since they can print as much as they require and are the monopoly issuers of the currency. Their policies, therefore, should not be shaped by fears of a rising national debt.

Understanding reserve accounting is fundamental to understanding MMT fiscal policy options. A sovereign government typically has an operating account with the country's central bank. From this account the government can spend and receive taxes and other inflows. Each commercial bank also has an account with the central bank, by means of which it manages its reserves (money for settling and managing interbank transactions). When a government spends money, its Treasury debits its operating account at the Central Bank and deposits the money into private bank accounts. This money increases the total deposits in the commercial banking sector. Taxation works oppositely: private bank accounts are debited and deposits in the commercial banking sector fall, adding to the Treasury account. All monetary instruments issued by the government are thus created or destroyed with spending and taxing or bond offerings. Taxation and its legal-tender-enabling power allow the government to discharge debt and establish fiat money as currency, giving it value by creating demand for it in the form of a private tax-paying currency.

MMT swaps the roles of fiscal and monetary policy. Standard economics sees the Federal Reserve as ensuring that there is full employment and stable prices, through monetary policy that manipulates interest rates. Under MMT economies should be guided by fiscal policy-government spending and taxation. With MMT the government prefers interest rates to always be at zero percent, allowing fiscal policy to make the adjustments. Proponents see the use of government-issued bonds bearing interest as a mostly pointless practice. Instead of raising interest rates to fight inflation you raise taxes. The budget restraint is replaced by an inflation constraint. MMT sees taxes not primarily as the means to provide the government with money to spend on infrastructure and fund social welfare programs, but as the tool to take money from an economy that is getting overheated. If there is too much money chasing products, the government should tax some of it, thereby taking it out of circulation. The idea of taxes as a deflationary measure means that government would need to find the courage to raise taxes in an inflationary environment. But tax policy is difficult enough to implement while inflation moves quickly. The central role of taxes, not surprisingly for a program supported by the Left, goes to the conceptual core of MMT, which is about how money originates and how it is removed.

Because the government can issue its own currency at will, MMT maintains that the level of taxation relative to government spending (the government's deficit spending or budget surplus) is in reality a policy tool that regulates inflation and unemployment, and not solely a means of funding the government's activities. MMT proponents say inflation and consumer demand can be managed both by cutting back on government spending (!) and raising taxes(!!). Taxes are used to control inflation. But trying to use fiscal policy to steer the economy is a proven failure because Congress and the President rarely act quickly enough to respond to a downturn. Politicians simply cannot be relied on to impose pain on the public through higher taxes or lower spending to squelch rising inflation. Raising taxes is politically unpopular, and inflation inevitably takes hold before any action could be taken, even if it did work out the way MMT proposes. The approach of MMT effectively reverses theories of governmental austerity. MMT's depiction of the reserve system first creating and then destroying money results in the misleading depiction of the flow of funds that actually occurs in the private banking system, following productive activity, by creating the illusion that the whole process starts and ends with the government.

Traditional economists see the role of government as setting taxes in order to raise revenue. That revenue is then used to pay for the things government needs to do: police, firefighters, building roads and bridges. This conception likens the government to a household budget. It cannot send out money until it has taken in money. Any extra money it spends must be financed by borrowing. MMT argues that the household metaphor is exactly backwards because the government has to create the money first in order to spend it, and only after it is put in circulation can it be taxed back. MMT says that the government does not impose taxes in order to find money. In the MMT framework spending and creating are the same thing. The government thus has two levers to propel or retard the economy-it can vary taxes and spending, up or down, in concert or independently. MMT proponents overestimate the potency of fiscal policy, assuming it can successfully control inflation. If inflation became a consequence of fiscal policy, Congress would have to determine how to adjust taxes in order to control it. This involves a learning curve that would prove very costly while inflation continued to destroy the economy. Fiscal manipulations of tax hikes and spending cuts to quell inflation are highly unrealistic, given politicians' aversion to fiscal austerity, not to mention the lags inherent in the budget process, especially in election years. Government borrowing is only deferred taxation; inflation is hidden taxation. Because it is harder for the public to understand what's happening when government money printing makes them poorer, there is a definite sense that taxation is honest while deliberate inflation is insidious. The printing press, and to a lesser extent government borrowing allows the politicians to get away with spending that the public would never agree to explicitly pay for through straightforward tax hikes.

MMT wants the nation's central bank to do the bidding of the Treasury. So, when the Treasury needs money, the central bank accommodates it with a keystroke-creating money from thin air by crediting the Treasury's checking account. Governments should be able to spend whatever is required to achieve their goals, deficits be damned. The deficit is the difference between all the cash the government has spent and all the taxes it has collected. A deficit indicates that the private sector is holding the difference. If the government is in deficit, then the private sector is in surplus, and vice-versa. There is a striking similarity of MMT claims to Hamilton's that the national debt was a blessing. "The national debt is the equity that supports the entire global credit structure."—and is in turn similar to Wynne Godley's sectoral balance analysis of England's economy. From the perspective of MMT and Godley, deficits are not the problem, they are the solution. The alternative is squeezing the economy in order to balance the government's books.

MMT is deemed "timely" and "relevant" as it is allegedly based on fresh insight showing how all the mainstream economists are locked into old habits of thought: thoughts such as if a government project is deemed unaffordable, due to lack of funds provided by taxes and conventional accounting, then it should also be denied funding through the printing press; thoughts such as the government has a moral obligation to make ends meet and satisfy the bottom line. Proponents write "the most important conclusion reached by MMT is that the issuer of a currency faces no financial constraints. A country that issues its own currency can never run out and can never become insolvent in its own currency. It can make all payments as they come due." MMT adopts the exogenous money theory (money created within the economy by government deficit spending or bank lending) and rejects the endogenous idea (that there is a finite supply of loanable funds out there, backed by gold, that private business produces and competes with government over.) Instead, they believe that loans by banks create money in accordance with demand, meaning private borrowers are not crowded out when government borrowing raises interest rates. Neither can the US government go bankrupt because that would mean it ran out of dollars to pay creditors; it cannot run out of dollars as it is the only agency to create dollars. To be sure, a currency-issuing government can always print more money when a bill comes due. That ability might seem to release the government from any financial constraints. But when the government prints money to pay a bill, it is, in effect, borrowing. Interest accrues, which might be paid by printing even more money. But the ever-expanding monetary base will have even further ramifications. You can print all the money you like as long as there is a corresponding increase in demand, and the response will be a currency of stable value. But aggregate demand will increase due to the wealth effect, eventually spurring inflation. The expansion of the monetary base decreases interest rates and reduces the real quantity of money demanded, reaching the point where the ability to print money has little further value. Given these circumstances a government may decide that defaulting on its debts is a better option than printing more money, as default would be preferable to hyperinflation.

Under MMT, fiscal policy (government taxing and spending decisions) is also the primary means of achieving full employment, by establishing the budget deficit at the stimulative level to achieve that goal. In mainstream economics, monetary policy (Central Bank adjustment of interest rates and its balance sheet) is the primary mechanism, assuming there is an interest rate low enough to spur employment and also avoid a liquidity trap. MMT rejects the modern consensus that economies should be steered primarily by the raising and lowering of interest rates. MMT proponents on the Left believe that the natural rate of interest in a world of fiat money is zero and that pegging it higher is a giveaway to the investor class. Tweaking interest rates is ineffectual, they claim, because businesses make investment and hiring decisions based on the prospects for growth, not the cost of money.

An essential element of MMT, therefore, is the national Jobs Guarantee (JG), something never tried in any developed economy. MMT says unemployment is the result of government spending too little while collecting too much in taxes. It says that those unable to find a job in the private sector should be given a minimum-wage "transition" job funded by the government and managed by the local community. The job guarantees intend to ensure full employment, and maintain demand, no matter what policies the government is employing to fight inflation. The suggested wage is $15 an hour, with benefits, in make work jobs, for anyone that wants one. A jobs guarantee acts as an employment buffer, when the government slows aggregate demand through higher taxes and regulation, that forces people out of the private sector. Instead of becoming unemployed the person enters the JG workforce. When demand recovers that person returns to the private sector. During downturns JG works as an automatic stabilizer, putting money in the pockets of laid-off workers and helping mitigate recessions. The purpose of MMT's claims about employment are to create the illusion that the government needs to spend to maximize the number of employees, a moral argument for full employment masquerading as a poorly constructed economic argument for full employment. Neutering the use of that discredits their ideologically motivated inflation theory. MMT cannot empirically show that JG does what they claim. As with any government expenditure that goes right to consumption, diversion of X billion from the private sector for a public "jobs bill" is epistemologically barren as it cannot determine either the source of changes in the number of jobs or the behavior of jobs in the absence of the bill. Furthermore, if the government is printing as much money as it takes to buy up all the unemployed labor, then the private sector will be starved of workers. Employees will be pulled out of productive, efficient, market driven companies into inefficient, make-work government jobs. Wage inflation will spiral up as the government's new money pours in, and workers demand higher pay in the private sector. You *can* cause inflation and you *will* cause inflation if you reach full employment, and you continue to try to increase spending. At full employment the economy's resources are all used. Any further government spending will necessarily be inflationary.

MMT suggests that government spending can grow the economy to its full capacity, enrich the private sector, eliminate unemployment, and finance major programs such as universal healthcare, free college tuition and green energy. The government should be able to print all the money it needs as long as that does not generate inflation. As long as there is unemployment and unused capacity it remains the case that it is unlikely that inflation will happen. But if you keep *spending* and cannot produce goods to meet that spending you also get inflation. Furthermore, when a lack of productive supply meets demand from excess cash, hyperinflation will be the result. Full employment is the upper limit of non-inflationary spending.

MMT believes it can effectively manipulate tools such as inflation and taxation to accommodate any amount of spending the politicians desire. MMT views spending not as something to be weighed against and limited by government revenues, like a checkbook, but as something limitless that is a nation's foremost tool for achieving full employment. MMT views taxes not as a front-end tool to fund the government but as a back-end tool to curb the inflation resulting from excessive government spending. In short, MMT creates a new pathway for higher levels of government spending by drawing down the bank accounts of American citizens through inflation and taxation, rather than pay for that spending by borrowing. So, the money supply is expanded exponentially, driving hyper-inflation, resulting in higher taxes to curb the pace of growth. Even beyond those problems, the amount of interest on the debt soon crowds out the ability of the government to pay for anything else-the military, infrastructure, or welfare. American citizens pay either way for increased government spending. MMT is designed to shrink the "wealth gap" by sapping the savings Americans already hold, through inflation, and transfer that wealth to an ever-increasing pot of government expenditures that they can direct in whatever direction they choose. The government's share will be protected and grow into perpetuity. Runaway inflation saps private wealth, destroys the value of the currency and thus eventually lessens the tax revenues, which in turn kill the spending plans. MMT is an inevitable failure.

MMT takes a Marxist and post-Keynesian framework and adds a bunch of modern understandings replete with inconsistencies and flaws. The new paradigm they try to form for public finance, not surprisingly, really just misconstrues reality. The correct parts of MMT aren't new and the new parts aren't correct. MMT is a state-centric view of the economy that tries to intervene, with the use of spending and taxation, for the purposes of ensuring full employment and financial stability. These interventions, incompatible with a capitalist economy, are formed from a misleading operational perspective of the monetary system. While it is true that in limited ways government can be a useful facilitating force in the economy, MMT has a strong tendency to overreach and misrepresent the degree to which this is necessary and helpful.

The effect of MMT is to give intellectual respectability to the notion that the government doesn't have to pay for everything it wants to do, with taxes or by issuing bonds. MMT claims to explain why budget deficits do not matter and why monetary ease-the printing of money-can cover the difference between spending and taxes and never cause inflation. The fact that leaders of the Progressive Party drew attention to, and support the idea, because its tenets conform to their policy views, makes one additionally skeptical. Politicians will always use whatever elements of this or that economic thinking which best supports their agenda. They never feel a need for coherence or further justification. MMT is being implemented today. It is used in policy debates to argue for Progressive legislation such as universal health care and the New Green Deal for which opponents claim there is insufficient money to fund. Despite the historical examples, proponents claim that large government debt and printing money aren't the precursors to collapse that we have been led to believe. In searching for radical theories to support radical policies, MMT apologists have come to endorse an approach to economic theory that flies in the face of centuries of economic research and historical precedent, without any empirical evidence of its own. Once those in government, academia and the media begin to speak honestly about what MMT is, instead of what they wish it was-when they cease conflating the theory with the policies its advocates happen to endorse-MMT will be exposed as a grossly inadequate foundation for public policy.

Without a sound dollar we will run into problems that dwarf any that plague us now. The value of fiat money is derived from the relationship between supply and demand and the stability of the issuing government. Fiat money is inconvertible and cannot be redeemed for gold. The Federal government stopped allowing citizens to exchange currency for government gold with the passage of the Emergency Banking Act of 1933. The gold standard ended completely in 1971 when the U.S. stopped issuing gold to foreign governments in exchange for dollars. Only an ongoing tax obligation (the full faith and credit), in concert with the diminishing private confidence and acceptance of the currency, now underpins its value (rather than gold). If people lose complete faith in the currency the money loses its value, and hyperinflation is again the result.

The Leftists proposing MMT purport that inflation doesn't always result from too-high aggregate demand which taxes can help cool. MMT in fact discounts its own effects on inflation. Instead, it *must* otherwise come from monopolists and predatory capitalists using their market power to push prices higher and can be best tackled by directly regulating those capitalists. They write that "class conflict theory situates the problem of inflation as being intrinsic to the power relations between workers and capital, which are to be mediated by a government within a capitalist system." That is, inflation gets out of control when workers and capitalists each struggle to claim a larger share of national income, and not from government spending. According to this view income policies such as government guidelines for wages and prices are another solution to high inflation. MMT advocates see these controls as a kind of arbitration in the ongoing class struggle. But while the government getting involved in price setting might improve the allocation of resources as a matter of simple theory, the complexity of the economy and the desultory history of price controls suggest that this solution too, is not practical. Actual governments in actual economies cannot increase general welfare by inserting themselves in the wage and price-setting process. The most novel policy prescriptions of MMT simply do not follow cogently from its premises. Most people would still use US dollars even if no taxes were paid. We use the US payment system primarily because it gives us access to a credible form of money that allows us to purchase the output denominated in that currency.

....

The orthodox roles of monetary and fiscal policy are separate and distinct. Monetary policy prioritizes a stable dollar with stable borrowing and investing opportunities through the gradual manipulation of interest rates. The stability of the dollar gives people confidence to lend to the government at relatively low rates. Appropriate rates drive liquidity into the marketplace, helping to propel the private sector and drive full employment. Traditional fiscal policy is managed by Congress and the Treasury and ostensibly prioritizes balancing the income from taxes with the spending on programs. When the government spends more than it takes in borrowing is necessary to sustain the deficit spending. The traditional separate treatment of fiscal and monetary policy tends to dampen inflation and pushes Congress to spend within its means. Both offer challenges to Progressives, who would like the government to spend more, and more easily, and who view private savings as a source of both inequality and the means to fund their own pet programs. In the conventional reading of the economy massive spending is seen as a problem because it risks destabilizing the otherwise steady forces that power growth. MMT, however, reinterprets spending as the foremost tool for growing the economy.

A corporation can issue short-term financial assets that are money-like, in effect spending those assets into existence and then charging for their goods and services. This is especially true of start-up firms issuing shares of stock without yet having proven that they can generate the cash flow to support present valuations. Their innovation, productive capacity and pricing power are what make those shares viable in the future. The firm is able to issue the stock because it has credible ideas and willing holders of its liabilities. It is the corporation's intellectual capital base that makes its asset holders confident enough to invest. When that capital base deteriorates investors lose faith and devalue the assets. If the company fails no one is hurt except for the willing investors.

A company's equity is the residual of assets and liabilities. We create equity when we produce real goods and services or increase the market value of our assets relative to their liabilities via productive output. The government produces nothing. It is illogical to claim that the government can just print equity out of thin air. A government has broadly diverse sources of capital but is overreaching if it thinks that it never needs funding or willing holders of its liabilities. While the government has an especially high level of credibility, we should not confuse that to mean it has unlimited credibility or that it does not rely on the productive private sector to fund its spending.

The US government does not actually issue money in the first instance. New money comes into being via production in the form of goods, then into the private banking system in the form of sales, then into the Treasury in the form of taxes. Any issuer of money needs to find willing holders of that money, so those holders are the financing agents for the currency issuer. It is only the income from taxes that provides the credibility that allows a government to borrow. A country with a large tax base can afford to expand their balance sheet more by leveraging, and to spend more because they have a larger potential funding source. Taxes fund government spending in that they give the government the ability to spend existing money (money that has been loaned into existence by commercial banks and is supported by an underlying resource-gold) without having to expand the government's balance sheet.

Government debt is the liability of the society that created it. In the aggregate government debt is the liability that must be financed by the productive output of that society. A government obtains its financial strength by leveraging the capital of its private sector, not the other way around. MMT says the government must supply financial assets in order for the private sector to operate when in fact the private sector supplies itself with production-created financial assets and formed the government to protect those assets. MMT confuses the concept of establishing a national currency with the idea of actually supplying those assets. It is more accurate to say that the private sector net worth is the equity that supports the domestic economy and government debt can, at times, serve as a useful insurance and liquidity instrument that supports that equity.

Saying the government's deficit equals private savings is one thing. Saying it *causes* private savings is another and implies that government debt is the backbone of the economy, after Hamilton. But government debt is financed by private sector income. Private resources necessarily and logically precede taxes. Trading preceded government. Without a highly productive, revenue producing private sector it is impossible for government assets to remain valuable. You cannot have tax receipts if there is no output, as happened in Rome. So sustainable and productive output must precede taxes. In an MMT world, all of our efforts to create and build things can be discarded by just more spending and printing. The money illusion is the idea that our wealth is determined by the amount of money in our pockets rather than the actual amount of goods in the world available to buy. But the only way to get more goods for tomorrow is to save and invest for today.

Since fiat money is not a scarce or fixed resource like gold, MMT theoretically gives central banks much greater control over its supply, which gives them power to manage economic variables such as credit supply, liquidity, interest rates and money velocity. In the real world, though, a currency tied to gold is more stable than fiat money *because* of its limited supply. There are more opportunities for the creation of bubbles with fiat money due to its probable overuse and the likelihood it will be put towards ambiguous political ends. Any attempt to extract too much from seigniorage-the printing of money-leads to an infinite upward spiral in inflation. In effect, the currency is destroyed.

Currency in an economy being managed on those principles would be unreliable; because no one wants to hold unsound currency, the demand for it falls, the value of the dollar is lessened, and inflation will erupt. This could happen even if no supply was added. A lower demand is sufficient to spark inflation. Bond, credit and foreign exchange investors essentially make daily bets on the health of national economies-and their currencies-by buying and selling government debt, based on how risky it appears to be. The credibility of a form of money is contingent on many things and a structured legal system is one element of this demand. Holders of a certain currency are confident using it because there is a government regulatory system and established courts that can enforce claims. In addition, though usually ill-timed, the Fed has decades of experience in learning how its policy tools affect the inflation rate. Monetary policy has before (1980's) and will continue to be a powerful, though blunt, tool for controlling inflation. So, while a government regulatory system is an important link in the demand for money it is not necessarily *the* driver of this demand.

The FX markets may decide they don't want to hold the currency of a country that is printing money to pay its bills. The bond markets may decide they don't want to buy the debt of a country that has no intention of curbing its deficits. The flight of productive capital out of the country coupled with short bets against your assets (see George Soros and Great Britain), might devalue the domestic currency on international markets. Foreign debt becomes much more expensive as a result. Even if everything MMT proposes is true, and money creation and deficit spending are not inflationary at the national level, runaway inflation will still kick in if foreign investors decide that MMT will make the nation's currency worthless, the government bankrupt, and the central bank default. When interest costs on government debt become as large as the state's revenue, investors will no longer believe the government to be solvent, will refuse to buy bonds or lend to the government at reasonable rates of interest. While the country might be able to stomach more debt eventually all revenue would be devoted to its retirement, with no funds available for *any* other spending item.

At some point the inflation becomes high enough to constrain all domestic public purpose. When the government's counterparties (the citizens and foreign countries) refuse to hold the currency any longer, the value of money is repriced, and hyperinflation turns into a full-blown collapse, in what is essentially an insolvency. Governments go bankrupt in real terms while households go bankrupt in nominal terms. When the supply of household money collapses you simply have no more money to spend. When demand for government money collapses you get high inflation. No one will hold the liabilities of an entity that has no chance of being able to redeem their liabilities in real terms since there is no output base upon which these liabilities can be given value. If there is no productive economy for government to tax at some level of output, then it has no credibility. Although a sovereign government has unique powers it is not immune to the reality that it can run out of viable counterparties. All money issuers need willing holders of their liabilities. The government's money is considered viable only when it has an underlying productive private sector that drives demand for that money. A productive private sector generates the domestic product and income, later taxed by government, that gives government liabilities credibility. The credibility of a money's value comes from the economy's underlying productive resources. So, it is the viability of the process of production that must in every case be preserved and maintained.

Mainstream theories of inflation emphasize this excessive growth in aggregate demand due to expansive monetary policy. All spending is inflationary if it drives nominal aggregate demand above the real capacity of the economy to absorb it. Additionally, the level of employment stems from the level of private investment, not government spending. The economy must have the capacity to grow in response to the added demand created by the increased money flows. MMT treats the entire private sector as if it can only create wealth if the government first expands its balance sheet. It treats the government as if it is an entirely exogenous entity; as if government liabilities are not the liabilities of the aggregated domestic economy. Government cannot tax in excess of underlying productive capacity, or they will create inflation with their excess spending. So, in the real world, government spending is constrained by the quantity and quality of its private sector's productive output. And the quantity and quality of income that the private sector can create is the amount of income that constrains the government's ability to spend.

MMT denies the existence of an upper limit on debt printed in a government's own currency. They therefore embrace using central banks to print money and monetize debt. But numerous examples demonstrate the causal relationship between currency printing and hyperinflation. Weimar Germany, Austria-Hungary, Brazil, Peru, Zimbabwe and Venezuela have all run into a solvency constraint only after running out of willing holders of its currency due to hyperinflation. MMT does not really have a coherent theory of inflation, instead giving people the idea that a sovereign government can afford anything denominated in its own currency. MMT cannot model the actual limit of that spending, cannot accurately predict the level of inflation, so there is no way to adjust what MMT claims is the true constraint for government spending. If one cannot correctly understand how government funds its spending, then how can MMT theorists properly understand how government spending will influence potential economic outcomes? The more variables the government tries to control in its efforts to manage the economy, the greater its failures.

MMT is dangerous and indefensible. Advocates for MMT are setting the stage for potentially disastrous policy making. As part of an anti-capitalist movement perhaps this is the intention all along. It has more in common with a political or ideological movement than it does a theory of economics. By asserting their policy goals, they assume away the barriers to achieve these ends. Is it sensible to pay for government spending with central bank money? Only if the authority over how much money is printed transfers from the Fed to the Treasury, and the rationale is no longer keeping a stable currency, but meeting the Treasury's deficit-spending needs. Accepting MMT also implies that there are no constitutional limits on what the government may undertake, that it is right and legal for the government to interfere with the economy, that an entirely new bureaucracy can be created that will intelligently administer jobs programs for 16 million persons, with the concomitant lessening of freedom all that would bring. It is irresponsible and irrational to argue that this is a good program when it is not been empirically tested in any useful form. Consolidating the supposedly independent Federal Reserve into the Treasury simply creates a fictional world in order to make their flawed accounting look correct. The most fundamental problem with MMT is its complacent attitude towards debt and deficits.

Inflation since 2008 has been dampened by requiring banks to retain more reserves while raising loan standards. The effect was to slow economic activity while strengthening banks, who had previously allowed reserve requirements to slack. At the same time trillions have been funneled into the stock market, destroying price discovery, and into the fool's gold of cryptocurrencies, lessening the effect on everyday consumer prices, though that has begun to change. Technology companies such as Amazon are terrifically deflationary by holding prices down.

Inflation is kept at bay only if economic growth exceeds the interest rate on public debt. A budget crisis might lead to draconian tax increases which stifle economic growth. The US will likely continue to experience recessions of varying degree, which generally cause the deficit to go much higher. A responsible government does not incur debts that are only manageable if everything goes well. Debt service means a redistribution from future generations to those alive today, an immoral taking from those who aren't even alive, educated or able to vote.

The MMT process is already beginning-leading to a loss of faith in the currency. Near zero interest rates that no longer stimulate production, efforts to raise punitive taxes on the same capital needed for business start-ups, discussions of multi trillion-dollar spending plans, guaranteed job programs, and direct payments to citizens are all proposed or already in existence. The test will come when there is a substantial and notable decline in the value of the dollar with no corresponding response from the government to support the currency value via base money contraction. This would mean at least a temporary end to central bank bond-buying and consequently no more printing press money. There would eventually have to be budget discipline and higher interest rates. Bonds would find yields better reflecting the real risks today.

Only after real trouble comes will we be ready to return to money based on gold. Over centuries the most successful countries have had reliable currencies giving them long-term success. This comes about when gold and silver, or their monetary equivalent, are the only things people will accept for large scale payment. The Federal Reserve wishes to issue fiat currency (paper not exchangeable for gold) without it ever being redeemed. The government is heavily in debt, and they hope to find a safe way of being dishonest. But only in relation to gold can the unit value of paper money be maintained.

Mathematics is the language of the technological age. It is an instrument of practical thought and communication in our daily lives. The men who organize and perform the practical tasks by which modern civilization is kept going think in the mathematical language while performing their jobs. If those who are entrusted with the general direction and political organization of a vast system, which depends throughout on the correct knowledge and use of mathematics, actually do not know, or do not understand the most elementary statement in that language, how can the system function and survive? If politicians and financiers will not believe logic or evidence that the value of the currency must remain stable, what will convince them?

When words are used without exact definition there can be no communication above a primitive level. If those who are supposed to express or influence public opinion cannot think in conceptual terms, what can be the outcome? What is most astonishing is that when the enemies of civilization have openly declared their intention to destroy it, and have explained how they mean to do so, those who are to be destroyed actually carry out the program of ruin. Keynes said: "Lenin was certainly right. There is no subtler, no surer means of overturning the existing basis of society than to debauch the currency. The process engages all the hidden forces of economic law on the side of destruction." Progressives have learned the lesson well.

General exchange must go on in an endless sequence through time and distance, to include variable quantities of raw materials existent in nature, labor applied to them, and end use, consumption or inactive possession. What is wanted is a medium of exchange, something for which everything else can be exchanged, so that it enters into every transaction as the unit of value and serves for an indefinite number of transactions. Money facilitates immediate exchange; it is a repository of value; and it carries exchanges through time on the long circuit of production. So the material for money must be durable, divisible, incorruptible, portable, not easily counterfeited, and found in nature in sufficient but limited quantity. Nothing but gold answers to these requirements. The supply of real money is increased as production of goods is increased. Gold is not given value by fiat, any more than any other commodity would be so given. It has value because it serves a vital need. A dollar is a certain quantity of gold. This is not a matter of opinion but by definition and by Law. A dollar bill used to be a certificate of deposit, a warehouse receipt for a dollar's worth of gold. The value of the paper dollar was in the metal on deposit. If the gold does not exist, or is destroyed or not delivered, the paper has no value. Real money, the unit in precious metal, is absolutely necessary for any extensive sequence of exchanges. The Left still attempts to persuade citizens that a "managed" currency consisting of nothing but printed paper is just as good or better. But if the paper currency is not actually redeemable on demand for gold; if the citizen cannot regain possession of his own property when he presents the certificate of deposit, because the members of government refuse to obey the Law, then what difference does it make whether the gold really exists or not? What difference would it make if the United States government has sold off its gold reserves, reputedly at Fort Knox? The government has no assets with which to meet its debts, because it is non-productive, and the creditor (the citizens) have no recourse in Law. The suspension of gold payments became unavoidable when the government was permitted to issue paper currency and borrow money. These are intrinsically dangerous powers. At present it is taken for granted that governments must have such powers, just as before kings and nobles had powers which were abolished with the establishment of republics. The method of the Left to gain their surreptitious objectives is the steady subtraction of value from money, and an increase in the national debt through borrowing from the banks. Nobody but a collectivist could imagine such a system. With a gold unit of value, labor hours, material and depreciation of machinery, and everything else that goes into the entire process can be reckoned by a common measure; and they must be reckoned somehow, in order to move anything from field to factory to shop; so the prices on the goods will show what can be bought for any given sum in that currency.

Real money is indispensable; prices are established by the total quantity of gold existent. The process in general exchange is greatly complicated by the numerous kinds of goods, the varying supply and demand, distances which add to the cost of transport, and deferred exchanges. It is by the comparison of quantities that prices are determined. Were there unlimited supplies of gold it would become useless as a medium of exchange and a price determinant. When paper currency is depreciated the difference must always be taken out of wages; heavy government expenditure causes a rise in taxes which means whatever pay a man receives will buy him that much less in goods which even now are more expensive. Moreover, the worker is deprived of a repository of value, as the amount saved loses buying power immediately. Conversely, increased production raises wages which will buy more. Real money is the only means by which the worker can have any independence. When the government seizes gold, and refuses to convert currency to gold on demand, it makes the worker helpless. If real wages are lowered by inflation the market for products is gone-nobody can afford it. Production must cease. The indispensable condition is that producers shall retain control of the production system so that there is something positive of which to return. When governments take over the total production of their nations, they continue only on the diminishing returns of their seized capital resources. Such nations cannot go back; the production circuits have been cut through and destroyed. Bureaucracies cannot be disbanded without internal anarchy; they are essentially the means of paying people not to revolt.

The survival of any nation depends entirely on the preservation of its capital resources, taking off only a minimum for the end product of government. Decentralization is the formula for duration. Goods must be produced on the complete circuit by men using private property freely. Time is on the side of a nation which increases its general production. Time is mortal on the nation which spends its capital reserves. The power from general production can be obtained only by free men choosing their own jobs of their own volition, for whatever reward work will bring. The creative man must find for himself the place and employment in which he can function; he must have a continuous choice of what he will do with his faculties, his time and his means. If he is assigned to a job at forced labor, all that will be got out of him is muscular power at what the prescribed task calls for. When he works as he chooses, finding for himself the market for his talent, there is no limit to the extent he may increase production. Left to themselves it is impossible to say how much innovation may be released into production by ambitious men. The engineering problem then is to organize the productive economy for free men. The whole problem of free volition of employment and free contract exchange is solved by observing throughout the principle of Contract. Contract is the principle of the true dynamic economy. A production system does not determine the moral relations of a society. The moral relations create the production system. Free men create it; it will not operate except in the private property, free enterprise society of Contract. It is only through Contract that a country preserves itself and its institutions from destruction. No despotism can indefinitely and independently maintain a machine economy. In the meantime, though, it can do enormous damage.

An engineering, technical and industrial economy *is* a hard money economy. It cannot work any other way. Authoritarian government, as with Rome, can only continue to function on the supply of goods extorted from the civilian production of the nation, until there is no more. Collectivists run their economy on the stolen portion of capital obtained from a money economy, embezzled from abroad or looted by military force. When they run out of other people's capital, their purposes must come to an end in financial and moral disaster. The same principle applies to finances inside a country; the government runs on the cut they obtain from the fraud of inflation and from the amounts they can expropriate through taxes. Hence nations of long duration are always based on principles of freedom and limited government. Production is the flow of energy; without it the country must stagnate. The appropriate type of organization is determined by the extent to which trade is developed, and Law is present. The Roman Republic was a far more advanced economy than the strict feudalism which followed in the Empire.

Sound money is the means by which the intelligence of individuals can be brought together in free co-operation, on large, productive enterprises. The right of an industrial concern to engage in business is derived from the right of its owners to invest their money in a productive venture-from the right to hire employees-from the right of employees to sell their services-from the right of all those involved to produce and sell their products-from the right of the customers to buy, or not to buy, those products-every link of this complex chain of Contractual relationships rests on individual choices and agreements. Every agreement is specified and subject to certain conditions dependent upon a mutual trade to mutual benefit. Private property, sound money, freedom, engineering and industry are all one system; they are the components of the high potential long circuit of production. When one element is taken out, the rest must collapse and cease to function. By virtue of his mind man works through time and space stemming from his creative and expansive faculty. Since production is carried on through time and distance, credit arises as a natural consequence. Otherwise, all transactions would have to be closed on the spot, as no credit would be given, nor loans made. This would be the soundest, though impracticable, possible production system, with no panics. Sound money is the best means of extending exchanges of goods into the future. Sound money is the only means by which deferred exchanges in goods can safely be effected with credit. But this has never been proposed by any theorist, because it calls for no control, no compulsion, no political job or power for the reformer. Men could stick to cash transactions if they wanted, but they don't. Credit helped to enable the modern system of production and trade to get under way. Accumulation of paid-up cash capital in the needed sums would have been almost impossible, or at least much slower. Banks facilitate payments for shipments to and from distant points and carry deposits of current funds, giving local credit. Sound money is the medium of a Contract society.

The use of gold, currency, a check, or a bond obscures the true nature of exchange transactions, which is the production of one item which buys another. The use of a medium simply expediates transactions along a reverse parallel circuit in which everyone is paid; the presence of rational men means everyone's knowledge is also increased through the trade. The entire process requires human intelligence and volition, whereby the succession of voluntary Contractual agreements allow the circuit to be completed. The inevitable breakdown of the circuit in a planned economy necessarily comes when the sequence is destroyed by rationing, restrictions and compulsion.

The first charge on any productive circuit is its maintenance and replacement. Next, food, clothing and shelter must be gotten for the producer. The mere allotment of a subsistence measure of food to be ingested by workers on compulsory jobs cannot maintain the circuit. It does not allow for invention or discovery. For the exercise of intelligence men must have some surplus materials, time and energy at his disposal, with freedom to seek whatever employment he prefers. For the exercise of volition, to route the profits into such channels that production can be maintained, every exchange of goods must be made by free Contract. The long circuit is a hard money economy; many politicians imagine they can abstract more and more profit from the circuit without consequences to the continuing flow. The authoritarian state is the final form to which every planned economy tends. Force consists of profit withdrawn from production and yielding no return. Conversely, energy flowing though the channel of private production is self-sustaining, self-augmenting and self-renewing. A credit collapse is rapidly liquidated, recovery is rapid, and a pathway to freedom is re-opened. Profit going to government is a dead loss, being used up immediately in consumption, corruption and dissipation. The most comprehensive and fatal error that can be made by government is to take most of the nation's profits for the subsistence of the bureaucracy and the idle. Then there is nothing left to draw on but the stockpile of raw materials, the machinery of production already in existence, which must wear out rapidly, and a workforce dealing with the depreciated assets until they are exhausted. Government produces nothing, not even its own maintenance. It is a losing formula; the nation must constantly become weaker.

It was not unusual that the obvious facts concerning capitalism were late in being perceived and the general laws governing its creation and maintenance slow in being formulated. Principles may be put in practice long before they are understood. This is what happens by the use of sound money, or by credit or other contractual agreements. There is a real, material, unbroken sequence of energy carried through in the long circuit of production, which is visible and easily traced. A farmer grows food to trade for his needs, he feeds the men who dig ore, make steel, manufacture motors, build and run railways and airlines; innumerable other products enter into the sequence; but it is the physical succession of material objects in motion and in process which brings a new tractor back to the farmer, coffee from Brazil, and gasoline from Texas. There can be no break in the line brought under control for those purposes. It would never run into those particular channels of itself, nor start again where seriously interrupted, without the intervention of intelligent men, and the presence of sound money.

The crucial test of private property *is* the attitude of government toward money. Devaluation of the currency (increasing the money supply causing inflation) is outright expropriation. The British empire was founded when its debased coinage was restored to standard during the opening years of the reign of Elizabeth I (1533-1603), on the advice of Gresham (of Gresham's Law). At the time, English trade was in distress, the national treasury was empty, the national credit was gone and mercantile credit shaky, war was threatening and rebellion a possibility. In such circumstances, governments usually resort to repudiation, confiscation, and fiat currency. Instead, England took the opposite course. The world came under her sway. The British Empire ended three hundred and fifty years later, when England again debased her coinage, defaulted on her debts, confiscated private property, and abrogated personal liberty.

CHAPTER NINE-STATES RIGHTS AND

THE NECESSITY OF VIRTUE

D.D. EISENHOWER
CLINTON ROSSITER

RUSSELL KIRK
IRVING BABBITT

ROSE WILDER LANE
ISABEL PATERSON

RALPH KETCHAM

"Estimate the percentage of men and women who are idle, selfish, commonplace and frivolous and consider what if any education is likely to improve them. It is folly to think of making all, or the many, philosophers, or even men of science and systematic knowledge. But it is duty and wisdom to aim at making as many as possible soberly and steadily religious; inasmuch as the morality which the state requires in its citizens for its own well-being and ideal immortality, and without reference to their spiritual interest as individuals, can only exist for the people in the form of religion. In fine, religion, true or false, is and ever has been the center of gravity in a realm, to which all other things must and will accommodate themselves.

Samuel Taylor Coleridge

"However pure may be a social system, or a religion, in the commencement of its power, the possession of an undisputed ascendency lures all alike into excesses fatal to consistency, to justice and to truth. This is a consequence of the independent exercise of human volition, that seems nearly inseparable from human frailty. We gradually come to substitute inclination and interest for right, until the moral foundations of the mind are sapped by indulgence, and what was once regarded with the aversion that wrong excites in the innocent, gets to be not only familiar, but justifiable by expediency and use. There is no more certain symptom of the decay of the principles requisite to maintain even our imperfect standard of virtue, than when the plea of necessity is urged in vindication of any departure from its mandate, since it is calling in the aid of ingenuity to assist the passions, a coalition that rarely fails to lay prostrate the feeble defenses of a tottering morality."

James Fenimore Cooper, *The Heidenmauer*

"Even those among whom the habitual desire to do right still operates, they are corrupted by the moral indifference of their neighbors: The whole prospect that environs them has become morally colorless; and they discern in their attitude towards the world without, what it must one day come to be towards the world within. It is a malady of the modern world-it is betraying itself every moment around us, in conversation, in literature, and in legislation."

WH Mallock, *Is Life Worth Living?*

"Cold will still freeze, and fire will never cease to burn; disease and vice will continue to disorder, and death to terrify mankind. Emulation, next to self-preservation will forever be the great spring of human actions, and the balance of a well-ordered government will alone be able to prevent that emulation from degenerating into dangerous ambition, irregular rivalries, destructive factions, wasting seditions, and bloody civil wars."

John Adams

"The scheme of the humanist might be described in a word as a disciplining of the higher faculty of the imagination to the end that man might behold, in one sublime vision, the whole scale of being in its range from the lowest to the highest under the divine decree of order and subordination, without losing sight of the immutable veracity at the heart of all development, which is the praise of virtue."

Sir Thomas Elyot, *Boke Named the Governour*

"Virtue is the health of the mind, and vice its disease and disorder. That nation is in a dreadful way, in which almost every mind is diseased and disordered"

Plato, *The Republic*

"We framed a general government on free principles-we placed the state legislatures between Congress and the people. We were then too cautious; and too much restricted the powers of the general government. But now it is proposed to go into the contrary, and a more dangerous extreme; to remove all barriers, to give the new government free access to our pockets, and ample command of our persons, and that, without providing for a genuine and fair representation of the people."

Melancton Smith, June 21, 1788

Concerning the natural, inanimate world scientific knowledge is possible. Men who observe how it acts can, within the laws of physics, predict how it will always act. It is controlled. Man, physical, intellectual and moral, is as much a part of nature, as surely a part of the cosmic process, as the humblest weed. He is an animal among animals and insofar as that is true is open to the scientific method. But when one attempts to base a complete explanation of conduct on such methods one must discriminate qualitatively between the behavior of man and that of an ant or a bee. Otherwise, you have naturalism gone mad. Man's living energy is different; it is creative and variable. It changes, and it changes the conditions in which it acts. This is the nature of human energy; individuals generate and control it. Each person is self-controlling, is responsible for his own acts, and thus, by his nature, is free. But a solitary man on this earth can hardly survive. His enemies are too numerous and too strong; to ensure his existence he must have allies of his own kind, a desperate necessity to combine their energies in order to live. This relationship creates the struggle for control of these combined energies. The problem is real. What controls them? The Old-World answer is Authority. The uses of human energy are innumerable; since no two persons are alike, they rarely choose to act in precisely the same way at the same time. The larger the number of individuals, the more difficult the problem. Each acts according to their belief in the nature of the universe. Each acts in accordance with his personal view of the good. Each acts within their own standard of values. Human relationships are so numerous and varying every moment, that no mind can begin to grasp them all. When the problem of control extends over hundreds of millions of unpredictable individuals, obviously no effort to control them all can possibly succeed. "It would not be difficult to prove, that anything short of despotism, could not bind so great a country under one government: and that whatever plan you might, at the first setting out, establish, it would issue in a despotism. If one general government could be instituted and maintained on principles of freedom, it would not be so competent to attend to the various local concerns and wants, of every particular district, as well as the peculiar governments, who are nearer the scene, and possessed of superior information…" (Centinel)

"It is possible that an individual may lay down a system of principles, on which government shall be constitutionally established to any extent of territory. But the practice upon those principles, as applying to the various and numerous circumstances of a nation, its agriculture, manufacture, trade, and commerce requires a decentralized knowledge of a different kind, and which can be had only from the various parts of society. It is an assembly of practical knowledge, which no one individual can possess; all forms of government are limited, in useful practice, from a similar incompetency of knowledge, degenerating, in time, into confusion, ignorance and incapacity. Need we any other proof of their wretched management, than the excess of debts and taxes with which every nation groans, and the quarrels into which they have precipitated the world?" (Paine)

It is impossible to conceive a system of government better capable of acting over such an extent of territory, and such a circle of interests, as is immediately produced by the operation of representation. A representative government concentrates the knowledge necessary to the interest of the parts, and of the whole. It places government in a state of constant maturity-never young, never old. It admits not a separation between knowledge and power and is superior to all the accidents of individual men. The representative system diffuses such a body of knowledge throughout a nation on the subject of government, as to explode ignorance and preclude imposition. In the representative system the reason for everything must publicly appear. Every man is a proprietor in government and considers it a necessary part of his business to understand. He examines the cost, and compares it with the advantages; above all, he does not adopt the slavish custom of following what in other governments are called LEADERS." (Paine)

The Federal government of the United States, with its expressly limited endowment of powers, was created by the people in, and for, the several states, each state acting separately and independently through conventions called for that purpose. If it had been practicable and desirable for a state to retain its sovereign and independent status it simply could have refused to ratify the Constitution. Clearly the people preceded the states, and the states preceded the Federal government. The formation of the states consisted of certain delegated powers from each individual, such as that of self-defense, and judging in one's own case. Ratification of the Constitution amounted to a subtraction of certain delegated powers from that reservoir of sovereignty in each state and a consolidation of those subtracted powers in the new Federal government.

The separate states already existed and had not yet ceded their full sovereignties to the original loose federation. Their natural resistance as political entities, in being, was strong enough to defeat proposals that their autonomy should be extinguished and obscure the future danger in that direction. The question was how to bring them together in a more perfect union without lapsing into a ruinous democracy. The prerequisite must be the conditions, or mode of association, which did not hinder development of the innate faculties so necessary for individual liberty. What was wanted was a Republic. If a true American Revolution can be said to have occurred, it came only with the successes of Jefferson and the Republicans in the Election of 1800. They were largely opposed by Alexander Hamilton and John Adams.

Chief Justice John Marshall drew on both Hamilton and Adams. Marshall conjured up judicial review in *Marbury v. Madison,* 1803. Adams placed him as Chief Justice and was rewarded with *Fletcher v. Peck*, 1810 (asserting the right of the federal government to invalidate state laws which are in conflict with or otherwise contrary to the Constitution). He carried on the great work of nationalism and centralization with *McCulloch v. Maryland*, 1819 (giving the federal government implied powers, even though the Constitution may not explicitly state them); with *Dartmouth College v. Woodward*, 1819 (strengthening the Contracts Clause and reinforcing individual property rights), *Cohens v. Virginia,* 1821 (asserting the Supreme Court's power to review state supreme court decisions when a defendant claims his Constitutional rights have been violated) and with *Gibbons v. Ogden*, 1824 (granting the federal government the power to determine how interstate commerce is conducted). By his asserting the power of the Court to invalidate laws judged unconstitutional, he put the last stone in place in the wall of conservative constitutionalism. Constitutionalism was admirably suited to capitalism's political purposes. Its substance blended Adam's faith in diffusion and balance, Jefferson's insistence on strict construction, Madison's devotion to the separation of powers, and Marshall's ideal of a stubborn judiciary standing guard over property. Majority rule was the object of most concern, for a popular majority in the seats of power threatened the positions, plans and properties of the business community. A constitutional theory that set unbreachable limits to the power of democratic decision was therefore a necessity. The Constitution was clearly intended to be just such a catalogue of limitations rather than a grant of powers. The Right made the Declaration's pursuit of happiness consonant with pure economic individualism. In its practical applications the constitutional theory of laissez-faire capitalism looked first to this strong, independent judiciary pledged to defend property and economic liberty with the weapon of judicial review. The legislature was to operate under severe restrictions; the only good legislature was an adjourned legislature. The Senate was there to slow down, and if possible, stop any leveling legislation coming out of the House. The ideal President was one who confined his activities to executing the will of Congress, and thus of the people.

The mass of Americans go through their lives without an understanding of the scope and purpose of the Constitutional system. It is rooted in the self-evident truths of the Declaration. Clearly stated is the idea that government is man's agent for the protection of the unalienable gifts of life, liberty and property. For the first time in human history Government was thus logically and categorically reduced from its traditional role of tyrannical mastery to the simple service and deliberate will of human nature. This unprecedented transition was the very essence of the American Revolution. The Founding Fathers knew that Government would not surrender its historical pre-eminence without a sustained struggle. All of man's strength and all of man's vigilance would be needed to hold Government in a subordinated position of servitude. To prevent a renewal of that tyranny the Founding Fathers tied it down with strong chains-the checks, balances and divisions of the American constitutional system. They not only proclaimed liberty-they defined it in the clear terms of strict constitutional limitations. Liberty has lived in this country because here every officer, department and division of government is intended to be limited by Law. True American Government is not superior to the individual, only permitted by it; it is Government by Law. The Constitution forbids. It exists to limit and restrain and check and hinder American Government. Superstition, that deep darkness in human minds, supports all other kinds of Government. The awe and dread and allure of power creates the belief that Authority controls individuals. It supports a living ruler's use of force. Until the American Revolution, Government always rested on such superstitious belief. An American politician swears to obey the Constitution that limits his power. Only his honor, and the next election, hold him to that oath. All the other incentives that human beings feel impel him to break it: If he wants to do good, if he wants to be re-elected, if he wants more money, if he needs more self-importance-he needs more power. The only thing that prevents him from doing this is Constitutional Law-words on paper. Its only force is moral, and it must be found in each American politician's conscience. That, in turn, is only possible by the self-government, self-restraint, and moral self-control of each American citizen.

Perhaps the strongest and most significant links in the constitutional chains are the 9th and 10th Articles of the Federal Bill of Rights, in which personal and state rights are underscored. Enumerating some rights was not to be construed as meaning that they were the only rights the people retained. Those powers not specifically delegated by the Constitution to the Federal government, nor prohibited by it to the States, were reserved to the States respectively or to the people. The Bill of Rights was not written as a protection against the administration of George Washington, but to protect the rights of American citizens in perpetuity. In years to come, when less conscientious administrators were in charge of Government, Americans could still rely on the protections afforded to them.

The constitutional reallocation of powers created a new form of government unprecedented in human history. Every previous national authority had either been centralized or else had been a confederation of sovereign constituent states. The new American system was a mixture of both, partly national and partly federal. Madison develcped the variation devised in Federalist #39. After first calling attention to the checks inherent in having officials in the several branches be elected for periods of differing lengths, he analyzed the Constitution in respect to "the foundation on which it is to be established; to the sources from which its ordinary powers are to be drawn; to the operation of those powers; to the extent of them; and to the authority by which the future changes to the government are to be introduced." The key to the new approach was the proposition that sovereignty embraced a large number and a wide variety of different specific powers: obviously these specific powers could be assigned to different governments, to different branches of the same government, or to different persons serving within the same branch of a government. Hamilton spelled out the implications in his opinion on the constitutionality of certain sections: "The powers of sovereignty, are in this country divided between the National and State Governments, and each of the portions of powers delegated to the one or to the other is sovereign with regard to its proper objects." It followed from this that "each has sovereign power as to certain things, and not as to other things. To deny that the Government of the United States has sovereign power as to its declared purposes and trusts, because its power does not extend to all cases, would be to deny that the states retained sovereignty because *they* were forbidden to do a number of things." No one contended that the combined powers of the state and federal governments were absolute, for there were some powers that remained beyond the reach of both. Logically those powers must reside somewhere else. The Ninth and Tenth Amendments are clear.

The division of power between the states and the federal government is *the* key part of the constitutional system. The Ninth and Tenth amendments are just as important as the First. Once this division was discredited, all permanent value was drained from the constitutional system. Nothing worth preserving remains. On the resulting ruins we must begin to start over again. To conserve is to preserve without loss or detriment-the ability to keep pure, unmixed, unadulterated by time and various taints; having the power to oppose diminution or injury. One thinks long, wide and conscientiously about the rightful expectations of future generations, with an enlarged inventory of national resources-not just forests and fisheries, but spiritual and legal resources, found in Roman Law, our Declaration and Constitution-that now need to be conserved. Without the constant support of those spiritual and legal resources the material and physical assets could never have been developed as they have in this country, as opposed to anywhere else in the world, ever. We now need to restore and revitalize those resources.

As long as the Constitutional balance between the States and the Federal Government was maintained there was no possibility of centralizing power, the first stop in taking over the country. Controlling the police and the ballot box soon follow. The 34th President wrote: "Unless the place of state governments, with the authority, the responsibility and the revenues necessary to discharge their duties is preserved, then we do not have America as we have known it. We will have some other form of government. If we allow the constant drift towards central government to continue, ownership of property will gradually drift there as well, and finally we will have a dictatorship as the only means of operating such a huge bureaucracy."

American history reveals that a prime ingredient of central power is this principle of expansion which is characterized by its steadily increasing rate of growth. Its slow start at the beginning was disarming and deceptive. Alexander Hamilton feared that the central government might succumb to the factional issues stemming from established state sovereignty. But, with ever increasing speed, and Hamilton's help, the centripetal force of his central power principle asserted itself in the ever-expanding influence of the federal establishment. This was no tyranny imposed suddenly and ruthlessly by the iron hand of a dictator. The American people asked for it-or were made to believe that they did-in contrived doses of "federal aid" that developed an insatiable popular appetite for more and more of the same.

Perhaps it was vain to expect that any centralized government could be restricted to the exercise of its few limited powers. By its very nature centralized power is dynamic and aggressive. All of its force is centripetal, wanting to expand. In the vortex of an Authority that is supreme in any one area, it is next to impossible for it to maintain a respect for the different principle of subsidiarity in all other areas. Sooner or later a government of one thing will become a government of everything. So, in spite of the clear mandate of the 10th amendment there is no longer an item or area of sovereign jurisdiction that the states may call their own. The consequence of not stopping to understand the imprescriptible rights of man in the abstract is later having the leisure to meditate on the imprescriptible rights of Authority in the concrete. The Founding Fathers were only partially metaphysically mad: they trusted too much in their parchment and political machinery to corral the corruption of human character and the paucity of human reason. If the Constitution cannot be relied upon as a barrier against appetite and force, if the most capacious human intellects ever assembled cannot apprehend a way to manage society, where may future security against power be found?

The Constitution is the agency Contract between citizens and the government and is the sole basis of their authority to act for us. Taxpayers see their trustee (Congress) violate the trust indenture (the Constitution) and dissipate the trust funds of the taxpayers with unauthorized payments here and around the world. There is no reference to sovereignty in the Constitution that prevents the trustor (tax-paying citizens) from pursuing a legal remedy for this malfeasance. The Constitution is being concealed by public officials who are betraying the public trust. They attempt to satisfy the desire for change at the same time that they do not offend the intentions of the Founders. But no anomaly is innocent, which makes the law either more difficult to understand or harder to arrange in a logical order. The Constitution of the United States, representing the rule of Law, remains but as a mere shell, presenting the greatest obstacle to reform and re-organization of the civil law. It has long been undermined, while any new positive law hides itself under its cover. There is at once a difficulty in knowing whether the new rule which is actually operative should be classed in its true place, outside the Constitution, or in its apparent place within, as the functioning law. If American law is ever to assume an orderly distribution, it will be necessary to prune away the legal fictions which are still abundant in it. The tyranny of government can be prevented only by constant vigilance. The popular controls that are necessary to guard against government's irresponsible action are inherently weakened in the proportion and to the extent that such controls are removed from the ready reach of the people who must exercise them. The federal government in Washington is so far removed from the control of anyone except its self-perpetuating bureaucracy that it has become a completely irresponsible despotism. What hope can there be of an assertion of rights against some unconstitutional violation by that government?

Why can't we enforce that Contract when our federal agents violate the letter and spirit of our agency, which each of them has sworn to uphold? Self-serving laws and Supreme Court decisions have left American citizens helpless to affirmatively enforce the Constitution against its violation by the government. All persons possessing any portion of power ought to be strongly and awfully impressed with the idea that they act only in trust and must be accountable in that trust to the public. The main purpose of the Constitution was to construct a hard and fast confinement for the expressly limited checked and balanced powers which it conferred upon the federal government. Whenever the government, through the activities of its agents or officers, steps over any of the walls marked out for it, it commits a trespass upon the areas reserved to the several states and/or to the American people. At that point it should be liable to suit in the same manner and through the same kind of proceedings that are available for other violators of privacy, property and liberty. But the Federal government must consent to such a suit through sovereign immunity, effectively removing a key method of protecting a citizen's rights.

Men are corrupt, their appetites need restraint; the forces of custom, authority, Law and government, along with moral discipline, are required to keep them in check. This sentiment may be traced through Hamilton and John Adams to the Calvinists and Augustine, to Marcus Aurelius and his Stoic preceptors, as well as St. Paul and the Hebrews. In Federalist #6 Hamilton argues against those who assume that thirteen independent states can live at peace with one another: "Have we not already seen enough of the fallacy and extravagance of those idle theories which have amused us with promises of exemption from the imperfections, weaknesses, and evils incident to society in every shape? Is it not time to awake from the deceitful dream of a golden age, and to adopt as a practical maxim for the direction of our political conduct that we, as well as the other inhabitants of the globe, are yet remote from the happy empire of perfect wisdom and perfect virtue?"

James Madison was just as outspoken, calling attention to "the infirmities and depravities of the human character" and the "injustice and violence of individuals." It was the determination of the framers to base their new government "on men as they are and will probably remain, not as we would like them to be or become. In establishing a government which is to be administered by men over men, the great difficulty lies in this: you must first enable the government to control the governed; and in the next place oblige it to control itself."

John Adams was equally skeptical. Freedom could be achieved and retained only by sober men who take humanity as it is, not as humanity could be. Adams entertained no exaggerated opinion of the wisdom and virtue possessed by the mass of mankind. What was needed were good and practical laws transcending the passions of the hour: "It is weakness rather than wickedness which renders men unfit to be trusted with unlimited power. Men must try to attain a balance of the affections and appetites, governed by reason and conscience. If they surrender the guidance for any course of time to any one passion, they may depend upon finding it, in the end, a usurping, domineering, cruel tyrant. They were intended by nature to live together in society, and in this way to restrain one another; but they know each other's imbecility so well that they ought never to lead one another into temptation. The passion that is long indulged and continually gratified becomes mad; it is a species of delirium; it should not be called guilt, but insanity. We may appeal to every page of history we have hitherto turned over, for proofs irrefutable, that the people, when they have been unchecked, have been as unjust, tyrannical, brutal, barbarous and cruel as any king or senate possessed of uncontrollable power. The majority has eternally and without one exception usurped over the rights of the minority. My opinion is, and always has been, that absolute power intoxicates alike despots, monarchs, aristocrats and democrats."

The Founders had a devotion to divided, limited, balanced government, following Montesquieu: "A legislative, an executive and a judicial power comprehended the whole of what is meant and understood by the term government. It is by balancing each of these powers against the other two, that the efforts of human nature towards tyranny can alone be checked and restrained, and any degree of freedom be preserved in the constitution." Adams preferred the concept of virtue to liberty; indeed, enduring liberty is the child of virtue. "We must not depend alone upon the love of liberty in the soul of men for its preservation. It cannot be discussed in the abstract as if it were totally independent of public virtue. Liberty must be under Law, but even the compass of civil laws does not sufficiently hedge liberty; under the best of laws freedom may still be infringed if virtue is lacking. The fallibility of man-his credulity, his egotism, his indolence, his violence-means that the best chance to attain justice and freedom lies in keeping power away from the hands of ambitious, corrupt men."

Man, being obliged by nature to live in society, without which he cannot survive, is obliged to preserve society in order to preserve himself. If men are in a state wherein they cannot exist without society, and have the judgement to discern what is capable of preserving that society, can he but conclude that he is obliged to follow those rules which conduce to that preservation? The purpose of uniting under governments is to preserve all men in their "Lives, Liberties, and Estates," which Locke calls by the general name of Property. To accomplish this goal, government must establish, "settled, known Law," which must accord with the Law of Nature; provide a known and indifferent judge, with Authority to determine all differences according to the established Law; to provide power to give such decisions, and execute them. Thus constituted, government can have no powers except such as are compatible with the end for which it is established; and it cannot act arbitrarily, depart from its own laws, take from any man his property without his consent, or delegate the law-making power to other hands. If government violates these strictures, it ceases to be legitimate and can be legitimately overthrown.

Virtue entailed firmness, courage, endurance, industry, frugal living, strength, manliness and an unremitting devotion to the weal of the Republic, a community of virtuous men. If public virtue declined so did the Republic, and if it declined too far, the Republic died. Manhood gave way to effeminacy, republican liberty to licentiousness, licentiousness to anarchy, and from there to tyranny. What was sought was a moral solution to the mortality of republics-make better people-rather than socio-political solutions-make better arrangements. Puritanism made any matter that might in any way contribute to strengthening or weakening the virtue of the public become subject to regulation by the public. Public virtue cannot exist in a Nation without private, and public Virtue is the only Foundation of Republics. Those seeking better arrangements cautioned against basing public good on private virtue, as public evils could just as well emanate from private vices. The trouble was that the world always contains a few wicked and designing men who were perpetually trying to destroy the polity, and it was against them that one must be vigilant.

John Randolph denounced the democratic proclivity to enlarge the sphere of positive law. The democratic passion for legislating was a menace to liberty. There exists the rage to make new and repeal old laws. "I do not think we would find ourselves at all worse off if no law of a general nature had been passed by either General or State Governments for the ten or twelve years past. Like Mr. Jefferson, I am averse to too much regulation." For Randolph, prescriptive right, common law and custom afforded the real guarantees of justice and liberty. Once men commence tinkering with government, lopping and adding and stimulating and new modelling, they imperil those old prerogatives and immunities which are the fruits of many generations of growth. Arbitrary intervention in the process is a short and nasty way to social calamity. When a people begin to think that they can improve society by incessant alteration of positive law, nothing remains settled: every right, every bit of property, every attachment to family, home and countryside is endangered. Such a people soon presume themselves to be omnicompetent, and the farther their affairs fall into confusion, the more enthusiastic they become for some legislative panacea, which promises to be the answer.

Randolph suggested habitually and regularly restricting the scope of government to its original, narrow limits and basing all government, and participation therein, upon practical considerations, rather than philosophical speculation. Let the objects of government be few and clearly defined, let all important powers be reserved to the states, outside the scope of federal authority. State powers must be asserted so that local and personal liberties may endure-the smaller the unit of government, the less possibility of usurpation, and the more immediate and powerful the operation of prescriptive influences. At the local level corruption and negligence is too conspicuous to pervade for any length of time. Few great abuses could be hidden as they are in today's trillion-dollar legislative bills. In the ideal community the personal, morally directed self-government of each person should be enough to generate the common good of all. In practice this burdens each individual with a maximum of responsibility which few of us are willing to assume and execute. There is an urge to push away this moral obligation each of us must embrace and discharge. The urge to escape responsibility then proceeds to rationalize the advantages of bigger, more remote, more centralized administration of troublesome problems. When mistakes are made the error is too far away for local revision. The original sin of personal irresponsibility comes full circle and personal liberty is ready for a permanent decline. The lesson for the people in the Federal government is clear-*keep the authority to raise money and the power to spend it as far away from their sources-the people-as possible.*

Madison affirmed the temporal and eternal personal responsibility of the individual citizen: "our entire political experiment swings upon our capacity to govern ourselves according to the moral law." The only people who can afford the great luxury of a civil government strictly limited by Law are those who recognize and are willing to live by the concept of Natural Rights. The Bill of Rights intended to withdraw entirely from political control the faculties of the individual and the instruments of initiative and enterprise. No law might be passed against the freedom of the mind, nor to restrict the interchange of ideas, nor the expression of private opinion from individuals directed towards the government. No man's home (private property) might be entered except on formal warrant in pursuit of specific charges authorized by law and confined to the named purpose; no private property might be taken for public use without just compensation. Furthermore, steps were taken to forestall attempts on the part of government to nullify theses safeguards by indirect means-excessive fines larger than the offense warrants meant to intimidate and confiscate property on any pretext. The restrictions contained in the treason clause go on to define guilt as personal, and property as belonging to the individual. Both are in opposition to the collectivist theory of the group as superior or antecedent to the individual, and to the Greek idea of generational guilt that follows members of a family. Heretofore in Europe laws allowed punishment for all the members of a family for the crime of any one member. Since the family was the political unit and honors were inherited and privilege pertained to all members of the family, it appeared equitable and logical that the whole family should suffer proportionately for the delinquency of any one member. Likewise, the family property was held to be forfeit altogether by the fault of the head of the family. Thus, with a charge of treason the secular ruler-many of the later Caesars-could use the family unit as a pretext for confiscating all the family property. He could fall back on the political system of feudalism where land was held in tenancy from the crown, and that tenancy lapsed when the tenant failed in allegiance.

If human nature in general cannot be much improved, each individual may bring his own impulses under control-shunning vice and cultivating virtue. Only through the moral striving of many men can free government be secured, and society made stable. The good man is conservative through habit and choice. He is alert to the identity and malignity of the vices to be shunned. Self-government is for moral men; those who would be free must be virtuous. Education starts a man on the path that leads through virtue to freedom, and consequently shapes civilization. Its great mission is to act as a conserving, civilizing force: to convey to each man his share of the inherited wisdom of the race, to train him to lead a moral, self-disciplined life and foster a love for order. He must be taught his community's values and be integrated into its structure. If men would cultivate individual virtues, social problems would take care of themselves. Reforming men will go just as far as limiting the size and scope of government. Some will say that limiting government *will tend* to the reformation of men. Edmund Burke wrote that "the happiness to be found through virtue in all conditions is the true moral equality of mankind; not the monstrous fiction, which by inspiring false ideas and vain expectations into men destined to travel in the obscure walk of a laborious life, serves only to aggravate and embitter that real inequality, which it can never remove; and which the order of civil life establishes as much for the benefit of those whom it must leave in a humble state, as those whom it is able to exalt to a condition more splendid, but not more happy."

In the unrolling of history, millennia of human experience have implanted proper judgements and means in the mind of the species. The foundation of human welfare is not divine providence but the development of reason. What then is the foundation of authority in morals and politics? By what standard may men judge the prudence of any particular act, and the justice of it? Natural Law has taught humanity, through thousands of years, a collective wisdom: tradition tempered by experience. Millenia of experience have taught man how to sublimate his wilder nature in a precarious restraint-consisting of myth, ritual, instinct and prejudice. "The ordinance of heaven is termed the natural law; the principle which directs us to conform our actions to the natural law is called the rule of moral conduct, or the right path; the organized system of rules of moral conduct which puts us on this path is called the doctrine of duties or of institutions."

Evil exists independently of social and economic maladjustments; we must search for the source of our discontents in defective human nature rather than a defective social order. Men, far from being malleable, are subject to cultural alteration only slowly and to a limited degree. They are mysterious and complex beings, and no amount of psychological probing will ever fully explain them. Man needs all the help he can get from education, tradition and institutions if he is to enjoy even a limited success in his political experiments. The collective wisdom of the community, itself the union of countless partial and imperfect wisdoms, is alone equal to the task. It is a product of centuries of growth, not something that can be dismantled and reassembled, without great destruction. It is natural in origin and natural in development. Laws and institutions are likewise the result of centuries of growth, not the fiat of one administration.

Rejecting the notion of a world subject only to impulse and appetite, conservatives expound the idea of a world governed by strong purpose. "You would not cure evil by resolving, that there would be no more monarchs, nor ministers of state, nor of the gospel; no interpreters of laws; no general officers; no public councils…Wise men will apply their remedies to vices, not to names." Christianity, the carrier of our heritages from Israel, Greece, and Rome has been a major support of American liberty and morality. What is necessary for man to further advance, though, is to base his ethic on reality, not faith. Only then can it be lasting. Change will continue to be the essence of American life and it should be channeled by the Right into areas of progress. If reality is a world without God and Authoritative Government, a wasteland of withered hopes and crying loneliness, then man should realize and accept this fact and work to make his world better. Until morality can stand without the sanction of religious faith or autocratic power Man will not progress. The desire of a certain type of conservative to re-instill the fear of God into society, is in effect the desire to return to the days when Kings invoked religion as their sanction on earth; it is the admission that men cannot develop the virtue and discipline necessary to govern themselves; it is a confession that men would rather live a lie than the Truth. It concedes that only a world of immaterial values can be the necessary counterpoise to the mutual envy and greed of man. The whole management and direction of human life depends upon the question of whether or not there is a God and a future state of human existence. Is there a power independent of our senses, independent even of our reason, to which we may appeal against our very selves? Do men have immortal souls, or do they not? Upon one's solution of this inquiry rests the basis of politics; for if men do not possess immortal souls, if there is no higher will, then they must learn the discipline of self-government, or perish.

The Federalist is flatly committed to the central proposition that man can govern himself, but there is no certainty that he will; free government is possible but far from inevitable. The strictures of the new Constitution were designed for men more likely to be moved by "momentary passions and immediate interests" than by "considerations of policy, utility and justice." Power must be diffused and checked, men's rights and property must be protected against the whims of arbitrary power, and the wise and virtuous man must be raised to leadership. Only in this manner can a Republican America enjoy a government based on "the natural authority of the people alone, without a pretense of miracle or mystery." Forms of government that place the power of final decision in one man or group or class or party are unnatural and doomed to failure. The state was made for the man, not man for the state. The American political mind says that the state cannot be anything but the individuals who make it up, and places man rather than the community at the center. America is not as sure of these principles today than it was a century ago. Some have launched the search for a substitute faith. The ideal of American government is one that exists only to protect the individual's rights and clear the way for his energies. The reality has been one of government that intervenes repeatedly to guide and reduce the free play of the individual's interests, always in behalf of a larger interest described as the public or the greater good.

The Left is purposely trying to wreck the Republic and make it again along the lines of an Old- World Government, one that uses force to control its subjects because they believe someone has to do so. It believes that force can produce economic results; they demand that men in Government control the growth of crops, the production of goods, and wages and prices and trade. They believe that men are just cells in a greater organism. All men are naturally dependent, obedient, and controlled by Authority. Government is the Authority, controlling the masses and responsible for their welfare. Therefore, the stronger the Government the better for the masses. If anyone is not willing to obey the Greatest Number, then make him submit and obey. This is not the reasoning of the Americans who wrote the Constitution that at one time protected individual freedom. It is not the reasoning of many Americans now. But they know that there are always enough stupid, dishonest voters to carry any election, when influenced by demagogues, vote-buying and outright fraud.

Americans at this moment are suspending their exercise of individual freedom. They are submitting more than willingly to

Government's control. The practical effect of all similar cases in history are the same; obedience to Authority stops the effective working of human energy to satisfy normal human needs. The use of force against the natural uses of human energy reduces the production and the distribution of wealth-of the material goods that nothing but productive uses of human energy can create. If men believe that Government is responsible for their welfare, the increasing poverty further increases their demand that men in public office control the individual's affairs. This demand further increases the use of force against productive energy. This use of force must progressively destroy all the protections of an American citizen's natural human rights and eventually his life.

CHAPTER TEN-ABRAHAM LINCOLN AND THE 1619 PROJECT

THEODORE WIDMER
CARL SANDBURG

FREDERICK DOUGLASS
RUSSELL KIRK

CLINTON ROSSITER
MARGARET COIT

“I have said that the Declaration of Independence is the ring-bolt to the chain of your nation’s destiny; so indeed, I regard it. The principles contained in that document are saving principles. Stand by those principles, be true to them on all occasions, in all places, against all foes, and at whatever cost.”

“How circumspect, exact and proportionate were all their (the Fathers of the Republic) movements! How unlike the politicians of an hour! Their statesmanship looked beyond the passing moment and stretched away in strength into the distant future. They seized upon eternal principles and set a glorious example in their defense. Mark them!”

“Now, take the Constitution according to its plain reading, and I defy the presentation of a single pro-slavery clause in it. On the other hand, it will be found to contain principles, entirely hostile to the existence of slavery. Interpreted as it ought to be, the Constitution is a glorious liberty document. If it were intended to be, by its Framers and adopters, a slave-holding instrument, why neither slavery, slaveholding nor slave can anywhere be found in it?”

But “fellow citizens, pardon me, allow me to ask, why am I called upon to speak here today? The rich inheritance of justice, liberty, prosperity and independence, bequeathed by your fathers, is shared by you, not by me, or those I represent. To drag a man in fetters into the grand illuminated ‘temple of liberty’ and call upon him to join you in joyous anthems, is an inhuman mockery and sacrilegious irony. Are the great principles of political freedom and of natural justice, embodied in those documents, extended to us? Above your national, tumultuous joy, I hear the mournful wail of millions whose chains, heavy and grievous yesterday, are, today, rendered more intolerable by the jubilee shouts that reach them. This day, to a slave, reveals to him, more than all the other days of the year, the gross injustice and cruelty to which he is the constant victim. To him, your celebration is a sham; your boasted liberty, an unholy license; your national greatness, a swelling vanity; your sounds of rejoicing empty and heartless, your denunciation of tyrants, brass-fronted impudence; your shouts of liberty and equality, hollow mockery; all your religious parade and solemnity, mere bombast and fraud; all a thin veil to cover up crimes which would disgrace a nation of savages."

"We need the storm, the whirlwind and the earthquake. The feeling of the nation must be quickened; the conscience of the nation must be roused; the propriety of the nation must be startled; the hypocrisy of the nation must be exposed, and its crimes against God and man must be proclaimed and denounced."

Frederick Douglass, from his speech *What to the Slave is the Fourth of July?* (1852)

"It were doubtless to be wished that the power of prohibiting the importation of slaves had not been postponed until the year 1808, or rather that it had been suffered to have immediate operation…It ought to be considered as a great point gained in favor of humanity that a period of twenty years may terminate forever, within these states, a traffic of which has so long and so loudly upbraided the barbarism of modern policy; that within that period it will receive a considerable discouragement from the federal government, and may be totally abolished, by a concurrence of the few states which continue the unnatural traffic…"

James Madison, *Federalist* #42

The Left has seemingly exhausted the possibilities of the old schools and forms, and flounders for a time in the search for new patterns and styles, new rules and disciplines. The 1619 Project is the perfect example. 1619 presents itself in the guise of the extraordinary patriotism of the oppressed rather than a movement to overturn traditional society which they see as illegitimate from its earliest beginnings. The aim of the 1619 Project is to create a historical narrative that legitimizes efforts of the Democrat Party to construct an electoral coalition based on the prioritizing of personal 'identities" -i.e., gender, sexual preference, ethnicity, and above all, race. It seeks to enlist slavery as an explanatory mechanism for a long list of grievances against capitalism. It is an attempt to reframe American history; there must be a mythology despite the lack of proof or facts. The left doesn't care what historians with decades of experience think, if it counters the narrative supporting their cause.

It has been tried before; Beard's *Economic Interpretation of History* (1913) was the first attempt to make selfish economic interest the purported purpose of the Declaration, Revolution and subsequent Constitution, rather than life, liberty and the pursuit of happiness for all. Current efforts also put ideology before historical accuracy and understanding. The Left wants to place the consequences of slavery and the contributions of Black Americans at the very center of the United States' national narrative. Slavery is portrayed as a uniquely American phenomenon and construed as a capitalist venture. The Project has been called a dramatic and necessary corrective to the blindly celebratory versions of the founding, to the fundamental lie of the American origin story. It holds that protecting the institution of slavery was *the* primary reason for the American Revolution, a claim for which there is simply no historical evidence. It also claims that *no* aspect of the country that would be formed here has been untouched by the years of slavery. Another of its arguments is that black Americans have been the only consistent contributors to American progress culturally, economically and politically. It puts bad history at the service of contemporary ideological and policy agendas. The Vice-President of the United States called the 1619 project a "masterpiece."

It is in fact a distorted economic history borrowed from the bad scholarship of trying to connect everything to slavery; presented in a biased way under the disguise of objectivity; it attempts to indoctrinate citizens to interpret American history as an ongoing drama of racial conflict. It is a divisive and revisionist account of history that threatens the integrity of the union by denying the true principles on which it was founded. It marks the first year when enslaved Africans arrived on Virginia soil as our nation's foundational date. This is an 'origin story', not a work of history. When journalists use the past in an effort to shape contemporary policy, the temptation to distort or ignore facts that do not fit their narrative or are unlikely to help realize the policy objective is overwhelming. This is not conducive to an accurate understanding of the past and how it shapes the present. Advocacy journalism, such as this effort by the New York Times, is held to a much lower standard of accuracy than scholarship and intentionally blends factual content with normative propositions aimed at producing a particular political stance. 1619's core economic argument is that many of the contemporary business practices, protocols and institutions that characterize modern American capitalism go back directly to the brutal world of Southern plantations. But double-entry accounting, depreciating assets on the books of a company, and futures contracts for commodities were developed either earlier or elsewhere, and for other purposes than the perpetuation of slavery. Their ideas put an ill-informed advocacy ahead of historical accuracy; the project's characterizations of slavery in early America reflected laws and practices more common in the Southern Antebellum feudal era than colonial times. It is the attempt to weaponize the brutality of the plantation system in order to launch a sweeping political attack on free market capitalism in the present day. It cannot be argued that slaveholders were practicing capitalism simply because they made money.

The 1619 Project lays claim to a competing black radical historiographic tradition, embodying significant errors which appears driven by a desire to promote a particular ideological outlook rather than providing historical truth. To the extent that the black experience and the role played by slavery in American economic history have been ignored or misrepresented-then it is a worthy exercise. But its problematical argumentation and absent or questionable sources will result in the perpetuation of misleading claims about slavery and its significance for American capitalism. It also encourages people to take a more favorable view of extensive government intervention in the economy, whether in the form of public ownership, greater regulation, or wider redistributions of income and wealth.

The Left wants to "reimagine" and revise the "narrative" of history rather than reexamine the facts. Instead of taking our bearings from the eternal truths enshrined in the Declaration the Left argues that slavery is the lens through which all of America's successes, and its failures, good and bad, must be understood. Leading historians on both sides have examined the contentions and found no evidence to support them. But as idealogues the truth or falsity of the assertions make no difference; it is the maintenance of the narrative that is more important. Manipulation of public opinion can make people reject obvious facts when catering to the existing perceptions and interests. You cannot change their minds even when you expose them to authentic information. A person who is de-moralized is unable to assess true information. 1619 is clearly an effort to tarnish contemporary American capitalism by associating it with slavery through giving exaggerated claims and partial and inaccurate accounts of history. It is seen as the way to encourage an acceptance of economic policies best described as Progressive or Democratic Socialism, as it implies that one way to address slavery's alleged effects is for the State to add to its power by taking on more government economic functions. The Left is working for the ideological destruction of capitalism so that society can more readily adopt the rhetoric and political ideals of the ruling party.

Slavery is among the world's oldest and most ubiquitous institutions. It was a cruel and brutal world that existed in the premodern societies of the West. Slaves were held in Greece and Rome and Persia and Africa, and almost everywhere else, but that does not discredit the positive contributions those civilizations contributed to our lives, nor does it require us to ignore those contributions, and beat our breasts in contrition. Native Americans held slaves for centuries before 1619. The formation and development of the United States cannot be understood apart from the international economic and political processes that gave rise to the New World. Slavery had existed since ancient times and became an international economic institution stretching from the heart of Africa to the shipyards of Britain, the banking houses of Amsterdam and New York, and the plantations of the South, Brazil and the Caribbean. Slavery was one inescapable and politically tragic legacy of the global foundation of the United States. Slavery flourished in the mercantile, feudal economic systems of the period from the late 1500's until the early 19th century, whereas slavery declined as capitalism began to emerge in the late 18th century. The US was not founded to protect slavery, but race relations *are* central to our story, without denying the roles of other influences or erasing the contributions of whites of good will. 1619 is untrue to the actual history because it leaves out so much. It paints a one-sided picture of American progress as simply a record of heroic black virtue triumphing over persistent white vice. An accurate picture of our history presents a comprehensive picture that 1619 theory seek to suppress.

The importance of teaching about slavery and racism as part of our history is undeniable. Blacks endured whippings, torture, hangings, mutilations, castrations, forced sterilizations, beatings, being water hosed and bitten by dogs. Slavery, Jim Crow, segregation, denial of civil rights, unfair housing, redlining, lack of equal education, unfair employment practices, police profiling, unfair sentencing and incarceration practices were and are reprehensible. Viewed from the perspective of those historically denied rights enumerated in America's founding documents, the story of the country's great men necessarily looks different. While to build the self-esteem of young blacks by teaching them about the truths of America might be a worthy mission, to build it on faulty and incomplete premises does not bode well for the long-term self-confidence of students who buy into the thesis without serious vetting against reliable sources of our history. Why indoctrinate students with a narrative that only further prevents them from assimilating and being successful? If assimilation is not the goal, then revolution and destruction of the current culture is all that is left. No effort to educate the American public in order to advance social justice can afford to dispense with the basic facts.

One can only enter such an enterprise believing that its major objective is to promote predetermined outcomes and political goals in the future. Therein lies the path to compromising the scholarly standards that help elucidate the truth of the matter. Poor blacks don't have the benefit of deriving from history any illumination of their present condition, any guidance for their judgments and policies, any guard against the rebuffs of surprise from the vicissitudes of change. The population that had scarcely adapted to a transition from bondage to freedom, from an agricultural basis to the industrial order and then to entrepreneurism is now required to adapt themselves once more to the information age.

The Founders were flawed. The nation is imperfect. The Declaration and the Constitution are nevertheless the summary of all man's attempts to emancipate himself from the burdens of arbitrary Authority. The Left is not seeking that end, but rather to re-submit themselves to a new elite. America is a nation born of debate and has developed through argument and even war, to resolve its political conflicts. To eliminate the "white" ideals and leading actors of the nation's history is also to teach a dishonest version of the facts. The civic impact of this kind of history can only be detrimental to the trust that is needed across the color line in America that enables racial and ethnic diversity to strengthen and not weaken our national unity. Making black Americans the only heroes of the story as they contested against their white oppressors serves to polarize our civic life and make problems increasingly difficult to solve within the framework of the Constitution, laws and courts. The fact that American history includes slavery and other injustices does not mean that the country was founded on and defined by racism and that our founding principles, our Constitution and our way of life should be overthrown. The American ideals that were to be realized only in a far-off future made them no less valid. The 1619 project ignores the fact that the first real anti-slavery movement in the world, that of the Northern abolitionists, took place in New England. Substantial numbers of white Americans worked, fought and died to free and educate the slaves, and then ensure that they had civil rights. The countervailing tendencies against racism, led by whites, have been just as an important theme in American history, alongside the black struggle for equal rights.

American history is the story of a people and a nation that always sought the improvement of mankind, the advancement of liberty and justice, the broadening of the pursuit of happiness for all. The Christian heritage of justice and virtue working on the English heritage of Law and liberty shaped the American tradition. A white people who have never had to think about how to wipe out an oppressive past have thought of liberty as a heritage to be preserved rather than as a goal to be fought for. The result, conceivably, was part of the reason that the movement towards ending black slavery in the country moved so slowly. There was no empathy for their situation. If the point of the 1619 Project is to think of the effort to live up to our ideals as part of the larger freedom story, that only makes sense if those founding ideals in the Declaration are indeed our founding ideals, which is exactly what the 1619 Project denies. If the nation's founding principles really are racism and oppression, then it is senseless to celebrate any effort to realize such ideals. To adopt the 1619 founding date over 1776 means to accept a particular understanding of the nature of what it means to be an American-one profoundly contrary to that expressed in both the nation's founding documents and subsequent amendments. It is the logical consequence of a certain conception of what America stands for-one that regards the nation as pledged to oppression, not liberation.

A political ideology is a set of principles aimed at establishing and maintaining a certain social system; it is a program of long-range action, with the principles serving to unify and integrate particular steps into a consistent course. It is only by means of principles that men can project the future and choose their actions accordingly. Conservatism's most celebrated principle, originalism, holds that the Constitution can only be interpreted and understood as an expression of the framer's intent. If that intent was profoundly shaped by their racism or self-interest as slaveholders, then this way of seeing the Constitution is problematic. The ideals of freedom and individual rights are not just part of a tradition but are the source of the country's legal existence. Institutional legitimacy is premised on the self-evident truths to which the founders pledged their sacred honor. Lincoln said that the Declaration's truths were the definitions and axioms of American nationhood, and anyone that denies their viability is supplanting the principles of free government. People have no choice but to believe in this literal interpretation of the principles in the Declaration. We cannot pick and choose what parts of history we think are important and what is not. The story that should have been told was the struggle of Americans whose ancestors were once excluded or exploited and whose victories are still too little known. It has only served an honorable purpose of viewing the civil rights movement in light of the covenants of American liberty. Everything that makes America great originates in the fact that Americans do not take the sale of human flesh as the source of their nationhood and are disgusted by what that would say about their nation.

The Revolution was not just the dissolving of political bands with England but a new direction for economics. The Wealth of Nations was also published in 1776. Far from accentuating the slavery-plantation-feudal economy, the Declaration and Adam Smith's book marked the beginning of its inevitable and uninterrupted decline. The decisive forces gaining power in this era are the developing economic energies. These changes were gradual, sometimes imperceptible, but with an irresistible cumulative effect.

Men, pursuing their interests, are rarely aware of the ultimate results of their activity. Yes, the commercial activities of the eighteenth century developed the wealth of Europe by means of slavery and monopoly. But in so doing it helped create the industrialism of the nineteenth century, which turned around and destroyed the power of commerce based on slavery and all its works. Since the existence of slavery was contrary to the trend of economic forces and moral convictions throughout the world, with the passage of time servitude would have faded away without the need for interference from the federal government. Government meddling and private fanaticism could imperil the Union but not resolve great social questions. Without a grasp of this, which was not presented anywhere in the 1619 project, any history of the period is meaningless.

The nation's founders recognized the evil of slavery and said repeatedly that it could not be reconciled with their principles. John Quincy Adams knew Jefferson, Washington, Madison and Monroe. He observed their lives and wrote that they all abhorred slavery. They all said that the doctrine of equality rendered slavery anathema. The wildest Abolitionist in the Northern states need only consult the writings of Jefferson, from the time of the Declaration and during the whole of his lifetime down to his very last year, to find a justification and confirmation for everything he (the abolitionist) thought on the subject of slavery, and a description of the horrors of slavery greater than they themselves could express, all written by the greatest of the Founders. These opponents of slavery were hardly fringe figures in American history. Adams insisted that the "wise rulers of the land" had counseled to "repair the injustice" of slavery, not perpetuate it.

The Constitution, forming the federal form of government, unhappily admitted the ambiguous expedient of slavery. That the subject was embarrassing is indicated by the language; the words slave and slavery do not appear. But the brute fact remained that there were slaves; the Constitution did not pronounce them free by right. The lasting injury of this inclusion of slavery was that it vitiated the principle on which the new nation came into being. Later emancipation could never be exactly equivalent to starting with liberty as a natural right from which the authority for self-government could be derived. The moral defect caused an equivalent structural defect, as it was bound to do. The Federal Union was so desirable that the point of returning slaves to their owners in the South, instead of freeing them as the laws of the Northern states required, was conceded. The conflict remained in abeyance, while the hope remained that slavery would be gradually extinguished. The Federal government's control of the borders meant that it had the authority to at least forbid further importation of slaves from abroad.

The divisions between North and South began as early as the late 1770's. It went to the heart of the fundamental disagreement rapidly emerging among American leaders over the virtuous character of the American people and the nature of the republican society being formed. One side was said to have the desire to reverse the Revolution and to establish an aristocratic and mercantile society that would allow full play to private interests. Such men laughed at virtue, were commercial and interested. If allowed to flourish they would eventually destroy America's experiment in republicanism. But it was the principles and manners of New England-the manners of a wise, attentive, sober, diligent and frugal people, that had produced that spirit which finally established the independence of America. Southern fears of leveling tendencies and the New Englanders' dislike of the aristocratic and luxurious manners of the South-an antagonism implicit from the beginning-became more and more exposed. By the early 1780's many New Englanders saw themselves as the last bastion of devout republicanism standing against the torrent of vice that was sweeping America, though changes were happening in places like Boston as well. What kind of people were Americans anyhow? This was the fundamental thought of the 1780's.

Men in the South so loved their life upon the soil that they sought out in literature and history peoples who had lived a similar life, so they might justify and further stimulate their own ways and set a high goal for themselves among the great nations which had sprung from the land. The people who they admired most were the Greeks and the Romans of the early Republic. Of the Greeks, their oratory, their philosophy, their art-especially their architecture-all appealed to the South. However, it was the Romans of the early Republic, before land speculators and corn laws had driven men from the soil to the city slums, who they most desired to emulate. It was Cincinnatus, who rose from the plow to lead in a troubled time, even more than Cato, who Southerners respected most. This agrarian society had its own interests, which in almost all respects diverged from the interests of the industrial system of the North. The two sections, North and South, had entered the Revolution against the mother country with the full knowledge of the opposing interests of their societies; knowing this difference, they had combined in a loose union under the Articles of Confederation. Finally, they had joined together under the Constitution, fully conscious that there were thus united two divergent economic and social systems, two civilizations, in fact. The two sections were evenly balanced in population and in the number of states, so that at the time there was no danger of either section's encroaching upon the interests of the other. This balance was clearly understood; without it the union would not have been possible. Even with the understanding that the two sections would continue to hold this even balance, the sections were very careful to define and limit the powers of the federal government lest one section with its peculiar interests should get control of the national government and use the powers of that government to exploit the other section. Specific powers were granted the federal government, and all not specifically granted were retained by the states. But equilibrium was impossible with expansion and growth; one section would become dominant and control the national government and either exploit the other section or else fail to exercise the functions of government for its positive benefit. Herein lay the struggle between the agrarian South and the commercial and industrial North, at least as important as the conflict between slavery and freedom. The industrial North demanded a high tariff so as to monopolize the domestic markets-especially the South-for the South, being agrarian, must purchase all its manufactured goods. It was an exploitive principle, originated at the expense of the South and for the benefit of the North. The South fought the tariff to the point of nullification and then to the extent of dissolving the Union. Southerners saw that what was good for the North was fatal to the South. The industrial North demanded a national subsidy for the shipping business and merchant marine, neither of which was important to the South. The industrial North demanded internal improvements-infrastructure-roads, canals and railroads, at national expense to furnish transportation for its goods to Southern and Western markets which were already hedged around for the benefit of the North by the tariff wall. The burden of this would be heavier on the South and the benefits greater for the North. The North favored a government-controlled bank; Andrew Jackson let its charter run out and paid off the debts of the country for the last time. The South believed that its re-institution would be to the sole benefit of the North. Nowhere in the Constitution were these matters specifically mentioned. The North was demanding positive action on the part of the federal government; the South was demanding that no action be taken at all. As a general principle the agrarian South asked little of the federal government in domestic legislation. These differences alone made the conflict inevitable; two different political philosophies had been developed and were evident in the very nature of the demands of the sections: centralization in the North and states' rights in the South. The North had interests which demanded positive legislation exploitive of the agrarian South; the South had interests which demanded that the federal government refrain entirely from legislation within its bounds-it demanded only to be let alone. Though language and religion were the same, and though race was not widely different, two distinct nations had grown up, clearly separated in their merits and their defects, in character, manners, aspirations and interests, resulting in profound and lasting differences between North and South.

In the early years of the Republic, all of the measurable factors were preponderantly in favor of the slave states. They had ample and varied natural resources; their products were in demand by a world market, affording cash and credit. They had the prestige bequeathed by their great statesmen as a political asset. Southern conservatism found its most able spokesman in John C. Calhoun-Secretary of War under James Monroe, elected vice-president under John Quincy Adams *and* Andrew Jackson, Senator from South Carolina, and Secretary of State under John Tyler-he embodied most of the contradictions present in the national debate over slavery. In trying to defend the patriarchal slave-plantation system, he spoke of the supremacy of the Southern cultural legacy, rather than of Natural Rights: "Man's social and political state is-the one for which his creator made him, and the only one in which he can preserve and perfect his race…Instead of being born free and equal, men are born subject, not only to parental authority, but to the laws and institutions of the country where born, and under whose protection they draw their first breath. It is a great and dangerous error to suppose that all people are equally entitled to liberty. It is a reward to be earned, not a blessing to be gratuitously lavished on all alike-a reward reserved for the intelligent, the patriotic, the virtuous and deserving-and not a boon to be bestowed on a people too ignorant, degraded and vicious, to be capable of either appreciating or of enjoying it. These greatest and dangerous errors have their origin in the prevalent opinion that all men are born free and equal-than which, nothing can be more unfounded and false."

Where Calhoun was perhaps right was his characterization of the causes and benefits of inequality: "Now, as individuals differ greatly from each other, in intelligence, sagacity, energy, perseverance, skill, habits of industry and economy, physical power, position and opportunity-the necessary effect of leaving all men free to exert themselves to better their condition, must be a corresponding inequality between those who may possess these qualities and advantages in a high degree, and those who may be deficient in them…It is, indeed, this inequality of condition between the front and the rear ranks, in the march of progress, which gives so strong an impulse to the former to maintain their position, and to the latter to press forward into their files. This gives to progress its greatest impulse. To force the front rank back to the rear or attempt to push forward the rear into line with the front, by the interposition of the government, would put an end to the impulse, and effectually arrest the march of progress." Liberty is the noblest and highest reward for the development of our faculties-moral and intellectual. The men at the top of the order formed the most natural and socially most valuable of all aristocracies: the aristocracy of personal achievement. Civilization was one long anxious search for just such individuals. Liberty and complete equality, far from being inseparable, are incompatible, if by pure equality is meant equality of condition. The natural aristocrat, elevated above his fellow men by his superior energy and ability, had the duty to act as the agent and trustee for his less well-off brethren. Calhoun was perhaps more realistic than most Americans about the facts of class warfare and worked to prevent the agrarian South from going the way of the industrial North. He cherished a way of life and strove ably and sincerely to save it from ruin.

Calhoun's doctrine of state sovereignty was fully evolved in South Carolina before the crusade had begun against slavery. State Rights was meant to protect things far more fundamental and larger than slave property. By upholding the doctrine of a rigid division of powers between state and nation and the literal interpretation of the Constitution such legislation as protective tariffs, ship subsidies, national banks, internal improvements at federal expense would be avoided. A policy of State Rights was the only safe bulwark between Northern exploitation and encroachment. To throw all the varied regional interests under one government would be to sacrifice all the minority interests to the one which was represented by the largest population and body of voters. The Southern idea was local self-government and decentralization so that each region should be able to defend itself against the encroachment of the other regions. An unmixed agrarian society such as Jefferson and Calhoun envisioned called forth no positive program; it called for only enough government to prevent men from injuring one another. It might not make for a neat and orderly system of government, but this was the price of social and economic freedom, the price of bringing into one Union so many different groups and interests.

The greatest vested interest was personal liberty, along with the old Anglo-Saxon principles expressed in the Magna Carta, engrafted finally in every state constitution as "bills of rights". These guaranteed freedom of religion, speech, assembly, petition and thought; freedom from arbitrary arrest and imprisonment, right of trial by jury, and prohibited the taking of property without due process of law-guaranteed, in short, the fundamental rights which Jefferson called the inalienable rights of man and Locke and Rousseau had called the natural rights-rights of life, liberty and property, and their free pursuit. The Virginia and Kentucky Resolutions of 1798-9 had been directed at the violation of these liberties. The Alien and Sedition laws which had been pushed through Congress during the John Adams administration struck at many. Under the Sedition Act men had been prosecuted for criticizing the President, members of Congress or judges, some had been sent to prison in violation of the Constitutional guarantee of freedom of speech. Opinion had been suppressed, arbitrary arrests made, men held without trial; in fact, the whole body of personal liberties had been brushed aside by the Federalist or centralizing party eight years after the signing of the Constitution. Jefferson and Madison proclaimed that the federal government had thus shown itself to be an unsafe protector of liberty. Jefferson, in his 1800 inaugural, announced that states were "the most competent administrations of our domestic concerns, and the surest bulwark against anti-republican tendencies. The founder of the agrarian party of the South and West upheld State Rights as the safest guardian of the liberties and the domestic interests of the people.

But before the Southern doctrine, which was the defense mechanism for its entire system of society, could be employed, it was confused with the issue of slavery, insuring its demise. Certainly, the slavery question furnished more fuel to sectional conflict and created more bitterness than all the other elements dividing the two sections. Because slaveholding was the acid test as to whether a state would remain agrarian or become industrial, the Northern leaders wished that no more slave states should be admitted from the Western territories. It was a question of whether the territories would be equally open to both or whether the North should have an exclusive right to found its own states and system and thereby destroy the balance of power and control the federal government in the interest of its own economic and social system. As state's rights was conflated with slavery so the North clothed their political arguments in the moral language of the abolitionist. It was good politics to speak of it as a struggle for freedom when it was essentially a struggle for power. The South, in the political atmosphere formed by the eighteenth century, did not realize its genius in time, but continued to defend itself inarticulately on the political terms of the North, and thus waited too long and lost its cause, allowing its rival to gain the ascendancy. The South might not have been defeated if it had been able to bring out a further body of doctrine setting forth its true conviction that the ends of men require more for their realization than mere politics.

Neither the victory of the Revolution nor the establishment of the United States solved the problem of slavery. The economic conditions for its abolition had not sufficiently matured. But the economic development of the United States-wage based industry in the North and the cotton, sugar and slave-based plantation economy in the South-intensified the contradictions between two increasingly incompatible systems. The corroding issue of Negro slavery forced the Southern gentry, and its political spokesmen, to re-examine the whole pattern of Southern life. The struggle to preserve an agrarian, stratified, slaveholding, essentially static society produced the implacable issues leading to the Civil War. Central to the middle-class revolution in the North was an unprecedented celebration of work-any work-and for wages, making the slaveholding South seem more anomalous than ever. Slavery required a culture of leisure that Northern labor-clerks, merchants, farmers and millworkers-held in contempt. The leisured gentry in the South were parasites living off the work of others.

Thus, the two sections clashed at every point. Their economic systems and interests conflicted. Their social systems were hostile; their political philosophies growing out of their economic and social systems were as impossible to reconcile as it is for two points to occupy the same space on a line. Their philosophies of life, growing out of the whole situation in each section, were as two elements in deadly combat. When the balance of power was destroyed by the rapid growth of the North, and the destruction of this balance was signaled by the election of Lincoln of a frankly sectional, hostile political party, the South dissolved its partnership with the industrial North.

The problem of slavery was inescapably linked with loose or strict construction of the Constitution and state powers. Preceding the War, the slavery controversy confused and blurred any analysis of political principle in the South; it was impossible to discern where interest in state sovereignty left off and interested pleading for slave property commenced. The whole grim slavery problem, to which no satisfactory answer was possible, warped and discolored the American political mind, on either side of the debate, for the first two-thirds of the nineteenth century. Southerners perceived that the drift of the world was not toward a tranquil, agricultural life but toward a consolidated and industrialized new order. The menace of a debased, ignorant, and abysmally poor folk, outside the protection of laws, except for their existence as protected property, and largely outside the influence of churches, must have been in the back of each white Southerners mind. A slave-class, disconnected with the whole fabric of established society, must tend to produce in the minds of the dominant people an anxiety to preserve every detail of the present structure of society, and be extra-vigilant about any innovation. Calhoun deliberately entangled the Tariff debate-at bottom a question of whether the industrial or agricultural interests should predominate in America-with slavery, so as to enlist in his camp a greater body which otherwise might have been indifferent to the issue: "Once the principle, that it is the absolute power of majorities to do as they like is accepted, the liberties of no section or class are safe." Having passed the 1828 Tariff of Abominations (setting a 38% tax on imported goods) and the Force Bill (empowering President Jackson to employ the Army to force South Carolina to comply with the law), the interests which reduced South Carolina to submission would proceed on to other conquests. "After we are exhausted, the contest will be between the capitalists and the operatives in the Northern cities; for into these two classes, it must, ultimately, divide society. The issue of the struggle here must be the same as it has been in Europe. Under the operation of such a system, wages must sink more rapidly than the prices of the necessaries of life, till the portion of the products of their labor left to them, will be barely sufficient to preserve existence." These words of Calhoun were written in 1828, twenty years before the promulgation of the Communist Manifesto, warning the old agricultural interest, the new industrial interest, and the yet inchoate masses of industrial labor that when law is employed to oppress any class or section, the end of constitutions and the substitution of ruthless power is at hand.

The Federalists believed that security of property, stable government, respect for religious conviction, recognition of distinctions between man and man-could be best protected by a strong central government, vested with extensive powers and capable of indefinite expansion. Southerners were convinced that consolidation, economic or political, would breach the wall of tradition, and establish in America a unitary state-arbitrary, omnicompetent, manipulated for the benefit of a dominant majority for the pursuit of the new industries. They preferred the slow process of natural change, guided by prescription and tradition, as distinguished from artificial innovation. The South was determined not to be taxed through the tariffs in order to support Northern industry. The independence of the Southern white made him resent government from any point more remote than his county courthouse. This inclination made the Southerners the most consistent advocates of local liberties and state powers.

Calhoun, as early as 1832, began to discern a necessity greater than 'liberalism' and 'progress' and 'equality.' He faced squarely, as few Americans have, the problem of protecting the many small interests against the relentless pressure of the general interest. One catches here a glimpse of a solitary, powerful, melancholy mind which had pierced through the cloud of transitory political haggling to see a future of social turbulence and moral desolation: "If there be a political proposition universally true, one which springs directly from the nature of man, and is independent of circumstances-it is, that irresponsible power is inconsistent with liberty, and must corrupt those who exercise it. On this great principle our political system rests. The truth is, the Government of the uncontrolled numerical majority, is but the absolute and despotic from of popular government; just as that of the uncontrolled will of one man, or a few, is of monarchy or aristocracy; and it has, to say the least, a strong tendency to oppression, and the abuse of its powers, as either of the others."

There is no natural right to exercise political power, no historical, physical or moral foundation. A proper foundation can only be drawn from a body qualified by tradition, education, station, property and moral nature, not merely the entire population of a country, lacking proper discipline, taken indiscriminately. The exercise of political power is not an immutable right, but a privilege to be extended to the intelligence and integrity of a population. Majority rule is no more a natural right than is equality. When we accept the principle of majorities in politics, we do so out of an expedient of process, not because it comes out of an abstract moral injunction. Democracy may be wholly bad, or admissible with certain restrictions, according to the time, circumstance and temper of the country. The smaller number possessing reason may be in the right while the larger number may be little else than impetuous appetite.

"We now begin to experience the danger of admitting so great an error (equality) to have a place in the declaration of our independence. For a long time, it lay dormant; but in the process of time, it began to germinate, and produce its poisonous fruits…Instead, then, of all men having the same right to liberty and equality, as is claimed by those who hold that they were all born free and equal, liberty is the noble and highest reward only to be bestowed on mental and moral development, combined with favorable circumstance." (Calhoun)

Calhoun said that a civil war would shake the nation to its foundations; and whatever the outcome of that war, the United States could never again be the same people under the same laws. He had believed that the Republic was guided by a benevolent popular reason; now it was manifest that if reason operated in the enactment of the new tariff, it was malignant reason, calculated to plunder the people of one section in order to benefit a class of persons in another. Given selfish interest sufficiently powerful, Calhoun saw that grasping majorities would warp the Constitution to suit their ends. It was clear that Congressmen who should uphold the popular sense of right had voted for the tariff of 1824 merely to gratify the avarice of their constituents.

Calhoun repeated the Antifederalist arguments of 1788: "The naked question is whether ours is a federal or a consolidated government, a constitutional or absolute one; a government resting ultimately on the solid basis of the sovereignty of the states or on the unrestrained will of a majority; a form of government, as in all other unlimited ones, in which injustice, and violence, and force must finally prevail. We have acted, with some exceptions, as if the General Government had the right to interpret its own powers, without limitation or check; under such operation of the system, we already see, in whatever direction we turn our eyes, the growing symptoms of disorder and decay-the growth of faction and corruption, and the decay of patriotism, integrity and disinterestedness. Mark the approach of the fatal hour; and come it will, unless there be a speedy and radical change-a return to the great conservative principles which brought the Republic into being."

"We should not judge whether a state is governed justly and freely by the abstract equality, or numerical preponderance of a portion of its citizens, but whether individuals are protected in their separate interests, against monarchs or majorities, by a constitution founded upon compromise. If a government by unequal fiscal action, divides the community into two principal classes of those who pay taxes, and those who receive the benefits, this is tyranny, however egalitarian in theory." So, Calhoun comes to the doctrine of concurrent majorities, his most important contribution to political thought. Calhoun proposes to weigh not merely the individual votes of particular persons, but the several wills of large groups in the nation. Differing economic elements, geographical sections, and other distinct interests are to be protected from the encroachments of one another by a mutual negative, or rather a negative commonly available to all. A true majority is not a simple headcount: instead, it is a balancing and compromising of interests, in which all important elements of the population concur, feeling that their rights have been respected. The first regards numbers only, and considers the whole community as a unit, having but one common interest throughout; and collects the sense of the greater number of the whole, as being that of the community. The second regards interests as well as numbers-considering the community as made up of different and conflicting interests, as far as the action of government is concerned; and it takes the sense of each, through its majority or appropriate organ, and the united sense of all, as the sense of the entire community. The former Calhoun called the "numerical or absolute majority" and the latter, the "concurrent or constitutional majority."

Calhoun rejected with scorn the demagogue's abstraction called "the American people." No people exist with identical, homogenous interests; in reality, there are only individuals with vastly differing scales of value. Polling the numerical majority is an attempt to determine the sense of the people, but it is unlikely to ascertain the sense of the true majority: for the rights of important groups may be altogether neglected under such arrangements. In his *Discourse on the Constitution,* he cites as an example the tendency of simple numerical majorities to throw all power into the grasp of an urban population, in effect disenfranchising the rural regions. Groping for a practical remedy, Calhoun turned to Nullification, derived from Jefferson's old Virginia and Kentucky Resolutions: A State might set at defiance any act of Congress clearly unconstitutional, refuse to allow that measure to operate within her boundaries, and appeal to other states for aid and comfort, so that the unscrupulous majority which had enacted the oppressive legislation might behold the power of Laws and be compelled to withdraw their plans. Application of the concurrent-majority principle would allow each region to shape its institutions according to its particular needs; a numerical majority tends to impose standardized and arbitrary patterns upon the whole nation. Historical origin, character of population, physical configuration naturally distinguishes one region from another; the means of protecting and perfecting these separate societies must vary accordingly. *This* is the doctrine of diversity, opposed to the doctrine of uniformity. In his writings Calhoun echoes Montesquieu and Burke.

Democratic institutions will be safer in a nation which has adopted the principle of concurrent majorities, and under such conditions the suffrage may be extended more widely than prudence would otherwise allow, without extending it all the way to the more ignorant and dependent portions of the community. Liberty forced on a people unfit for it is a curse bringing only anarchy. Calhoun's theory of a concurrent majority *was* a conservative, constitutional check: "It is this mutual negative among its various conflicting interests, which invests each with the power of protecting itself-and places the rights and safety of each, where only they can be securely placed, under its own guardianship…it is this negative-the power of preventing or arresting the action of the government-be it called what term it may-veto, interposition, nullification, check, or balance of power-which in fact, forms the Constitution." Had it been adopted, this method of testing majority rule would have brought the Roman Tribunal's veto power full circle to the present.

Government is a contrivance of human wisdom to provide for human wants. Society requires not only that with individuals, but with the mass and body of the people, the inclinations of men should frequently be thwarted, their will controlled, and their passions brought into subjection. This can only be done by a power out of themselves, and not, in the exercise of its function, subject to that will and to those passions which it is its office to bridle and subdue. Calhoun believed that the common inconvenience would dissuade the chief interests from petty interference in the conduct of affairs. Promptness of action is diminished, but a compensating gain in moral power occurs, for harmony and unanimity and the confidence of security from oppression are gained by the nation. The slowness and clumsiness of the law must be tolerated for the sake of the safeguards to liberty and property that wither away in any legal system which accords pride of place to speed. Laws and courts do require constant scrutiny and cautious renovation or improvement; but though they may sometimes even require wholesale reformation, still, when that comes, it ought to be conducted with an eye toward ancient prerogatives, with every precaution to make sure that no person or class suffers a particular injustice in the name of some general benefit, with a solicitude for old ways and private rights. The tribune power could be accompanied by another Roman device, the plural executive, the approval of each being required for the ratification of acts of

Congress. Necessity could provide sufficient incentive to obtain efficient action by the state. Calhoun cites the Roman Republic as his example and confesses the existence of no obstacle which practice and forbearance could not surmount.

Calhoun's philosophical principle is one of the most sagacious and vigorous suggestions ever advanced by American conservatism. The concurrent majority itself; representation of citizens by section and interest, rather than by pure numbers; the insight that liberty is a product of civilization and a reward of virtue rather than an abstract right; the acute distinction between moral equality and equality of condition; the linking of liberty and progress; the strong protest against domination by class or region, under the guise of numerical majority-these concepts give Calhoun a place beside John Adams as one of the two most eminent American political writers.

Calhoun subjected the philosophy of the Founding Fathers to critical analysis; pointed out wherein he conceived it to be faulty; cast aside some of its most sacred doctrines; and provided another basis for the democratic faith he professed. That his own interest in the stability of a feudalistic society, and in slavery, was repugnant to the new cause of freedom, as with the development of Roman Law in the midst of slavery, does not take away from the intellectual achievement of either. Calhoun's concurrent majority was the belief that each minority must have the power to defend itself against public policy determined by mere weight of numbers. While Calhoun failed in his effort to save the Union, he gave Southern conservatism a political philosophy in his unequivocal description of the forbidding problem of the rights of individuals and groups menaced by the will of overbearing majorities.

For the last eighteen years of his life Calhoun sought for some means of reconciling majority claims with minority rights, under the Rule of Law. Nullification succeeded just so far as to prove power can be successfully opposed only by power. Yet the essence of civilized government is reliance not upon power, but upon consent. Can the rights of minorities be adjusted to this grand principle of consent? If not, government is an imposition. For, said Calhoun, governments at heart are designed chiefly to protect individual rights. Preponderant majorities need no protection-they have naked force to maintain themselves. The authors of the Constitution had recognized that the government is the shelter of the individual and had done their best to afford protection by strict limitation of federal powers and the added guarantee of a Bill of Rights. These had not sufficed. When he had finished his work of constitutional reconstruction, Calhoun had reduced Jefferson's philosophy to one of idealism and misplaced humanism. He completed the work of Randolph in demolishing Jefferson's abstract equality and liberty, the rights of which he had assumed to be complimentary, while working to devise an effective check upon numerical preponderance and a tyranny intent upon the manipulation of positive law.

Calhoun concluded, with Plato and John Adams, that "man is left to perfect what the wisdom of the Infinite ordained." Constitutions are in a sense the voice of God expressed through the people; but nature and God work through historical experience, and all sound constitutions are effective embodiments of compromise, reconciling the different interests or portions of the community with one another, in order to avert anarchy. "All constitutional governments take the sense of the community by its parts and regard the sense of all its parts as the sense of the whole, and hence the great and broad distinction between governments is, not that of the one, the few or the many, but between that of the constitutional and the absolute."

While the Constitution abounds in manifold restrictions thought necessary by its framers for the purpose of securing the self-command necessary for the country to remain a nation, the history of the United States has shown that it is not safe to leave unsettled *any* important question concerning the exercise of public powers. The Founders neither guaranteed slavery nor attempted to regulate it, or to provide for its gradual extinction, thrusting the subject of slavery as far as they could from their own sight. The authors of the Constitution purposely declined to apply their political wisdom to a subject which they knew to be all-important, and which would result in a bloody and costly war. The points on which the controversy of slavery turned on were embedded in the original construction of the Constitution, and the fact that the ablest men in the country later took opposite sides proved them to be still unsettled at the critical time. There was no authority recognized by both sides by which the issue could be satisfactorily adjudicated on and decided. It was useless to appeal to the law as, from the South's point of view, the law had been abusively put into operation. It was useless to appeal to the electoral bodies of the country, as they were severely partisan. War was the last resort.

The Civil War in the United States was as much a war of revolution as the break with England; it was a war carried on by adherents of one set of principles and one construction of the Constitution against the adherents of another body of principles and another Constitutional doctrine. The affection for state sovereignty and the traditions of Southern society surrendered to superior force along with General Lee at Appomattox. Consequently, the great majority of people never apprehend the doctrines of Randolph and Calhoun as more than an apology for slavery. The way was cleared for the radical state constitutions of Reconstruction days, demolishing the structure of the South's old society, and the near permanently blighting of the character of Southern political life. From the hurricane-fanned conflagration of reforming enthusiasm and appetite which became Civil War and Reconstruction, American moral and political conservatism has not yet recovered, and perhaps never can. For the nation was irretrievably changed. The Northern idealists, when the war was burned out, discovered aghast that from its ashes writhed the same corruption, brutality, and baneful ignorance which were supposed to have been burned away with all the lives of the war dead.

Historians are accustomed to speaking of the heroism of the American colonies in repudiating imperial taxation and asserting and achieving their independence against all the force of Great Britain. But no one who looks carefully into the history of the country will doubt that the Southern States, in the War of Secession, exhibited an incomparably higher level of courage, tenacity and self-sacrifice. But it was countered with an equal tenacity and with far greater resources; the North crushed the revolt and established its authority over the vanquished South.

In the end neither sovereignty nor tradition did much to impede the advance of those impulses toward consolidation, secularization, industrialism and leveling which were everywhere the characteristics of nineteenth-century social innovation. The South alone had hardihood sufficient for an appeal to arms against the new iron order of Authority-King Numbers-which was inimical against the sort of humanity they knew. Grant and Sherman, and the factories of the North, ground their valor into powder. Randolph and Calhoun nonetheless revealed how intricately linked are economic change, state policy, and the fragile tissue of social order.

Henry Adams, great-grandson of the Founder, from his home on Lafayette Square, wrote: "The doctrine of states' rights was in itself a sound and true doctrine… as a starting point of American history and constitutional law, there is no other which bears a moment's examination."

……………………………………………………………………
………………………..

Democracy had been tarnished by corruption, insider deals and broken promises. It had been degraded, specifically by the Slave Power, aggressively intensifying its assault on the basic human rights that the Republic had been founded upon. The 3/5 Clause was a compromise of the Constitutional Convention, concerning representation in Congress, to be based on the total number of inhabitants of the state. Northern opponents correctly pointed out that slaveholding states had more representatives than if only the free white population was counted. By 1793 slaveholding states had 47 congressmen but would have only 33 if not for the compromise. During the entire period before the Civil War slaveholding states had a disproportionate influence on the Presidency, the Speakership of the House of Representatives and the U.S. Supreme Court as a result. By the 1830's abolitionists cited the same clause in their arguments that the federal government was dominated by slaveholders. With Abraham Lincoln's election, though, the people had drawn a line. Slavery had no place in such a man's vision. It made Democracy look absurd. It violated every one of the rights proclaimed by the Declaration-not just life, liberty and the pursuit of happiness, but the general idea that a government derives legitimacy from consent. Liberty and reason seemed a stretch for a nation's capital where enslaved Africans were ubiquitous, performing the labor which kept legislators comfortable in the sweltering city. Regional tensions, unscrupulous leaders and a dysfunctional Congress were all coming to a head. Hostility to the Declaration, with its soaring claim of human rights, was as fundamental to the Confederacy as Lincoln's embrace of it was to the Union. It was not merely that the Founders contradicted one another-and themselves-changing their stories as they aged. It was not merely that slavery seemed unstoppable; even more insulting was the fact that the Slave Power now claimed to be the genuine voice of America. The country was being run by "blusterers and braggarts," wrote Walt Whitman. It was as if the other parts of the story were being erased, as the ink faded a little more from the Declaration every year. As Lincoln examined the labyrinth of the Founder's writings, he could see that they made it difficult for anyone to alter the edifice they had built, including all the protections that subsequent Southern politicians had built into the architecture of power. Was the country not likely to end as so many other imperfect Republics cited by the Federalist Papers-Carthage, Rome and Venice-in a pile of toppled Corinthian columns, broken under the weight of the Founder's ambitions? The persistence of the ancient forms was once a reminder of the power of ideas to endure. Democracy was in retreat around the world, and the failures of the French Revolution of 1848 had not increased the confidence of the people. A daring claim for human dignity had been proclaimed, along with independence, at the beginning of the experiment. If Americans could conquer their demons, perhaps they could show the world a better way. Lincoln's quest was to save the very form of government that the Founders, with all their imperfections, had bequeathed. Lincoln read Euclid for pleasure, but also to improve his ability at presenting a proposition in court. He praised the six books of the Greek mathematician's *Elements* as the foundation of his thinking. He tried to reduce problems to their essentials. Years later, the Gettysburg address would owe something to Euclid's idea that a proposition was not true until proven so.

The Northwest Ordinance (1787) forbade the expansion of slavery into the new territories (the soon to be states of Illinois, Indiana, Michigan, Ohio, Wisconsin, and part of Minnesota) and provided for religious toleration, criminal procedures, protection of property and education-this was the first piece of legislation passed under the Articles of Confederation and then renewed with the Constitution in 1789. The 36*30' line, part of the Missouri Compromise (1820), forming the borders of Missouri and Arkansas, Tennessee and Kentucky, Texas and Oklahoma, New Mexico and Arizona is the remnant of a line drawn to separate slave from free states in 1820. The Kansas Nebraska Act of 1854 ostensibly was about the route for a transcontinental railroad. It concerned the territory encompassing the present states of Kansas, Nebraska, Montana, and the Dakotas. The reality of it left it to new states to decide the question of slavery (popular sovereignty) and repealed the 1820 line of the Missouri Compromise. It was the prelude to civil war.

The emergence of the Democrat Party in the 1820's was to oppose the *Republican* principles of the equality of all citizens. Before, in the colonial period, Southern whites didn't have to invent any racist arguments to justify the lowly status of blacks. The whole world of inequality and hierarchy was taken for granted. In a hierarchical society you don't need to justify or explain slavery or the unequal treatment of anyone. Endowments and skin color were irrelevant to the immorality of slavery. Assuming that working with the hands was despicable and mean was what justified slavery. Democrat racism, saying that blacks were inferior, developed in the succeeding decades because in a free Republican society, Southern Democrat whites needed a new justification for keeping blacks in an inferior and segregated place.

Chief Justice Roger Taney, laying out forever the precedent for first stating one's opinion and then divining its source in the Constitution, wrongly claimed that the "right of property in a slave is distinctly and expressly affirmed in the Constitution." But the Constitution contains no legal protection for slavery. In 1857 the Supreme Court under Taney issued a 7-2 ruling in *Scott versus Sanford* stating that people of African descent "are not included, and were not intended to be included, under the word 'citizens' in the Constitution, and can therefore claim none of the rights and privileges which the instrument provides for and secures to citizens of the United States." He concluded that the enslaved African race possessed "no rights which the white man was bound to respect." Taney supported his ruling with an extended survey of American state and local laws from the time of the Constitution's drafting that purported to show that a 'perpetual and impassable barrier was intended to be erected between the white race and the one which they had reduced to slavery."

It was such men who manufactured the lie of American white supremacy. They were opposed every step of the way by men such as Adams, Frederick Douglass and Abraham Lincoln. Douglass correctly maintained that the Founders deserved blame for not doing more to eradicate slavery but the notion that they were insincere or disingenuous was "a slander upon their memories." It would have meant "that they were the verist impostors who ever practiced against mankind," something he denied. The 1619 Project says that the failure to abolish slavery, either in 1776 or in 1789, proves that the fundamental intent was to protect and prolong slavery. Lincoln observed: "We had slavery among us, we could not get our constitution unless we permitted them to remain in slavery, we could not secure the good we did if we grasped for more, and by necessity having submitted to that much, it does not destroy the principles that are the charter of our liberties. Let that charter be our standard."

Yes, the founders deserved blame for not doing more, but progress *was* being made. Nothing in the Declaration or Constitution established a color line; the country forbade the slave trade after 1807, prohibited its spread in the Northern half of the country; in fact, when the Constitution was ratified, black Americans were citizens in several states and in places could even vote. The fact that many of the Founders might have been hypocrites by not freeing their slaves on July 4, 1776, does not prove that the Declaration excluded non-whites nor that the Constitution guaranteed slavery. Those who claim it does have the burden of proof. It was slavery's defenders, not its opponents, who should fear the Constitution, as secession proved. The Democrat slaveowners saw its real nature and wanted out. When the Founders wrote of equality they had, in Lincoln's words, "no power to confer such a boon" in that instant. But that was not their purpose. Instead, they "set up a standard maxim for a free society, which should be familiar to all, and revered by all, constantly looked to, constantly labored for, and even though never perfectly attained, constantly approximated, and thereby constantly spreading and deepening its influence, and augmenting the happiness and value of life to people of all colors everywhere." *That* constant labor, in the generations that followed the Civil War, is the real source of everything that has truly made America exceptional. An honest portrayal of Lincoln and American history would contradict the 1619 claim that "black Americans fought back alone" to "make America a democracy." A dubious goal in any case. The interracial character of the Abolitionist movement, especially writers such as Harriet Beecher Stowe and fanatics such as John Brown do not appear in the essays and deserve to be remembered. So too would a single mention of the 2.2 million

Union soldiers who fought and the 365,000 who died to end slavery.

In Independence Hall it would be difficult to find a structure that more accurately captured the contradictions of the American story. Escaped and re-captured slaves were once interned in the very building where the Constitution was debated. On his way to Washington for his inaugural, Lincoln spoke in front of the building, in defense of the Declaration. It was still alive. America needed to live up to its founding ideals. He celebrated the equal rights that inhere in all people. Inside each person a fundamental worth could be found-an unfettered potential to make the most of one's ability. The words permitted no equivocation. There was a religious mysticism, a sacred significance, beneath Lincoln's attachment to the document. He actually *believed* that its premises were true. This made him dangerous to a system that had grown quite comfortable with its moral rot. To Southern Democrat politicians, the idea that African Americans had rights was anathema. Lincoln thought that the document applied to all, and America's moral influence in the world depended on the fact. It gave "hope to the world for all future time." The tendency to pick and choose which ideals were convenient violated both his ethics and his mathematics-as Euclid knew, thousands of years earlier, equal meant equal. If the experiment was to succeed, it would give hope to all people, in all places, for all time. As a result, African Americans began to invoke the Declaration in their own cause. By denying equality, slavery did the opposite. It created a permanent caste system and made a mockery of the words in the Declaration, which should always inspire people to renew the battle which their forefathers began. Lincoln's entire political career had led to this moment.

He continued. The cause of self-government mattered to all people on earth. Something more than common had united Americans when they threw off the yoke of British rule. Their yearnings had given courage to other peoples. A remarkable catalogue of rights had been woven into the country's founding documents, suggesting that human beings *were* capable of governing themselves. They had articulated "something that held great promise to the people of the world for all time to come." He concluded his remarks with a stunning statement, that he would be "one of the happiest men in the world" if the country could be saved with its great idea intact-but added that he would "rather be assassinated on this spot than to surrender it." Lincoln had reset America's moral compass. In the course of his visit to the national shrine, he had restored the radical promise inherent in the Declaration. It was another in the progressive steps of African emancipation leading to the eventual consummation of the work. To be able to speak about the Declaration, in the spot where it was signed, gave voice "to the feelings that had been really the feelings of my whole life." In effect he had repeated the act of the signers, swearing to give his life to defend his principles. And with his speech he had restored integrity to Independence Hall.

Congressman Lincoln had introduced a bill to end slavery in Washington, in January 1849. The slave pens he saw from the windows of the Capital during his only term were still there upon his arrival as President in 1861. His inauguration would spell the end for all of the exceptions carved out of what were thought to be binding arrangements, so many hidden protections for the Slave Power, including the Fugitive Slave Law. In an attempt to further weaken the Confederacy Lincoln declared "that on the first day of January, 1863, all persons held as slaves within any State, or designated part of a State, the people whereof shall then be in rebellion against the United States, shall be then, thenceforward, and forever free, and the Executive government will recognize and maintain the freedom of such persons, and will do no act or acts to repress such persons, or any of them, in any efforts they may make for their actual freedom."

Later that year, after the dreadful battle, Lincoln gave his Gettysburg Address:

"Four score and seven years ago our fathers brought forth, upon this continent, a new nation, conceived in liberty, and dedicated to the proposition that "all men were created equal."

"Now we are engaged in a great civil war, testing whether that nation, or any nation so conceived, and so dedicated, can long endure. We are met on a great battlefield of that war. We have come to dedicate a portion of it, as a final resting place for those who died here, that the nation might live. This we may, in all propriety do. But in a larger sense, we cannot dedicate-we cannot consecrate-we cannot hallow, this ground-the brave men, living and dead, who struggled here, have hallowed it, far above our poor power to add or detract. The world will little note, nor long remember what we say here; while it can never forget what they did here."

"It is rather for us, the living, that we be dedicated to the great task remaining before us-that, from these honored dead we take increased devotion to that cause for which they here, gave their last full measure of devotion-that we here highly resolve these dead shall not have died in vain; that the nation, shall have a new birth of freedom, and that government of the people, by the people, and for the people, shall not perish from the earth."

Late in the war Lincoln visited the Richmond capitol and addressed a group of negroes working nearby. "My poor friends, you are free-free as air. You can cast off the name of slave and trample upon it; it will come to you no more. Liberty is your birthright. God gave it to you as he gave it to others, and it is a sin that you have been deprived of it for so many years. But you must try to deserve the priceless boon. Let the world see that you merit it and are able to maintain it by your good works. Don't let your joy carry you into excesses. Learn the laws and obey them; obey God's commandments and thank him for giving you liberty, for him you owe all things. As long as I live, you shall have all the rights which God has given to every other free citizen of this Republic." The final price of freedom *was* self-discipline and self-restraint. But

Blacks were no more prepared for liberty in 1865 than were the Russian people in 1991. Freedom is not the absence of discipline, for it calls for discipline by internal constraint in contrast with the external control of Authority, an ethic built up over time through many generations.

For years, it had been fashionable to claim that America was less lovely than Europe because it lacked picturesque ruins. Now the South was littered with them, its Greek revival banks and courthouses shattered, like the temples of old, as if two thousand years had elapsed. In Richmond, the State Capitol had survived the bombardment, but from its hilltop, it now surveyed a landscape of utter destruction. Lincoln would be amused by our wish to seek him now, through an elaborate Greek portal such as the Lincoln Memorial, a perfect Doric temple that would have been unrecognizable in the settlements of his childhood. But it has become a place where Americans come to talk to one another about what kind of country they would like to live in, a more perfect union than the one we know. It embodies Lincoln's idea that all of us who believe in the Declaration can step inside a "temple of liberty" open to all. In that sense, the Greek shrine works perfectly, remembering the candor of the Ancients as they also grappled their way toward something better, all those centuries ago.

By 1865 Victor Hugo was writing that "America has again become the guide among the nations" and hopes for democracy were revived around the world. The point of history, Lincoln had mused, was not so much to blame people for their shortcomings as it was to gain wisdom for the struggles yet to come.

The North had the invaluable personal enterprise of a free population. Suddenly the free economy reached out and began to take over a greater territory than the area which had accrued to slavery. The wealth and power of the free states doubled and re-doubled. The South lost the Civil War, as it was bound to; and the question of state sovereignty was dismissed as an adjunct, set aside by the verdict on slavery. It had resorted to war and committed the moral error of repudiating a contract after taking special advantage through it; the Federal government was clearly obligated to maintain itself against aggression. An intelligent observer realizes that there must have been a fault in the structure as sure as in a fallen house. The operation and consequences of the Reconstruction, however, raised grave doubts whether there could be moral authority for perpetuating by force a union of voluntary origin. Nor was it justifiable to alter the terms of contract when one of the parties is under duress. Despite being made by force the rebuilt structure still contained a physical defect corresponding to the moral defect. The Reconstruction Act wiped out the states as political entities. Though the Act eventually lapsed the damage was done. In politics the specific act implies a continuing power. Even if denominated as an exception, a temporary expedient, the rule has been laid down that such expedients may be used. The Northern states could not consent to any extension of Federal power over the Southern states without making themselves liable to the imposition of the same power against themselves in the future.

The Civil War was the great divide of American Conservatism. The victory of the Northern armies assured that the discussions of slavery and the nature of the union, issues that had fed the fires of political thought since the beginning of the Republic, were effectively settled. The Grant administration was also a dividing line in the country's history, between what we had hoped for, and what we had become. Change is the transformation of values or institutions in which the government plays no part; reform is a transformation through the conscious use of political power. After the Civil War it became apparent to some that government alone was equal to the challenge of some changes, and the discussion became one of the constitutional legitimacies of the reforms, and this menace is what roils the nation to this day.

Democracy became the secular religion, with the Constitution becoming the symbol of national unity, while becoming less and less useful in its role of a delaying mechanism. The major point of debate became the right and capacity of the now all-powerful national government to regulate enterprise in the general interest of the community and in the specific interest of its less fortunate members. The root cause of the struggle over the future of America was now to be industrial capitalism. Change-rapid, massive and unsettling-was the dominant characteristic of the American scene. Leaders on the Right, as the chief agents of change, were confident that the new mines and mills would bring them profit without disrupting the established order. Leaders on the Left served as the chief advocates of reform, convinced that only positive action by federal and state governments could shore up democracy against a rapidly increasing inequality of property and currents of panic and depression. The South was reduced to a poverty of economy and spirit from which it only recently has fully recovered, and the country was exposed to a regime of corruption which left its permanent stamp on the character of the United States. The America of Jefferson and John Adams *was* being effaced; Hamilton's scheme was triumphant. Political centralization and industrialization were destroying rural virtues and loyalties, sapping the influence and vigor of the small towns. Could the country be restrained from further destroying its own past, shattering its own Constitution, or cured of its ruin of leadership? The test of any change to the Constitution is threefold: Does it deny the rights of individuals? Does it weaken the bases by impairing the states as political entities? Does it add to the bulk or improper distribution of the weight of the superstructure? As the structure cracks, sags or sways, disrupting the private economy, the alternating attack by the zealous opposition will be plied more furiously. There is a progressive increase in chronological frequency of amendments to the Constitution, including the outright ignoring of its fundamental Law. The full consequences are compounded and cumulative, becoming manifest after a lapse of time all at once in a general collapse. They are aggravated by a concurrent drift in judicial decisions, and further extensions of political power by simple usurpation.

It was not the liberation of the slaves which extinguished state sovereignty. Liberty is a pre-condition which the Constitution should have recognized as a primary. The destruction was done by the usurpation of state powers by the Federal government as a right of conquest. If the Federal government won the war, the states must have lost. The stabilizing function of the mass inertia vote of the House was lost with the Sixteenth Amendment. When the interest of every voter was practically the same, the center of gravity was a constant even though the citizens were mobile. But the power of the Federal government to take from some to give to others opened the field wide for corruption. Furthermore, the need and power to tax increases with time, as proceeds tend to go into things requiring upkeep and yielding no return (public buildings and political jobs). Productive possibilities had been converted into static forms, which necessitated more diversion to carry the dead-load. "We already see, in whatever direction we turn our eyes, the growing symptoms of disorder and decay-the growth of faction, cupidity and corruption; and the decay of patriotism, integrity and disinterestedness." (Calhoun)

The question remains open: did the Civil War break on slavery, state rights, or the cleavage between an agrarian and an industrial economy, the latter fueled by the National Bank? Distribution of sovereign powers between a federal government and its component states is no simple matter; the past is strewn with the wreckage of leagues and federations. By the Left's reckoning, all stipulated powers are accounted strength in a national government; the absence of any conceivable power is considered a degree of weakness. The usual recourse is further centralization of powers, which is to say, an increase in the bulk of the superstructure and the diversion of more resources into it. Utter incompetence in government is finally achieved by what is called absolute political power, whether under the name of democracy or as outright despotism. The worst thing which can happen to Law is its over-extension, its expansion into fields in which it cannot be competent; then disrespect for Law in all its capacities becomes general.

"It appears that the Congress under this constitution will not possess the confidence of the people, which is an essential requisite in a good government: for unless the laws command the respect of the great body of the people, so as to induce them to support it, when called on by the civil magistrate, they will be executed by force, which is inconsistent with every idea of liberty; for the same force that may be employed to compel obedience to good laws, might and probably would be used to wrest from the people their constitutional liberties." (Centinel)

The truth is that powers which are improper, being contrary to the moral order of the universe, are weakness, and so are powers allotted to an inappropriate agency. They impose weight and stress which no structure of government can support. Beyond the correct proportions and powers, this is fatal; unless the resistance from the base is greater than the weight of strain of the superstructure, the whole must fall. Feeble governments are those which have no adequate and legitimately instrumented opposition from the regional bases (the states), the mass veto of the House, or the stability of the Senate. In the country's beginning both the states and the Federal government were too weak by the claim of improper powers and the improper allotment of a proper power. The latter nullified a vital tribute of sovereignty, its space dimension. Unless the distinction between stipulated powers and intrinsic strength is understood there can be no relevant vertical division of power. States are required to stand against pressure from above which tends to thrust them apart, making them buckle outward. A structure collapses from weakness, not strength. If the country is torn apart it must be from uncompensated stresses. This can be either from inadequate bases or excessive and an unequally distributed superstructure. If slavery had not been admitted into the Constitution on tolerance, its original design was largely sound; its inclusion, though, introduced both faults. It made the bases unequal to the task of opposing the superstructure. The extradition clause gave the slave states a point of pressure against the free states. Slavery afforded an excuse for adding excessive weight to the superstructure and distributing it unequally. If a structure is defective, the fact that it was the best the builders could do will not avert the physical consequences. But since human affairs are in the realm of moral law the outcome may confound all measurable probabilities. The relations are nevertheless unaltered. Freedom and private property are the two necessary conditions, with firm state bases for the federal structure. The potential of a nation cannot be computed quantitatively, in material wealth at a given date; it consists in abstract ideas, in its axioms of human relations expressed in its organization. These ideas deeply express the most essential conditions of economic growth and human progress. The quest for calculable rationality in human affairs defies the incalculable subjectivity of human beings and the danger and indeterminacy of all human life.

Burke wrote on just this subject, as it applied to England: "One of the first and most leading principles on which the commonwealth and its laws are consecrated, is lest the temporary possessors and life renters in it, unmindful of what they have received from their ancestors, or of what is due to their posterity, should act as if they were the entire masters; that they should not think it among their rights to cut off the entail, or commit waste on the inheritance, by destroying at their pleasure the whole original fabric of their society; hazarding to leave to those who come after them a ruin instead of a habitation-and teaching these successors as little to respect their contrivances, as they had themselves respected the institutions of their forefathers. By this unprincipled facility of changing the state as often, and as much, and in as many ways, as there are floating fancies and fashions, the whole chain and continuity of the commonwealth would be broken. No one generation could link with another. Men would become little better than the flies of a summer." Thus, all three of the disputed causes of the Civil War entered into one cause, with the apparent problem masking the real problem. The apparent problem was the preservation of the Union. But the antecedent condition of the federal union was the existence of the states. The real problem was the preservation of the states. If that proved impossible, the Union must presently disintegrate or fossilize into a mass.

The Sixteenth Amendment was a devastating indignity for Americans, a plenary power in Congress to ignore all of the other constitutional restrictions upon the federal government. It was conceived in class hatred as an instrument of vengeance and plays right into the hands of collectivists. In effect it repealed the Fourth Amendment guarantees of privacy and property. It opened up our homes, our papers and our effects to the prying eyes of government agents and set the stage for inquiries into our private affairs whenever the government decides. Constitutional government cannot be restored while the Amendment is in effect. Congress has the right to authorize the confiscation of any or all of the income of citizens using calculated discrimination, in any manner and by any procedure that a federal agent may deem expedient. Our vaunted government of enforceable laws has long since disappeared into a huge maze of completely uncontrollable government by unpredictable men.

The final stroke in disestablishing the states was the Seventeenth Amendment, which took the election of Senators out of the State Legislature and gave it to the popular vote. Since then, the states have had no connection to the Federal government; representation in both Houses of Congress rests only on a dislocated mass. As a counterweight to the Federal Government the states ceased to exist. The immediate appearance of an enormous bureaucracy was the natural consequence of a structureless nation. Concurrently and by interaction with these events the productive economy was distorted, and wealth diverted into the political channel. The Civil War precipitated the sequence. Afterwards there was no government, only force, the moral control having been disconnected. People had lived by the moral order; they cannot survive otherwise; but the ancient and erroneous identification of government with force and Authority became plausible again.

Likewise, politics became lucrative. Government employees are not aware of any objective in political life except parasitism. Larger salaries, perquisites and more ostentatious buildings must be provided to maintain the dignity of their office, lest they be mistaken for lackeys. The cost and display of government is always in inverse ratio to the liberty and prosperity of the citizens, as with the impoverished nation and magnificent monarchy of Louis XIV, and his expensive court at Versailles.

When the separate States agreed on carefully defined conditions to enter into a bond of union, they never meant to surrender the right, which they had so recently vindicated against Great Britain, of seceding from it if the main body of their citizens desired it. This was the doctrine of Calhoun, and it was supported by a great weight both of argument and authority. One cannot understand how those who had been so lately preaching in the most unqualified terms that all large bodies of men had an absolute, unimpeachable, indefeasible right to choose for themselves their form of government, and that the growing recognition of this right was one of the first conditions of progress and liberty, could support or applaud the Federal government in imposing on the Southern States a government which they detested, and in overriding by force their evident and unquestioned desire. Unable to argue coherently on these grounds, the North was represented as fighting for the abolition of slavery, or at least its extension to the new territories, which would upset the balance of power in Congress. It was at once felt that the question at issue was one of national preservation, to which all other considerations must be subordinated, and by preserving the integrity of the Republic, even against the wishes of an immense section of the people, they were serving the best interests of the country.

After the War, the Northern temper was one of expansiveness, and now it was no longer shackled by the weight of the conservative Southern tradition. Likewise, it was impossible for the South to resume the give and take of ideas which had marked her ante-bellum relations with the North. She retired within her borders and endured, in a rage, ten years of persecution, leaving her the less capable of uniting gracefully with the life of the Union; for that life in the meantime had been moving on in another direction. The South was physically impaired and has ever since been unable to offer an example of its philosophy in action. The American Progressive principle has developed into a pure movement without any check, with no substantial barrier, from a Southern minority whose voice could no longer be heard.

Thoughtful men were very much concerned with the erosion of the quality of individual life by the forces of industrialization and the uncritical worship of material progress as an end in itself. It was not their assumption that one first achieved material well-being, then used it to further the more spiritual side of life; on the contrary, they insisted that any attempt to divorce economics and labor from this side of one's life brutalized the labor and cheapened the humanity. The way had been cleared for the materialistic reorganization of society that in effect brought a spiritual disorganization. What the Agrarians were saying, at a time when few Americans worried about such things, was that if the Republic was to live up to its Founder's ideals and be what it could be, then it had better look long and hard at what it was in danger of becoming and devote conscious effort to controlling its own destiny, rather than continuing to drift along on the tides of economic materialism. We should order the country's economy, social arrangements, and political actions accordingly, refusing to be determined by events rather than attempting to determine them, instead of letting the foundations of our values and conduct go unexamined. Man functions best in a society that takes account of his limitations. In the zeal for the benefits of modern scientific civilization, he is placing so high a value on material gain that he ignores his own spiritual welfare and his moral obligations to society. In place of beauty and truth he erected a new ideal, that of Progress. Man was losing contact with the natural world; his quest for gain blinding him to all that makes life worth living. The tenuous and frail spiritual insights of western civilization, achieved so arduously over the course of many centuries were being sacrificed. The result could only be dehumanization and chaos. The correct vision of the good life is one of a more harmonious, aesthetically and spiritually rewarding kind of human existence. A way of life that omits or deemphasizes the more spiritual side of existence is necessarily disastrous to *all* phases of life. Man's life cannot be divided into segments; there is no such thing as economic man, political man, and social man; there was only man, and his various activities must be considered as parts of one human life.

For a century and a half, the South preserved its agrarian economy and fought to the death for principles now clearly defined, as representing the cause of agrarianism against industrialism. The South lost its battle, and what is worse, lost the peace. After the South had been conquered by war and humiliated and impoverished by Reconstruction, there appeared to remain something which made the South different-something intangible in the realm of the spirit. As with today's Progressives, that too must be invaded and destroyed, a conquest of the mind calculated to remake every opinion, impose a different way of life and thought upon the country, and write "error" across the pages of the country's history. Thus, the war of intellectual and spiritual conquest now being waged against all, the Progressives sitting in judgment and attempting to impose its philosophy of living upon anyone who dares to object.

One great cause of the current degradation of American politics is the extreme facility with which votes have been given to ignorant persons who have no experience in public life and no real interest in the well-being of the country. Following emancipation, the enfranchisement of the negroes added a new and enormous mass of voters, who were utterly and childishly incompetent. The influence of property and intelligence in the South was completely broken, and the negro vote was ostensibly made supreme. A host of vagrant political adventurers from the North poured into the Southern provinces, and, in conjunction with the mean whites, undertook the direction of the negro votes. Then followed, under the protection of the Northern bayonets, a grotesque parody of government, a hideous orgy of anarchy, violence, unrestrained corruption, undisguised, ostentatious and insulting robbery, such as the world had seldom seen. State debts were profusely piled up. Legislation was openly put up for sale. At length the Northern troops were withdrawn, but the carpetbaggers had had their day. A more curious picture of the effects of democratic equality among a population who were entirely unfitted for it has never been presented, perhaps, again, until 1991 in Russia.

In disrupting and disorganizing the economic life of the South, the Civil War jolted from power and status the most articulate Agrarian group known to American history, leaving no effective check to an industrial dominance in national public policy, particularly in tariff matters. It forced a dependence in the South on a one-crop system, temporarily reinforced by unusually high prices for cotton. It terminated slavery without removing Negro labor. It created a vacuum for an economic invasion, with the region becoming a suppliant for outside aid and thus yielding much of its economic destiny. By 1876, though, the cotton crop was approximately the size and value of that in 1860, employing the tenant and crop lien credit system as a replacement for slavery.

The ruin of the South deprived the nation of that region's conservative influence. Civil War opened the way for previously unheard-of tariffs, for exploitation of the resources of the West, for the triumph of urban interests over the rural population, for a system of life in which culture was wholly subordinated to economic appetite. Later states were, in effect, creations of the Federal government rather than of the citizens of the state, in one case designated solely to secure a political majority in the nation; the newer states tended to look to the Federal government for special legislation. The increase of government power concomitantly destroyed the natural power of the individual. The power being there, it was bound to be used. The result was factional interests inevitably seeking to use the Federal power for partisan advantage. And in that the Western states got their first political training.

From the quagmire following the War, the fact that the South did survive the horrors of the Reconstruction period is perhaps the most heroic fact in all American history. Reconstruction could never have occurred had the military forces of the United States not controlled the Executive governments of the Southern States, with virtually no class of the population, except the negroes, being represented in the Southern Legislatures. The War of Succession, itself a Revolution, was succeeded by a period of several years during which the institutions of both the Southern States and the greater part of Federal government were violently distorted to objects not contemplated by the framers of the Constitution. The attempt to find his place in the world is the story of the Negro since 1865. Reconstruction did little to remedy the Negro's defects in preparation. He discovered himself as a political power, but the benefits of that power were garnered by someone else, as they are today. The political training which he received was the worst possible; it was a training in corruption, oppression and revenge. When the carpetbaggers left, the Negro found he had mortgaged his best capital; that capital was the confidence of the Southern white man with whom he had to live. The rehabilitation of this confidence in the Negro is part of the white man's story since 1880.

1619 discredits the Revolution and the Civil War as elaborate conspiracies to perpetuate racism. By its reckoning, nothing has changed. Slavery was replaced with Jim Crow segregation, and this has given way to the permanent condition of white racism that is the inescapable fate of the country. What is left out of the 1619 tale is breathtaking; the invocation of permanent white racism takes the place of any serious examination of the economic, political and social history of the country. The project ignores the actual social development of the African American population over the last 150 years. That Martin Luther King does not fit into the 1619 narrative is perhaps its greatest indictment.

The defining moment of the American civil rights movement *was* Dr. King's iconic speech, appropriately enough, in front of the Lincoln Memorial, with allusions towards the Gettysburg address. "Five score years ago, a great American, in whose symbolic shadow we stand today, signed the Emancipation Proclamation. This momentous decree came as a great beacon of hope to millions of slaves, who had been seared in the flames of withering injustice. It came as a joyous daybreak to end the long night of their captivity." He refers to the fact that "one hundred years later, the Negro still is not free." In earlier speeches he had noted the gap between the American Dream- "a dream as yet unfilled"-and reality, for Negroes, saying that the "federal government had scarred the dream through its apathy and hypocrisy, its betrayal of the cause of justice." Dr. King suggests that "it may well be that the Negro is God's instrument to save the Soul of America."

From the Washington speech: "In a sense we have come to our Nation's Capital to cash a check. When the architects of our great Republic wrote the magnificent words of our Constitution and the Declaration of Independence, they were signing a promissory note to which every American was to fall heir. This note was a promise that all men, yes, black men as well as white men, would be guaranteed the inalienable rights of life, liberty and the pursuit of happiness. It is obvious today that America has defaulted on this promissory note insofar as her citizens of color are concerned. Instead of honoring this sacred obligation, America has given its colored people a bad check, a check that has come back marked 'insufficient funds.' But we refuse to believe that the bank of justice is empty. We refuse to believe that there are insufficient funds in the great vaults of opportunity in this nation. So, we have come to cash this check, a check that will give us upon demand the riches of freedom and the security of justice."

"We have come to this hallowed spot to remind America of the fierce urgency of Now. This is not time to engage in the luxury of cooling off or to take the tranquilizing drug of gradualism. It would be fatal for the nation to overlook the urgency of the moment and to underestimate the determination of its colored citizens. This sweltering summer of the colored people's legitimate discontent will not pass until there is an invigorating autumn of freedom and equality. 1963 is not an end but a beginning. Those who hope that the colored Americans needed to blow off steam and will now be content will have a rude awakening if the nation returns to business as usual."

"I have a dream that one day this nation will rise up and live out the true meaning of its creed. We hold these truths to be self-evident, that all men were created equal. I have a dream that my four little children will one day live in a nation where they will not be judged by the color of their skin but by the content of their character."

"I have a dream that one day every valley shall be engulfed, every hill shall be exalted, and every mountain shall be made low, the rough places shall be made plains and the crooked places will be made straight and the glory of the Lord shall be revealed, and all flesh shall see it together. With this faith we will be able to work together, to go to jail together, to climb up for freedom together, knowing that we will be free one day. This is our hope. This is the faith that I will go back to the South with. With this faith we will be able to hew out of the mountain of despair a stone of hope."

For the 1619 Project to claim that Lincoln, King and many others had no hand in ending slavery and discrimination simply has no factual basis. It shows an ignorance of history, and/or a deliberate misrepresentation. Historical literacy is foundational to how we think about ourselves as citizens of the state. Historians are concerned with uncovering and increasing understanding about the truth of the past, no matter how difficult and complicated that truth may be. The Left writes history as if there was no actual record of what happened and as if what matters is not truth but who is in control to write it down. "Our democracy's ideals were false when they were written", says the author of the Project. The Left seeks to define the United States by its shortcomings-while it magnifies and romanticizes the contributions and culture of black Americans. It is the inverse of the long-time failure of educational texts to describe or even acknowledge the historical contributions of blacks. This is likely to become the accepted Story of America in the coming decade unless there is significant pushback. "Our popular narratives about the past inform what we think is possible in the present," say the Project's organizers. But where are the African principles of self-discipline, of self-government, or a demonstration that slavery was unprecedented in history, unique to America and absent from Europe, Africa and Asia? 1619 rejects Dr. King's common humanity idea of politics for a noxious zero-sum brand of the politics of envy and enmity. Left wing politics supporting social justice and egalitarianism is in effect a critique of meritocracy. They claim that the development of the poor can only proceed when excessive differences in status, power and wealth are eliminated. This can only mean bringing others down, since they offer no program for raising the poor to an acceptable level of each.

Somehow, thinks the Left, by creating enough hatred for the nation's founding, its ideals and America's majority group, justice and harmony will somehow emerge. We must resent and reject our past; possess an aggressive, contemptuous and disobedient attitude; punish the old transgressors and rule in their stead. Not a civilized self-rule but one of fanaticism and self-destruction. Such a spirit of vengeance will lead neither to political stability nor to justice. While they deny they are fomenting a race war, the 1619 authors bear responsibility for the political conclusions and consequences of their false and misguided arguments. Praise for rioters and looters does not add to their credibility.

Being a patriot means believing that America is basically good; its sins are aberrations rather than central to its history. The US has largely been redeemed from slavery by the Civil War and from segregation by civil rights legislation and twenty trillion dollars of reparations. Just as 1619 sees the landing in Virginia as the country's Original Sin so did the country spill its blood and spend its treasure in propitiation of that sin. With 1619, slavery is viewed and analyzed not as a specific economically rooted form of the world exploitation of labor but rather as the American manifestation of white racism. If, as its proponents claim, it is embedded in the DNA of whites then it must persist independently of any political or economic conditions. The reference to DNA is part of the growing attempt to derive racial antagonisms from innate biological processes. Such an absurd claim serves to legitimize the Left's view, entirely compatible with the political perspective of Marxism-that blacks and whites are hostile and incompatible species, and the dialectic between them must be exploited in order to correct past errors and gain power now and in the future. The myth of a white supremacist founding serves the emotional needs of people who cannot quite reckon their place in contemporary society with what they feel is their due.

Black Americans such as Dr. King forced whites to take their ideals seriously. Blacks represent the most stringent testing of the American Republic and the possibility of its greatest achievement. Blacks have from the first (late 1700s) advanced the cause of a greater alignment of political practice with stated American principles. If the Left wanted to show what a nation that is really founded on slavery looks like they should point to the Confederate Constitution along with the secession ordinances and declaration of causes issued by Democrat-led slaveholding states. The 1619 arguments don't imply any difference of those with the Constitution of the United States. Black people have the responsibility of having their ideals and images recognized as part of the composite image that is part of the still-forming American people and give compelling demonstrations that those ideals are worthy of further transmission. Demands for reparations by people who were never slaves from people who were never slave holders is not such a demonstration. An honest accounting of the nation's past would tell both the story of white Americans' effort to live up to the Declaration and the Constitution, and many other triumphs of black and white together that composed the American civil rights struggle.

The whole course of history was repeated before the eyes of nineteenth-century Americans. One man in his lifetime could see it all, if he cared to; theories and arguments were put to the test by demonstration. Looking back to Europe he could see the system of Status still in force or perhaps yielding to various modifications. He could observe the portent of a new and terrible tyranny-The State-emerging in its ancient guise of absolute power. He could discern the ultimate position of men as subjects of that absolute state; they were economic slaves. He could contrast the difficulties of the lives of savages with the rewards of civilization. He could see free men in free association making and building, working for no one, but still industrious, and meeting as equals without disorder. Clearly then their behavior and mode of association was practicable, and must have deducible principles, intrinsically different from those of Europe. The presence of slaves gave the answer. A man was either free or not free. Where it had formerly been assumed that some men were not fit for freedom, it was now thinkable that nothing but freedom was fit for all men.

The Left claims that Republicans today are somehow the heirs of an institution (slavery) that in reality owes its defense and longevity in American history almost entirely to the historical Democrat party. They say that current Republican opposition to Democrat policies are clearly downstream of a style of political combat that came to fruition in the defense of human bondage. Despite the massive resistance to school desegregation, civil and voting rights legislation on the part of the Democrats, they accuse the Republican Party of what they, the Democrats, actually did to oppose the rights of blacks. When these mistaken ideas such as CRT and 1619 are introduced to the education in K-12 we have crossed the line from education to indoctrination.

Slavery was abolished, segregation was overturned, and the struggle today is carried on by people ultimately driven by their commitment to the principle that all men were created equal-that same principle articulated at the nation's birth. It is precisely because millions of Americans have never bought the notion that America was built as a slavocracy and were willing to lay their lives on the line to make good on the promissory note of the Declaration. What makes America unique is not slavery but the effort to abolish it. Today's Constitution, especially the 13th, 14th, 15th amendments, has much more to do with what happened in 1865 than in 1776 or in 1619. Redemption through struggle has been the history of America.

The history of liberty is the history of the limitation of government's power. When we resist the concentration of power, we are resisting the process of death, because a concentration of government's reach always precedes the death of human freedom. So now the Left wishes to erase the country's past and begin anew with their radical ideas. The revolt of the masses against the social establishments, property, and intellectual traditions of the West, commencing in 1789, has continued with only intermittent truces to this day. Progressivism is a movement for control over property, trade, work, amusements, education and religion. The popular detestation of the past, once awakened, does not limit itself to annihilation of governments and economies; if the arts and sciences seem prerogatives of the minority, or if they appear to impede gratification of popular appetites, then genius, talents and learning from the most enlightened periods, are liable to become objects of proscription and casualties of the general catastrophe. Progressivism is the transition from Christendom, aristocracy, and family economy to an overwhelming utilitarian collectivism. If you refuse to move in the prescribed direction, you are not simply different, you are arrested and perverse. Tradition is suspect; the Left insists upon reform, revision, and restatement.

The real enemy of mankind is not social institutions, but the devil within us; the fanatic improver of mankind through artificial alteration is in truth the destroyer of souls. Only one species of reform really is worth attempting: reform of individual conscience.

In *Earth's Holocaust,* Nathaniel Hawthorne describes the destruction of the past by modern innovating mankind, carting off to a bonfire, Savonarola style, everything that the dead ages venerated. Pedigrees, noble crests, badges of knighthood, and all the trappings of aristocracy are tossed in; a despairing gentleman cries, "this fire is consuming all that marked your advance from barbarism, or that could have prevented your relapse thither." But purple robes and royal scepters follow; and strong drink, and tobacco, and the weapons of war, and the gallows-and presently marriage certificates, and money, and all deeds to property, and all written constitutions. The bonfire is augmented, very soon, by millions of books, the literature of the ages. "The truth was, that the human race had now reached a stage of progress so far beyond what the wisest men of former ages had ever dreamed, that it would be a manifest absurdity to allow the earth to be any longer encumbered with their poor achievements." To replenish the flame, the people soon drag up surplices, mitres, crosiers, crosses, fonts, chalices, communion tables, pulpits-and the Bible. Because it flourishes on the rootlessness of the masses, the total state detests, and endeavors to obliterate, knowledge of the past. But a sense of history is far more basic to the maintenance of freedom than hope for the future. Hence the relentless effort to destroy memory and discourage real scholarship. And hence the ingenious techniques for abolishing the social allegiances within which individual memory is given strength and power of resistance. When every vestige of the human past has been destroyed in this magnificent reform, mankind may once again luxuriate in its primitive innocence.

Twenty-first century America is a nation tormented by self-inflicted crime, urban vice, massive political corruption, family decay and increasing polarization; amid this scene the commanding voice is not a Savonarola's, but a chorus of sociologists proclaiming that egalitarianism will cure every social cancer. Throughout history books have been burned so that the weight of the past should be removed from the present. So now the left wishes to erase the country's past and begin anew with their radical ideas. Cancelling is the new, Progressive form of blacklisting and book-burning.

CHAPTER ELEVEN-MARX, PROGRESSIVISM AND CRITICAL RACE THEORY

ISABEL PATERSON
ROSE WILDER LANE

AYN RAND

"The strong will help the weak, the rich will share with the poor, and it will not be called charity, but it will be known as justice. And the man or woman who fails to do his duty, not as he sees it, but as society at large sees it, will be held up to the contempt of mankind."

Edward Mandell House, from his *Philip Dru, Administrator,* 1912

Critical Race Theory (CRT) is an offshoot of Marxism, which built its political program on the theory of class conflict. Marx believed that the primary characteristic of industrial society was the imbalance of power between capitalists and labor. The solution to that imbalance was revolution: the workers would gain consciousness of their plight, seize the means of production, overthrow the capitalists, and usher in a new socialist utopian society. In practice Marx's ideas unleashed the prisons, show trials, executions and mass starvations with a body count totaling in the hundreds of millions. Forced collectivization, government induced famine, terror campaigns, diseases, war and high mortality rates in the Gulag-this happened to political opponents, kulaks, ideological rivals, suspect party members, cautious military officers, former societal elites, ethnic and religious groups, along with the relatives and sympathizers of all the above. Intellectuals, though, realized that middle class America, with ever-improving standards of living, were unlikely to similarly revolt along Marxist lines, having never developed a sense of class consciousness or class division. The US working class has never nor will ever be organized into radically led unions, so building Marxist class division was more difficult here than anywhere else. CR theorists, masters of language construction, realize that neo-Marxism would be a hard sell. Its supporters instead deploy a series of euphemisms to describe CRT including equity, egalitarianism, social justice, diversity and inclusion, reimagined and/or stakeholder capitalism. Equity sounds non-threatening and is easily confused with the American principle of equality. But the distinction is vast and important. CR theorists explicitly reject equality-the principle proclaimed in the Declaration of Independence, defended in the Civil War by Republicans against slave holding Democrats, codified into law in the Thirteenth, Fourteenth and Fifteenth Amendments, the Civil Rights Act of 1964 passed by Republicans against Democrat objections, the Voting Rights Act of 1965, passed again by Republicans against Democrat objections, a hundred other acts of Congress and a like number of court decisions. To CR theorists, equality represents mere non-discrimination and provides camouflage for white patriarchy and oppression. Equity, however, as defined and promoted by CR theorists, is little more than reformulated, outcome-focused

Marxism. This revolutionary movement lost out in the '60s to the civil rights movement, led by Martin Luther King, which instead sought the fulfillment of the American promise of freedom and equality under the Law. Americans then preferred the idea of improving their country rather than overthrowing it. Under CRT the idea of treating everyone as an individual who is equal before the law and meant to be judged on the content of his character, and the merit of his work, is considered only a myth that keeps minorities down. In the 1990's CRT was re-built on the intellectual framework of identity-based Marxism. Abandoning Marx's economic dialect of capitalists and workers, the left substituted race for class and sought to create a revolutionary coalition of the dispossessed based on other categories as well. Therefore, racism and sexism were combined to form a broad coalition of the people's movements in order to win a decisive majority in elections. The left uses the concept of equity to mean, not political, but metaphysical equality-the equality of outcomes not due to personal attributes and virtues, regardless of natural endowment or individual choice, performance or character. It is nature, and reality, that they propose to fight. Since nature does not endow all men with equal beauty or equal intelligence, and the faculty of volition leads men to make different choices, the egalitarians propose to abolish the "unfairness" of nature and of volition, and to establish universal equality in fact. Since personal attributes cannot be "redistributed" they seek to deprive men of their consequences-of the rewards, the benefits, the achievements created by personal attributes and virtues. They can only make men equal by treating them unequally, therefore dismissing any idea of meritocracy.

Equity is predicated on the idea that the only certain measure of equality is outcome-educational, social and occupational. Equity pushers assume axiomatically that if all positions at every level of hierarchy in every organization are not occupied by a proportion of the population that is precisely equivalent to that portion in the general population, then systematic prejudice (racism, sexism, homophobia) is definitely at play, and there are perpetrators who must be regulated, limited or punished. This theory assumes that racial prejudice is sufficient explanation for the differential representation of individuals in various organizational positions. It is an impossible equation to solve because there are too many organizations, strata of positions, and identities of the group sort to possibly treat in the equitable manner demanded by idealogues. Many people have multiple group identities and further sorting that out is technically impossible without the introduction of an authoritarian overseer. Major, multi-disciplinary social interventions inevitably produce unintended counter-productive large-scale consequences. We can only hope that the doctrine of equity contains so many internal contradictions that it will actually be the death of the radical left.

An equity-based form of government would mean the end not only of private property but of individual rights, equality under the law, federalism and freedom of speech. These would be replaced by race-based distribution of wealth, group-based rights, active discrimination against whites, and omnipotent bureaucratic authority. CRT has nevertheless permeated the collective intelligence and decision-making process of American government. Under its increasing sway, the ostensibly neutral administration of Law, originally oriented towards broadly held perceptions of the public good, is increasingly being turned against the American people. The public debate has largely been ceded to these people pushing anti-American ideologies, as most on the right have been intimidated and developed an acute fear about speaking up about social and political issues. Relegated for many years to universities and obscure academic journals, CRT has increasingly become the Left's default ideology, being injected into government agencies, public school systems, teacher training programs, exercises in diversity by corporations, public policy frameworks and school curricula. No longer just an academic matter, CRT has become a tool of political power. It is fast achieving cultural hegemony in America's public institutions, which have become monocultures: hostile, dogmatic and suspicious of any opinion contrasting with theirs. Human resource departments serve as political offices, searching for and stamping out any dissent from the official orthodoxy. CR theorists demand priority, leading to a series of undisciplined, silly, self-destructive articles and books published by law reviews and universities. Stories, parables, chronicles and narratives replace logical reasoning as a means of getting in the way of a shared understanding of our legal and political discourse. There is re-education occurring in the workplace, schools, corporate America, the military, and the halls of government.

Few societies have been content to rest their moral codes upon so frankly rational a basis as economic and political utility. For the individual is not endowed by nature with any biological disposition to subordinate his personal interests to those of the group, or to obey irksome regulations for which there are no visible means of enforcement. Morals, then, were initially endowed with religious sanctions, because mystery and supernaturalism lent a weight which could never attach to things empirically known and genetically understood; men were more easily ruled by imagination than by science. Religion gave to a people that unity of morals and belief which seems so favorable to statesmanship. But as knowledge grows or alters continually, it clashes with mythology and theology, which change with glacial leisureliness. Since the natural inequality of men dooms many of us to poverty or defeat, some supernatural hope may be the sole alternative to despair. Destroy that hope and class war is intensified. There is no cure for such antipathies except a broadened education. The members of the Left have become frustrated with the eternal inequalities among men, prompting their demands for immediate justice; they have rejected religion as one of those many inventions by which men have sought to bear evil patiently, and to face life with hope; that there would be an inevitable working out of a law, unjust for one's life in the moment, but perfectly just in the end. To accept evil and to find for men some scheme in which they may too, accept it, is the task which most religions have attempted to fulfill.

It offered at least the consolation that man must bear only the consequences of one's own acts; unless it questions all existence, it can accept perceived evil as a passing punishment, and look forward to tangible rewards for virtue borne. But religion is a weak broth for the ills of minority neighborhoods. Without such a consolation there is insecurity, hopelessness, immorality and unmitigated despair. There is no thought today that religion is any restraint on the actions of men. Conduct, deprived of its religious supports, deteriorates into chaos, and life itself, shorn of faith, becomes an insufferable burden. There is soon a paralyzing disillusionment with every dogma and idea. Life for the inner-city poor is beset with a thousand dangers, and seldom ends naturally. For the oppressed another myth must arise, giving new form to human hope, new courage to human effort, and attempts to build another civilization. The proponents of Critical Race Theory have proposed just such a new mythology complete with all of the elements necessary to replace religion; a new fable of the fall from Eden, the corruption of the philosophical descendants of Greece and Rome, implying the possibility of a single act of redemption embodied in a revolution.

Elites see social contentment as an impediment to their power. According to CRT, racism is an unsolvable problem. As with all other leftist grievances there can be no endpoint where an issue is successfully addressed. True progressivists intend to have a program so elastic that they can always propose new worlds to conquer. If their Utopia were really practicable, and if the progressivist should secure it, they would have to defend it from further progress, which would mean his transformation from a progressivist into a conservative. This is simply to say that Progressives never define their ultimate objective but thrust their victims at once into an infinite series. The intention of being infinitely Progressive cannot permit of an established order of human existence. It is the abandonment of the fortress of tradition in order to take a new one that its proponents hope will be unassailable. Progressives never lose the sense of anger against an order, the tradition of which forces them at every step to fight for themselves and their ideas. They are driven, by the law of their being, to deny the foundations of the world they hope to conquer. Between themselves and its spirit is an unbridgeable, fundamental contradiction of principle.

Structural white privilege is described by them as a system of white domination that creates and maintains belief patterns that make current racial advantages and disadvantages seem normal. These belief patterns survive and thrive even though they fail to provide equitable outcomes for people of color. The system supports powerful incentives for maintaining white privilege and its consequences, and powerful negative consequences for trying to interrupt white privilege or reduce its consequences in meaningful ways. The system includes internal and external manifestations at the individual, interpersonal, cultural and institutional levels. From the CRT perspective, white skin is akin to owning a piece of property, in that it grants privileges to the owner that a person of color would not be afforded. White privilege refers to the "unquestioned and unearned" set of advantages, benefits, entitlements and choices bestowed on people solely because they are white. Racially privileged people are inherently racist and everyone else is inherently oppressed. Racism is a zero-sum conflict that was arranged by white people so that no one else can have a real chance in society. The Left doesn't want to admit that the current hierarchy might be attributed to competency. The fact that some people fail is not necessarily the result of another social group's success. The chief idea that two races are on unequal footing can be found not in proof of differential treatment but in differential outcome by race. This makes it easy for the left to ignore all the personal characteristics of character and behavior which lead to success. To prove racial inequality, one need not show animus or discriminatory policy. All one must now show is unequal outcome. But all human groupings will show differential outcomes. When culture is taken into account disparities can be even more deeply rooted. Discrimination would still not be the cause of such disparity.

Generally, white people who experience such privilege do so without being conscious of it. White privilege is a way to willfully refuse to engage; anything that prevents whites from confronting their racism through CRT; anything that maintains white comfort should be considered suspect and in need of disrupting. Saul Alinsky writes that the organizer must first rub raw the resentments of the people of the oppressed community; then fan the latent hostilities to the point of overt expression. An organizer must stir up dissatisfaction and discontent; provide a channel into which people can pour their frustrations-agitate to the point of conflict. CRT tactics insert racism into every interpersonal transaction in every situation. That means you have to find and focus upon the hidden racism in your workplace, your school, your neighborhood, your town, the books that you read, your church-all the time. CRT believes racism is present in every aspect of life, every relationship, every interaction and therefore its advocates look for it everywhere. They look for hidden problems that they assume must be present in everything they scrutinize. This makes all of our relationships and social systems extremely fragile and tense. CRT sees that individualism, freedom and peace are only a mechanism for keeping the marginalized in their place by obscuring larger structural systems of inequality. The accumulated and interrelated advantages and disadvantages of white privilege are reflected in racial/ethnic inequities in life expectancy and other health outcomes, income and wealth, in part due to differences in access to opportunities and resources. These differences are maintained in part by denying that they exist and refusing to redress them or eliminate the systems, policies, practices, cultural norms and other behaviors and assumptions which maintain them. Free society is a mirage, fooling people into believing they have more freedom and choice than societal structures actually allow.

The violence and looting during the summer of 2020 demonstrated that the intention was not justice but chaos and crisis. The whole intent is to keep the law-abiding citizenry alarmed and fearful. The role of keeping the middle class unsettled is very important to the left; hence the pass given to Antifa and BLM as they destroyed America's Democrat-run cities. The statist-collectivist groups hover over the remnants of capitalism, hoping to pounce on the remains, and to accelerate that end whenever possible. Their minimal goal is just to make trouble-to undercut, to confuse, to demoralize, to destroy-then take over. To the Progressive leadership, groups such as BLM and Antifa are only cannon fodder-to riot, to go to jail, to lose their careers and their future. Leadership did not create the cause of rebellion but as professionals they did know how to attack an intellectual vacuum left by a prostrate right. Normal men, at a time when they need it most, are left without a remnant of philosophical guidance. If they struggle to make sense out of what they see, they encounter so much irrationality, such a chaos of inexplicable evil, that they begin to believe in the reality constructed by the Left's imagination. One cannot fight what one does not understand, especially when the appeasers keep striving to obscure the nature of the enemy. This is not the time for compromise and self-deception. It is necessary to fully understand the nature of the enemy and his mentality, and how small the enemy is that is claiming our lives.

It is impossible for whites to do anything to correct racism because whatever they do must be in their own self-interest. You can signal that you will give in to their demands, which will then continue to come and to escalate. But giving into their ultimatums will not appease them. You didn't do it earlier, or faster or better, because of your racism. Disagreement with their program becomes evidence of the dissenter's unconscious bias or internalized white supremacy; your defensiveness or anger are really feelings of guilt or shame. Compromise means forgetting your silly ideals of freedom and individual striving, moving in the direction of pure socialism, in order to show those who want to destroy you that you are not close-minded and ignorant. Responding to their jargon is only for fools and sociopaths-they preclude objection, they disconcert and disunite opponents. CRT rejects the concepts of truth and merit as expressions of political dominance and rejects the Rule of Law. Being complicit in racism that includes capitalism, individualism, freedom, limited government, and peace means traditional society can do nothing to satisfy CRT. The left questions the fairness of any procedure the outcome of which does not accord with their pre-determined endpoint. Hate is any disagreement with Progressives. Racists are anyone who opposes Progressives. Fear mongers are anyone who argues with Progressives. Be quiet and accept your complicity in white supremacy.

CRT calls into question whether objectivity is desirable or even possible. CRT prefers their narrative of Black lived experience to any empirical evidence. The vacuousness of their complaints is demonstrated in the belief that symbolic narratives are more important than literal truth. This is a central feature of CRT discourse. The incremental truths produced through the painstaking weighing of legal evidence is too slow for CRT. For the Left, abstract analysis and formal empirical research are less appropriate than stories for communicating the understandings of people of color. When their rhetoric is combined with transgression, provocation and transcendence, especially in the absence of any critique to provide discipline, is it any wonder that CRT attracts those who are chomping at the bit to chuck traditional scholarly rigor and self-restraint? The norms of academic civility hampers readers from challenging the accuracy of the researcher's account. Discouraging white legal scholars from entering the national conversation about race has generated a cynicism in white audiences, precisely the reverse intended effect of CRT.

Now, everyone is separated by race, gender, wealth and politics in order to enable an elite to divide the country along Marxist ideas and attempt to gain complete control. The whole idea is to sow chaos where before there was peace-or at least progress. It is to disrupt any sense of community one might have had. CRT attempts to make the "oppressed" see the contradictions between the official story of universal freedom and equality and their actual inability to have real control over their lives. The job of revolutionaries is to heighten or accelerate those contradictions. The goal is to intensify social divisions and to contribute to an atmosphere of mutual suspicion and anger, even rage, that weakens the nation and makes it difficult to govern. The ultimate goal is to provoke unrest and discontent which brings about the change they are seeking. In each of its principles and tactics, Critical Race Theory mimics the writings of Marx and Engels, Lenin and Stalin. Until the rise of the Progressives, the American political mind had refused to think in terms of classes. Progressives though, and the Left in general, need a straw man to beat up on, be it a distinction of wealth, intelligence and ability, religion, ethnic origin or political party.

With Critical Race Theory, the many threads of Marxism come together. White privilege is a set of dominant cultural assumptions about what is good, normal or appropriate that reflects the Western European white world views and dismisses or demonizes other world views. Institutional white privilege are policies, practices and behaviors of business and government that have the effect of maintaining or increasing accumulated advantages for those groups currently defined as white and maintaining or increasing disadvantages for those racial or ethnic groups not so defined. This variety of Marxism determines which people count as full moral and political persons, and therefore sets the parameters who can contract into the freedom and equality that the social contract promises. Some persons, especially white men, are full persons according to the racial contract. They are seen as fully human and therefore deserving of equality and freedom. Their status as full persons accords them greater social power. This racial contract determines the bounds of personhood and parameters of inclusion and exclusion in all the other contracts that come after it. It is an agreement by white Europeans to identify themselves as fully human, and to identify all others as non-white and not fully human. So race is not just a social construct but more especially a political one, created to serve a particular political end, and the political purposes of a specific group. The racial contract makes possible and justifies some people, in virtue of their alleged superiority, exploiting the peoples, land and resources of other races. According to this theory racism is not just an unhappy accident of Western democratic and political ideas. One of the secret purposes of the Constitution, then, was to keep hidden from view the true political reality-some persons will be accorded the rights and freedoms of full persons, and the rest will be treated as sub-persons. It is not just the case that we have a well-conceived political system imperfectly applied. CRT says that American social life, political structures and economic systems are founded upon race, which in their view is a social construct. Racism actually lays the foundation of the very structure of our political systems and forms the basis for the continuing oppression of non-whites. Our society has been informed by the systematic exclusion of some persons in the realm of politics and Contract. Racism is ubiquitous, having been absorbed into our institutions of custom, practice and Law. Systematic racism has been internalized and as such there have been significantly different legal and economic outcomes between racial groups. It is most often evidenced as white inaction in the face of black need, manifesting itself both in inferior material conditions and in access to power. Differential access to quality education, sound housing, gainful employment, appropriate medical facilities and a clean environment comprise the other material differences cited by its accusers. Advocates of CRT use their focus on race to emphasize the importance of identity politics. For political identitarians, simply not being racist is not enough. The only way to undo racism, in their view, is to endlessly identify and describe it-and then dismantle it. The only way to end racism is through a social revolution that unmakes the current society entirely and replaces it with something engineered by CRT. 1619 says the founding was illegitimate so everything that followed is illegitimate. No amount of reverse racism will ever fix the effects of slavery. The objective of the 1619 Project and

CRT is not reparations but a total transformation and re-alignment of the country.

CRT says that Law is not objective or apolitical. It does not see Law as neutral, principled or dissociated from social considerations. CRT says that racism is codified in Law, woven and embedded into social structures. CR theorists hold that the Law and legal institutions in the US are inherently racist insofar as they function to create and maintain social, economic and political inequalities between whites and non-whites. The Law is actually complicit in maintaining this unjust social order, as seen in the rhetoric of neutrality of our founding documents, through which whites justify their disproportionate share of resources and social benefits. CR theorists attack the very foundations of the liberal legal order, including equality theory, legal reasoning, Enlightenment rationalism and neutral principles of constitutional Law; it challenges the incrementalistic, step-by-step approach of traditional civil-rights discourse. They reject the liberal embrace of affirmative action, color blind laws; instead relying on political agitation rather than the traditional rights-based remedies. Unlike the Civil Rights movement, which sought to work within the structures of American democracy, CRT challenges the very foundations of the traditional order.

The attempt to influence the courts with CR theory uses political and ideological factors rather than precedent and accepted principals of legal reasoning. Foreswearing analysis for narrative and repudiating reasoned argumentation in legal studies only reinforces stereotypes about the intellectual capacity of non-whites. CR scholars believe that political liberalism is incapable of adequately addressing the fundamental problems of injustice in American society, notwithstanding the legislation and hundreds of court rulings of the '50s, '60s, and beyond, and the trillions of dollars spent in reparations in the feckless "war" on poverty. CRT feels that the emphasis on equal treatment-color blindness-under the Law renders society incapable of recognizing the less overt and racist practices, those that are indirect, subtle and systematic.

Liberalism is also faulted for presupposing the apolitical nature of judicial decision making and for taking an incremental or reformist approach that prolonged unjust social arrangements and afforded opportunities for retrenchment and backsliding through administrative delays and conservative legal challenges.

The CRT vision argues that integration is not a one-way street where blacks must absorb 'white' norms. For blacks, the invitation to integrate has come to mean a form of assimilation that demands self-erasure rather than engagement of black contributions and experience. All traditional standards are therefore inherently racist. CRT criticisms of meritocracy and 'whiteness' include politeness, punctuality, education, being well-groomed and well-dressed, hard work, self-reliance, use of logic, planning and family cohesion. None of these are "white" but CRT frames them that way. The Left even criticizes math and science, whose knowledge is objective, neutral and universal. Those subjects are just politics by other means. The left has gone so far as to publish social constructionist treatments of mathematics claiming racial bias rather than objective truth, calling it reflective of the values and interests of those who produce it. CRT sees science as a white and Western way of knowing; it therefore encodes and perpetuates white dominance and thus isn't really fitting for black people who inhabit a political culture of Blackness. Whose rationality and whose presumed objectivity underlie the scientific method? Whose interests are served by science, as though that is a relevant question to ask of a universalist discipline? CRT thus cripples the people it claims to help-it undermines their ability at critical, empirical thinking, teaches them an unrealistic, us-versus-them way to see the world, that rigorous methods of logic are what white, not black people use. Affirmative action and special or lowered admission standards have resulted in students who struggled with college coursework and the social aspects of the college experience.

The left continually redefines what *is* racist. It has conditioned its clients against adopting the virtues, morals and behaviors which would make for their success, as this would betray their race/class and be an admittance that their own ways don't work. It is the Left that has formed the constructs in which the poor are trapped. To tell a black youth that he cannot make it without the help of the white Democrat is to internalize racism and contribute to feelings of inequality. The Left sells a pessimism which destructively enervates the black community. Anything that incites Americans to look at inner-city blacks as different from themselves or suggests to those blacks that their future is anywhere but the mainstream, is a dangerous thing.

The function of the social justice concept is to blame someone else for your own problems. It is merely an assertion of desire. Social justice is a term of entitlement, indicative of a claim on a good and a declaration to use the language of rights to acquire that good. Since the program of social justice inevitably involves claims for government provision of goods, paid for through the efforts of others, the term actually refers to an intention to use force to acquire one's desires. Not to earn desirable goods by rational thought and action, production and voluntary exchange, but to forcibly take goods from those who can supply them. Nobody can pretend any longer that the goal of such policies is the elimination of racism-particularly when one observes that the real victims are the better members of these privileged minorities. The small home and shop owners are the unprotected victims of every riot. The minority's members are expected by their egalitarian leaders to remain a passive herd crying for help (which is a precondition of the power to control a pressure group). Those who ignore the threats and instead struggle to rise through individual effort and achievement are denounced as traitors to the racial collective-to the incompetence or unwillingness or lethargy or malingering of the rest.

Does the authentic black experience in America require that they withdraw from mass culture like the Amish? Doesn't the middle class have the right to protect the national culture? Middle class values include stability and a high material standard of living, a respect for the conventions and proprieties, high ideals of education, professional competence and personal ambition. Today's dropout will be tomorrow's criminal. The black who rejects education merely condemns himself to further years of what he despises. Emphasis on the command of the English language is now considered Jim Crow. The implication is that standard English is being foisted on millions who are otherwise perfectly well-adjusted in their own culture, for the sole purpose of keeping them down. But mastery of the hegemonic language is always a determiner of social standing in complex societies. CRT says that language is itself a function of the powerful to impose their own views, to differentiate between knowledge and myth, reason and emotion, objectivity and subjectivity. For the Left, understanding what society deems worthy of calling knowledge depends on a prior inquiry into the social situation. Culture precedes epistemology. CRT claims that cultural bias sets standards for performance in terms of the tendencies, skills or attributes of white America, and it is against these standards that all other groups are measured. So how can blacks be authentic members of a community when, at best, they are measured by standards not of their own creation and, at worst, by standards that help justify racial domination? But what standards would CRT adopt? What subjects will be taught in school, by whom and to which students? If science, math, reading and speaking English well come to be seen as a White Thing, what will induce black students to pursue these subjects?

According to CRT, it is unfair that only producers can obtain good health care, education, housing, or any commodity in short supply, that in their view should be rationed, not competed for. These methods do not provide the inferiors with any part of the virtues of their superiors, but merely frustrate and paralyze the practice of virtue. This premise, once introduced into a culture, grows geometrically, pushing the freeloaders forward and creating more where before none existed. Weakness of any sort-intellectual, moral, financial or numerical-is today's standard of value, criterion of rights and claim to privileges. The demand for an institutionalized inequality is voiced openly and belligerently, and the right to a double standard based on race is proclaimed self-righteously. Resistance to change and "progress" is regarded as reactionary if demonstrated by a majority but hailed if demonstrated by a minority. We are told, as the majority, to tolerate and understand the minority's values and customs-while at the same time the minority proclaims that its soul is beyond the outsider's comprehension, that no common ties or bridge exist, that it does not propose to adopt any aspect of the majority's values, customs or culture, and will continue to hurl epithets at the majority's faces. All contribute to the Decline of the Law.

Is society not to recognize and reward superior virtue, talent and performance, without being confronted with charges of oppression and calls for egalitarianism? In what way are men equal, and to what extent must democracy treat them as equals? What can be done for men beyond establishing equality of opportunity and making the appropriate education available, if they will not adapt the character traits necessary to take advantage? Can the proposals of the Left be logically and historically related to any one of the original natural rights? Why does earned property necessarily become exploitive political power? Why shouldn't the leaders of the country be chosen by a meritocracy? It is said that the desires of the masses should prevail over the meritocracy of the few. True, if the constitution of a country is only a problem of arithmetic. But nature has furnished, in the form of successful men, the materials for a meritocracy which the wisely conducted state will recognize and honor, always reserving, as with democracy, a counterpoise to ambition.

Just as it is a fact of nature that the mass of men are ill qualified for the exercise of political power, so it is written in the eternal constitution of things that a few men, from various causes, are mentally, physically and spiritually better suited for social leadership. The state which rejects their services is doomed to stagnation and destruction. It is wise and just and in accord with the laws of nature that such persons should exercise a social influence much superior to the average citizen, and beyond their own numbers. A true natural meritocracy is not a separate interest in the state, or separable from it. It is an essential integrant part of any large body rightly constituted. Leadership by men of ability, birth, and wealth is one of the most natural, and most beneficial, aspects of civilized life. Domination of society by mediocrity is contrary to nature. Society ought to be designed to encourage the highest moral and intellectual qualities in man; the worst threat of the democratic system is that mediocrity will not only be encouraged but may be enforced. No effort to improve the quality of the electorate by characteristics of intelligence or property would even obtain a respectful hearing. If you lower the suffrage you must either have a strict construction of the constitution or resort to some type of plural voting for those of education and means.

In hardly any other country does the best life and energy of the nation flow so habitually apart from politics. It seems a strange paradox that a nation which stands in the very foremost rank in almost all the elements of a great industrial civilization, which teems with energy, intelligence and resources, should permit itself to be governed in the manner above described. In twenty-five centuries, where man has shown his genius in ten thousand forms of adaptation and invention, society should have discovered a more successful method of governing itself.

Edmund Burke writes: "To be bred in a place of estimation; to see nothing low and sordid from one's infancy; to be taught to respect one's self; to be habituated to the censorial inspection of the public eye; to look early to public opinion; to stand upon such elevated ground as to be enabled to take a large view of the wide-spread and infinitely diversified combinations of men and affairs in a large society, to have leisure to read, to reflect, to converse, to be enabled to draw upon the wise and learned of the past; to be formed to the greatest degree of vigilance, foresight, and circumspection, in a state of things in which no fault is committed with impunity, and the slightest mistakes draw on the most ruinous consequences; to be led to a guarded and regulated conduct, from a sense that you are considered as an instructor of your fellow-citizens in their highest concerns; to be employed as an administrator of law and justice; to be amongst rich traders, who from their success are presumed to have sharp and vigorous understandings, and to possess the virtues of diligence, order, constancy, and regularity, and to have cultivated an habitual regard to commutative justice-these are the circumstances of men, that form what I should call a natural aristocracy, without which, there is no nation."

Does that describe *anyone* on the Left attempting to wield power, or their clients? Physical and moral anarchy is prevented only by general acquiescence in social distinctions of duty and privilege. If a natural aristocracy is not recognized among men, the demagogue exercises power in the name of a faceless 'people'. The country would no doubt exchange good leadership for "the intoxication of self-expression and the negation of discipline" of the Progressive program. The people's appetites are flattered by demagogues, who satisfy the popular impulse toward action by the exhibition and spectacle of incessant change. Upon acceptance, though, of natural, inescapable differences among men rests the orderliness of the human race. Burke again: "Tranquility will be obliterated, for indefinite periods, by wild snatches at perfection such as the Left projects in their political plans. A little learning of the wrong kind might hazard that all old principles are to be discarded, while decorum and discipline are to be destroyed; anarchy and insecurity of property will be introduced. Nations will soon wish their books in ashes, seek darkness and ignorance for the citizens, restore superstition and fanaticism as blessings, and follow the standard of the first mad despot who will endeavor to lead them." No society can exist without the social differences of birth, manners, attainments, character and social condition. If these go, eventually civilization will follow.

It is folly to believe that, men naturally being unequal, society will be perfect when some state of equality enters into legislation.

Because all nature cries out that men are unequal from the very constitution of things. Those who expect to reform society upon the basis of equality are ignorant of the real character of progress. Equal opportunity gives job seekers an equal chance to compete within the framework of goals and the structure of established rules. It is seen as the procedural value of fair treatment by the rules. Striving for equality of opportunity necessarily brings about certain inequalities of outcome. People by nature have differing levels of ability and initiative which result in some having better outcomes than others. The ability to convert equal opportunities into income is affected by a multiplicity of individual and social differences that mean some people will earn more than others. It is therefore impossible to ensure equality of outcome without imposing inequality of opportunity. Striving for equal outcomes means discriminating against one group to achieve a better outcome for another. Attempts to provide equality of outcome may reduce the relative poverty of one group but taken to its usual extreme it leads to greater overall poverty. It destroys incentives to work harder. This is akin to the desire of the left to do away with legal procedural due process in favor of results based, imposed outcomes by the courts. One is fairness and transparency in the processes by which decisions are made while distributive justice means some imposed equality in physical goods. Established theories of justice holds that fair procedure leads to equitable outcomes even if the requirements of egalitarian justice are not met. Equalities of outcome disregard any idea of a meritocracy or equality before the law. It means that people will be paid the same regardless of their performance on the job and that they cannot be fired for underperformance.

Equality of outcome is the politics of envy. The difficulty is of people having different starting points at the beginning of the socio-economic competition. A person born into a middle-class family will have greater advantages by the mere fact of birth than the person born into single-parent poverty. But Utopias of equality are biologically doomed and the best to hope for is an approximate of legal justice and educational opportunity. A society in which all potential abilities are allowed to develop and function will have a survival advantage in the competition of groups. We cannot say how much potential ability and genius lurk in the chromosomes of the harassed and handicapped poor, were it allowed to be exposed. A child born into a poverty- stricken, dangerous neighborhood with rotten schools is significantly disadvantaged in his attempt to discover and maximize his talent, no matter how fine his work ethic. But what to tell the young black child who gives up in hopeless despair after being told by CRT that this earth is a realm of misery, futility and doom, where no happiness or fulfillment is possible? It is the Left which lends its sanction to such spiritual murder.

The programs they propose are the culmination of Marxism, the inception of a moral convulsion from which society will not recover, until the revolt against reason has run its course. To check it, we oppose the ideas of Aristotle, Cicero, Ibn Khaldun, Locke and Hayek. Men are saved from anarchy only by prescriptive wisdom. The Founders opposed a rigid standard to the mere flux of popular impulse and made sure that the standard was appropriately embodied in institutions. The natural inequality of men, education as a process of discovering and exploiting superior talents and energies, justice as a fair division of rewards according to achievement, a natural aristocracy based on virtue and self-discipline, and the improbability of a successful democracy are the tenants of the creed on the Right. It is an attempt to save the new civilization from the vulgarity, degradation and disillusionment of the old. It is the expectation of a conservative to measure all men by the high standards of performance and morality he imposes on himself.

In its greatest era, the United States was the freest country on earth, attracting men of all races here, from every obscure, impoverished country, who accomplished feats of productivity which would have remained stillborn in their statist homelands. Today, though, the problem is growing worse; America has become race-conscious in a manner reminiscent of the worst times, except in reverse. The cause is the same; the growth of collectivism and statism. A mixed economy disintegrates the country into an institutionalized civil war of pressure groups, each fighting for legislative favors and special privileges at the expense of one another. The pretense of any political philosophy, any principles, ideals or long-range goals have disappeared; the country is floating without direction, at the mercy of the short-term power game played by various statist gangs, each intent on getting hold of a legislative gun for any special advantage of the immediate moment. This pattern has been damaging to the country in every respect. But it has been surpassed by the current policies of black leaders. So long as they were fighting against government enforced discrimination-right, justice and morality were on their side. But that is not what they are fighting any longer. The confusions and contradictions surrounding the issue of racism have now reached their climax.

If some men are entitled by right to the products of the work of others, it means that those others are deprived of rights and condemned to labor for others. There are only political rights, not economic ones. But the advocates of the latter have all but destroyed the former. Those who advocate capitalism are the only supporters of individual rights. Rights are a moral principle defining proper social relationships. Just as man needs a moral code in order to survive (in order to act, to choose the right goals and to achieve them), so a society needs moral principles in order to organize a social system consonant with man's nature and with the requirements of his survival. Men who deny others their individual rights cannot claim, defend or uphold any rights whatsoever. The hallmark of such mentalities is the advocacy of some grand public good without regard to context, cost or means. If men have grasped some faint glimmer of respect for individual rights in their private dealings with one another, that glimmer vanishes when they turn to public issues. Regardless of the purpose-personal aggrandizement or the unearned benefit of the underprivileged-it makes no difference to the productivity of a nation. Producers, when chained, cannot produce. The national interests of the Progressives can only be achieved by sacrificing the rights, property and interests of individuals. Motives do not alter facts. The paramount requirement of a nation's productivity and prosperity is freedom. Men will not produce under compulsion and controls.

The liberals, following Rousseau, advocate the sacrifice of *all* rights to unlimited majority rule. Those who deny individual rights cannot claim to be defenders of minorities. This accumulation of contradictions, of cynical contempt for principles, or irrationality, has reached its breaking point with the latest demands. Instead of fighting against discrimination, they are demanding it be legalized and enforced. Instead of fighting for color-blindness in social and economic issues they are claiming that color should be made the primary consideration. Instead of fighting for equal rights, they are demanding special privileges. They do not merely demand special privileges on racial grounds-they demand that white men be penalized for the sins of their ancestors, who may not have owned slaves, who may not have even lived in the country. It means that whites are charged with collective racial guilt, the same principle that the worst racist charged all Negroes with for any crime committed by an individual black. That absurd policy destroys the moral base of the Negroes' fight. Their case rested on the principle of individual rights. If they demand the violation of the rights of others, they negate and forfeit their own. There can be no such thing as the right of some men to violate the rights of another. Yet the entire policy of the black leaders is moving in that direction. It is indicative of the philosophical backwardness of those leaders that the people who most need the protection of individual rights are in the vanguard of their destruction.

Racism is the quest for an automatic evaluation of men's characters that bypasses the responsibility of exercising moral judgment. To ascribe one's virtues to racial origin, is to confess that one has no knowledge of the process by which virtues are acquired, and most often, that one has failed to acquire them, any personal identity or individual achievement; one seeks the illusion of self-esteem gained from membership in a group of others just like him. It means, in practice, that a man is to be judged, not by his own character and actions, but by the characters and actions of a collective of ancestors. It is the notion that a man's intellectual traits, his moral, social and political significance is produced and transmitted by his internal body chemistry. It says that the content of his mind is inherited; that a man's convictions, values and character are determined before he is born, by factors beyond his control. Racism has only one psychological root-the racist's sense of his own inferiority. Racism is a variant of collectivism; statism is the political corollary of collectivism.

The mystique of racism is a crucial element in every variant of the absolute state-Germany, Russia, and now the United States. The philosophy of individualism and laissez-faire capitalism are the only antidotes to racism. It is not a man's ancestors that count in the free market; it is his current productive ability. Capitalism is the only system that functions in a way that rewards rationalism and penalizes all forms of irrationality, including racism. Capitalism abolished serfdom and slavery in all the civilized countries of the world. It was the capitalist North that destroyed the slavery of the agrarian-feudal South in the United States. The rise of collectivism in all its forms has reversed the gains made by the country in its first 150 years. When men began to be indoctrinated again with the doctrine that the individual possesses no rights, that moral authority and power belong to the group, they naturally gravitated toward the simplest collective to join, the least demanding to join-race. If for whatever reason the individual's society seems to become remote and purposeless, that they feel the victims of discrimination and exclusion, nothing will prevent them from looking for the kind of surcease that comes with membership in a social or moral order seemingly directed at their very souls. But the question must not be whether a group recognizable in color, features or culture has any rights as a group. No, the question is whether any American individual, regardless of color, features or culture, is deprived of his rights as an American. If the individual has all the rights and privileges due him under the laws and the Constitution, we need not worry about groups and masses- these do not, in fact, exist, except as figures of speech to be used as clubs in the political spoils game that our country has become.

The ethos of a community does not break down in a day, even when the convictions that sustain it have been undermined. Old habits remain from earlier traditions even while the idealists work to destroy them. But the old habits do not survive indefinitely. The goal of the liberals had been to smuggle the country into welfare statism by means of single, concrete, specific measures, enlarging the power of government one step at a time, never permitting these steps to be summed up into principles, never permitting their direction to be identified or the basic issue to be named. The Progressive movement saw early on that governments and society may be fundamentally transformed, without producing any great convulsions or catastrophe, if the continuity of habits is preserved, if the changes are made by slow, gradual and almost imperceptible steps. "If this constitution becomes oppressive it will be by degrees. It will aim at its end by disseminating sentiments of government opposite to republicanism; and proceed step-by-step in depriving the people of their share in the government." (Melancton Smith, June 21, 1788)

Statism was to come, not by vote or violence, but by slow rot. One of the evils of the present Progressive Party is its attempt to greatly accelerate this program. The liberals' program requires that the concept of capitalism be obliterated. The actual nature, principles and history had to be smeared, distorted, and misrepresented, because socialism has not and cannot win in open debate, neither on the grounds of logic nor economics nor morality nor historical performance. The Left needs a new straw man and racism fills that void nicely. The technique is to smear the social system of capitalism with the epithet in order to discredit the whole. Racism is far more plausibly related to the Democrat Party, though, through its association with slavery, the KKK, its opposition to civil and voting rights legislation, and its avowal of collectivism.

CHAPTER TWELVE-WEALTH AND POVERTY: THE PROBLEMS

GEORGE GILDER
ISABEL PATERSON

ROSE WILDER LANE
IRVING BABBITT

AYN RAND

"The principle that the sovereign power resides in the people, who may change the Constitution and government whenever they please, has proved a chimera. This admirable system is, with the empires of antiquity, destined to a speedy dissolution; it must, in time, through the degeneracy of the people, and a corruption of its principles, of necessity, give way to a system of remediless tyranny and oppression."

Nathaniel Chipman

"A nation which wishes to preserve republican institutions cannot afford to allow its legislatures to become engaged on a large scale in the promiscuous distribution of special subsidies and favors. Once this occurs, there is no protecting the interests of the community at large, and, what is more important, there is no protecting the political institutions themselves."

Henry C. Simon

"Despots do plunder their subjects, though history and experience tell them that, by prematurely exacting the means of profusion, they are in fact devouring the seed corn from which the future harvests of revenue are to spring. Why, then, should we suppose that the people will be deterred from procuring immediate relief and enjoyment by the fear of distant calamities-of calamities which perhaps may not be fully felt until the times of their grandchildren?

Thomas Macaulay

"It was impossible for any man at Athens to live a dissolute life unreproved: for every man was liable to be sent for by the Areopagites, to be examined, and punished, if guilty. At Rome the Censors had the same power. We Christians may be as wicked as we please. Our governments encourage vice for the benefit of the revenues."

James Burgh, *Political Disquisitions*

"In the writings of medievalists, and the rantings of the socialists, one can observe the unmistakable longing for a society in which man's existence will be automatically guaranteed to him-that is, in which man will not have to bear responsibility for his own survival. Both characterize their ideal society by freedom from change or challenge or the exacting demands of competition; a society in which each must do his prescribed part to contribute to the whole, but in which no one will face the necessity of making choices and decisions that will crucially affect his life and future; in which the question of what one has or has not earned, and does or does not deserve, will not come up; in which awards will not be tied to achievement and in which someone else's benevolence will guarantee that one never bear the consequence of one's errors. The failure of capitalism to conform to this view of existence is essential to the indictments of a free society. It is not the Garden of Eden that capitalism offers men."

Ayn Rand, *The Virtue of Selfishness,* 1961

"What if it comes to be believed that the policies of the New Deal brought about the downfall of the region that nurtured them and gave them to the nation? I will tell you what will happen. There will be a response of bitterness and reaction that will approach in duration if not intensity the response of the South to its defeat in what we now call the War Between the States. It would be one thing to lose, as it were, the Northeast. It would be a very different and vastly greater blow to lose the tradition of national liberalism that the Northeast did so much to give the nation."

Daniel Patrick Moynihan

The familiar criticisms of capitalism by the left include that it perpetrates gross immorality: racism, sexism, inequality, environmental abuse, that it is a practical failure in that it brings periodic bouts of inflation or unemployment, and its scope prevents the emergence of the large-scale planning that is indispensable to a world in the time of ecological crisis, resource scarcity, and rising expectations in the Third World. Above all capitalism creates and perpetuates inequality-between rich and poor, men and women, black and white-and destroys balance-between man and nature, consumption and conservation, individual appetites and social needs. Analysts of the left quickly become bogged down in the static and mechanical concern with distribution, fret over inequalities and speculate on possible government interventions to alleviate the problems. To the Left, slavery, discrimination and deprivation allegedly stemming from capitalism have so abused the black psyche that all sorts of new ministrations and therapies are needed to redeem it; racism and the resulting unemployment still inflict such liabilities that vast new programs of public works and affirmative action are required to overcome them. The reasonable inference arises that even though blacks are not genetically inferior, that racism and poverty have made them so. Such attitudes perpetuate the idea that the poor are incapable of helping themselves without the aid implicit in government programs.

Expanded welfare and in-kind benefits have effectively lifted all but a small proportion of Americans above the poverty line. But the expansion of the welfare rolls halted in its tracks an ongoing organic improvement in the lives of poor blacks and left behind a wreckage of broken lives and families worse than the aftermath of slavery. Although intact black families are doing better than ever, the condition of poor blacks has radically worsened. Poverty is less a state of income than a state of mind; the government dole enervates most of the people who come to depend on it. Since 1964 the moral blight of dependency has been compounded and extended to future generations by a virtual plague of family dissolution. No one contemplating the lives that have been maimed and demoralized in the wreckage of broken homes and lives can call it a victory over poverty without depriving the word of all meaning.

The refusal of American leaders to tell the truth about blacks is most important when it comes to the issue of poverty. The prevailing expressed opinion is that only racism and discrimination are needed to explain the low income of blacks. Not only does this slander white Americans it deceives and demoralizes the poor. This is to obstruct the truth and perpetuate and encourage the falsehood that blacks cannot make it without vast federal assistance, without the very government programs that account for the worst aspects of poverty and promise to extend it. The program to lift by transfers and preferences the incomes of less diligent groups breaks the psychological link between effort and reward, which is crucial to long-run upward mobility. People must feel deeply and understand that what they are given depends on what they give-and they must supply labor in order to demand goods. Parents and schools must inculcate this idea in their children both by instruction and by example. Nothing is more damaging to achievement than the belief that effort will not be rewarded, that the world is a bleak and discriminatory place in which only the predatory and the specially preferred can get ahead. Such a view in the home discourages the work effort in school and shapes future earnings capacity. If a capitalist system is to expand, it must give social and educational rewards and reinforcements to discipline and morality. As with so many things, work effort begins in family experiences. This means that successful families must take care in choosing their associates and those of their children. Parents who fail to warn their children of these Leftist pitfalls and protect them from those who profess a morbid egalitarianism of leveling down rather than summoning up, should not be surprised when their children end up stuck in the lower class. For liberals to pander to lower-class behavior is to assign them to permanent poverty, erode the requirements of growth and opportunity, and foster processes of cultural and economic deterioration. It is cultural and behavioral problems which lock people into poverty.

The psychological immaturity of children, carried into adulthood, leads men to expect life-sustaining goods to come from some undefined, effortless supply already extant. There is a positive hatred by the Left of any suggestion of persons helping themselves by their own individual efforts, by the non-political means which imply no power over others, with no compulsory apparatus. For it is true that nothing but the political means will yield them unearned public adulation. The social and economic relations of collectivism admit neither the biologically natural but mathematically irregular and interwoven order of the family, nor the creative faculty of the individual. The specter of the unpredictable man defeats the purpose of the totally planned society. Otherwise, there could be convenient arrangements for enforcing equality of condition, the complete instrumentation and functionalization of humanity, according to scientific laws and blueprints, in the gratification of their lust for power and the destruction of all ancient institutions, in the interest of the newly dominant elites.

The Grand Plan requires that the public be kept constantly in an emotional state closely resembling that of a people in crisis or at war: this lacking, obedience and cooperation wane. The mold must be set to preclude variation. The Left longs for static societies. The world transformed by capitalism had shifted beneath their feet; their minds take refuge in a fantasy of a world which should not be subject to change. There is an unending search for security in an inevitably insecure world. The self-interest of Progressives leads not to the entrepreneurial giving of one's wealth and time to the realm of chance and fate, shaped by the decisions of others in the market; rather it leads to a quest for power *over* others, in an effort to impose the fantasies of social change and egalitarianism contained in the radical politics of the sterile and predatory Left. Businessmen provide the continuing challenge and reproach to those who refuse a practical engagement in the world, men who demand power over others in the name of their ideology, without first giving and risking their wealth. Capitalism offers nothing but frustrations and rebuffs to those who wish-because of some claimed superiority of intelligence, credentials or ideals-to get without producing, to take without risking, to profit without sacrifice, to be exalted without humbling themselves to meet the ever-changing demands of others in an always perilous and unpredictable life. It is not surprising, then, that there is a broad misunderstanding and undisguised contempt of capitalism by the self-proclaimed intelligentsia who refuse to acknowledge the paramount role of individual enterprise in the progress of man. Equality of results always involves a coerced transfer of income of wealth or income from the productive to the lazy. It attempts to equalize how people end up rather than how they begin. This effectively ignores all differences in effort, character, education, morality, values, and basic human striving to better one's condition. Making people equal means treating them unequally. Coercion by the government is always necessary in attempts to achieve this. The expectation of those wanting unearned societal benefits without providing anything in the way of contributory work or ethical behavior leaves most people without equality *and* without opportunity.

The social surplus spoken of by collectivists is in fact the product of the labor and ingenuity of particular men of ability. The dependent class in the US assume that they are entitled to this surplus; that welfare is somehow summoned by the invisible hand of government rather than contrived by the specific exertions and sacrifices of men on the frontiers of enterprise. From their knowledge of failure, entrepreneurs forge success. In accepting risk, they achieve security for all. In embracing change, they ensure social and economic stability. While entitled children bemoan the absence of worthwhile work, entrepreneurs hold three jobs at once, knowing that civilization swiftly declines and decays on forty-hour weeks. Capitalist success comes from sweat and toil; natural resources gain value only by the ingenuity of man; money has value only if there is something to buy. It is entrepreneurs who produce the wealth over which politicians posture and contend. When capitalists are thwarted, deflected or dispossessed, the left is always surprised at how fast the physical means of production deteriorate into scrap iron, broken concrete, snarled wires, and ruined land. The calculable means of production are impotent to generate wealth and progress without the creative men of capitalist production, the entrepreneurs.

A welfare system of direct money grants financed by anonymous taxpayers through the choices of their elected representatives completely disassociates the earning and the spending of accumulated capital. Welfare beyond a minimal level becomes deeply problematic. Excessive welfare demoralizes its recipients and reduces them to an addictive dependency that ruins their lives. It is indeed difficult to transfer value to people in a way that actually helps them. Real wealth is the morals and ingenuity of the people. If you removed welfare payments, you will have produced nothing inside of its recipients that would allow them to go on by themselves. The receipt of unearned monies erodes the very qualities needed to be free of the welfare bureaucracy. The difference between healthy capitalism and sterile socialism is not natural resources and industrial plants. It is ideas and attitudes. Because capitalism is chiefly an intellectual and psychological arena its far greater creativity is combined with less apparent stability. Capitalist economics stress the dynamic supply of new products, focusing on the processes of production and innovation, rather than stressing aggregate demand for goods and services; emphasizes the generation of demand through the production of goods rather than through manipulating the value and supply of money.

In poor communities, capital, in its human form of work effort combined with education and savings, does not adequately accumulate to provide opportunities of income and wealth. Men's links to children and the future are too insufficient to induce work and thrift. Such men cannot bring themselves to work, save and forgo immediate rewards in the name of an unseen and unknowable future. It is the firm links between work, wealth and marriage that creates a future oriented psychology in the mass of men. The act of marriage is necessarily one which stands centrally in the whole complex of social behavior. It stands centrally to a man's attitude towards time, saving and capital. A condition of widespread illegitimacy and family breakdown can be a sufficient cause of persistent poverty, separating men from the extended horizons embodied in their children. The analysis of poverty that begins with family structure and marital status explains far more about the problem than differences in income, education, race, discrimination and any other items cited in leftist academic journals. The first priority of any serious program against poverty is therefore to strengthen the male role in poor families. Unattached young males are defined largely by lacking any orientation to the future. Confucius remarked "the man who does not take far views has near troubles." Living from day-to-day and hand-to-mouth, lower-class individuals are unable to plan or save or keep a job. Short time horizons are a deep-seated psychological defect affecting millions of the poor, mostly single, divorced and alienated men, who in their conspicuousness set the tone for the entire community. Their style of instant gratification and concentration in ghettos multiplies their impact on young directionless black males. This short-sighted outlook of poverty stems largely from the breakdown of family responsibilities among fathers. Civilized society is dependent on the man's submission of his short-term sexual behavior to the extended maternal horizons of women. The woman gives a man a unique link to the future, and he gives her faithfulness and a commitment to a lifetime of work and support. It is marriage that converts the short horizons of youth and poverty into the long horizons of career and child rearing. It is familial anarchy among the concentrated poor of the inner city in which flamboyant and impulsive youths, rather than responsible men provide the themes of aspiration. The result in the former case are boys brought up without authoritative fathers in the home to instill in them the values of responsible paternity, and the adverse pattern is extended into future generations.

The supreme test of any civilization is whether it can socialize men by teaching them to be fathers-creating a culture in which men acknowledge their paternity and willingly raise their offspring. This is largely absent in the poor black community. What is more likely is unattached men living off the welfare that single mothers receive from the government. It is not surprising, then, that young people from single-parent homes are two to three times more likely to have emotional, behavioral and learning problems, and commit more crimes, than children from homes with two parents. The father, if present in the poor black home, gives the female children a role model of how to form healthy relationships with men, and for the son he provides a role model for how to treat women in his future dealings. Blacks have no appropriate role models whereby young men and women can see what is possible in their lives. In a father's absence, there are no models for discipline and self-control. Peer pressure preys on these vulnerable kids. It is heartbreaking to see generation after generation waste themselves on drugs, promiscuity, ignorance and dependency.

Benefit levels destroy the father's key role and authority. In the welfare culture money becomes not something earned by men through hard work, but a right conferred on women by the State. Welfare tells the man he is not a necessary part of the family; his wife knows he is dispensable, and his children sense it. Sooner or later the pressures of the subsidy state dissolve the roles of fatherhood, the disciplines of work, and the rules of marriage. Indexing the benefits to the price level makes them even more reliable and attractive, still more preferable in every way to the taxable, inflatable and interruptible earnings of a father. All wage earnings, moreover, entail the hazards of foregoing Medicaid, food stamps, housing and public social services. Only in the ghetto, among the most visible, concentrated and identifiable poor, have the insidious seductions of the war on poverty and its well-paid agents fully prevailed over home and family. Protest and complaint replace diligence and discipline as the sources of income. Poor blacks are not taught the virtues necessary to secure and keep a job, but rather the steps necessary to procure welfare payments, generation after generation. Boys grow up seeking support from women. Nothing is more destructive to all the male values than the growing recognition that when all is said and done his wife and children are better off without him. His role as provider, the definitive male activity throughout history, has been seized from him; he has been cuckolded by the compassionate State. His response is that very combination of resignation and rage, escapism and violence, short horizons and promiscuity that everywhere characterizes the life of the poor. He tries to maintain his self-image by the use of muscle and bluster and turns to the street for his male affirmations. Poverty and unemployment are chiefly reflections of the family breakdowns caused by the Left.

Acquisition of a primary job creates incentives for mature and responsible behavior and the assumption of long-term family commitments. Secondary, dead-end jobs foster the erratic and short-term perspectives associated with the lower class and discourage a real break with the impulsive behavior of youthful male groups, where job disciplines are derided and undermined. There is no motivation to face the tedium and frustrations of daily labor; child support provisions for absent fathers reduces the amount of money going to the children, by effectively diminishing the welfare allotment and transforming the father's payment from a morally affirming choice into an embittered legal requirement. Such men cannot long be made to work to pay for children whom he rarely sees, kept by a woman who is living with someone else. Work requirements are particularly futile because they focus on women with small children, the official welfare clients, rather than on the unlisted beneficiaries-the men who subsist on the system without joining it, who live off welfare mothers without marrying them. There are millions of these men. They are the counterpart to the masses of welfare mothers who preoccupy all the social workers and reformers. These women live and bear children of dubious paternity, with a succession of men working from time to time in the cash economy of the street, leaving their children with a grandmother receiving disability payments for a sore back. The anomalies and perversities of the system become serious chiefly as the benefits rise to the point where they affect the life choices of whole generations. Every attempt of the left to ameliorate some perceived inequality involves "redistributing" something one person has earned and giving it to someone who hasn't. Focusing on re-distribution rather than production means smaller and smaller amounts are left until there is equality in poverty.

Our welfare system creates moral hazards because the benefits have risen to a level higher than a man could earn would he marry the woman and support his children. For an ill-educated man from the welfare culture to support a family at that level requires delay of marriage and childbearing until after the development of economic skills and then the faithful performance of work over a period of years. These requirements are essentially moral and familial. The attempt to elicit them by legal pressures while deterring them remorselessly by contrary financial incentives is as hopeless a venture as has ever been undertaken by government. The most serious fraud is committed not by the members of the welfare culture but by the creators of it, who conceal from the poor the most fundamental realities of their lives: that to live well and escape poverty they will have to keep their families together at all costs and will have to work harder than the classes above them. In order to succeed, the poor need most of all the spur of their poverty. In an evolutionary sense all life is struggle, the effort to become fully human, to reach one's full potential. The difficulties encountered, in order to realize their existence are precisely what awaken and mobilize their activities, their capacities. Political philosophies which promise to save us from all the pains, the grievances, which the common course of life entails will lead us, instead, into deeper torments. But the pains and sorrows of our life are essential to the balance of our character; with them lacking, the human race would be distorted and destroyed by endeavoring to separate from our nature qualities upon which all our other attributes depend. A guaranteed job denies the crucial fact that all jobs are to some extent created by the worker; only he can guarantee the job, by the act of supplying labor, undergoing hardship, achieving distinction, and thus becoming part of the struggle by which human life improves itself. These differences, palpable in the very texture of the job, are what distinguish real work from make-work. One way to gain the consent of the governed is to give them jobs and money. Government can thus assimilate its own constituency. But the counterproductivity of public employees lowers efficiency, engages ever more scarce resources, and drags down the entire economy. Job guarantees give what cannot be given. It implies that everyone could diminish their effort and slackly accept pay without causing the entire system to decay. If, under guarantees such as exist in civil service, all workers merely performed to the minimal level, the US standard of living would collapse. Crucial to a real job is the risk of being fired if the work is not performed. A guaranteed job implies that the work is mostly optional and thus no real job at all. At the same time, performers of hard, productive labor can derive deep satisfaction from their jobs. By expanding the realm of subsidized work and welfare the government undermines the morale of the entire country.

Most affirmative action rules are ostensibly designed to shield the poor and vulnerable from the costs of change, but regardless of the cosmetics of egalitarian policy, the chief effect is to deny to the lower classes the benefits of a progressing economy. Risk and competition, death and change, are the very essence of the human condition. The effort to fight unemployment by subsidizing make-work jobs merely makes the problem worse and foists them onto the public at large in a stagnant economy. In general, the most important effect of the government attempt to shield itself and its client from uncertainty and risk is to place the whole system at peril. It becomes unable to react resourcefully to the new shocks and sudden challenges that are inevitable in a dangerous world.

Neither can welfare be justified in economic terms. The attempt to deny and plan away the dangers and uncertainties of our lives violates the spirit of capitalism and the nature of man. A government devoted to suppressing uncertainty finds itself forever having to channel or depress the human will to risk. The effect is to drive an economy from positive and creative avenues to negative and destructive ones.

As with business the welfare state grows by making its product more acceptable, more appealing to potential recipients, by offering more attractive packaging, calling it workfare instead of welfare. All public sector work that is created to "develop jobs" rather than to accomplish a needed purpose may be assumed to represent waste. Beneath it all is the same old trap of dependency and demoralization. Since make-work jobs do not contribute to the economy, the cost of them comes from the output of productive jobs elsewhere, either through increased taxes, expanded federal borrowing, or the directly inflationary creating of money. All three take away from the wealth available for investing in the real economy-capital equipment, goods and services, or savings to be lent in mortgages for home building. By competing with private business, government jobs deprive ghetto businesses of low-cost labor; by requiring and paying a minimum wage, the easier welfare jobs reduce the employment pool available for start-ups. Potential permanent jobs involving real work are replaced by artificial jobs that offer a deceptive and demoralizing experience that once again deprives the poor of an understanding of their real predicament: the need to work harder than the classes above them in order to gain upward mobility.

Cynical administrators transmit to impoverished youth their own contempt for the world of work. Make-work is only welfare in disguise. The 'hassle" of the jobs themselves is resented because it deceives neither the recipients nor the supervisors about what is going on and whether the jobs are done well or not. Far more at fault is the political order that fosters this self-destructive and socially erosive behavior-the adults who create these insidious systems of dependency and self-indulgence. Welfare shields people from the realities of life and so prevents them from growing up and finding or creating useful tasks. A desultory labor market creates desultory laborers-the problems of young black men begin long before their first rejection for a job and persist long after they receive one. The attitudes of the secondary work force are a significant source of instability for small businesses. But good jobs are not enough to create good workers; the sloth and the suspicion in the welfare culture remains. Productivity matches those of primary workers only when no concessions are made on quality, deadlines or work attitudes. Large companies know they cannot win if pitted against government civil rights lawyers, so they capitulate whenever offered tolerable terms. But the lesson companies learn is to avoid at all costs any entanglements with government social programs. It is usually easier to bypass EEOC lawsuits and hiring quotas by building plants in the suburbs rather than in inner cities, as most large companies do. Incalculable gains came from the civil-rights effort that brought the energies of some blacks more fully into the economy and transformed cities such as Atlanta.

A person, like a nation, who is forced to experience the economic foundation of his life, gains valuable knowledge, which renders him to a greater degree an economic man. He becomes a person better able to find his most useful role in the division of labor and more likely to invent a profitable job or business. Entrepreneurism asserts a firm hierarchy of values and demands a hard discipline. It is the source of all we are and can become, the hope of the poor and the true redemption of the oppressed. The risks and exigencies of one's life define its bounds and possibilities. Much of the productivity and growth of entrepreneurs comes from intangible accumulations of knowledge and efficiency which are the invisible profits of the system. One of the key moral hazards entailed in government job programs and other insurance schemes is this loss of knowledge-the debauchery of human capital-a real capital loss-that is inflicted on citizens who never learn their own best abilities and opportunities. As these debits accumulate, the economy declines.

Then there is the reproach that nearly every other group presents to the failure of black communities. Because blacks have been at the bottom of social statistics for decades now, economists miss the dynamism within the American system. Many men from other ethnic groups have overcome similar barriers by entering business, studying at night, working two jobs, finding the employers who value leadership and productivity more than years at school. Japanese Americans were interned, by a Democrat president, in concentration camps during World War II, but thirty years later they had higher per capita earnings than any other ethnic group in America except for Jews. Three and one-half million Jewish immigrants arrived on our shores around the turn of the twentieth century with an average of nine dollars in their pockets. Six decades later the mean family income of Jews was almost double the national average. Yet social scientists who live in the midst of these convulsions of change can still declare that there has been no shift in the distribution of wealth and income in the country in the last one hundred years. All American ethnic groups in the past rose out of poverty partly by learning proper English and by downplaying their own culture. Today's young blacks are thought to require the freedom to speak in their own polyglot for reasons of ethnic pride. Most importantly, every successful group in our history rose up by working harder than other classes, in low paid jobs, with a vanguard of its men in entrepreneurial roles. But it is supposed that the current poor can leapfrog all the drudgery with the aid of therapeutic government, a view which depicts the poor as a race so alien to the entire American experience, so radically different in motive and character, that one can speak in terms of a new form of liberal bigotry. Past racism can explain a good deal about today's racism. The demoralizing blandishments of the War on Poverty and the explosion of welfare explain much more. The black community needs a scapegoat for its own failures. It is far more correct to say that Progressivism, not racism, accounts for the enduring poverty of blacks in America. The Left claims that the poor's willingness to work is unaffected by levels of welfare and in-kind support substantially higher than the prevailing wage. The poor, however, choose leisure because they are paid to do so. They are assumed to be relatively unshaken by the plague of family breakdowns-joblessness, drinking and drug consumption, philandering, little support for education-and any lower income or unemployment levels are said to be due to discrimination, and the behavior of poor black youths to be little influenced by the absence of fathers. Poor men are assumed to be unaffected by the higher relative incomes available to single mothers from welfare and in-kind payments, which are alleged to have no relationship to high rates of unemployment and illegitimacy.

Any welfare system will eventually extend and perpetuate poverty if its benefits exceed prevailing wages and productivity levels in poor communities. As long as welfare is preferable to what can be earned by a male provider, the system will deter work and undermine families. Whatever the changes and reforms, welfare families will readjust their lives to qualify for what they see as their best available economic opportunity. Welfare exerts a constant, seductive, erosive pressure on the marriages and work habits of the poor, and on poor communities. Welfare continuously mutes and misrepresents the necessities of life that prompted previous generations of poor people to escape poverty through the invariable routes of work, family and optimism. The prevailing dogma that effective father substitutes exist, in the network of government support poor black women enlist to raise their children, is a myth. The truth is really to be found in the intergenerational transmission of poverty, ignorance, crime, and misogyny. It is out of poverty and ignorance that crime and family disorder come. The pattern of poverty and destructive gender and parenting behavior is the single greatest cause of chronic failure among poor blacks.

The black family was better off by nearly every measure-education, out-of-wedlock births, dual parent families, and work ethic-before the war on poverty and the expenditure of twenty trillion dollars on their behalf. The war on poverty reduced the effectiveness of the civil rights movement by converting its moral authority based on rights to just another political interest group seeking entitlements, blocking change and social mobility for those who need it most. Not political empowerment but social development is the crucial challenge for the underclass. For now we are left with a permanent lower class with gender and race attitudes that are emotionally and socially brutalizing, and physically self-destructive; the posturing, pathological narcissism of "cool pose" masculinity, with its predatory, sociopathic sexuality, soul-numbing addictions; the daily and nightly carnage on the streets of Democrat-run cities, the grim statistics on child and spousal abuse, rape, poverty, illiteracy and suicide, the overwhelming prevalence of out-of-wedlock births, the belief that education is "white." Motherhood becomes a source of self-affirmation; single motherhood has deep roots in the lives of black women. Conduct is considered a kind of protest when the acts are openly expressive of an oppositional social or political point of view. Kind of like performance art. Stealing a car for the purposes of posturing and joyriding is actually an act of free speech. As such it is of course entitled to constitutional protections. A youth boiling with hormones will wonder why he should not give full freedom to his desires; if he is unchecked by family, custom, morals or laws; he may ruin his life before he matures sufficiently to understand the need for restraint, if it is not to consume in chaos both the individual and the group.

The government creates maximum incentives to qualify for benefits, maximum rewards for familial strife and disruption. The goal of welfare is to help people out of dire but temporary problems, not to treat temporary problems as if they were permanent ones, and then make them so. The best that any program can achieve is to relieve poverty without creating a welfare culture that perpetuates it. Welfare now erodes work and family and thus keeps poor people poor. What is worse is the ideology which sustains a whole system of federal and state bureaucracies that also operates to destroy their spirit. The ideology takes the form of false theories of discrimination and spurious claims of institutional racism as the dominant forces in the lives of the poor. There is little talk among activists about racial integration. They declare that integration will be almost as bad as segregation if it results in complacent, middle-class, interracial society.

It is psychological forces that above all else shape the performance of an economy along with given resources and technology. It is ambition and resolve that fosters the impulses of growth, enterprise and progress. Heavy taxes on personal incomes stifle the drive to excel and succeed. Steeply progressive rates may have an idealistic ring, but their effect is to reduce incentives for economic success, work and risk, and to force the highly productive to seek the advantages of insurance and security, political power and leisure time. High marginal rates continuously undermine the very diligence and determination that are necessary to accomplish any useful work in the world. They diminish the motive to move up, negatively impact taxable economic activity, work effort and productivity, and promote the impulse to pull out and return to the dole.

Obstacles, and problems overcome, elicit motivation and creativity and impel progress, much to the chagrin of the welfare industry. The antidiscrimination drive can only reap a harvest of demoralization, work-force withdrawal, and family breakdown, and a decay in the spirit of work, family and optimism on which enduring upward mobility depends. The crucial goal of all antipoverty programs must be to lift the incomes of males providing for families and to release the poor from the honeyed snares of government jobs and subsidies. Such a policy, though, is the opposite of the ones favored by academics and government, secure within their academic tenure or civil-service protection, which is one reason poverty amid American riches is unlikely to end soon. The intoxication of the power to unleash egalitarian taxation, along with introducing a new "Progressive" cultural force in America, devoted to "meaningful work" and "social change," without a real sense of costs, is overwhelming. As an instrument for deliberate social alteration, the income tax has supplanted the industrial revolution. That force, at the end of the 1970's and now again has met a counterforce of tax revolt, inspired by the need to re-establish the foundations of the country within the rule of Law.

The positive influences that the egalitarians would vitiate-home, family, church, and community-are, in fact, the only influences that work. The egalitarian program can destroy lives, taxing away the earnings of the successful, penalizing ambition and productivity, but it is not capable of fostering upward mobility among the groups that lack strong community and familial cultures. America is described as racist and exploitive in order to vindicate sweeping new powers for government and its administrative bureaucracy. There developed a need of federal lawyers to make up for a lack of careerist drive and aggressiveness in the black community. The lower class has little to lose in clamoring for the re-distribution of wealth. The problem of impoverished blacks is not at all new, subtle or insidious. It is essentially the problem of most previous generations of American poor: how to make up by the dint of effort and ambition for a lack of family background and educational qualifications. The welfare state is manifestly an obstacle. Furthermore, the emphasis on education and the credential system to sort applicants out depreciates the assets of diligence, determination and drive when they do exist. The ideology of Progressive schooling, like that of discrimination, and the culture of welfare, demonstrably haunts the ghetto mind and discourages the efforts and ambitions that are indispensable to progress. The lack of social capital in poor neighborhoods is also telling-that being a shared vision and willingness of residents to intervene and create social trust (a sense of engagement in neighborhood goals and ownership of public spaces); it is a public good provided by citizens who participate to build up their communities that is essential to maintaining order.

Black resentment and feelings of inadequacy do not add up to racism on the part of whites. You simply cannot assign every discrepancy of outcome between whites and blacks to racism, without any mention of the paucity of effort to reform poor black families, neighborhoods, communities and cities, by the very people claiming victimhood. Are income, housing, educational achievement, employment, infant mortality and out of wedlock birth discrepancies and inequalities only attributable to racism? The value of a society's goods ultimately derives from the values of its people. The moral order defines the order of value that defines the prices and worth of a society's goods. The worth of housing derives from the social values and disciplines of a familiar community and access to schools not dominated by the lower class. Housing values increase with distance from poor neighborhoods, particularly those of broken welfare families that produce the bulk of America's violent criminals. Because welfare clients receive their apartments free, they value them commensurately. Decent housing is an effect of, not a cause of middle-class values. Someone in public housing has no incentive to maintain the cleanliness, safety or appearance of something he does not own. The forced movement of welfare blacks into communities of middle-class whites is an act of social disruption, particularly when done with the subterfuge of rent or mortgage subsidies. Black cultural pathologies make the idea of structural racism simply a crutch in the search for black moral leadership in efforts of self-reform. Working to divide America along the lines of race is simply the old Marxist class warfare argument that embroiled the world in revolution and war for a century and cost two hundred million lives. Is that what the proponents of 1619 and CRT are after? If they survive, the children of the poor are thrust out on the street to shift for themselves; Chicago and New York are shooting galleries and drug meccas. What is there to conserve in such a society? It is the curse of a populace cut off from the continuity of humanity, deprived of religious consolation, political tradition, decency of existence, true family life, education and any possibility of moral improvement. Never have so many been bored and hopeless, condemned to monotonous labor when they are willing to work at all, in a world where material success and moral individualism are otherwise so readily visible and available.

The apparent manifestations of racial and ethnic prejudice are in fact expressions of economic class-the natural disinclination to accept lower-class values. Racial antipathies have some roots in ethnic origin, but they are also generated, perhaps predominantly, by differences of acquired culture-of language, dress, habits, morals, behavior and religion. In order to escape such tensions, the upper economic classes will send their children to schools dominated by their own class. In their efforts to educate their offspring as best they can, whatever the cost, these families are making a major investment in the future of the country, in which coming generations will depend. What is reprehensible is the effort to force lower middle-class families to dispatch their children to ghetto schools dominated by gangs of fatherless boys bearing knives. The worst thing that liberals do is depict as racist the desire of parents to protect their children from the schools that liberal policies have largely ruined, and that black parents, if they could, would flee as rapidly as white, and that white liberal parents would no sooner accept for their children. Inner city black children fail because their families and communities devalue study and academic achievement. Having to speak proper English means a giving up of a part of the black identity.

The institution of the family is disintegrating before our eyes because it has been deprived of its old economic and educational advantages. So it is with aristocracy, religion, local government and the other elements which bound man to man for centuries. National debts recklessly increased until they are repudiated, ignorance of a higher law, along with the continual revision of common law are evidence of what an age without historical veneration does for itself and its successors. Prejudice and prescription are delicate growths, slow to rise, easy to injure, hardly possible to resuscitate. The Left works against prescription in the form of local rights and private property, and habits of life, against prejudice that favors the old decencies, the family, and religious dogmas which can still be forces of great power among the masses. Immensely expensive systems of state schooling have succeeded in permanently damaging private character and public life when Leftist ideas began to supplant mainstream opinion. Democracies press against their proper limits, to convert political equality into economic levelling, to invade every personal right and privacy, to insist that equal opportunity to succeed to any height becomes only mediocrity; they set themselves above the Law; they substitute mass opinion for justice. The strong inclination of democratic peoples to invade the traditional securities of private life is a shocking perversion. No prescription, no Law should operate against their wishes. We may cherish democracy but not in it unlimited and lawless forms. The abstract Leftist and fanatic reformer, intending to cleanse society, may find he has scrubbed it clean away.

The lawless policies and approaches the country has adopted in our concern about race will likely be applied to the millions of others now flooding across our southern border. The potential injury that will be inflicted on our economy and on those poor is quite incalculable. But on the basis of the long and thoroughly unambiguous experience of our government in blighting the lives of Blacks and Native Americans-the previous minorities reduced to a state of bitter dependency by the government-one can only predict the damage to be tragically great. In the midst of the American poverty in the inner cities which the Left bewails, it admits strangers both to the country and its moral principles. How will you feed them? How will you clothe them? How will you house them? To get a grip on the problem of poverty one should forget the idea of overcoming inequality by redistribution. The effort to take income from the rich, thus diminishing their investment, and to give it to the poor, thus reducing their work incentives, is sure to cut American productivity, limit job opportunities and *perpetuate* poverty. Rather than learning the clear lessons of the American experience, the Washington bureaucracies are rushing to accommodate new immigrants within the old formulas of discrimination and poverty. Far worse is the indefensible program of bilingual education which undermines any entry into American life and culture, segregating it into presumably separate but equal classrooms. The refusal of government to insist on literacy in English effectively removes poor blacks and immigrants from any chance at economic success and insures their dependency. It would be a blessing for the newcomers to somehow avoid the blandishments of the welfare culture as it reaches out hungrily towards the endless arrivals. What has the Left done to maintain the family as the basic unit of society? Welfare payments only create dependency, with all of its associated evils of drug and alcohol abuse, family disintegration, depression, crime and intergenerational transmission of habits, and behavior likely to result in more of the same.

Even were the country to be created as a slavocracy, 600,000 men died in the Civil War which ended the institution. The nation's history has been a series of episodes haltingly seeking to redeem itself through legislation, court decisions and reparations. Blacks complain that it is difficult first to obtain resources to be deployed in their communities and subsequently to control those resources. This despite the expenditure of twenty trillion dollars in the 'war on poverty' since 1964. Those monies went almost directly to consumption and little if any saved to consolidate capital for productive enterprises. Neither equality nor moral wholeness has come out of the guilt money of white liberals, in "reparations" spent to try to settle the presumed debt. The narrative collapses in light of the struggles and successes of countless Americans of all races who *have* found the country to be a refuge and a land of opportunity. Moral hazard is the danger that a policy will encourage the behavior or promote the disasters that it insures against. If the insurer state attempts to absorb all the risks of individuals and businesses-of unemployment, inflation, foreign competition, waning demand, accident and disability-it will find itself overwhelmed with larger perils and responsibilities than it can manage. A siege of insurance can bring about some of the very dangers that motivate it. Most fundamentally people experience a steady erosion of the link between conduct and its consequences, effort and reward, merit and remuneration. With the welfare state the insurance principle emerged as the commanding theme of federal policy.

This is the moral hazard of the welfare state. Unemployment insurance causes unemployment. Aid For Families and Dependent Children makes more families dependent and fatherless. All means-tested programs promote the value of being poor and thus perpetuate poverty. Furthermore, the welfare state has not only been displacing private charities and schools but also private savings and insurance. The diastolic process whereby the system pulls in the savings that sustain it has faltered. The particular moral hazards of various policies accumulate and coalesce into a collective danger of national sclerosis, an economy that is closed to the necessarily risk-fraught and unknown future. The principle of averaging and equalizing risk informs many policies that do not ostensibly resemble insurance, but which share the effect of spreading the consequences of economic misfortune or change. The result of all this activity-the shifting, diffusing, concealing, smoothing, evading and collectivizing the real risks and costs of economic change-is to desensitize the economy. It no longer responds well to the news of scarcity and disequilibrium-the high prices that signal new opportunities, and no longer provides information about invention, creativity and entrepreneurship. If Progressive redistribution from the rich to the poor, or from white to the black could relieve social stresses, the time since 1964 should have been golden years rather than a period of growing frustration and social unease. The war on poverty took away any identity and possible feelings of self-worth from black males.

The Democrat party has forced, not whites, but African Americans, into the social construct and internalization of racism. It is now central to the purposes of the Left to have blacks enlisted in their cause. Blacks inexplicably support their (the Democrats) supremacy and dominance by maintaining and participating in the set of attitudes, behaviors, institutions and ideologies that undergird the party's power. People of color no longer have the ultimate decision-making power over their lives and resources. As a result, blacks believe that white Democrats know more about what needs to be done for them than *they* do. An underlying theme of 1619 is that wider access and more integration into various government programs is the way forward, despite considerable evidence to the contrary. Structurally there is a system in place that rewards an intervening class of race hustlers who take their direction from the Democrats, so it is passed along as coming from blacks. Reformers focus on changing institutions rather than individuals. They first should endeavor to conform political arrangements to the dictates of Natural Law, and be profoundly familiar with the world of reality, before tinkering with the structure of society. Weak-minded humanitarians and community agitators wrongly think that established traditions must be the cause of their afflictions. Avarice, disorderly appetites, and other vices are the actual causes of the storms that trouble life. Social problems are the result of individual incompetence rather than signs of a social structure in need of drastic repairs.

The problem in many instances is not really discrimination at all, but the attitude that wealth is possible without work and thrift; that life's setbacks and frustrations are the fault of others; that good intentions of bureaucrats are better than good results; that what is needed to put the world right is simply a vision of free goods that teaches people to believe that they are not responsible for their lives and choices; there the problem inevitably grows. Furthermore, poor blacks are more likely to go on welfare because many of them are concentrated in inner-city communities, where all the therapeutics of the social-service bureaucracies can be focused on them. Welfare perpetuates the causes and effects of poverty. For half a century the United States Government has housed, clothed and fed a significant portion of the nation's citizens, at the rest of the country's expense. The Left's conception of social progress is defined only in terms of improvement in the material conditions of living for the masses; visions of an endless upward sweep of democracy in which every individual shares increasingly in the "public surplus," intoxicating the pliant imaginations of people loosened from traditional social moorings. The ideals and Utopias that float before the popular imagination point to great social and industrial changes, to redistributions of wealth, and to a dissolution of the present fabric of society. When the promised heaven on earth keeps failing to show up, it is never the fault of the ideas of liberals. The Progressive cannot conceive of an unprovoked suffering; it cannot be that the criminal culture of fatherless black males was caused by the programs of the Great Society. Liberals cannot believe that their true religion of saving the world hasn't yet delivered the equity and social justice that they know is just around the corner and keep promising. There has to be an Other.

The public establishment of ideas about black poverty by government officials, academic social scientists and complicit media leaders, is a crime. Blacks are told that the world is against them, and the prevailing powers want to keep them down; that racism and discrimination are ubiquitous except under the order and surveillance of the law; that jobs are unavailable; that slumlords gouge their clients, that police are universally guilty of bias and brutality; that the only allies of young blacks are poverty lawyers, social workers and liberal politicians. This image of a racist and venal country, this image of a corrupt and immobile society incapacitates all of the poor who believe in it. Upward mobility is at least aspirational; necessary is an accurate perception of the nature of the contest and as admiration for the successful. Education and credentials are the most important for government employment; in the real-world diligence, discipline, dedication, hard work, ambition and a willingness to take risks are more important.

What is missing in poor black communities is evolutionary optimism-the biology of hope, the spirit of moral community-all needed for upward mobility. All are necessary to sustain the spirit of work and enterprise against the setbacks and frustrations it inevitably meets in a difficult world; it inspires trust and cooperation in an economy where they will often be discouraged; it prompts the forgoing of present pleasures in the name of a future which may go up in smoke; it promotes risk and initiative in a world where all rewards vanish unless you get in the game. In order to save without the certainty of future value, in order to work beyond the requirements of the job in hopes of promotion, one has to have confidence in a law of compensations beyond the immediate and distracting struggles of existence. Work, family and optimism are being eroded now by the intellectual and political leaders of the Left in perhaps the freest and most prosperous of all the world's societies.

To believe in subliminal racism, de facto segregation and concepts like the ghetto are vague and out of date reminders of racial grievance and sequestration. It is as if there were some strong current in American Leftist thought that cherishes the idea of racism, that cannot, indeed, do without it. Yes, there is the fear lurking in many a liberal heart that blacks cannot prevail in a truly free competition. And if racism is dead blacks and their political patrons will not much longer be allowed to run the bureaucracies-or subsist intellectually on the rationales-of civil rights, affirmative action, EEOC lawsuits, expanded welfare and compensatory employment programs.

The government makes the dubious claim that it can use wealth more productively than a capitalist; they will raise the always adverse odds of successful enterprise with taxes to the point where an investor no longer has any interest. The poor man swings between welfare and the lottery while the rich man alternates between risk-taking in business and tax-free municipal bonds. The conversion of political power to the ends of a levelling humanitarianism uses the blunt instruments of the graduated income and inheritance tax. These devices were irresistibly tempting to social reformers, almost impossible to restrain within the strict necessities of limited government. Property must follow power; a people possessed of universal suffrage, and just then beginning to nibble at the bait of social planners-this people could not be withheld from experimenting with their new engine of change. The rights of property, in a nation increasingly industrialized and experiencing rapid growth, would inevitably be contrasted with the supposed rights of man. Property being the most important of the social rights to be protected nevertheless does not make for a good bumper sticker slogan.

A growing sense of the omnipotence of Congress has made the notion of a single written instrument creating and limiting the government decidedly obsolete. All moral and Natural Law limitations on Congress are now deemed strictly theoretical, without binding legal meaning, and relevant only to the extent they impinge on the minds of lawmakers. Most could no longer conceive of the constitution as anything anterior or superior to government and ordinary law. The constitution was merely the original frame of government with no lasting effect on future legislation. All law, customary and statutory, comprise the "living, breathing" constitution which is a Progressive euphemism for arbitrary law-the chief characteristic of the law under any dictatorship.

CHAPTER THIRTEEN-INDOCTRINATION OF THE MIND

AYN RAND
RENE DUBOS

ISABEL PATERSON
ROSE WILDER LANE

"For in dealing with a mob, a philosopher cannot influence them by reason or extort them to reverence, piety and faith; nay, there is need of religious fear also, and this cannot be aroused without myths and marvels. For thunderbolt, aegis, trident, torches, and lances in the arms of the gods are myths and so is the ancient theology. But the founders of states gave their sanction to these things as bugbears to scare the simple minded. Now, since this is the nature of mythology, and since it has come to have its place in the social and civil scheme of life as well as in the history of actual facts, the ancients clung to their system of education for children and applied it up to the age of maturity; by this they can satisfactorily discipline every period of life. But now, the writing of history and present-day philosophy have come to the front. Philosophy, however, is for the few and myths are more useful to the people at large."

Strabo (64 BC- AD 24)

"I exist, and I have senses through which I receive impressions; the cause of my sensations is outside of me, they affect me whether I have reason for them or not; they are produced and destroyed independently of me…Thus other entities exist besides myself. I find that I have the power of comparing my sensations, so I am endowed with an active force for dealing with experience." The next step is reasoning. "I see design in a thousand instances, from the structure of my eyes to the movements of the stars; I should no more think of attributing to chance, however often multiplied (a la Diderot), the adjustment of means to ends in living organisms and the system of the world, than I would ascribe to chance the delectable assemblage of letters in printing the Aeneid."

Rousseau, speaking through the Vicar, in his *Emile, or on Education, 1762*

"The proper process does not offer the content of the mind but the order for that content-the exercise of attention, observing, comparing and classifying. The mental attitude acquired by such an exercise leads the child to make observations on his environment, observations which prove as interesting to him as new discoveries, and so stimulate him to multiply them indefinitely and to form in his mind a rich context of clear ideas. Language then comes to fix by means of exact words the ideas which the mind has acquired."

Maria Montessori, *Dr. Montessori's Own Handbook,* New York, 1965.

"It is important to inculcate the duties of behavior, the 'must' and 'must not' of individual obligation, as soon as possible. Later on, more liberty is allowed. The well-grown boy is made to understand that his future will depend on his personal effort and capacity; and he is therefore left, in great measure, to take care of himself, being occasionally admonished or warned, as seems needful…Throughout the whole course of mental and moral training, competition is not only expected but required…The aim is the cultivation of individual ability and personal character-the creation of an independent and forceful being."

Lafcadio Hearn

"Experience has ever shown, that education, as well as religion, aristocracy, democracy and monarchy, are, singly, totally, inadequate to restraining the passions of men, of preserving a steady government, and protecting the lives, liberty and properties of the people."

John Adams

"The education system of the United States is designed to strip students of whatever moral principles they brought with them and send them out into the world with nothing in the way of values or understanding to help them come to terms with reality."

Russell Kirk

"This class, the professional organizers and administrators, who control the executive government, the machinery of organized labor and organized capital, now wish to assume, not only the direction of all our great productive undertakings, but, through the control of education and doctoring, the private lives of all the citizens."

Douglas Jerrod

"Among the strange notions which have been broached since I have been in the political theater, there is one which has lately seized the minds of men, that all things must be done for them by the Government, and that they are to do nothing for themselves: the Government is not only to attend to the great concerns which are its province, but it must step in and ease individuals of their natural and moral obligations. A more pernicious notion cannot prevail. Look at that ragged fellow staggering from the whisky shop, and see that slattern who has gone there to reclaim him; where are their children? Running about, ragged, idle, ignorant, fit candidates for the penitentiary. Why is all this so? Ask the man and he will tell you. "Oh, the Government has undertaken to educate our children for us."

John Randolph

"In the early stages of that great movement which has made the whole of the West democratic, there was only discontent and a desire for such relatively small changes in the mode of government as would increase its efficiency and make it serve the interests of the discontented. A philosophy was invented to justify the malcontents in their demands for change; the philosophy was elaborated; conclusions were relentlessly drawn; and it was found that, granted the assumptions on which the philosophy was based, logic demanded that the changes in the existing institutions should be, not small, but vast, sweeping and comprehensive…becoming familiar such a dogma automatically becomes right."

Aldous Huxley, 1927

"Upon this Empire, as upon that of Rome, calamity has at last fallen. A host of intellectual barbarians has burst upon it, and has occupied by force the length and breadth of it. The result has been astounding. Had the invaders been barbarians only, they might have been repelled easily; but they were armed with the most powerful weapons of civilization. They were a phenomenon new to history, they showed us real power in the hands of real ignorance; and the work of the combination thus far has been ruin, not reorganization. Few great movements at the beginning have been conscious of their own tendency; but no great movement has mistaken it like modern Progressivism. Seeing just too well to have the true instinct of blindness, and just too ill to have the proper guidance from sight, it has tightened its clutch upon the world of thought, only to impart its own confusion. What lies before men now is to reduce this confusion to order, by a patient and calm employment of the intellect."

W.H. Mallock

Progressives place a universal and comprehensive system of education at the top of their agenda, reasoning that the modernization of society requires the compulsory education of all children even where the parents object. The belief that society can be scientifically controlled begins with a child's earliest teachers. A government that desires to intelligently and scientifically direct the social and economic development of society should institute a universal and comprehensive system of education, regulate competition, and connect the people on the alternative basis of opportunity and co-operation. Before such a science of society can be formulated, Progressives have to destroy the ideas that have held sway over America since its founding. Freedom, individualism and capitalism are the specific targets of their continuing legislative forays. In large, complex and rapidly growing societies human freedom (according to the Left) can only be achieved by a strong government acting in the interest of the victimized individual. It is not enough to establish an equal right to liberty by ensuring that people do not physically interfere with each other and by having laws that are impartially formulated and applied. Equality of results further compels more proactive and coercive measures which disregard individual differences in values, ability and character. The underlying assumption, the measure of individual freedom, is now not how much the state leaves people alone but how an overeducated elite can direct a malleable public to ends not of their choosing.

To transform the thinking and behavior of the population-de-moralization-the moral fiber and integrity of the country is put into question, thereby creating doubt in the minds of the people. To do so, manipulation of the media and academia is required to influence the young. As the next generation embraces new/old values, such as Marxism and Leninism, the older generation loses control simply through attrition. True facts do not matter at this stage, but rather the creating of perceptions. The next step is to change the country's economy, foreign relations and defense arrangements. The intent is to create a massive government permeating society and becoming intrusive in the lives of the citizens. Here, entitlements and benefits are promised to the populace to encourage their support. Basically, the people are bribed so they will accept the programs. Next, a crisis of large proportions happens to the country, or even is engineered by the government, upsetting and dividing the people and creating panic. Remedies will include and require circumventing the Constitution and altering the checks and balances of government. Subversion of our political system has involved the undermining of our American ideology, philosophy and founding principles, which slowly, quietly and methodically has destroyed our systems, traditions and institutions beginning with academia, the media and the courts. The citizens become unable to come to sensible conclusions about what is going on and so become unable to defend themselves.

The Left is the product of this cultural disintegration; it is bred not in the slums but in the universities; it is not the vanguard of the future but the terminal stage of their failed programs. A precarious mixture of freedom and controls, our mixed economy includes injustice, insecurity, confusion, the pressure group warfare of all against all, the amorality and futility of randomness, and the pragmatist, range-of-the-moment policies to be found in such a philosophical vacuum. Without opposition, the hoodlums of the left are crawling out from beneath this intellectual wreckage to protest against reason, progress, technology, achievement and reality. The most destructive influence is not the thugs themselves but the cynicism of mainstream media that hail them as idealists.

Civilization is not inherited; it has to be learned and earned by each generation anew; if the transmission should be interrupted, civilization will die. Education is not merely the painful accumulation of facts and dates and reigns, nor merely the necessary preparation of the individual to earn his keep in the world, but the transmission of our mental, moral, technical and aesthetic heritage for the enlargement of man's understanding, control and enjoyment of life. There is no significant example in history of a society successfully maintaining a moral life devoid of guiding principles. Morality is customs and manners, conscience and charity; a Law built into the spirit, generating at last that sense of right and wrong, that order and discipline of desire, without which a society disintegrates.

Part of the function of parentage is the transmission of such moral codes. Civilization is an accumulation, a treasure house of arts and wisdom, manners and morals, from which the individual, in his development, draws nourishment for his mental life; without that periodical reacquisition of the intellectual heritage by each generation, civilization would die a sudden death. It owes its life to education, the transmission of skills and the training of character. Biologically, man is badly equipped for civilization, since his learned instincts provide only for traditional situations; every vice was once a virtue, necessary in the struggle for existence; it became a vice only when he survived the conditions that made it indispensable; vice, therefore, is not an advanced form of behavior, but usually an atavistic throwback to ancient and superseded ways. Greed, acquisitiveness, dishonesty, cruelty and violence were for so many generations useful to men that not all our laws, all our education, our morals and our religions can quite stamp them out; for some they doubtless have a certain survival value even today. It is one purpose of a moral code to adjust the unchanged-or slowly changing-impulses of human nature to the changing needs and circumstances of today's social life.

A child has humanity thrust upon it day by day as it receives the moral and mental heritage of the race. As they grow up so does their fear. They become aware of their own impotence in the face of a reality as unknown to them as it was when they were very young, only now it confronts them with menacing, demanding problems they cannot handle. The production of wealth requires the personal responsibility of dealing with reality; the formulation of philosophical ideas requires the personal responsibility of observing, judging and integrating the facts of reality on an enormous scale. The economic and psychological parasites of the Left have a mental development arrested by a determined quest for the unearned, an overwhelming terror of reality and the desire to escape it. Man's need for self-esteem is the nemesis of the Left. The success of a man who deals with reality augments his self-confidence; those on the Left experience panic. The man of authentic self-confidence is the man who relies on the judgment of his own mind. He is inflexible in regard to the absolutism of reality, in seeking and demanding truth. There is only one source of authentic self-confidence: reason. Hence the hatred of the Left for reason, all of its manifestations and consequences-of intelligence, of certainty, of ambition, of success, of achievement, of virtue, of happiness, of pride. All these are from a universe that will destroy the members of the Left.

The Church, which alone survived the downfall of the Roman Empire, dominated the intellectual, political and religious life of

Western Europe for about a thousand years. There was little evidence during this period of a shift in interest from other worldliness to progress of the human race in the known world. Scholastic philosophy identified the search for truth with the attempt to rationalize Church dogma, and as a consequence the teleology of history remained largely a matter of Christian theology. Western Reason had always played the ostrich by sticking its head in the Supernatural. Scholasticism tried to use reason, science and nature as instruments of defense for the protection of the other than reasonable, the other than empirical, the other than natural. For a time, this performed a tremendous feat of spiritual unity. At some point it took its head out and got so used to the natural setting, perhaps like the man in Plato's cave, and found it to be good. The Church knew that the only way to restrain the practical impulse to follow that was to proscribe any divergence from its dogma. Once Scholasticism introduced reason through which the Christian church could be contemplated and enjoyed, without its tenets being corrupted by too much use, some began to see the practical possibilities of knowing more about Nature. The symbols and myths of religion meant that nature was largely an inviable whole; once the symbols and myths proved not to be natural facts, but unnatural fictions that fitted into no logical series tolerable to the rational mind, the curtain fell away.

There was little knowledge of Greek science, and the schooling of the Middle Ages was largely formal and dialectical. Interest in nature was necessarily stifled by a philosophy which renounced the world. The barrenness of Scholastic learning could not fail to irk men of an empirical turn of mind, as well as those inclined toward speculative philosophy and mysticism. There began a growing interest in nature and science, encouraged by the study of Aristotle's works on physics and by the Arabian schools of Spain. The revival of letters in the fifteenth century accelerated the process whereby the Church lost control of Western thought and prepared the way for a philosophy favorable to views of terrestrial progress. The philosophy of the Renaissance was in the main the history of the process in which the natural science mode of regarding the world was gradually worked out from the humanistic renewal of Greek philosophy. Renaissance philosophy reflects the re-discovery of Greek civilization on the one hand, and the excitement generated by scientific and geographical discoveries on the other. Columbus' voyage to America, Magellan's fleet which toured around the world, proving the hypothesis that the earth is a globe; the astronomical works of Copernicus, Kepler and Galileo, and numerous studies in mathematics, physics and biology fired Renaissance thinkers with an intense zeal for knowledge about nature. These events were productive of a metaphysical view of the world which in a sense underlies all doctrines of progress, namely Natural Law. Copernican astronomy that placed the sun at the center of the universe and located the earth among the planets was the primary source of this notion, inasmuch as the conception of an infinite universe destroyed the traditional distinction between heaven and earth. This introduced grave incompatibilities between Church doctrine and the theories of Renaissance scientists and philosophers. The fiery fate of Giordano Bruno illustrates how serious was the conflict.

The Middle Ages were an era of mysticism, ruled by blind obedience to the dogma that faith is superior to reason. The Renaissance was specifically the rebirth of reason, the liberation of man's mind, the triumph of rationality over mysticism-a faltering, incomplete, but impassioned triumph that led to the birth of science, individualism and freedom, finally reaching its culmination in the Enlightenment. The men of the Renaissance said throw over the spirits and symbols, which are irrational anyhow, and find those quantities in nature which *will* work. The tale of modern human life is a parade of unfolding rationality and purpose first envisaged in Greece and carried on from there. Reason also leads to individualism and competition from which ineluctably follows capitalism. Reason is the faculty that identifies and integrates the material provided by man's senses. Reason is man's only means of grasping reality and acquiring knowledge.

The rejection of reason means that men should act regardless of and/or in contradiction of the facts of reality. Hatred of reason leads to a fear of reality; since fear has always been an intense motivation of the leftists, it is fear that they have always used as their chief psychological tool of propaganda, apparently in the belief that it has as irresistible power in the consciousness of others as in their own. The philosophers of the Left want to sever the connection between the mind and reality by playing on human weaknesses, doubts and fears.

That ideas matter means that knowledge matters, that truth matters, that one's mind matters. The certainty of that is the most profound, earnest and solemn aspect of life. No matter what corruption one observes, one is unable to accept it as normal, permanent or metaphysically right. Somewhere, a proper, human way of life is possible to humans, and justice matters. It takes years to realize that one lives among the not-fully-human. It also takes many years for a man (and many, many centuries for mankind) to grasp the fact that, in order to live, man needs a comprehensive view of existence, which he relies on, consciously or not. While other men are struggling to live, the haters of man on the Left are undercutting their means of survival. The realm of philosophy has become an abandoned vacant lot, to be filled in by the professors in our universities which turn out so many frightened children to face the world defenseless.

These activists and their clients are fully, literally, loyally, and devastatingly the products of the modern philosophy taught in colleges the last seven decades-epistemological agnosticism (anti-logic), avowed irrationalism (divorcing reason from reality), and ethical subjectivism (a range-of-the moment perspective on life). But people go to college to learn theoretical knowledge to guide them in practical action. The left avoids questions about the application of their ideas to reality. Its students graduate from university believing existence is an un-chartable maze and that fear and uncertainty are man's permanent state; that these are socially valuable traits leading to tolerance of differences and a willingness to compromise. Chronic doubt, therefore, was the guarantee of a peaceful, democratic society while intellectual certainty was the mark of a judgmental mentality.

Any Authority must promulgate some sort of distant goals and moral ideas in order to justify its rule and the people's immolation; in time its contradictions are thrown back in its face. Its best subjects are the most intelligent and the most honest, hence these are the first to be silenced. The Greeks and Socrates, the Catholic Church and Galileo, the Soviets and Solzhenitsyn. Their dedication to ideas drove these dissenters to the supremacy of truth no matter the cost to themselves. They could not do otherwise. For the most part similar men are disappearing in silence, unknown and unnoticed. Sometimes they perish, extinguishing their minds before they have a chance to grasp the nature of the evil they are facing. They go from confidence to bewilderment, to indignation to resignation, to obscurity. How can man preserve his sacred fire if he knows that jail is the reward for a loyalty to reason?

Reason is the individuating attribute for men. The exercise of the intellect in abstract reasoning will lead intelligent men to like conclusions through logical sequences, and at the same time develop their individuality, because thinking is an individual function. When it is directed toward the mastery of nature, the ordering of inorganic matter by knowledge of natural law, it is creative, not only in material goods but in enrichment of human personality. Therefore, the collectivist, to obtain his objective of supreme power, the collective society or state, seeks the one type of organization, the political agency, which is directly prohibitory and must tend to stop men from thinking and acting.

The power that determines the establishment, the changes, the evolution, and the destruction of social systems is philosophy. The role of chance and accident stands in inverse ratio to the strength of a country's philosophical basis. A culture has an emotional atmosphere created by its dominant philosophy, by its view of man and his existence. Western civilization had an Age of Reason and an Age of Enlightenment. Their achievements were the intellectual drive of that era, creating a corresponding sense of life, and fostering those values. Today we live in the Age of Envy. It is all around us, we are drowning in it, yet men continue to evade its existence and are afraid to name it, as people in the Dark Ages were afraid to pronounce the name of the Devil. It is the hatred of the good for being the good. It is felt primarily by persons plagued with self-doubt. It is demonstrated in the attitudes of people who resent the success, happiness, achievement or good fortune of others, and who experience pleasure at someone else's failure. The essential characteristic of this corruption is the fact that what the mind recognizes as a value is transmitted to its emotional mechanism as an object of hatred, not admiration.

The appeasement of evil has been the undertow of mankind's cultural stream all through the ages. It took the form, from Greece forward to the Reformation, of abject humility before omnipotent gods. Today, the profiteers are men with a vested interest in mankind's psychological devastation, who burrow their way into positions of moral-intellectual leadership. Journalists, teachers, tenured professors, and power-hungry politicians provide the haters with unlimited means of rationalization, dissimulation, excuse and camouflage, including ways of passing off vices as virtues. They slander, disarm and confuse their victims. Their stock-in-trade is any system of thought or of belief aimed at keeping men small. The policy in action is to destroy the men of achievement so the rest will give up and obey.

Man's cognitive process is the interaction between his conscious mind and the automatic functions of his subconscious. At birth, both are blank. He faces an immense chaos which he must learn to perceive by means of a complex mechanism which he must learn to operate. After learning to focus his eyes, he must perceive the things around him by integrating his sensations into percepts and grasp the process of concept formation whereby he orders his life. This acquired skill, this seriousness about the knowledge of reality, is what is lacking on the part of the Left. The left teaches that the mind of man is impotent, that there is no such thing as reality, and we wouldn't be able to perceive it if there were-there you have the magnitude of the treason involved.

At the age of three a child's cognitive development is just beginning; his mind is in a state of impatient flux; he is unable to catch up with the impressions bombarding him from all sides; he wants to know everything and all at once. For him, the world has just begun; *it* is intelligible-the chaos is in his mind, which he has not yet learned to organize. This is the next, the conceptual task. The first five or six years of a child's life are crucial to his cognitive development. The subconscious is the integrating mechanism. Man's conscious mind observes and establishes connections among his experiences; the subconscious integrates the connections and makes them automatic. Once a child learns to walk, for instance, there is no longer a conscious awareness of its difficulty at that age. Similarly, a mind's cognitive development involves a continual process of such automatization. As an adult, the efficiency of your mental operations depends on the kind of context your subconscious has automatized. The process of forming, integrating and using concepts is a volitional process. It is not innate, but an acquired skill; it must be learned, and all of man's other capacities depend on how well or how badly he learns it. The method by which he acquires and organizes knowledge programs his subconscious computer, determining how well or how badly his cognitive process will function. It is a child's early experiences and observations that determine this programming. Thereafter, the interaction of content and method establishes a certain reciprocity: the method of acquiring knowledge affects the mind's content, which affects the further development of the method, and so on. He develops an eager curiosity about every new experience and a desire to understand it. The perception of reality, the learning of facts, the ability to distinguish truth from falsehood, are exclusively individual capacities; there is no such thing as a collective brain. The refusal to sacrifice one's mind and one's knowledge of the truth to any social pressures-intellectual integrity-is a profoundly selfish attitude. The purposeful, disciplined use of his intelligence is the highest achievement possible to man. To succeed in producing the atrophy of intelligence, one must get hold of the child at an early stage; hence, the government's real interest in supplying daycare for single mothers. The philosophers of the Left want to sever the connection between the mind and reality by playing on human weaknesses, doubts and fears, from the earliest age.

Does a child conclude that the world is intelligible, and proceed to expand his understanding by the effort of conceptualizing on an ever-widening scale, with growing success and enjoyment? Or does he conclude that the world is a bewildering chaos, where the fact he grasps today is reversed tomorrow, where the more he sees the more helpless he becomes, and consequently, he retreats into the cellar of his own mind, locking the door? Does a child grasp the distinction between consciousness and existence, between his mind and the outside world, which leads him to understand that the task of the first is to perceive the second, which leads to the development of his critical faculty and of control over his mental operations? Or does he remain in an indeterminate daze, never certain of whether he feels or perceives, of where one ends and the other begins, which leads him to feel trapped between two unintelligible states of flux? Does a child learn to identify, to categorize, to integrate his experiences and thus acquire the self-confidence needed to develop a long-range vision? Or does he learn to see nothing but the immediate moment and the feelings it produces, never venturing to look beyond it, never establishing any context, which leads him eventually to a stage where, under the pressure of any strong emotion, his mind disintegrates, and reality vanishes?

The principles of epistemology are the rules by which humans are to acquire knowledge, by which the mind automatizes certain processes, turning them into permanent habits. The result is that by the age of seven a child acquires the capacity to develop a vast conceptual context which will accompany and illuminate his every experience, creating an ever-growing chain of automatized connections, expanding the power of his intelligence with every year-or a child shrivels as his mind shrinks, leaving only a nameless anxiety in the vacuum that should have been filled by his growing brain. Whatever a child's natural endowment, the use of intelligence is an acquired skill. It must be acquired by the child's own effort and automatized by his own mind. Adults can place him in an environment that provides him with evidence of a stable, consistent, intelligible world which challenges and rewards his efforts to understand-or in an environment where nothing connects to anything, nothing holds long enough to grasp, nothing is certain, where the incomprehensible and unpredictable lurks behind every corner and strikes him at any random step. Adults can, and do, accelerate, hamper or even destroy the development of his conceptual faculty.

The Progressive education does not merely neglect the cognitive training that a child needs in his early years: it intentionally stifles his normal development. It conditions his mind to an anti-conceptual method of functioning that paralyzes his rational faculty. Children are robbed of their full potential, their further development impeded and slowed down. If such complex skills are not acquired by a certain age, it becomes too late. The longer their development is ignored, the greater their fear of reality and the slimmer their chance of ever recapturing the desire to face it, to know, to understand. Thereafter, there is little motivation to correct the deficiency; they have cause to dread reason, reality and truth.

The Progressive schools teach the wrong method of mental functioning; now students are expected to begin acquiring mental content, i.e., ideas, by such means as they possess. They are indoctrinated with the kinds of ideas that will make any intellectual recovery unlikely, if not impossible-and it is done by a method that continues and reinforces the conditioning begun in earlier schools. Memorizing belongs primarily to the perceptual level of learning while understanding is associated with being able to form concepts. To understand means to focus on the context of a given subject, as against merely its sensory input: to isolate its essentials, to establish its relationship to the previously known, and to integrate it with the appropriate categories of other subjects. Integration is the essential part of understanding. From the time a child learns to speak his education requires a progressively larger scale of understanding and progressively smaller amounts of memorizing.

When applied to conceptual material, memorizing is the destroyer of understanding and of the ability to think. Memorizing becomes the student's dominant method of mental functioning. They have no other way of coping with the school's curricula that consist primarily of random, haphazard, disintegrated snatches of various subjects, without context, continuity or systematic progression; the educational system works to multiply his inner conflicts. This leads to a nameless resentment, to a wordless feeling, to a growing hostility without object. The student concludes that the pursuit of knowledge is senseless, that education is an enormous pretense for something he cannot understand, and thus is started on the road to mental stagnation. The nameless emotion growing in his subconscious is hatred for people.

The supremacy of the group is forced into the student's mind by every means available. Progressive education has as its object to train the child for co-operative action. Group activities and interests become predominant. The ruling power is always the sentiment of the class in which the child is enrolled. It is always the rule of the many over the one. It is political correctness now transmuted into the cancel culture and public ostracization. The further objective is the teaching of the Progressive social ideal of the purest altruism in the communal cult. One's right to live rests solely upon the willingness to serve the community. Every member of a community must carefully watch the conduct of his fellow members. No man's time or effort can be considered exclusively his own. There is no right to personal initiative or choice, no possibility of doing what one pleases in terms of a productive life. Even the language reflects the altruistic code of ethics, by avoiding the use of personal pronouns, and modifying them to a social meaning.

They are being taught, by implication, that there is no such thing as a firm, objective reality, which man's mind must learn to perceive correctly; that reality is an indeterminate flux, that truth and falsehood is determined by majority vote. Reason, thinking, and intelligence, therefore are of no importance. No matter what premises a child forms in his grade- and high-school years, the educational system works to multiply his inner conflicts. They graduate as good little collectivists, reciting the correct dogma. Progressive schools condition the mind to an anti-cognitive method of functioning, reinforced in later years; struggling with snatches of knowledge, the student learns to associate the process of learning with dread, resentment and self-doubt. College completes the job.

Most people retain some hold on their rational faculties; the symptom of that desire is the quest for a comprehensive view of life. No matter how badly organized, a young person's mind still gropes for answers to fundamental questions. The years from fifteen to twenty-five are the crucial formative years. This is the time when he confirms his impressions of the world, of other men, of the society in which he lives, when he acquires conscious convictions, defines his moral values, chooses his goals and plans his future. On the conscious level, the countless alternatives confronting him make him aware of the fact that now he has to make choices and that he does not automatically know what to choose or how to act. The thinking youth has been frustrated in his longing to find people who take ideas seriously-he believes that he will find them in college-the alleged citadel of reason and wisdom. Things do not make sense to him, but they do to some in the world, and he hopes they will make them intelligible to him as well.

A major symptom of a culture's intellectual and moral disintegration is the shrinking of the vision and goals to the range of the immediate moment. The manifestation of a disintegrating consciousness is the inability to think and act in terms of principles. It is only by means of principles that one can set one's long-range goals and evaluate the alternatives of any given moment. It is only principles that enable a man to plan his future and achieve it. Our culture is one in which all major values are being betrayed while selling out its future for some spurious advantage of the moment. Modern philosophy is a sustained attempt to invalidate reason and any integration of knowledge, leaving students without an understanding of the nature, function or practical application of principles. The mentally paralyzed, anxiety-ridden college graduates with their epistemological irrationalism and ethical subjectivism, seek relief to escape from the absolutism of reality with which they feel themselves impotent to deal. They grope blindly through an incomprehensible, complex industrial civilization, struggling and ultimately giving up in terror.

The overpowering presence of whim as the ruler of everything means these helpless, frightened, unformed children are left without guidance and ordered to act as a mob. Protest, accusations and unwarranted demands are their protective devices. Their groping sense of time continuity-of the reality of the future-is stunted, shrinking their concern and awareness to the range of the immediate moment. Cut off from reality they are plunged into the world. How can they be sure of what is true and what is not, what is out there and what is only in their mind? They feel only fear, confusion and helplessness. The stronger the fear, the more aggressive the behavior. The more uncertain the assertion, the louder the voice. Why bother solving problems if they can be wished away, as when they were children? Why struggle to discover the world if you can make it whatever you wish, with a tantrum? They will not know, until much later, by what imperceptible steps, they became an outcast from the world. Out of revenge, or frustration or aimlessness, they threaten, cajole, imitate and deceive the members of their group so that they fit in. Now the intangible face of the pack stands between them and reality, with the will of the pack as the dominant power.

Such men acquire no incentive, no motive to develop an intellect. Of what importance can reality be to him if his fate depends on the group? Reality, to him, is no longer an exciting challenge, but a dark, unknowable threat, which evokes a feeling of failure and impotence in his own malfunctioning mind. The group is the only realm he knows where he feels at home; he needs its protection and reassurance. An overwhelming hostility toward all men is his basic emotion, his automatic context for the concept "man." Every prop supporting his mind is absent: he has no self-confidence-no concept of self-no sense of morality-no sense of time continuity-no ability to project the future-no ability to grasp, to integrate or to apply abstractions-no values. They are released into the world, as impotent creatures, unable to think, unable to face or deal with reality, creatures who combine brashness and fear, creatures deprived of their means of survival, doomed to limp and stumble through life, in search of some nameless relief supplied by the people they hate.

The hater's mental functioning remains on the level of a child-a random store of unprocessed material that comes and goes at the mercy of chance. Reality does not obey him, it frustrates his wishes, it is impervious to his feelings. He attempts to circumvent reality by manipulating others. Gradually, these subconscious conclusions are automatized in his mind, leading to the only emotion he will ever experience: fear. He is able to grasp the given but unable to integrate it to anything. He is trapped between yesterday and tomorrow. He senses that there is something wrong with him, with his mind. To conceptualize is to identify, to organize, and to integrate the content of his mind. The chronic fear is of what the collectivist is supposed to know, and his pretentious posturing is intended to hide the fact that he hasn't the faintest idea. Since he was prevented from conceptualizing his early cognitive material, the accumulation of unidentified experiences and perceptual impressions is now such that he feels paralyzed. When he tries to think his mind runs into a blank wall; his mental processes seem to dissolve into a labyrinth of question marks and blind alleys. His subconscious is cluttered with the irrelevant, the accidental, the misunderstood, the un-grasped, the undefined; it does not respond to his efforts. He uses concepts by a child's perceptual method; without definitions, integrations or specific referents the only context is the immediate moment. His concepts refer to a foggy mixture of partial knowledge, his own feelings and memorized responses. He gives up, once again, in fear.

The result, in adult life, is the absence of moral freedom-the absence of the ability to act according to one's own conviction of justice. Indeed, there can be no concept of justice, if the sole authority is that of the mass, of the collective, of the government in the ultimate resort. The prevailing philosophy with which pupils are indoctrinated is that of pragmatism, which denies that there are any universal or permanent moral values and standards. Neither evidence nor logic can penetrate the fog in which they have been reared, as if there can be no facts or connected mental processes, which would lead to one conclusion over another, or distinguish a conviction from a feeling. They have been trained to accept the class, the group, or the social trend as the sole authority. They have been reduced to parts of a collective body, ready to be manipulated, instead of individuals capable of self-government and initiative. Social media makes it far easier to control them. An immense proportion of those who still read never read *anything* but social media-very probably social media intended to inflame or mislead them-and the half-educated mind is particularly open to political utopias and fanaticisms. The modern reading public suffers from an increasing incapacity for continuous attention, so the people, suffering from chronic boredom, are easily roused to action-and then, commonly, ignorant action. In such an order of things socialism finds its fulcrum. All contribute to the Decline of the Law.

The survival of mental parasites depends on blind chance; an unfocused mind is unable to know whom to imitate, whose motions are safe to follow. They are the men who trail after any destroyer who promises to assume the responsibility they evade:

the responsibility of being conscious. Such men exist by destroying those who are capable-those who are pursuing a course of action proper to man. The men who attempt to survive by means of force do so by the method of animals, by rejecting reason and counting on productive men to prey on. Rational men's survival means the terms, methods, conditions and goals required for the survival of a thinking being throughout his lifespan, in all those aspects of existence which are open to his choice. His own life is the ethical purpose of every individual man. It means one's acceptance of the responsibility or forming one's own judgments, never sacrificing one's convictions to the opinions of others, never acting without knowing one's purposes and motives, never seeking values against the total integrated sum of one's knowledge. It means the rejection of any form of non-sensory, non-rational, supernatural source of knowledge.

Man's mind is his basic means of survival-and of self-protection. Reason has to be used in and by a man's own mind, and its product-truth-makes him inflexible, intransigent, impervious to the power of any group. Deprived of the ability to reason, men become docile, pliant, impotent chunks of clay, to be formed by others for purposes not theirs. They are told there is nothing wrong with them-it is the undefined "System" that is abnormal. The System is anything that can be blamed for their inner misery, creating a paranoia; that they are innocent victims pursued by dark powers, which only goes towards increasing their rage. They are a product of society and society made a bad job of it. When they hear that all their troubles are caused by the political and economic systems, that the enemy is Republicanism and Capitalism, they accept it as self-evident. Their minds are set to chant and respond to slogans; armed with nothing but meaningless phrases, they scream their indignant, bewildered protests. They are left with nothing but the terror of chronic anxiety, the blind urge to act, to strike out at whatever caused it, and a boiling hostility at a universe which ignores them. They are just waiting to be told what to do. Like temper-tantrums with a child, after such an education, why should we be shocked by the spectacle of riots and demands for power-without knowledge, preparation or experience-and for reparations? The three-year old screaming child has become a twenty-year old rioter. The Left confounds rights with desires and aspirations, ever a plague on society. With such confusion, the mass of men must feel that some vast, intangible conspiracy thwarts their attainment of what they are told is their inalienable birthright. This fixes upon the poor a permanent grudge and frustration, encouraged by their self-appointed spokesmen. Vainglorious men in the role of guide, equipped with a map compiled from their own abstractions, will lead society to destruction. The rioters are the Left's greatest accomplishment: they go obediently along, never questioning the basic premises inculcated in their lessons, clinging to the belief that mankind can be united into one happy pack-by force. The rioters' claim that they have no way of attracting attention to their demands, and of getting what they want, except by violence, is a throwback to their earliest thought that a tantrum was the only thing required to achieve their childish wishes. Their enemy-reality-though, is implacable.

There can be no greater stretch of Authority's reach than required to seize children from their parents, teach them whatever the authorities decree they shall be taught, and expropriate from the parents the funds to pay for the procedure. If this is not understood, let any parent holding a particular religious faith consider how it would seem if his children were taken from him by force and taught an opposite creed. The principle is the same. Everything about public schools is compulsory, not free; the true nature of the institution has developed so fully along its own lines with the passage of time, against the wishes of parents, that they are now helpless when it is apparent that schools are for indoctrination, not the transmission of venerated ideas; for the secure employment of teachers rather than the education of children. The parents must still deliver their children into the power of those teachers or face fines and punishment. All Progressives want is that the state should prescribe their own specific doctrines to be taught. They are not the least concerned with freedom of thought, speech or person. They have no conception of personal rights or just authority. They do not ask whether a teacher should have the moral prerogative to instruct pupils what parents do not want taught. They do not question the political control of education; they only want to use it for their own ends. They do not inquire whether such control is not, by nature, bound to legislate against statements of fact, in prescribing a curriculum, in the long run. The most exact and demonstrable knowledge will certainly become objectionable to political Authority at some point, because it will expose the folly of such Authority and its vicious effects.

A thousand years after the Saracens, a revolutionary leader named Thomas Jefferson realized the dream of his life when he created the University of Virginia. He wrote to a friend: "We shall allow the students uncontrolled choice in the lectures they shall choose to attend. Our institution will proceed on the principle of letting everyone come and listen to whatever he thinks may improve the condition of his mind. In both the old and new world cases, there will be no tinge of the belief that minds acquire knowledge, not by actively seeking to know, but by passively being taught whatever Authority decides that they should know."

In such private schools, there is considerable competitive variation in curricula offered. Each must strive for objective truth, as there is no public authority to control opinion and nowhere will there be any inducement to teach the supremacy of the state as a compulsory philosophy. Once that doctrine is accepted it becomes an almost impossible task to break the stranglehold of the political power over the life of the citizen. It has had his body, property and mind in its clutches from infancy. A tax-supported, compulsory educational system is the complete model of the totalitarian state. If a parent sends their child to private school or teaches at home, it is with the permission of the state, not a right, and the educational standard is prescribed, and the tax must still be paid. The standards of education were much higher years ago than they are now.

Children could read, write and do simple math before they entered school. Now they may not be able to do that upon *leaving* school.

The vast majority of the knowledge this writer considers useful, on a daily basis, was garnered *after* graduating from college. Simple literacy is not sufficient education in itself, but the elementary key to the much more important and indispensable part of education found in the principles of civilization. But that further education in civilization cannot be obtained at all under the full political control of the schools. It is possible only to a certain frame of mind in which knowledge is pursued voluntarily and independently, as in a private course of reading. Americans find prosperity first of all in their own free minds. The free mind persisted in the United States, in spite of the steady intrusion of political power into the primary field of education, because choice and personal effort were still the governing factors in getting an advanced education. One pursued such studies as were selected on each student's own initiative, following Jefferson's ideal, afterwards taking his chance of making a living as best he could, getting a varied experience of using both hands and head, with no ineradicable class distinction to cut off his speculative intelligence from practical application. But education under political power has but one end; to route human energy into the dead-end political channels of non-profit, journalism or bureaucratic positions. The question remains; why would anyone willingly entrust their children to the Left and pay them for teaching them? Why do they have to extort their fees and collect their pupils by compulsion?

When the economic principle-competition-that has resulted in the superlative efficiency of American industry is permitted to operate in the field of education, the result will be a revolution. When the state assumed financial control of education, it was logically appropriate that it progressively assume control of the content of education. But when a government enters the field of ideas, when it presumes to prescribe in issues concerning intellectual content, that is the death of a free society. The government removes children from the home and subjects them to educational training of which the parents may not approve; the wealth of parents is expropriated to support an educational system which they may not sanction, and to pay for the education of children not their own. It is in the interest of Statism to foster the delusion of free public education, in order to throw a smokescreen over the indoctrination that is really occurring. Were schools private, parents could determine where and what their children would be taught, by the curriculum offered. No one would choose the present situation, were there better alternatives in a free society. The need is clear for a voucher system.

The worst of the Progressive era has effected a fundamental change in the methods and purposes of education. It no longer imparts positive facts and principles. It encourages immature self-expression, removes personal responsibility from the rule of obedience for children, weakens character by eroding individualism, and teaches the child to form ideas through his feelings, rather than through formal logic. The compulsory education of children in the United States results in the postponement of a child's maturity. He passes from the authority of his parents to the Authority of the State. His situation does not require him to develop self-reliance, self-discipline or responsibility. It keeps him from discovering the reward of a rigorous mental effort that overcomes any difficulty.

Men cannot be enslaved politically until they have been disarmed ideologically. The country at large is bitterly dissatisfied with the stale slogans of welfare statism, and desperately seeking an alternative. Without a firm, consistent ideological program and leadership, the people's desperation will be dissipated in the blind alleys of Statism. The doctrines of the Left have achieved the exact opposite of its alleged goal: instead of creating unity and agreement, it has disintegrated and atomized the country to such an extent that no communication, let alone agreement, is possible. It is not unity, but intellectual coherence that the country needs. That coherence can only be achieved by fundamental principles, the primacy of ideas.

It is true that a great many men do feel themselves to be strangers and afraid in a world they never made. It is true that man differs fundamentally from all other species, by virtue of possessing a rational, conceptual faculty. It is true that for man survival is a problem to be solved by the exercise of his intelligence. It is true that every man is alone, separate and unique. It is true that thinking requires independence. Those are the facts of man's existence. Why would one choose to regard these facts as a terrifying cosmic paradox, and to see in them the evidence of the tragic human problem? The Left resents the fact that their lives are their own responsibility and that the task of their reason is to discover how to maintain it. There are men who find thought unnatural and abnormal. There are men who find their existence as separate, independent entities an unendurable burden. The Left declares that capitalism has been a disastrous failure in solving the problem of man's alienation. In the feudal Middle Ages man had a distinct, unchangeable, and unquestionable place in the world from the moment of birth; he was rooted in the structured whole of religion, and thus life had a meaning which left no place, and no need for doubt. The social order was the natural order. The complete lack of control over any aspect of one's existence, the ruthless suppression of any form of intellectual freedom, the paralyzing restrictions on any form of individual initiative and independence-those were the cardinal characteristics of the Middle Ages. But all this, along with the famines and plagues, the exhausting labor from sunrise to sunset, the suffocating routine, the superstitious terror, the brutality of men's dealings with one another, the use of legalized torture as a normal way of life, sanctioned by the Church-is swept aside, so entranced is the Left's vision of the world in which men do not have to invent and compete, they only had to submit and obey. In liberating man from medieval regulation and authority, in breaking the chains of ecclesiastical, economic and social tyranny, in destroying the stability of the feudal order, capitalism and individualism thrust upon man an unprecedented freedom that was bound to create deep feelings of insecurity, powerlessness, doubt and anxiety.

With the collapse of medievalism and the emergence of capitalism, man was compelled to assume total responsibility for his own survival: he had to produce and trade-he had to think and judge-he had no Authority to guide him, and nothing but his own ability to keep him in existence. No longer could he, by virtue of the group to which he belonged, gain his sense of personal identity: henceforward, he had to achieve it. This posed a devastating psychological problem for men, intensifying their feelings of isolation and separateness. To offer men a chance to enjoy an unprecedented material well-being is, apparently, to sentence them to alienation; whereas to hold them down to the stagnant level of welfare recipient is to offer them the chance for spiritual fulfillment. How, the Left demands, can a man not feel alienated and victimized in a system where his wishes are not omnipotent, where the unearned is not to be had, where personal growth is rewarded, and stagnation is punished? But man's conceptual level of consciousness gives him a way of relating to the world around him immeasurably superior to that enjoyed by any other species. It does not alienate him from nature: it makes him its master. The Left chants that reason is unnatural, that the necessity of choice is an awful burden, that self-responsibility is frightening, that the achievement of personal identity is a social problem, and that the political answer to this is socialism. But alienation is really a response of an organism's alarm signal that he is existing in a psychological state improper to him-that his relationship to reality is wrong.

Man's power of abstraction enables him to project many alternative courses of action. Such questions are possible only to a being whose cognitive faculty is exercised volitionally-a being who is self-directing and self-regulating in thought and in action, and whose existence, therefore entails a constant process of choice. How a man exercises his capacities to satisfy his needs-how he chooses to deal with the facts of reality, how he chooses to function, in thought and in action-constitutes his personal identity. His sense of self-his implicit concept or image of the type of person he is-is the cumulative product of the choices he makes. To choose to think, to identify the facts of reality, to assume the responsibility of judging what is true or false, right or wrong, is man's basic form of assertiveness over nature. To the extent that a man chooses to think, his premises and values are acquired first-hand and are not a mystery to him; he experiences himself as the active cause of his character, behavior and goals. A strong sense of personal identity is the product of independent thinking and the possession of an integrated set of values.

The formation of philosophical ideas requires the personal responsibility of observing, judging and integrating the facts of reality on an enormous scale. When and to the extent that a man chooses to evade the effort and responsibility of thinking, of seeking knowledge, of passing judgment, his action is one of abdication, an admission that one is incompetent to deal with the facts of reality. To the extent that a man attempts to live without thinking, he experiences himself as passive, his person and actions are the accidental products of forces he does not understand, of his range of the moment feelings and random cultural influences. By his default, such a man allows himself to be turned into whatever the social determinist wants him to be; he is an empty mold waiting to be filled at the mercy of whoever and whatever is around him. If a man holds contradictory values, these necessarily do violence to a sense of personal identity. To escape his broken self, he will seek to escape by means of evasion, repression and rationalization-to escape a problem created by a failure of thought, he suspends thinking. He displaces his sense of self downward from his reason-the active, initiating element-to his emotion, which are a passive, reactive elements. Moved by feelings he does not understand and contradictions whose existence he does not acknowledge, he suffers a progressive sense of self-estrangement. A man's emotions are the product of his premises and values, of the thinking he has done or failed to do. But the man who is run by his emotions, attempting to make them a substitute for rational judgment, experiences them as a force bent on his destruction.

Such men feel outside the human race, metaphysical outcasts seeking to escape from themselves, desolated by an inner sense of spiritual impoverishment. The solution for such men is to seek a second-hand identity, through the mindless conformity to the values of others.

A large portion of an individual's self-identity might be formed from his perceived membership in a relevant social group. The development of self-identity for individuals from minority groups involves the integration of their own perceptions of the group as well as of the often negative, societal views of that same group. A collective identity is only formed through the group member's acceptance of shared cultures and traditions, often revealed in a narrative or myth. Individuals recognize that they share certain orientations in common and on that basis decide to act together. Group harmony is highly valued, and its members are perceived to experience equal standing amongst themselves. This perception is thought to impact goal formation in that people from marginalized groups tend to emphasize collectivist over individualistic values, they prefer equality over freedom. Rigid conformity within the group, and contempt for those without, characterizes such people. Membership boosts the individual's self-esteem as their opinions are seldom challenged within the group. Members seek a positive distinctiveness whereby the stability and legitimacy of the group is enhanced, at the cost of achieving self-esteem through their own action. Failures as individuals take refuge in these groups for a second-hand re-enforcement of their self-worth.

Collective consciousness just means you have surrendered your ability to think and act to the mob who you believe will act in your stead. The individual imagines the group collectively has attributes which the individual lacks. The manner in which a person acts is dependent on how the other people in their group act. Once submitted to a group it is unlikely for an individual to break free and re-assert himself. Indeed, in collectivist cultures there are found rules which focus on promoting selflessness and altruism. If the individual is not important then neither is freedom, nor are rights or individual hierarchies of values. If all power is centered around a state which holds the monopoly of force the benefits obtained from the division of labor in a pluralistic society disappear. In the name of equality government shifts from its constitutional role of protection to the arbitrary role of re-distributor of income and property. The greater the number of recipients the greater their political power. Thus, the Left needs a permanent underclass always dependent on them for their subsistence. As one group succeeds in this act of plunder so do others, including business, lobby for their own special privileges. Not content to rely on persuasion these groups depend on the use of coercion, through the attainment of government power, for the achievement of their objectives. It becomes evident that the government cannot please every group; the burden of taxation has its limits. They then employ the hidden tax of converting budget deficits into inflation of the money supply through bond illusion. When the state obtains funds in this manner, it removes funds from the capital market, raises interest rates and reduces the business opportunities that otherwise would have existed. The regimentation of economic activity is brought about by bureaucracies structured to implement such programs. Those who administer the countless forms of intervention in the economy have a vested interest in justifying the law they enforce. Thus, both the beneficiaries and the administrative agencies share the belief that this looting process is essentially fair. A society of conflict emerges as each special interest group sees the other as an adversary in the attempt to loot.

Collectivism tends to the idea that morality is fundamentally social: it is about national unity, the brotherhood of man, the welfare of the group, or collective redemption. Collectivism is the idea that the fundamental unit of the species that thinks, lives and acts towards goals is not the individual but some group-the city, class, society, race, gender, nation or even world. The group exists as a super-organism separate from individuals: it makes its own decisions, acts apart and in contest with the actions of individuals, has interests and competes for resources apart from the individuals who compose it. The idea is that society is a separate, singular moral agent from which we gain some value and to which something is owed in return. The individual has an obligation to give back to the community for any success he earns. Social democrats think it is appropriate for the society's leadership to punish any individuals that disagree with the will of the people, or that will not sufficiently contribute to what the leaders/majority deem to be the common good. But fundamentally it is only individuals who think, act and live, not groups of any size or type.

Reason identifies and integrates the information provided by man's senses. It is the faculty that man has to exercise by choice. In any hour, and over any issue, man is free to think or to evade that effort. Man can focus his mind to a full, active, purposefully directed awareness of reality, or he can un-focus and let himself drift, his mind making any random, associational connections it might happen upon. Man cannot provide for his simplest physical needs without a process of thought. No instincts will tell him how to plant a seed, light a fire, build a tool, or produce a silicon chip. Only a volitional act of his consciousness, a process of thought, can provide it. It is neither automatic nor infallible. Man must initiate it, sustain it and bear responsibility for its results. He must discover how to tell what is true or false and how to correct his errors; he has to discover how to validate his concepts, his conclusions, his knowledge, he has to discover the rules of thought, and the laws of logic to direct his thinking. Nature gives him no automatic guarantee of the efficacy of his mental effort. Nothing is given to man on earth except a potential and the material to actualize it. The potential is his consciousness which he must discover how to use and keep in constant action. The material is the whole of the universe, with no limits set to the knowledge he can acquire and to the enjoyment of his life that he can achieve.

Ethics is an objective, metaphysical necessity that answers the questions about the right goals and values that man's survival requires. Man has to hold his life as a value, learn to sustain it, discover the values it requires and practice his virtues-all by choice. A code of values accepted by choice is a code of morality. Since everything man needs has to be discovered by his own mind and produced by his own effort, the two essentials of the method of survival proper to a rational being are thinking and productive work. It is asking a great deal of schooling, especially now that it has been nationalized by the Left, to inculcate a respect for legitimate authority, to redress real wrongs by peaceful and constitutional means, and to honor the property of others when it comes to compensating for desperate social ills.

Humans do not know automatically what facts are true or false, right or wrong, good or evil. Yet they need that knowledge in order to live. They are not exempt from the laws of reality; they are a specific organism of a specific nature that requires specific action to sustain their lives. That which their survival requires is set by their nature and is not open to their choice. Knowledge, for any conscious organism, is the means of survival; to a living consciousness, every *is* implies an *ought*. Man is free to choose not to be conscious, but not free to escape the penalties of that evasion. Such men are motivated by fear and a desire to escape it. They are so overwhelmed by the terror of existence that they unleash their resentment and hatred against those who do not share the same state, those who are able to live, as if, by destroying the confident, the strong and the healthy, they can convert their impotence into some sort of effectiveness. An irrational society is one of moral cowards, men paralyzed by the loss of standards, principles and goals. If a moral code is inapplicable to reality, if it prescribes irreconcilable contradictions, if it offers no guidance except a series of arbitrary, groundless, out of context commandments, to be accepted on faith and practiced automatically, as blind dogma, its practitioners cannot properly be classified as human. On some middle-aged morning, such men suddenly realize that they have betrayed all the values they had once admired, wonder how it happened, and slam their minds shut to the answer, telling themselves that their fear was correct and pursuing values has no chance in this world. Such a society is ready to be taken over by anyone willing to set its direction.

It would never occur to a person of independent judgment that one's identity is a thing to be gained from or determined by others. The wailing of the 2020 rioters is almost incomprehensible, the cry of those who are moaning that it is someone's duty to supply them with a sense of belonging, that the system must provide them with self-esteem. This is the psychological root of the modern Left's mystique of the Middle Ages, of the dazed wishing for that style of life, and of the massive evasion of the actual conditions of existence during that period. The Middle Ages represents a system in which man's dread of independence and self-responsibility was proclaimed to be a virtue and was made a social imperative. Whenever a man, in any age, attempts to evade the responsibility of intellectual independence, and to derive his sense of identity from belonging to some group or another, he pays a deadly price in terms of the sabotaging of his mental processes thereafter. The degree to which a man substitutes the judgment of others for his own, failing to look at reality directly, is the degree to which his mental processes are alienated from reality. He senses dimly that he is out of contact with reality, that something is wrong with his grasp of the world around him. But he attempts to remedy the situation second-hand, through slogans and phrases repeated by others.

The theme running through all of environmental writing is that Man is the element of the universe which doesn't belong. He is radically different from all other living species, he is estranged from nature, he is overwhelmed by isolation; he has lost, in the process of evolution, the undisturbed tranquility of other species. The source of his curse is the fact that he possesses a mind. Self-awareness, reason and imagination disrupted the harmony which characterizes animal existence. But man is not equipped to adapt himself automatically and unthinkingly to his environment. Man is conscious of life and death as an issue and must solve the problem of survival. Once he emerged from the Garden of Eden with a brain, he had transcended nature and could never go back.

There is only one fundamental alternative in the universe: existence or non-existence. On the physical level the functions of all living organisms are actions generated by the organism itself and directed to a single purpose: the maintenance of the organism's life. No choice is open to the organism in this issue, that which is required for its survival is determined by its nature, by the kind of entity it is. If the organism fails in the basic functions required by its nature the organism dies. Life can be kept in existence only by a constant process of self-sustaining action. If an organism's life is its standard of value, that which furthers its life is the good, that which threatens it is the evil. Without an ultimate goal there can be no lesser goals or means which make the existence of values possible. The validation of value judgements is to be achieved by reference to the facts of reality. All of man's knowledge and all his concepts have a hierarchical structure. The foundation and starting point of man's thinking are his sensory perceptions; on this base, man forms his first concepts, then goes on building the edifice of his knowledge by identifying and integrating new concepts on a wider and wider scale. If man's thinking is to be valid, this process must be guided by logic, the art of non-contradictory identification-and any new concept man forms must be integrated without contradiction into the hierarchical structure of his existing knowledge. Aristotle's Law of Identity (A is A) is the paramount consideration in the process of determining his interests. He does not permit himself to hold contradictory values, to pursue contradictory goals or to imagine that the pursuit of a contradiction can ever be in his interest. A rational man does not hold any conviction without relating it to the rest of his knowledge and resolving any possible contradictions. To introduce into one's consciousness any idea that cannot be so integrated, an idea not derived from reality, not validated by a process of reason, not subject to rational examination or judgment, an idea that clashes with one's concepts and understanding of reality-is to sabotage the integrative function of consciousness, to undercut the rest of one's convictions and kill ones' capacity to be certain of anything. Man's need of self-esteem entails the need for a sense of control over reality-but no control is possible in a universe which, by one's own concession, contains the supernatural, the miraculous, or the causeless. There is only one reality-the reality knowable to reason. It was not by contemplating the non-existent that men lifted himself from the cave and transformed the material world to make human existence possible on earth.

As sensations are the first step of the development of a human consciousness in the realm of cognition, so are they its first step in the realm of evaluation. The pleasure-pain mechanism of the body serves as an automatic guardian of the organism's life signaling the right course or one that requires action to correct it. A plant has no choice of action; the goals it pursues are automatic and innate, determined by its nature. It acts automatically to further its life; it cannot act for its own destruction. The range of actions required for the survival of the higher organisms is wider: it is proportionate to the range of their consciousness. An animal has no choice in the knowledge or skills that it acquires; it can only repeat them generation after generation. An animal has no power to extend its knowledge or to evade it. An animal lives its life with no power of choice-it cannot evade its own perceptions nor ignore its own good. Man has no automatic code of survival, no automatic course of action, no automatic set of values. Humans can retain and integrate sensations into perceptions which give them a heightened awareness of the reality confronting them. In humans, consciousness is the faculty that registers that evaluation, discovers the answers to those questions and has to select a course of action. Man's particular distinction from all other living species is the fact that his consciousness is *volitional.*

Just as a plant's automatic values for directing the functions of its body are sufficient for its survival, but not for an animal's, so the automatic values provided by the sensory-perceptual mechanism of an animal are sufficient to guide it, but are insufficient for man.

Man's actions and survival require the guidance of conceptual knowledge, which cannot be acquired automatically. A concept is a mental integration of two or more perceptual concretes. It is by organizing his perceptual material into concepts, and his concepts into wider and wider concepts that man is able to grasp and retain, is able to identify and integrate an unlimited amount of knowledge, a knowledge extending beyond the immediate perceptions of any given, immediate moment. The process of concept-formation-integrating percepts into concepts-is not automatic. It is an actively sustained process of identifying one's impressions in conceptual terms, of integrating every event and every observation into a conceptual context, of grasping relationships, differences, similarities in one's perceptual material and of abstracting them into new concepts, of drawing inferences, of making deductions, of reaching conclusions, of asking new questions and discovering new answers, and expanding one's knowledge into an ever-growing sum. The faculty that directs this process is reason; the process is thinking.

There must be an integration of acquired knowledge into systems which may be used to guide our lives. There is only one human discipline which enables men to deal with large scale problems, which has the power to integrate and unify human activities, and that discipline is philosophy. Man first came into his own in Greece, some two and a half thousand years ago. The birth of philosophy marked the beginning of his adulthood; not the content of any particular system, but the *concept* of philosophy-the realization that a comprehensive view of existence is to be reached by man's mind. Philosophy is the goal toward which religion was only a helplessly blind groping. The grandeur, the reverence, the exalted purity, the austere dedication to the pursuit of truth, which are commonly associated with religion, should properly belong to the field of philosophy. Aristotle live up to it, as did Aquinas and Averroes-but how many others?

Most men are usually unable to form such a comprehensive view on their own; all need it, and most men, consciously or subconsciously, directly or indirectly, accept what the popular culture offers them by default. The integration of factual data, the maintenance of a full context, the discovery of principles, the establishment of causal connections and the implementation of a long-range vison-these are the tasks required of a philosopher, particularly one involved in politics. It is political philosophy that sets the goals and determines the course of a country's practical politics: one must identify, explain and evaluate the trend of events, discover their causes, define the problems and offer solutions. Politics is the study of the principles governing the proper organization of society; it is based on ethics, the study of the proper values to guide man's choices and actions. Both have been branches of philosophy since its birth in Greece. Ethics and politics are inseparable; the decay of one produces the decay of the other. Conservation of the political order must be preceded by the conservation of our moral order. Society cannot subsist unless both of its constituent elements thrive. Philosophy is the science that studies these fundamental aspects of the nature of existence. The task of philosophy is to provide man with a comprehensive view of life. This view serves as a base, a frame of reference, for all his actions, mental or physical, psychological or existential. This view tells him the nature of the universe with which he has to deal (metaphysics); the means by which he is able to deal with it, i.e., the means of acquiring knowledge (epistemology), the standards by which he is to choose his goals and values, in regard to his own life and character (ethics), and in regard to society (politics), the means of concretizing this view is given to him by art (aesthetics). It is not a question of whether a man chooses to be guided by a comprehensive view: he is not equipped to survive without it. The nature of his consciousness does not permit an animal's percept guided, range of the moment form of existence. His survival requires a conceptual method of mental functioning, an awareness that is volitional. He needs to project his actions into the future and to weigh their consequences; this requires a conceptual process requiring some context. In the early stages of mankind's development that view was provided by religion; the mystic, antireality nature of this view was the cause of man's incalculably long stagnation of the Dark Ages. Philosophy attempts to bring something of consciousness and order to the total perspective, the brave and hopeless inquiry into the first causes of things, and their final significance, of ideal men and states with a naturalistic view of man, a citizen rather than a subject; it would emancipate the educated classes from ecclesiasticism and superstition and attempt a morality independent of supernatural aid. Most men stumble through the transition from the predominantly perceptual functioning of childhood to the conceptual function of adulthood with various degrees of success. The Left is comprised of people who did not make the transition. The psychologically immature have concluded that reality is the enemy, that the truth will defeat them, and that they had better not be concerned with it. Reality does not obey them, it frustrates their wishes, it is impervious to their feelings, it does not respond to them as adults did when they were children.

The fundamental unit of the human species that thinks, lives and acts towards goals *is* the individual. This means that as adults we can form judgments, act on our conclusions, and disagree with the choices of others. One is not linked to others who do his thinking for him. Each adult individual has the ability to consider what is in his own best interests. Each can act on his own private motivations and values and can judge other people as good to form relationships with, or bad and to be avoided. Each can decide whether or not to cooperate with others to solve problems. Each can think about the conclusions that the majority of others in a group come to, accepting or rejecting them as indicated by his own thought. Humans think individually, often disagree, and do not automatically cooperate. The idea of a collective mind is refuted by the personal experience of every individual through their education, experience and introspection.

When people interact, they do so with the understanding that their respective perceptions of reality are related, and as they act upon this understanding their common knowledge of reality becomes reinforced. Since these things are negotiated by people, human institutions and language come to be presented as part of objective reality, particularly for future generations who were not involved in the original process. For children these conventions are practical givens which cannot be changed. Things which emerge with the shared experiences of a civilization or society are called social constructs. If things are the way that they are only because of our social conventions, as opposed to being so naturally, then it should be possible to change them into how we would rather have them be. Thought and innovation can be disturbances of regularity and are tolerated only for indispensable readaptations. Trade was the first great disturber of the primitive world, for until it came, bringing money and profit in its wake, there was no property, and therefore little need for government. Next, the evolution of law passed from personal revenge to the payment of damages; from trial by ordeal to the obligation of a state first to punish and then to attempt to prevent wrongs. So, the general body of common law was derived from the customs of the group and added to the body of positive law derived from the decrees of government. True justice should largely rise from the interactions of the people and not simply be dictated from the law-giving power of government. To determine whether a system of collectively enforced social arrangements is legitimate one must look for agreement of the people subject to it, not to one group's notion of justice based on an authoritative political ideology.

Every creature pursues goals that keep them alive. The ultimate goal of this activity for any organism is its continued life as the type of organism it is. Every organism pursues goals specific to its own identity. The question for humans is the type of self-sustaining goals to be pursued. Is it for themselves or for a group? Morality is a code of values and behaviors guiding chosen human action towards a chosen end. Morality is needed as all humans are living creatures with definite requirements for their long-term survival and happiness, and they do not automatically act in accordance with those requirements. Thus, the proper role of morality is to guide human actions towards the sustenance of their life. If individuals are the sovereign entities that act and live then this implies that morality should be a guide for individuals in how best to act, so as to achieve happiness in their own lives. Individuals are the moral agents; there are no larger units of humanity to which they must submit themselves. The right to act in one's self-interest is derived from his nature as man and from the function of moral values in his life. It is that individual's physical and mental well-being and happiness that is his ultimate goal. He exists as an end in himself, to live the fullest, happiest life he can.

Individualism holds that each person has a mind and *can* act rationally to support his life. To act rationally he must be free to act on his own judgment, according to his own understanding of the facts. Thus, each individual should have his own political rights, if he is to survive and be happy over a lifetime. These most basic political rights are life, liberty, property and freedom of action. To survive and prosper humans need to own, use, and control certain things including the products of their work; thus, property is necessary for that freedom. Individualism implies that the role of government is to protect the aforementioned rights and nothing else. A government gains no moral power to violate individual rights by the number of people that support it. The issue is not whether humans can survive better or be happier with or without some sort of social interaction, but whether each adult individual can properly judge for himself whether to associate with certain other individuals, or whether he must mindlessly obey some group and pursue *its* alleged welfare as the goal of his life, even if *their* mode of happiness might make *me* miserable.

Ethical standards arise out of the shared meanings and practices which are sustained by discreet cultures or societies. The standards for what are appropriate or normal have evolved in the interactions of people as communities grew from individuals supplying all of their own needs to an economy with a division of labor. Government is established through a contract to guarantee equality and protection for all. Under this theory of politics men give up certain rights to combine with others to make those same rights more secure. Edmund Burke wrote: "If civil society be made for the advantage of man, all the advantages for which it is made become his right. It is an institution of beneficence; and Law itself is only beneficence acting by rule. Men have a right to live by that rule; they have a right to do justice, as between their fellows. Whatever each man can separately do for himself, without trespassing upon others, he has a right to do for himself; and he has a right to all which society, with all its combinations of skill and force, can do in his favor. In this partnership all men have equal rights; but not to equal things."

To benefit from such cooperation each man agrees to conform his behavior to a certain model and to work in order to trade his product with that of others. Those outside of the Law or the benefits of a community of exchange have difficulty identifying, transmitting and living up to these standards and values that, while perhaps not self-selected, have nevertheless proven to provide the moral guidance necessary for our survival. A given society is just if its substantive life is lived a certain way, that is a way faithful to the shared understanding of its members. When economic relations and political mastery replaced groups as the principle of social organization, it was supplanted at the bottom by the family and at the top by the state. Government took over the problem of maintaining order, while the family assumed the tasks of production and carrying on procreation of the race.

For the real source of social order originally *was* the family; and the omnipotence of the father is best expressed not as a backwards condition of society but a preference for familial rather than political government. A weaker government requires a strongly organized and disciplined family structure to take the place of a far-reaching and pervasive central authority. Freedom was initially conceived in terms of the family rather than of the individual; for (the family being the economic unit of production as well as the social unit of order) success or failure, survival or death, came not to the separate person but to the family.

The passage from hunting to agriculture brought a change from tribal property to family property; as the family took on more and more a patriarchal form, with authority centralized on the oldest male (primogeniture and entail), property became increasingly individualized, and personal bequest began. Frequently another enterprising son would leave the family unit, go beyond traditional boundaries, and by hard labor, gain land he guarded jealously as his own, which was eventually recognized by society. As the process was repeated in an ever-widening circle and society became more complex, individual ownership became the order of the day. The individual was hardly recognized as a separate entity in primitive society; what existed was the family and the clan, the tribe and the village; it was these groups that owned land and exercised power. Only with the coming of private property, which gave him economic authority, and the coming of the state, which gave him a legal status and defined Contractual rights, did the individual begin to stand out as a distinct personage. Liberty is a luxury of the security provided by the state's sanctions; the free individual is a product of and a mark of civilization.

CHAPTER FOURTEEN-WEALTH AND POVERTY-THE ANSWERS

GEORGE GILDER
RUSSELL KIRK

IRVING BABBITT
W.E.H. LECKY

AYN RAND
ISABEL PATERSON

ROSE WILDER LANE

"None but the people can forge their own chains; and to flatter the people and delude them by promises never meant to be performed is the stale but successful practice of the demagogue. Being weak, man may be trusted with his own freedom, but he cannot be trusted to respect other men's liberty, unless the great forces of prescription and veneration demarcate his sphere of governance. Positive law, recently decreed by some transitory Congress, lacks this buttressing and circumscribing influence of tradition and prejudice; therefore, the public should enact new positive law only under the stress of urgent necessity. Constitutionalism has been subsumed by common law, rather than restricting it. It is not sufficiently venerable to restrain the appetites of ambitious men and classes. The potentialities for the increase of power hidden in some of the clauses are ominous for the future liberties of America. Once men have got into the vice of legislating indiscriminately for immediate purposes and special interests, only force can withstand the masked arbitrary power of ‘laws’ that are no better than exactions.”

John Randolph

The twenty-first century conservative is concerned for the regeneration of character and spirit, a recovery of moral understanding which cannot be merely a means of social restoration. The conservative is concerned with the recovery of true community, local energies and co-operation. Free community is the alternative to compulsory collectivism. The urban renewal of the Left has resulted in riots, crime and violence, the uprooting of classes and communities, and the boredom that engenders addiction to narcotics. Community building, not mass welfare, is the answer. It would be well to direct our energies to the examination of voluntary and private associations, rather than to the planning of new activities for the unitary state. Explode the superstitions of the childhood of the race while reaffirming the existence of a natural moral order. Let us recognize diversity and variety, rather than the standardization of life, to admit the virtues of order and class, to encourage the development of talented leadership, rather than the praise of universal mediocrity. The embittered and impoverished dupes of ideology in Democrat-run cities challenge the great traditions of the civil social order. The era of patience draws to its end, inflamed by the Progressive wing of the Democrat Party. The lust for change never lacks agents; in them lies the urge to sweep away the patrimony of civilized man. The conservative confronts the tremendous dual task of restoring the harmony of the person and the harmony of the Republic: neither can endure long if the other has surrendered to the Left.

The power without and the power within must remain in balance; every diminution of power on the part of the state should be accompanied by an increase of self-control in individuals. The Federal Constitution, the Senate and the Supreme Court and other checks upon immediate popular impulse are to the nation what the higher will is to the individual. Where we succeed, individually or as a nation, it is in consequence of this restraining influence in our individual thought and political structure; where it fails, it is in consequence of our sentimental humanitarianism. Leadership can only be restored by the slow and painful process of developing moral gravity and intellectual seriousness, turning back to the strength of traditional doctrines. Our spiritual indolence can be overcome only by a re-examination of first principles. In our submission to the collectivist humanitarians, we have lost sight of standards; upon the restoration of standards depends the preservation of our civilized life.

There must be a defense of the old morality against a Leftist humanitarianism that, without conservative opposition, would devour its own sustenance incontinently. The proper reaction is essentially to answer action with action, to oppose to the welter of circumstances the force of discrimination and selection, to carry the experiences of the past to hedge the diverse impulses of the present, and to move forward in an orderly progression. Conversely, the morality of flux rapidly sweeps through the stage of Leftist humanitarianism into the stage of collective compulsion. We see the weakness of such a creed when confronted with the profound problems of life; we discover its inability to impose any restraint on the passions of men or produce a government with appeal to the experiential past. Humanitarians, having dissolved all the old loyalties and prescriptions, find themselves defenseless before reality. Too stupid even to glimpse the necessity for revering and obeying the traditions and prescriptions that shelter the country from social revolution, democracy has become both the ally and the tool of collectivism. Civil war would seem to be the natural ending of the democratic philosophy.

How shall society be guided to suffer the coercion of a Left which has none of the insignia of an old prescription to impose its Authority? They are not aware that civilization is a thin and precarious crust erected by the personality and the will of a very few, and only maintained by rules and conventions skillfully put across and guilefully maintained. They have no respect for traditional wisdom or the restraints of custom. As cause and consequence of their state of mind, they completely misunderstood human nature, including their own. The conservative humanist can only counter this current radicalism by winning men to an alternate system of ideas. Forms and restrictions will not keep society from destroying itself, if ideas are lacking. America must be convinced that man cannot remain human unless he restrains his appetites. It is such exercise of will that distinguishes man from beast. Intent upon an egalitarian condition of society, the humanitarian tries to extirpate those spiritual essences in man which make possible truly human life. The humanist of today contrarily believes that man must take on the yoke of some definite doctrine and discipline, must do obeisance to something resembling Law, or he will lose all direction.

Democracy exhibits a tendency to repudiate leadership, to insist that any leader be wanting in any strength or originality of mind which might tempt them to act out of harmony with the wishes of the people they represent, to do what their many headed master bids them. The "party of progress" has foolishly deprecated the role of strong and intelligent men in civilization. But upon the encouragement and recognition of these men depends civilization. Compulsion is not needed where men of Ability are secured by adequate rewards and incentives. A state may compel labor, but no Authority can force Ability to perform its natural function. Under compulsion Ability sinks to the level of labor; no man will exert unusual talents if he is to get no reward. Abolish the true leadership of Ability, restrained by a traditional moral and political system, and the laboring classes, after an interval of terror in which they will be as helpless as sheep, must submit to new masters whose rule would be harder, more arbitrary, and less humane, than the old. Socialism first repudiates legitimate leadership, and then, in reaction to its own failure, demands a dictator.

Napoleon was no accident. He was the true heir and executor of the French Revolution, as society cannot go on without discipline of some kind. What became apparent was the affinity between an unlimited democracy and the cult of ruthless power. The governments whose legitimacy had been called into question took alarm, and, having entered into an alliance, invaded France, and invited the dawn of a new political era. The coming together of whole nations for mutual massacre go back to this period. Such new national enthusiasm supplied France with soldiers so numerous that she not only repelled her invaders but began to invade other countries in turn, theoretically on a mission of emancipation. In the actual stress of events, however, the will to power turned out to be stronger than the will to brotherhood, and what had begun as a humanitarian crusade ended in Napolean and imperialistic aggression. This aggression awakened in turn the new national sentiment in various countries and did more than all other agencies combined to prepare the way for a powerful and united Germany. France ceased to be the Christ of nations, especially after its invasion of Switzerland.

A century later, egalitarianism was so attractive to Western intellectuals that they quietly justified the murders of landowners, capitalists and wealthy kulaks who resisted the changes intended to bring about socialism in the Russian and Chinese "experiments." It has two meanings: in the political, legal sense of equality all people should be treated as equals in terms of political, economic, social and civil rights. As a social philosophy it means equality of results advocating the removal of economic inequality. This means social ownership of the means of production because in that case the profits accrue to the population as a whole as opposed to private owners. The failure of capitalism to finally end the periodic flirtations with socialism, have only given us Stalin and Mao and Hitler, the gulags, the deaths of hundreds of millions, and suffocating bureaucracies. Dictators know that if men are to be ruled then the enemy is reason, and everything that it implies-intelligence, ability, achievement, success, self-confidence, self-esteem.

The Democrat party is a combination of all the miscreants in society who claim entitlement to resources based on their victimization, while offering nothing in the way of civil behavior or work in recompense. Pushing CRT and 1619 drives the American public to the right and ensures that anything that the Left offers is reflexively rejected. Slavery's legacy and anti-black racism exist partly because the left continues to bring it up as a useful cudgel in their class warfare ideology. As long as blacks can intellectually beat up on white people and make the world think that everything that went wrong is due to them, and blacks had nothing to do with it, then they are robbed of the impetus, the motivation, the inspiration for personal change and responsibility. No people can be genuinely free if they look to others for their deliverance. It is the wise man who understands that his condition remains his responsibility whether or not society is fair. His purpose is to realize himself, to live the fullest possible life, and he alone is responsible for this, like all men, no matter how society treats him. Black entrepreneurs will no doubt have a tougher time than their white counterparts but it is clear that entrepreneurship will give minorities a stake in the economic system and an opportunity for personal and financial growth, and thus in turn aid their local community. Successful black entrepreneurs have overcome fear, self-pity, plain inertia, and an anti-commercial ethic ingrained in black culture, and refuted the idea that money is made only through exploitation. But CRT says the notion that blacks should aim at control of their own destinies is useless if not destructive. To point out exceptions of Black achievement is only a ruse to systematically mislead and deceptively encourage them.

Liberal orthodoxy states that any non-white male is trapped in circumstances beyond their control. Any challenges, failures or misery one encounters are not their fault. There is nothing they can do to change their circumstances. Is there anything more hopeless or dystopian that could be sold to young people? They consequently have little knowledge of the freedoms and opportunities, the standards and possibilities, the values of family and optimism, that are indispensable to all wealth and progress and are capable of extending the boundaries and lifting the goals of individual lives. There are no individuals in CRT. With CRT every person has to be understood in terms of the groups they inhabit. The idea that racial groups have differentiated access to opportunities and resources ignores individual variations that are obvious.

In America the electoral triumph of the Left was sudden and complete; it came to society as well as to politics; it came late in the history of the Republic and found the opposition only half dug in. There were such promises of effortless liberty and prosperity that genuine opposition dissolved. Nowhere in the world did the Progressive egalitarian mode of thinking so completely invade the mind of an entire people. Nowhere was the right forced so abruptly into an untenable position. Conservatives yielded ground in a manner which must only be described as a rout. The timid Right, cowed into submission, had to accept the ground rules of a corrupt democracy or lose even further ground politically. Conservatism was a certain way to social non-conformity and political suicide. Its intellectual performance has been inexcusably feeble, sterile and disordered. It repudiated, or at a minimum failed to defend, some of the most sacred articles of Conservatism. Conservative ideas, inexpertly explained, could not resist the unreasoning forces of centralization and the leveling impulse. Self-described conservatives lacked the discernment and articulateness to move the right ideas forward. Some "conservative" politicians were even more comfortable with the liberal or even radical members of their own profession than with conservatives to their right. They disliked the anti-statism and focus on free-market economics found there and had no use for political philosophy. The Left offers a more adaptable group of principles-democracy and egalitarianism, than the Republican's limited government and individualism. The Right frankly became too busy manufacturing airplanes, building bridges and pumping oil to build a philosophical system to withstand the Left. The field of political and social speculation, always the preserve of the Left as critics of society, has been theirs to dominate without effective challenge. The men of action on the right have been too heavily occupied to read or reflect and have conceded the battle to the Progressives, just wanting to be left alone. In the realm of ideas, the American conservative has proved an impotent failure. The more savagely the Left baits the conservative, challenges his position, criticizes his actions, and proposes changes in the rules of the game, the more defensive he becomes.

The Left early on discovered, and then manipulated, the conditions and motives that impel men to shun work in the quest for security. But the passion for unearned personal security is an opiate which tends to destroy the virile characteristics which made us great. If liberty prevails unimpaired-if a man can work and sacrifice and save without the nagging intervention of an officious government-he will win the only kind of security that is really certain: the kind he wins for and by himself. No government can give security to men for any length of time without dulling their spirits, undercutting its own solvency, and looting the pockets of other men who have sought *to provide security for themselves.* Security is the new label for equality and equality is the old enemy of liberty. The better the people the less necessity there is for government.

Many philosophers attempted to break the traditional monopoly of mysticism in the field of ethics and to define a rational, scientific, non-religious morality. But their attempts consisted of accepting the ethical doctrines of the mystics and of trying to justify them on social grounds, merely substituting *society* for *God*. This means, in practice, that society is the source, standard and criterion of ethics; since the good is whatever it wills, whatever it asserts, the good is whatever it chooses *because* it chooses to do it. So any group that claims to be society's spokesman is ethically entitled to pursue anything they desire, while other men are obliged to live their lives in that service. This radical tendency has become wide, deep and active in the American people. Ceasing to regard anything as sacred or venerable, spurning what is old, injuring what is fixed, setting adrift all religious, domestic, and social institutions, they borrow nothing from the past and ignore the lessons of experience.

The arrested moral development of Americans has reached the end of its course. Never having discovered a proper code of values to guide their choices and actions, the same choices and actions that determine the purpose of their lives, they lash out at the unfairness of life, never daring to question their own path. Arbitrary human convention-unrelated to, underived from and unsupported by any objective facts of reality-means that ethics is the province of personal emotions, social edicts and mystic revelations-the subjective irrational-rather than a metaphysical, unalterable condition of man's existence according to the moral order of the universe.

Nathaniel Hawthorne well describes the state of our nation, and the need for a return to principles, in his *Mosses from an Old Manse:*

"It was impossible, situated as we were, not to imbibe the idea that everything in nature and human experience was fluid, or fast becoming so; that the crust of the earth in many places was broken, and its whole surface portentously upheaving; that it was the day of crisis, and that we ourselves were in the critical vortex. Our great globe floated in the atmosphere of infinite space like an unsubstantial bubble. No sagacious man will long retain his sagacity, if he lives among reformers and progressive people, without periodically returning into the settled system of things, to correct himself by a new observation from the old standpoint."

Hawthorne held the conviction that moral reformation was the only real reformation; the projects of enthusiasts will always be corrupted by those who leave human frailty out of account. Progress is a delusion, except for the infinitely slow progress of individual conscience. The formation of philosophical ideas requires the personal responsibility of observing, judging and integrating the facts of reality on an enormous scale. Rationality means a commitment to the principle that all of one's convictions, values, goals, desires and actions must be based on, derived from, chosen and validated by a process of thought, directed by as ruthlessly strict, precise and scrupulous an application of logic, as one's fullest capacity permits. Formulate true general principles. Collect and verify the historical facts to which the general principles must be accommodated. Bring moral and social sentiments into harmony with objective conditions which no contrary sentiment can permanently alter. Establish your dogmas, a conservative system of thought, on such a scientific basis, in clear relation with the hierarchical structure of human knowledge, and we will ungrudgingly grant them a place in our system. Then translate these into a moral and rational synthesis by which human beings can live. No popular movement has ever succeeded without a political philosophy to guide it, to set its direction and goal. The United States-history's greatest example of a country created by political theorists-has abandoned its philosophy and is falling apart. We are intentionally being divided by the Left, intending to collapse the country and take it over. The debasing of civilization follows the coming of life without principle, in which the ordinary motives to integrity that had governed the operation of Western society since Charlemagne would be dissolved. Men, having been deliberately instructed that there are no supernatural sanctions for moral conduct, must be made to conform and to labor either by naked force or by elaborate social machinery. But the study of the past instructs us that a people deprived of the study of laws, social institutions and the history of morals cannot discern the future at all, merely drifting through impulse and confused desire to arrive at social apathy.

Capitalism was destroyed, despite its incomparably beneficent record, due to the lack of a fully explained philosophical base. It was in fact, the last, but incomplete, product of an Aristotelian influence, through Ibn Khaldun, one of its intellectual architects. Its alleged defenders regarded it as compatible with government controls, ignoring the meaning and implications of the concept of laissez-faire. Since controls produce further economic distortions which prior government interventions had created, and necessitate further controls and subsidies, it is the statist element of the economy that wrecks it; it is the free, capitalist element that takes the blame.

There will come a time when America finds itself a country, crowded, strained and morally perplexed, and will be obliged to fall back on its founding principles, adopt a new regimen of optimism, concentrate its strength, restrict its vagaries, and trust the best, not the average members. We will stand in need of steady methods, sober views, with grown-ups handling the ship of state. The new frame of mind must develop out of the old; it must retain all that is good and healthy in it, and it must bear direct relation to the traditions and realities of *American* life, using the familiar symbols, rituals and myths having some connection with the realities of the past and present and with the possibilities of the future. The Conservative stands firm in the belief that his principles are grounded in the nature of things and men.

The conservative ideal should be the exercise of great care and discretion in imposing new forms of government intervention and also a constant effort to reduce the area already occupied by government. Since every program has its own constituency, there must be a program of education to inform the recipients how they are actually better off without its benefits. There needs be a reduction in the regulatory activities of government through a constant revision of laws and reduction of administrative machinery to permit self-discipline to grow. Regulation has a deadening effect on the initiative and energy of free men. The burden of proof rests entirely on those who advocate increased government activity. In many areas the sum-total of national legislative intervention in the private affairs of men does much more social harm than good. There is a strong preference for local action over state and state over national to deal with any problem that demands a societal remedy.

There are only two ways open to the left for achieving de facto equality. One is to raise all men and the other is to hold back all the achievers. The first method is nearly impossible because it is the faculty of volition that determines a man's stature and actions; the closest approach was demonstrated by the early United States and capitalism, which protected the freedom, the rewards and the incentives for every individual's achievement, each to the extent of his ability and ambition, thus raising the intellectual, moral and economic state of the whole society. The second choice is actually impossible, because, if mankind were leveled down to the common denominator of its least competent members, it would not be able to survive. Yet it is the second method the egalitarianists are pursuing. The greater the evidence of their policy's consequences-the greater spread of misery and *inequality* throughout the world, the more frantic their pursuit.

From the basic fact of moral equality comes the right for all to find and exploit their talents up to their natural limits (equality of opportunity); men are equal before the law, with a right to justice on the same terms as other men (political equality). Beyond this we are unwilling to go. Recognizing the infinite variety among men in talent, taste, appearance, intelligence and virtue, we see that men are grossly unequal-and can never be made equal-in all qualities of mind, body, and spirit. But the Capitalist social and economic order is organized in such a way as to take advantage of ineradicable natural distinctions among men. Men find their level and equality of opportunity keeps the way open to ascent and decline. In a rational government the wish becomes to seek out the best men, characterized by talent and virtue and place them in positions of authority.

....

Throughout history, the most common view of the universe is that it was static, motionless, limited, and controlled by an Authority, be it government or religion. All individuals are, and by their nature should and must be, controlled by something outside themselves. As a child, everything that we want and must have comes from a power outside ourselves, one enormously stronger that we can conceive. And this power, at this time, actually does control the conditions of our life. Many can still not imagine that any security, order, or justice can exist among men who are not controlled by some intangible Authority. This false assumption underlies all the thought of the Old World, through its whole history, to this day. It underlies a great deal of current American thinking. No Old-World thinker has ever questioned it. But men do not remain babies all their lives. They grow up. A time comes when every normal person is responsible for himself. He is then free and self-controlling. Individual energy, constantly generated and acting, creates the physical necessities of human existence, and creates all human relationships-societies, nations, and civilizations. Ordinary American men and women, using their abilities, make our civilization and keep on making it, every day, every hour, and nothing but their constant individual efforts make it and keep it existing. The civilization does not create them. One result of all this individual planning and control is an enormous waste of things. No one can estimate its colossal total, for normally three hundred million persons are adding to it every day, every hour. Since individuals actually control their own energy, any change in its uses can only come from their efforts, experiments at new methods of production, and attempts to create things that do not yet exist. Most of those efforts inevitably fail, causing loss and waste. Communism prevents such waste by preventing individual initiative. This also prevents economic progress.

Since history began, all the people of the Old World lived in what is now called a "planned economy." This is the control of human energies used in producing and distributing material goods, by an Authority consisting of a few men, and according to a plan made by those men, and enforced by the police. The Old World does not waste an atom of anything. It never has. A planned economy does not waste any material thing. It wastes time, human energy and human lives. Under communism, the men who establish the government plan its economy. They can only plan it on the level of the living conditions that have already been created in that place at that time. They always establish economic equality. At whatever level of living conditions a commune is established, at that level or lower the commune remains for as long as it lasts. No man is permitted to live his own way; that would not be communism, it would be individualism. So no one living under communism can use his ability in a new way. He cannot even assert his will against the Authority, as long as he believes it is necessary. There can be no individuals until one person, like the man in Plato's cave, shakes his comrades' faith in the controlling Authority. This faith is all that keeps the commune in existence. Only an Old-World mind can think in terms of a fixed standard of living. A realist now thinks in terms of dynamic, creative energies, working to promote an unknowable future. This planet gives nobody food, clothing or shelter.

Men in Government have no more power to control others than an individual has. What they have is the use of force-command of the police and the army. Government, The State, is always a use of force, permitted only by the general consent of the governed. In any civilization the use of force is the whole difference between Government and any other organized group of men. The need for Government is the need for force; where force is unnecessary, there is no need for Government. But the use of force is not *control*. No force can compel a man to act. It can only hinder, restrict, or stop his acting. A "planned economy" is believed to be a Government's *control* of the productive uses of human energy. It is believed that men in Government can control, for the general good, the men who produce and distribute material goods. In thousands of years, they have never been able to do it.

Men in Government who imagine they are controlling a planned economy *must* prevent the economic progress of individuals, as in the past they always have done. For economic progress is a change in the use of men's productive energy. Only individuals who act against the majority opinion of their time will try to make such a change. And if they are not stopped, they destroy the existing (and majority approved) Government monopoly. The owners of river steamboats would never have encouraged the building of railroads, nor the owners of railroads the development of airplanes. When men in Government have a monopoly, they have the use of force to prevent anyone from attacking it. A planned economy, therefore, is a use of force to prevent the natural use of human ability. Its effect throughout history has been to prevent material progress. What the planned economies did was to prevent the development of civilization. Every time they almost achieved it, during the upheavals and disorganization of Government-which were called the "rise" of Egypt or Persia or Greece or Rome or France or Spain-they ended up establishing a firm, good, Government, an Authority supposed to control them. In turn each enforced a planned economy with increasing firmness, restricting the use of natural abilities until men could no longer eat nor their taxes support their government. What followed was the "fall" of each Government. That is the history of planned economies for thousands of years.

The problem of human life is the problem of finding the method of applying combined human energies to this earth to get from it the necessities of living. This problem has never been solved by assuming that an Authority controls individuals. To the degree that men in Government assume this authority and responsibility and have used their actual police force in attempting to control the productive uses of human energy, to that degree the energy has failed to work. The planned economy invariably causes the destruction of whatever Government that tries to enforce it. This is because Government has no means of knowing real costs, and these costs automatically increase at a growing rate until the people can no longer pay them. What they take must be used to serve Government's proper function, which is the use of force. When an unprotected monopoly charges too much the customers decline to buy the product. That company knows it must reduce costs or close up shop. But this threat of desertion does not exist for men in Government operating a "planned economy.' A Government monopoly need not depend on or please its customers, nor make a profit. It takes whatever it wants. They have no means of knowing the real costs in lost human production and the people who pay these costs have no peaceful means of registering a protest that these costs are too high. The important question is, what amount can government take *safely?* Because they use force, they have no means of knowing the answer to that question. The tragedy of the Old World is that the *only way*-regulation-by which Authority can maintain a social order must inevitably destroy that social order and any form of Authority that tries to maintain it. When men in Government try to control the natural uses of human genius in producing and distributing goods, the amount of produced wealth that they take must constantly increase, and the amount of production that they subtract from the economy must constantly increase as well. Every tax dollar Government extracts to support the bureaucracy, and to support the people who the bureaucracy tends to, must be increased as those demands increase, and the economy increasingly staggers under the load.

But an organization dependent for its existence upon the multitudes of individuals whom it serves, encounters a natural check to this waste. There is a natural limit to the amount of human energy that Government can waste as well. But because men in Government are using force, they have no means of knowing what this natural limit is. Recently it has been the limit of the majority's willingness to endure their increasing poverty that results from the increasing waste of energy. No one can know that limit, as it depends on a great number of individuals, no two of which think exactly alike. The actual limit can only be discovered by reaching it. Too much energy is deducted from human productivity. At that point it is all over for the men in Government.

Nobody can plan the actions of even a thousand living persons, separately. Anyone attempting to control hundreds of millions must divide them into classes and make a plan applicable to these classes. But those classes do not exist. No two are in the same circumstances; no two have the same abilities; beyond the bare necessities no two have the same desires. In real life, a planned economy comes up against the infinitude diversity of human beings. Naturally, by their nature, men escape in all directions from regulations applying to non-existent classes. It becomes necessary to increase the number of men who supervise their actions, and more men to watch the supervisors. Still, men will act individually, in ways that *they* plan. These ways do not fit the Authority's plan. So still more men are needed to stop or supervise and more men to co-ordinate the constantly increasing complexity of all this supervision. Bureaucracy by its nature must increase. It needs another bureau, to comb out of it all of its orders which productive men, behaving in unpredictable ways, have made obsolete. A super bureaucracy, arrogating to itself functions that cannot properly appertain to government; the planned economy, encompassing not merely the economy proper, but the whole moral and intellectual range of human activities, is the result. In the new-style collectivism, power is loved for its own sake; regulation becomes an end rather than a means, seeking to gratify by the acquisition of power their loneliness and their nameless anxieties. The intellectual servitude of this class is described unforgettably by Czeslaw Milosz, in *The Captive Mind.* They are at once jailers and jailed.

A Progressive reasons on this ancient assumption that some Authority controls all men. He takes it for granted. Since all men are equal, no man can be an Authority controlling other men. It must therefore be some intangible Authority. The Authority that controls men must be his situation. The Frontier created the United States. Economic Necessity controls men. But ordinary experience makes it hard to believe that this Power is wholly intangible. Anyone who believes that Authority controls human beings, and who does not believe that this superhuman Authority is wholly intangible, must believe it resides in a few living men whose nature is superior to the nature of most men. Those simple men have believed that it creates a superior *kind* of man to act as his agent-the Pharaohs of Egypt, the Emperors of Rome, the Kings of England. Therefore, they obey these men, supposed to be their superior, who are the Government. Progressivism is the total self-surrender of the individual to the will of this Authority, the purpose of which of course is always The Good. Progressives believe that history is not the mere record of men's acts, but of the Power that controls them. In practice, though, no effort to make this theory work, from Lycurgus to Lenin, has ever permitted human energy to produce effectively, because it does not recognize that individuals control themselves.

True American Government is not superior to the individual, only permitted by it; it is Government by Law. The Constitution forbids. It exists to limit and restrain and check and hinder our American Government. Superstition, that deep darkness in human minds, supports all other kinds of Government. Until the American Revolution, Government always rested on superstitious belief. The awe and dread and allure of power created the belief that Authority controls individuals. It supports a living ruler's use of force. An American politician swears to obey the Constitution that limits his power. Only his honor, and the next election, hold him to that oath. All the other incentives that human beings feel impel him to break it: If he wants to do what he thinks is good, if he wants to be re-elected, if he wants more money, if he needs more self-importance-he needs more power. The only thing that prevents him from doing this is Constitutional Law-words on paper. Its only force is moral, and it must be found in each American politician's conscience.

The more men in Government are dependent upon satisfying popular demands, and the more Americans believe that Government is a controlling Authority, the more this Government is compelled to use force to hinder and restrict the exercise of natural individual freedom; that is, to prevent human energy's working under its natural control and for its natural productive purpose. The State has lost completely the moral and intellectual authority it once possessed. It does not any longer represent God on earth. It represents the party which secured the most votes in the last election and is administered by men whom no one would make trustees of his property or guardians of his children. When I read accounts of the glorious future that awaits us as soon as we get the proper amount of state interference with our private concerns, for the benefit of the masses, administered by the Know-Nothings currently in Washington, I confess I am lost in amazement.

Modern populations possessing presumption without knowledge are resolved to extend the functions of government immeasurably beyond the duties of defense and maintenance of internal order. The public is fascinated with the possibility of obtaining necessities and comforts through the action of the state, even to the exclusion of those liberties which once were so important. Economic appetites, now the master of all classes, incline the public to demand a paternalistic regime; that encourages a variety of cheap Utopian fantasies; that leads invariably to the manipulation of the value of money by the state, with its consequent inflation and insecurity; the poor are an excuse for abusive public revenue and expenditure; it furthers the delusion that prosperity depends upon the action of government. The belief of many persons is in the idea that the stock of good things in the world is practically unlimited in quantity, contained in a vast storehouse or granary, and that out of this it is now doled in unequal shares and unfair proportions. It is this unfairness and inequality which Progressive law will someday correct. This is not to deny that at various times during the history of man that narrow oligarchies have kept too much of the wealth of the world to themselves, or that false economic systems have frequently diminished the total supply of wealth, and by their indirect operation, have caused it to be irrationally distributed. But if wholly triumphant, Progressivism leads to a common poverty of body and mind which masquerades as common gratification. In this world the poor have ceased to be content with their poverty. We must face the problem as it is presented to us. Corrupt and stupid governments may be tolerated when their activities are confined by prescription to a small and certain sphere; in this age of aggrandizement, though, corrupt and stupid government delivers us up to class warfare and economic collapse.

A rational man knows he must achieve his goals through his own effort; he knows that neither wealth nor jobs exist in a given, limited quantity, waiting to be divided. He knows that all benefits have to be produced, that the gain of one man does not represent the loss of another, that a man's achievement is not earned at the expense of those who have not achieved it. He never imagines that he has any sort of unearned claim on another human being. If a man speculates on what society should do for the poor, he accepts thereby the collectivist premise that men's lives belong to society, which has the right to set their goals, dispose of them in any manner and plan the distribution of their efforts. The man who is willing to serve as the means to the ends of others will necessarily regard others as the means to *his* ends. The more a person acts from this psychology, the more he will devise schemes "for the greater good of mankind' or of "society" or "the public" or of "future generations." There is no such dichotomy as human rights versus property rights. Rights are conditions of existence required by man's nature for his proper survival, and the right to property is their only implementation. No human rights can exist without property rights. Material goods are produced by the mind and effort of individual men and are needed to sustain their lives; if the producer does not own the result of his effort, he does not own his life. Whoever claims the right to redistribute the wealth produced by others is claiming the right to treat others as chattel. If one wants to uphold and protect individual rights, capitalism is the foundation. Individual rights are the means of subordinating society to moral law, and this recognition represents the most profound achievement of the United States. The government's role was changed from the role of a ruler to the role of a servant. The Constitution was written to protect man from the government. The Bill of Rights was directed not against the public but against the government, as an explicit declaration that individual rights supersede any public or social power.

What is called the middle class is not a class at all; it is a different form of society, a classless one, a free society, the Society of Contract. Every reference by members of this class stressed the fact that they were free men, and they lived by Contract law. Trade and money inevitably washed away the enclosing walls of the Society of Status. The stream flowed from continent to continent. The Arab Empire came into being, occupying much the same terrain as Carthage and with many points of resemblance, especially lacking in stability and a fixed center. It recaptured Spain and thrust into Europe, beyond the borders of France, only to finally meet repulse. But the impact loosened the European Status system instead of consolidating it. Nothing but money could furnish, pay, transport and subsist a sufficient defense; nothing but trade could supply the money. The Roman legal heritage of Europe was reasserted, and under adversity it remained cohesive. The Turks were a declining power from the moment they blocked the great trade routes, both overland and by water (the Silk Routes), and thus cut the supply source for their armies. They imposed a static society in their area, just as Europe was emerging from Status. With the trade routes to the East barred, Europe at last caught up with Pytheas and looked across the Atlantic.

The axiom of liberty, realized from the secular principles deduced by Greece and Rome, remains associated with America, persisting in spite of the prompt and atrocious contradiction offered by the treatment of the Indians and the early importation of African slaves. Europe was looking for an outlet for its energy; it had been cut off from the land route to the Orient. The voyage of Columbus was like the leap of an electric spark across an arc. His objective was Japan, China and India, and he was to be rewarded with a percentage of the trade to be opened by his route. If ever a nation and dynasty had the physical components of empire thrown in its lap by mere chance and all at once, it so happened to Spain. It controlled the richest parts of Europe, the dominant position in respect to the Mediterranean, and the wealth of America soon poured into its coffers. But an ocean does not tolerate monopoly. Making contact with the Americas, Spain picked up vast amounts of precious metals which were convertible into European currency. Yet there was the spectacle of treasure ships unloading bullion year by year in Seville, as the people were increasingly impoverished by an inverse ratio until reduced to hunger and rags. Every ordinance now recommended and applied in the name of a planned economy was tried out in Spain during that period on the same pretext of public necessity, with the inevitable consequences of stopping production. Commerce and industry were at a standstill, agriculture in decay, and no money in circulation. Everything went into government; and the government was always bankrupt. Yet its functions, alleged as the reason for such measures, were carried on with grotesque inefficiency. In France, Louis XIV threw the whole energy of the country into war, taxed his subjects into famine, anticipated several years revenue, depreciated the currency and still found himself penniless. The scope and pretensions of government in Spain and France increased continuously. The claims of government in England were no less persistently prosecuted, until refuted, diminished, and qualified. The balance of power fell to England only because for a while it allowed the energy of trade to flow most freely, which is to say that England conceded the most liberty to the individual by respecting private property and abandoning by degrees the practice of political trade monopolies. Of course, this did not happen all at once, and it was the remains of monopoly which precipitated the American Revolution.

The degree of a country's freedom is the degree of its prosperity. The basic conflict of our time is not merely political or economic, but moral and philosophical; the dominant philosophy is a revolt against reason, with the re-distribution of wealth being only one manifestation of that creed. There is only one power that determines the course of history, just as it determines the course of every individual life: the power of ideas. If you know a man's rational convictions, you can predict his actions. If you understand the dominant philosophy of a society, you can predict its course. In order to win, the rational side of any controversy has nothing to hide, since reality is its ally. The irrational side-the Progressive-has to deceive, to confuse, evade and hide its goals. Every evasion and contradiction helps the goal of destruction; only reason and logic can be the basis of progress. Evil wins only by default: by the moral failure of those who evade the fact that there can be no compromise on basic principles. When a society insists on pursuing a suicidal course, one may be sure that the alleged reasons and proclaimed slogans are mere rationalizations. The question is only: what is it that these rationalizations are hiding? It is the exhausted cynicism of a bankrupt culture, of a society without values, principles, convictions or standards, leaving a vacuum for anyone to fill. They are doing so. To work on a blank check held by every creature born, by men whom you'll never know, whose ability or laziness or fraud you have no way to learn and no right to question, just to work and work with others deciding who will consume your effort, the dreams and the days of your life, is all that men will have to look forward to. When men give up reason and freedom, the vacuum is filled by faith and force. Wealth acquired by force is somehow rightful property, but wealth earned by production is not; looting is somehow moral, but producing is not.

The ambitious agenda of contemporary liberalism simply ensures the government will do nothing well, except to expand itself as an obstacle of growth and innovation. Government best supports the future by refraining as much as possible from trying unduly to shape it, for the impact of government policy nearly always conforms with the current incidence of political power, which derives from the configuration of existing capital and labor. The phenomenon of government support for mismanagement, inefficiency and short-sightedness reaches far beyond business. Comfortable failure will always and inevitably turn to politics to protect it from change. Just as declining businesses turn to the state, people and groups that shun the burdens of productive work and family life will proclaim themselves a social crisis and a national responsibility-and, sure enough, they become one. The more federal aid that is rendered to the unemployed, the divorced, the deviant and the prodigal, the more common will their ills become, the more alarming will be the graphs of social breakdown. A government preoccupied with the statistics of crisis will often find itself subsidizing problems, shoring up essentially morbid forms of economic and social activity, creating incentives for unemployment, inflation, family disorder, housing decay, and budget deficits.

It is among the simplest of economic truths, that by far the largest part of the wealth of the world is constantly perishing by consumption, and that if it is not renewed by perpetual toil and adventure, that community which consumes without producing will be extinguished or brought to the very verge of extinction. The wealth of mankind is the result of influences effecting a continuing process, everywhere complex and delicate. If we alter the character or diminish the force of these influences, it is sure that the wealth will dwindle and disappear. Experience shows us that wealth may come very near to perishing simply through diminished energy in the motives of the men who produce it. A government may impoverish a country more by its action upon motives than by its positive exactions. The destruction of the vast wealth accumulated under the Roman Empire, one of the most orderly and efficient of governments, and the decline of Western Europe into the Middle Ages, can only be accounted for on the same principle. You have only to tempt a portion of the population into temporary idleness by promising them a share in a fictitious hoard lying in an imaginary strong box which is supposed to contain all human wealth. You have only to take the heart out of those who would willingly labor and save, by taxing them into misery, even for the most laudable of philanthropic objects. For it makes no difference to the motives of the thrifty and industrious part of mankind whether their financial oppressor be the few or the many. What motives will Socialism substitute for those currently acting on men? The motives which at present impel mankind to the labor and pain which produce wealth in ever-increasing quantities, are such as infallibly entailing inequality in the distribution of wealth. They are the springs of action called into activity by the strenuous and never-ending struggle for existence. There can be no grosser delusion than to suppose this result to have been obtained by socialistic legislation. It has really been obtained through the sifting of the most able by natural selection. It all reposes on the sacredness of Contract and the stability of private property-the first the implement, the second the reward of industriousness.

Since the Russian Revolution the Communist Party has been following Lenin's instruction to "first confuse the vocabulary." Thinking can only be done in words. Accurate thinking requires words of precise meaning. Communication is impossible unless words are used whose precise meaning is understood. Today, when you hear the word democracy, what does it mean? The United States and Britain, of course, and economic security and compulsory insurance, a vote for everybody, and freedom and human rights and human dignity and common decency. That is, the word has no meaning. Its meaning has been destroyed.

Similarly, the use of terms such as racist, extremist and selfish are artificial and rationally unusable terms designed to replace and obliterate some legitimate concept-in this case, capitalism-terms which sound like a concept but are incongruous, contradictory elements taken out of any logical conceptual order. The defining characteristic must be that which distinguishes it from everything else; thus, the Left attempts to subsume all its criticism of capitalism under those smears. The purpose is to make public discussion unintelligible, and if possible, to end it; to induce the same disintegration in the mind of any man who accepts them uncritically, making him incapable of clear thinking or rational judgment. If one destroys the concept of capitalism, one destroys the knowledge that a free society did and can exist. Confucius, when asked what would be his first concern, if the reins of government were put into his hands, replied that it would be to define his terms and make words correspond to things.

What really happened in Moynihan's Northeast was sort of a derangement of entrepreneurism-the energies of job creation that should have fueled the growth of capitalism instead found their outlet in the enterprise of expanding government. After the protests of the 60's, characterized by anti-war and anti-business sentiments, there were few places for their energies to go but to journalism and the government. Their greatest accomplishment was to create an interdisciplinary mass of social healers and, to keep them busy, added provocateurs and community agitators. The crucial event was the display of an aggressive fostering of growing government but with no fiscal limits. The jobs created-sufficient to launch a thousand businesses-turned out to not be jobs at all but seats at the trough, where the workers consumed their own human capital and the income of the state with all the assurance that they were serving the cause of social change and progress. Let's dispense with the idea that politicians are in government for any reason except to promote their own interest. The government boom, in the name of full employment, in the vision of job entitlement and insurance, will end by reducing the availability of real work at inviting levels of pay. Production is the source of all demand, and as the supply of marketable products decline, so does the worth of the specious jobs and blue-sky pensions of the public sector.

The members of mobs styling themselves as irreconcilable refuse to submit their opinions to the arbitration of anyone; they hold their beliefs as men once held religious opinions. They cling to their creed with the same intensity, the same immunity of doubt, the same confidant expectation of blessedness to come quickly, which characterizes the disciples of an infant faith. They insist on the immediate redemption of the pledge, and they utterly refuse to wait until a popular majority legitimately gives effect to their opinions. Nor would the vote of any such a majority have the least authority with them were its sanction to include *any* departure from their principles. The new rulers sternly insist that everything shall be brought into strict conformity with the central principles of the system over which they preside; and they are aided by a number of persons to whom the old principles were hateful, whether from their fancy for ideal reforms, from their impatience of a monotonous stability, or from a natural destructiveness of temperament. What a modern Democracy pretends to fight with is privilege; it knows no rest until this is trampled out. What really opposes it is the reproach of ability. To the left the sight of achievement is a reproach, a reminder that their own lives are irrational and there is no escape from reason and reality. Why do the non-producers and non-achievers merit prestige, or reward, or notice at all?-this hatred-eaten human ballast that men of the mind have to drag along, to feed and be martyred by, through all the millennia of mankind's history.

Of all modern irreconcilables the Progressives appear to be the most impracticable, and Republican government the least likely to cope with them successfully. Nobody can say exactly what Progressivism is, and the dangerousness of the theory arises from its vagueness. It seems full of the seeds of future convulsion. It appears to assume that men of one particular race suffer injustice whenever they are placed under the same political institutions with men of another race. The fact is that any portion of a political society, which had a somewhat different history from the rest of the parts, can take advantage of the theory and claim victimization, and thus threaten the entire society with dismemberment. There is no more effective way of attacking a Republic than by admitting the right of the majority to govern but denying that the majority so entitled is correct in the manner in which they govern.

CHAPTER FIFTEEN-DEMOCRACY AND FREEDOM

W.E.H. LECKY
SIR HENRY SUMNER MAINE

"The sole and only legitimate end of government is to protect the citizen in the enjoyment of life, liberty and property, and when the Government assumes other functions, it is usurpation and oppression."

Constitution of the State of Alabama

"The people authorized their rulers to make and execute laws to govern them, but always provided they retain a right and power to choose a sufficient number from among themselves, to be a representative body of the whole people, to have a voice in the making of all such laws, and in the management of the most weighty concerns of the state."

John Adams

"As there is a degree of depravity in mankind which requires a certain degree of circumspection and distrust, so there are other qualities in human nature which justify a certain portion of esteem and confidence. Republican government presupposes the existence of these qualities in a higher degree than any other form."

(Publius, #55)

There is no place in which the worst passions of human nature may operate more easily and more dangerously than in the sphere of politics. There is no worse criminal than the adventurer who is gambling for power with the lives of men. There are no crimes which produce vaster or more enduring suffering than those which sap the great pillars of order in the State, and destroy the respect for life, for liberty, for property and for law on which all true progress depends. Anyone who through such motives, as a desire for wealth and power, makes a revolution which destroys a multitude of lives, ruins the credit and commerce of a nation, scatters the seeds of anarchy, disaster and depression, deserves a prompt and ignominious death as much as a murderer. The future only can tell whether the energy of the American people can be sufficiently roused to check these evils, and to do so before they have led to some great catastrophe.

A trick of the Left is to generalize-rapidly framing, and confidently uttering general propositions on political subjects. Nothing can be simpler. Abstraction consists of dropping out of sight a certain number of facts and constructing a formula which will embrace the remainder; the comparative value of general propositions turns entirely on the relative importance of the particular facts selected and of the particular facts rejected. Crowds of men can be got to assent to general statements, clothed in striking language, but unverified and perhaps incapable of verification, and thus there is formed a sort of sham of concurrent opinion. There is a loose acquiescence in a vague proposition and the voice of the people is assumed to have spoken. The voice of the people is to many politicians the sum of all wisdom, the supreme test of truth or falsehood. It is even more than this: it is invested with something like the spiritual efficacy which theologians ascribe to baptism. It is supposed to wash away all sin. However unscrupulous, however dishonest, however unconstitutional, may be the acts of a party or statesman, they are considered to be justified beyond reproach if they have been condoned or sanctioned at a general election. It has led many politicians to subordinate all notions of right or wrong to the wishes or interests of majorities, and to act quite audaciously on the maxim that the end justifies the means. The root idea of this practice is the belief that the moral law has no deeper foundation and no higher sanction than utility, and that the greatest happiness of the greatest number is its supreme test and ideal. From this it must be inferred that minorities have no rights as against majorities.

Democracy, in the sense of direct and unlimited democracy is the death of liberty. Rousseau was the most uncompromising theorist and advocate of *direct* democracy. The force and universality of the movement towards direct democracy makes the question what form it is likely to take and the means by which its characteristic evils can be best mitigated. Rousseau was resolutely egalitarian. Any attempt to carry out his program leads one to break down standards in the real world in favor of purely chimerical ideals. Such men know no good but to please a wild, indetermined, infinite appetite. This conceit is closely associated in unregenerate man with envy and jealousy of anyone else whose conceit seems to set up rival pretensions to his own. We have seen that a tendency to direct democracy does not mean a tendency toward true representative government, equality or freedom. Strong arguments may be adduced, from both history and from the present nature of things, to show that democracy more than often leads to the direct opposite of freedom. In ancient Rome the old aristocratic republic was gradually transformed into a democracy, and it then passed speedily into an imperial despotism. In France a corresponding change has more than once taken place. A despotism resting on a plebiscite is as natural a form of democracy as a constitutional republic. Has the Progressive movement towards American direct democracy raised the country to a higher plane of liberty than in the past? Equality is the idol of democracy but with the infinitely various capacities and energies of men, this can only be attained by a constant, systematic, stringent repression of the natural development of the tendencies which are distinctly adverse to its formation. Of the many functions which government is expected to discharge the most important to the happiness of mankind is that of securing equal justice between man and man. But no one can follow American history without perceiving how frequently and seriously the democratic principle has undermined this first condition of true freedom and progress. The tyranny of the majority is not only shown in tyrannical laws. Sometimes it is shown in an assumed power to dispense with all laws which run counter to the popular opinion of the hour, sometimes in the tainted administration of existing laws.

There is no greater folly than to set up a political body without considering the hands into which it is likely to fall, or the spirit in which it is likely to be used. The ancient form may be preserved, but the spirit of the Constitution will evaporate. It means that democracies cannot permanently remain the supreme power among the nations of the world. Sooner or later, they will sink by their own vices and inefficiencies into a lower plane. It is only too probable that some great calamity or the stress of a great war may accelerate the change.

When a country has a formal political organization, taxation is already authorized; the channel is there, to divert profits from production into government expenditure. The welfare state further attaches this instrument of government to the dislocated, unemployed masses; whenever that mass is disturbed, it must wrest the instrument out of control and nullify its function. What was intended as interim financial help between jobs has transformed into half of the citizens of the country receiving some form of financial aid from the government. This is what happens in a democracy; it releases force in such a manner that there can be no control. For the government is under no control by the citizen in a democracy. The voters must somehow retain in their private control a corresponding but preponderant power of resistance to any misapplication of the power delegated to their representatives.

In the days when government was mainly in the hands of classes who were largely influenced by traditions, precedents and the spirit of compromise, tacit understandings, unrecognized by law, were sufficient to define the provinces of, and at the same time to limit, the powers of the different parts of the Constitution. Power has now passed into other hands; another spirit prevails, and this movement should be clearly recognized and accurately limited by new Law. The modern spirit is in everything the direct denial of practical reason. It asserts the unrestricted right of man to subject religion, morals, and politics to his own will, passion or caprice. This is inevitably fatal, as it stimulates insubordination and disorder, setting everything afloat, and breaking apart that moral solidarity which makes possible so delicate a government as democracy. The continual degradation of the suffrage to lower and lower strata of property and intelligence attacks institution after institution; representation to all portions of country, irrespective of their circumstances and characters, commonly means the end of constitutional government. It is always demoralizing to extend the domain of sentiment over questions where it has no legitimate jurisdiction. The demise of democracy is the consequence of general mediocrity in mind and character straying bewildered through the labyrinth of civil society. The Left believes that the state must do more than govern the nation, it must transform as well as reform its subjects; perhaps create them anew. Tocqueville, as are we, was terrified of such a planned human race. Socialism is the vehicle of this standardization and dehumanization of man, using the centralized, egalitarian state as the means. An interminable vista of gray uniformity, regimented and hedged in remorselessly, individuals totally absorbed in the body politic, stretched before his eye. The futility of opposing the monstrous deaf and blind tendency of the times made Tocqueville painfully conscious of his impotence and insignificance. But he never lost hope of ameliorating those problems which resulted from the levelling inclination of society.

Machiavelli wrote that “all human Constitutions are subject to corruption and must perish, unless they are timely renewed by reducing them to their first principles. Yet everyone knew that reducing the constitution to its first principles was impossible if the people themselves had become corrupted and sunk in vice. Until the society itself had been infected, until there was “a general depravity of morals, a total alienation from virtue, a people cannot be completely enslaved.” If the diseases remain unremedied, if the constitution cannot be restored to first principles, then the fault can only be the people’s. “Nothing is wanted but the people’s virtue; indeed, all men might be free, had they virtue enough to be so.” (Mather)

Eighteenth century intellectuals, Montesquieu foremost among them, had worked out the ambiguous but necessary and mutual relation existing between the moral spirit of a society and its political constitution. “Empires carry in them their own bane, and proceed, in fatal round, from virtuous industry and valor, to wealth and conquest; next to luxury, then to foul corruption and bloated morals; and last of all, to sloth, anarchy, slavery and political death.” Comparative histories written by Plutarch only too grimly showed the fate of empires grown too fat with riches. While the Romans maintained their love of virtue, their simplicity of manners, their recognition of true merit, they raised their state to the heights of glory. But they stretched their conquests too far and their Asiatic wars brought them luxuries they had never before known. From that moment virtue and public spirit sunk apace: dissipation vanished temperance and independence. That corruption soon descended to the common people, leaving them enfeebled and their souls depraved. The gap between rich and poor widened and the society was torn by extortion and violence. With the character of the Roman people so corrupted, dissolution had to follow. “The empire tottered on its foundation, and the mighty fabric sunk beneath its own weight.”

The analogy with the present situation of the United States is truly frightening. The increasing debt, the rising prices and taxes, the intensifying search for artificial distinctions of race, wealth and gender by more and more people-are evidence of our present degeneracy and impending destruction. Envy is a poison softening the once hardy character of the American people, sapping them of the will to fight for their liberty, leaving them as weakened prey to the designs of the Progressive Party. The American people are now too corrupted, too enfeebled, to restore their constitution to its first principles and rejuvenate their country.

One of the worst results of democracy, especially of the American example upon politics, is the tendency which it produces to overrate the importance of machinery, and to underrate the importance of character in public life. It is not surprising that it should be so, for the American Constitution is the best example which history affords of wise political machinery. Nor are the great men who formed it to be blamed if their successors degraded the electorate while removing the barrier of double election. There is no political advantage which is not too dearly bought if it leads to a permanent lowering of the character of public men and of the moral tone of public life. In the long run, the increasing or diminishing importance of character is perhaps the best test of the progress or decline of nations. It is an ominous sign for a nation when its governors and legislators are corrupt, but it is a still worse sign when public opinion has come to acquiesce placidly in their corruption.

American democracy carries with it at least as much of a warning as of encouragement, especially when we remember the singularly favorable circumstances under which the experiment was tried, and the impossibility of reproducing those conditions again. Its modest successes can be attributed to a written constitution, securing property and Contract, placing serious obstacles to change, and restricting the power of majorities. In America such safeguards were provided for a time, and to this fact America mainly owed its stability. The Senate originally did not rest on the democratic basis of mere numbers and could thus exercise even more restraining power on the House of Representatives. The Constitution was under the protection of a great, independent law court, which made it impossible for the government to violate contracts, or to infringe any fundamental liberty of the people, or to carry any constitutional change, except where there is the amplest evidence that it is the clear, settled wish of an overwhelming majority of the people. An amendment requires the votes of two-thirds of both Houses of Congress or an application from the legislatures of two-thirds of the states. No amendment can become law unless it is ratified by three-fourths of the States, by both local houses, or by conventions specially summoned for that purpose. It takes the concurrence of at least sixty-six separate legislative chambers, when the approval of three-fourths of the states are added to the Senate and the House of the Federal government, to amend the Constitution, it is evident why the Left prefers to ignore the amendment process in favor of positive legislation.

The most illustrious example of a great controlling aristocratic assembly is the Senate of ancient Rome, a body which existed for no less than 800 years, and which during the period of the Republic, contributed more than any other to mold the fortunes and the character of the only State which both achieved and long maintained supreme power in the world. It watched over the security of the State, and even had a right in time of great danger to suspend the laws and confer absolute power on the consuls. During the last days of the Republic, and under the Empire, the Senate went through other phases; though greatly changed and greatly lowered it survived every other element of Roman freedom, and even after the establishment of the Byzantine Empire and amid the anarchy of the barbaric invasions it played no small part in Roman history. Though neither an elective nor a hereditary body it owed its power chiefly to the number and importance of great functions that were confided to it.

The American Senate was designed to be such a balance wheel, one which adjusts and regulates the movements of the country. In the Continental Congress the vote had been by States. Smaller states refused to join in the new federation unless they obtained, in at least one House, the similar security of an equal vote, and were thus guaranteed against the danger of absorption by their larger colleagues. By this process a powerful counterpoise was established to the empire of mere numbers which prevailed in the Lower House. Two members represented the smallest as well as the largest State, and they were initially chosen, not by a directly popular vote, but by the State legislatures. Montesquieu had maintained that a senator ought to be chosen for life, as was the custom in Rome and in the Greek republics. Alexander Hamilton, the foremost political thinker of America, desired to adopt this system; but it was ultimately agreed to adopt a limited period of six years, one third of the permanent body being renewed every two years by the State legislatures. It was the object of its framers to combine a considerable measure of that continuity of policy which should be one of the first ends of a legislator with close and constant contact with State opinion; to place the Senate above the violent impulses, the transient passions, the dangerous fluctuations of uninstructed masses, but not above the genuine and steady currents of national feeling. Its merits have not been wholly retained. The excellent system of indirect double election of the Senate, which the framers of the Constitution considered the best way of freeing democracy from its baser and more foolish elements, has not been able to withstand the pressure and the ingenuity of Party. Similarly, the men who are entrusted with the task of voting for the President have long since been deprived by their electors of all liberty of choice and are strictly pledged to vote for particular candidates. But when there is no longer a check in the people's chamber, and the Senate and President have given in to Party and ceased to do their jobs as protector of the Constitution, the conservative influences are insufficient to prevent too rapid/revolutionary/destructive change. The influences working for change acquire an enormously augmented force, the dangers to the country are incalculably increased. It has been the steady action of the Progressives to disintegrate and degrade representative government, to support every measure in the direction of anarchy and plunder. It is impossible to foretell with accuracy in what form societies will organize themselves should, under the pressure of direct democracy, our present system of representative government break down.

The people are the only real check, but the vast proportion of the expenditure of the State is now intended for the express purpose of bribing them. No longer is government a penurious institution, jealously scrutinizing every item of public expenditure, denouncing as intolerable scandal the extravagance of unneeded programs, and viewing with extreme disfavor every enlargement of powers of the State. It has now become a government of lavish expenditure, of rapidly accumulating debt, of constantly extending State action. A large portion of the increased expenditure is also due, not to subsidies, but to the increased elaboration of administrative machinery required by the system of constant inspection and almost universal regulation. Nothing is more characteristic of democracy than the alacrity with which it tolerates, welcomes and then demands coercive government interference in all its concerns.

It is evident to any impartial observer the fact of the declining efficiency and lowered character of democratic government. A growing distrust and contempt for representative bodies is evident. It means constantly shifting government, ruined finances and the systematic manipulation of constituencies. National government has fallen under the control of men of an inferior stamp, of skillful talkers or intriguers, of demagogues, of sectional and even local interests. The great decline in the weight of representative bodies has advanced with the growth of direct democracy. It may clearly be traced to the general establishment of universal suffrage as the basis of representation, without effective Constitutional controls. It is generally being discovered that a system which places the supreme power in the hands of mere majorities, consisting of the poorest and most ignorant, does not produce a Congress of surpassing excellence. Intriguers and demagogues, playing successfully on the passions and the credulity of the ignorant and of the poor, form one of the great characteristic evils and dangers of our time. Skillful leaders commit their party by their own will to a new policy which has never been maturely considered or accepted.

The old understandings and traditions, on which deliberations had been for many generations successfully conducted, have largely disappeared, and new and stringent regulations have been found necessary by those in power. The effort by Progressives is to degrade, dislocate and paralyze the deliberative machine until their objects are attained; the contagion of their example and the connivance through party motives has been more than evident. The dreary torrent of idle, divisive and insincere talk that now drags its slow lengths through so many months of deliberation does not add to the Party's reputation. To carry highly complex measures of legal reform through a body like the American Congress is utterly impossible; thus much needed reform is never likely to be accomplished until the Constitution is so far changed as to severely limit the objects on which the government may operate. All real progress, all sound national development, must grow out of a stable, persistent, national character, deeply influenced by custom and precedent and old traditional reverence, habitually aiming at the removal of practical evils and the attainment of practical advantages, rather than speculative change. An appetite for such change is one of the worst diseases that can affect a nation. Institutions can never attain their maturity if their roots are perpetually tampered with.

The apportionment of political power between distinctly separated classes has been one of the oldest and most fruitful ideas in political philosophy. It existed in Athens even before the days of Solon; Solon, in his revision of the Athenian Constitution, divided the citizens into four classes, according to the amount of their property, subjecting each class to a special proportion of taxation, and giving to each class special and peculiar privileges in the State. In the Roman republic the citizens were divided into six different classes, according to the amount of their property, the lowest class comprising the poorest citizens; each class was subdivided into a number of 'centuries,' proportioned to what was considered their importance in the State, and each century had a single vote in enacting laws and electing magistrates. Cicero claimed for this system that it gave some voice to every class, but a greatly preponderating voice to those who had most interest in the well-being of the State.

To place the chief power in the most ignorant classes is to place it in the hands of those who naturally care the least for political liberty, and who are most likely to follow with an absolute devotion some strong leader. It is the upper and middle classes who have chiefly valued constitutional liberty, and those classes it is the work of democracy to dethrone. At the same time democracy does much to weaken the love of liberty. The instability and insecurity of democratic politics; the spectacle of dishonest and predatory adventurers climbing by popular suffrage into positions of great power in the State; the alarm which attacks on property seldom fail to produce among those who have something to lose, may easily scare to the side of despotism large classes who, under other circumstances, would have been steady supporters of liberty. This is the despotism resting, for as long as it can last, on the material prosperity created by and stolen from others, and not upon constitutional liberty.

The propertied class has interests indissolubly connected with the permanent prosperity of the country and, who by conducting businesses among the people, have acquired the kinds of knowledge and of capacity that are most needed in political life. The position of a public man is essentially that of a trustee, and interests of the most enormous importance depend largely on his character. It is absolutely indispensable to the working of the whole machine that it should be in the hands of honest and trustworthy self-governing men, of men determined to subordinate on great occasions their personal and party interests to the interests of the state. Wherever such sentiments pervade the public service men will soon learn to recognize that public servants cannot be bribed or corrupted. If such men cannot be found, then there is no constitution which can be enforced. And thus the management of great political interests have passed into the hands of mere scheming adventurers.

When such men are numerous enough, they will naturally alter the whole action of politics and may seriously impair the representative character of Congress, by submerging genuine informed opinion with great uniform masses of ignorant and influenced voters. Their power of numbers becomes so absolute that they exert an outsized control over the well-being of the country. Thus one of the great divisions of our day is coming to be whether the world will be governed by its intelligence or by its ignorance. According to one party the ultimate source of power should be with education and property; to the other, the preponderate power, the supreme right of appeal and control, belongs legitimately to the majority of the nation simply by headcount-in other words, to the poorest, the most ignorant, and the most incapable, who are necessarily the most numerous.

It is a theory which assuredly reverses all the past experiences of mankind. In every field of human enterprise, in all the competitions of life, by the inexorable law of Nature, superiority lies with the few, and not the many, and success can only be attained by placing the guiding and controlling power in the former's hands. Government must inevitably deteriorate if it is placed under the direct control of the most unintelligent classes. Nothing in any ancient alchemy is more irrational than the notion that increased ignorance in the elective body will be converted into increased capacity for good government in the representative body; that the best way to improve the world and secure rational progress is to place government more and more under the control of the least enlightened classes. The day will come when it will appear one of the strangest facts in the history of human folly that such a theory was regarded as liberal and progressive.

Aristotle observed that the propertied class was the section of the community that the chief power in government would be most wisely and profitably given. It is not the class most susceptible to new ideas or most prone to great enterprises, but it is distinguished beyond all others for its political independence, its caution, its solid practical intelligence, its steady industry, its high moral average. It sooner feels more than any other class the effects of misgovernment, whether that take the form of reckless adventure and extravagant expenditure, or whether it disturbs settled industries, drives capital to other lands, and impairs the national credit, upon which the whole commercial system must ultimately rest. There are multitudes in every nation who contribute nothing to its public opinion; who never give a serious thought to public affairs, who have no inclination to take any part in them; who if they are induced to do so, will act under the complete direction of individuals or organizations of another class, for the purpose of accumulating these votes to further the aims of the latter. The demagogue will try to persuade the voter that by following a certain line of policy every member of his class will obtain some advantage. He will encourage all Utopias. He will appeal to all class jealousies and antipathies. He will hold out hopes that by breaking contracts, or shifting taxation and the power of taxing, or enlarging the paternal functions of government, something of the property of one class may be transferred to another. All the divisions which naturally grow out of class lines and the relations between employers and employees will be studiously inflamed. Envy and covetousness will become great forces in political propagandism. Every minor grievance will be aggravated into a major one. Every redressed grievance will be revived; every imaginary grievance will be encouraged. If the poorest, most numerous and most ignorant class-vague and childlike-can be persuaded to hate the smaller, most productive class, and to vote solely for the purpose of injuring them, the Progressives will have achieved their end. Without knowledge and without character, the instinct is to use the power which is given them for predatory and anarchic purposes. To set the many against the few is their object.

Such men, while perhaps shrewd within the circle of their own ideas, are as ignorant as children of the consequences of constitutional changes, or the great questions relating to commercial or financial policy, on which a general election frequently turns. If they are asked to vote on such questions all that can be safely predicted is that their decision will not represent either settled conviction or real knowledge. To break up society, to obtain a new deal in the goods of life, will naturally be their object.

We can hardly have a more impressive illustration of the truth that universal suffrage wholly fails to represent the best qualities of a nation. Corruption does much to lower the character of Governments and to alienate from them the public spirit and enthusiasm that should support their activities. The forms of corruption practiced in a pure democracy are in general far more detrimental to the prosperity of nations. Wars, overgrown armaments, policies that shake credit and plunder large classes, laws that hamper industry, the forms of corruption which bribe constituencies or classes with great public expenditure, by lavish, partial unjust taxation-these are the things that really ruin the finances of a nation-lowering the national credit, driving out of a country great masses of capital, dislocating its industry and trade. To most of these evils unqualified democracies are especially liable. Few national diseases are more insidious in their march, more difficult to arrest, more disastrous in their ultimate consequences. The immediate stimulus which a program might provide masks its ultimate and permanent effects of adding to the debt service. Such governments take the short view and are eagerly looking for immediate support. All the lines of policy that are most fitted to appeal to the imagination and win the favor of an uninstructed democracy are lines of policy involving increased expenditure towards enlarging the functions and burdens of the State. When great sections of the people have come habitually to look to the Government for support, it becomes impossible to withdraw, and exceedingly difficult to restrict that support. Public works which are undertaken for political motives, and which private enterprise would refuse to touch, are scarcely ever remunerative. A false security grows up, until the nation at last slowly finds that it has entered irretrievably on the path of decadence. It is scarcely to be expected, under such conditions, that the tone of public life should be very high. The idea that a citizen's vote establishes a claim to a personal reward has rapidly spread. The old idea, that the representative Chamber is pre-eminently a check upon extravagance, a jealous guardian of the public purse, armed with the people's veto power, seems to have almost vanished in democratic countries. Instead, each representative seeks to secure a livelihood out of the public taxes for the greatest possible number of their electors.

The number of office holders in the United States quadrupled just in the lawless period from 1860 to 1870, and those appointments were systematically made through party motives, irrespective of the capacity of the claimant. These men were assessed to pay the political expenses of campaign. The extreme elaboration and multiplication of committees and organizations for the purpose of accumulating and directing votes along party lines, which add or subtract from party strength, turned the politics of the State into a business so absorbing that no one could expect to have much influence in it unless he made it a main business of his life. The vast number of men who hold office, and aspire to such, furnish the parties with innumerable agents, who work for their livelihood, while the tribute levied upon these officials supplies an ample fund for corruption. The great and growing volume of political work to be done in managing primaries, conventions and elections for the city, State and national Governments, which the advance of democratic sentiment and the needs of the party warfare evolved from 1820 to about 1850, needed men who should give to it constant and undivided attention. Those whose income depended on their party, might be trusted to work for the party, to enlist recruits, and play electioneering tricks whenever necessary. It is these spoilsmen who depraved and distorted the mechanism of politics. It is they who packed the primaries and ran the conventions, so as to destroy the freedom of popular choice; they who contrived and executed the election frauds of ballot stuffing, obstruction of the polls, and improper counting. "Politics has now become a gainful profession, like advocacy, stock-broking, the dry-goods trade, or the getting up of companies. Place hunting is the career; an office is not a public trust, but a means of requiting party services, and a source whence party funds may be raised for election purposes." The practice continues today in a geometrically advanced form. It all contributes to the Decline of the Law.

It makes contests which should be about principle mainly ones for plunder. There is no subject on which the best minds in America are so fully agreed as upon the absolute necessity of putting an end to the bureaucratic spoils system, if America public life is ever to be purified from corruption. The growth of the bureaucracy, which is a natural consequence of a corrupt spoils system, is also part of the prevailing tendency to extend the functions of government. The period following the Civil War was one peculiarly fitted for the growth of corruption: the sudden and enormous increase of debt, the corresponding multiplication of officials, the paralysis of political life in the Southern half of the nation, and the many elements of social and political anarchy that still prevailed all made the task of professional politicians easy and lucrative. The growth of a service which could be used for political ends was a rapidly growing menace to republican government. There were sales of monopolies in the use of public thoroughfares, enormous abuses in patronage; cities were compelled to buy, at enormous overcharge, otherwise unwanted property for parks; they graded, paved and sewered streets without inhabitants in order to award corrupt contracts; they made or kept the salary of an office unduly high in order that its tenant might pay largely to the party funds. No one can wonder at it. It was the plain, inevitable consequence of the application of the methods of extreme democracy to government. Is it possible to conceive conditions more fitted to serve the purposes of cunning and dishonest men, whose object is personal gain, whose method is the organization of the vicious and ignorant elements of the community into combinations that can turn elections, levy taxes and appoint administrators?

The withdrawal of the control of affairs from the hands of the minority who, in the competitions of life, have risen to a higher plane of fortune and instruction; the continual degradation of the suffrage to lower and lower strata of intelligence, quite irrespective of their circumstances and character; attacks upon institution after institution; a systematic hostility to the owners of property, are the directions which the Progressive Party wishes to move. To destroy some institution or injure some class is commonly their first and last idea in constitutional policy. There is no constructive ability and even less power of arriving at a perception of the evils arising or of the new remedies that are required. It has been the practice of the Progressive party that by adopting a very low suffrage it would be possible to penetrate below the superficial region where crude Utopias and habitual restlessness prevail, and to thereby even reach and corrupt the strong settled habits, the enduring tendencies, the deep conservative instincts of the nation.

The educational changes that introduced into constituencies a much larger proportion of ignorance, indifference, and credulity soon altered the conditions of politics. Politicians learned to think less of convincing the reason of the country than of combining independent groups or touching some strong chord of widespread class interest or prejudice. Men have become very indifferent to earning respect provided they can succeed by such methods in winning a majority and obtaining power and office. Such a coalition depends on the concurrence of many distinct groups, governed by different motives, aiming at different objects, representing different shades of political feeling. Progressives are obliged to consolidate by separate policy bribes these different tribes, or discover some cry that may rally them, some active and aggressive policy that may secure their support, and to which they will each subordinate their special objects. In a closely divided nation, a group of men representing opinions and aiming at objects which are only those of a small minority of the nation, may obtain a decisive influence if it keeps apart from the great party organizations, subordinates all other considerations to its own objects, and when a few votes can save or destroy the larger Party, makes the attainment of those objects the price of its adhesion. The process called logrolling involves one minority agreeing to support the objects of another minority on condition of receiving in return a similar assistance; a number of small minorities aiming at different objects, no one of which is really desired by the majority of the nation, may attain their several ends by forming themselves into a political syndicate and mutually cooperating. The first step is for some extreme politicians, often exercising disproportionate power, always to mark out some ancient institution for attack in order to rally their followers. Personal vanity here concurs powerfully with party interests, for men who are utterly destitute of real constructive ability are nonetheless capable of attacking an existing institution; there is no other form of politics in which a noisy reputation can be so easily acquired.

The toleration of change and the belief in its advantages are still confined to the smallest portion of the human race-the immobility of society is the rule; its mobility is the exception. The process is, however, familiar. A small minority obtain the ear of the governing part of the community and persuade it to force the entire people to conform itself to their ideas. These ideas appear to arise in a very small degree from intelligent conviction, but really to a very great extent from the remote effects of words and notions derived from broken-down political theories. If modern society is normally not changeable, attempts to conduct it safely through the exceptional process of political change is not easy but extremely difficult. What is easier to understand is what has come to man through long-inherited experience. Constitutions, gradually developed through the accumulation of experience, appear to have an advantage over speculative assumptions remote from empirical evidence. Let the new institutions of the Left be extraordinarily wide of experience and inconvenience becomes imminent peril.

When the balance of power between the different elements of the Constitution was still unimpaired, when the strongly organized conservative influences of class and property opposed an insuperable barrier to revolutionary change, suffrage might be safely extended. In the conditions of the present day, however, no serious thinker can fail to perceive the enormous danger of placing the essential elements of the Constitution at the mercy of a simple majority, composed, perhaps, of heterogeneous and discordant factions, combined only for a party purpose, and not larger than is required to pass the simplest of bills. With the multiplication of groups this evil is constantly increasing, and it is in this direction that many dangerous politicians are mainly working. It is absurd to suppose that, if the lowly worker and the needy become the depositories of power, and if they find agents through whom it becomes possible for them to exercise it, that they will not employ it for what they may be led to believe are their own interests. What is to be the nature of the legislation by which the lot of the worker is to be not merely altered for the better but exchanged for whatever station and fortune they may think it possible to confer on themselves by their own authority? The problem is how, with the growth of the numbers of poor, can property rights can be protected from confiscation at the hands of the non-producing classes? Suffrage not only protects the holder of the vote from aggression, but also enables him to aggress upon the rights of others by means of the taxing power. The most successful steps taken in the direction of reform have been those limiting the power of corrupt bodies, of restricting by constitutional laws the extent of their dishonesty. Long and bitter experience has convinced the people that legislators will roll up the debt unless positively forbidden to go beyond a certain figure.

Can anyone suppose that a theory of taxation and representation so palpably and grotesquely at variance with the reality of things has any real prospect of enduring? Looked at another way, the complete submission of all taxation to the will of a mere numerical majority is an end towards which we are manifestly travelling. The inevitable result is to give one class the power of voting taxes which another class almost exclusively must pay, and the chief taxpayers, being completely swamped, are for all practical purposes completely disfranchised. It would be difficult to conceive a more flagrant abandonment of that principle about the connection between taxation and voting, which in former generations was looked on as the most fundamental principle of freedom. Democracy pushed to its full consequences places the whole property of the country in the hands of the poorest classes, giving them an unlimited power of helping themselves.

Partial, inequitable taxation, introduced for the purpose of obtaining votes, is an evil which in democratic societies is too likely to increase. The nature and magnitude of new, replacement contributions, the form it is to take, and the areas over which it is to be distributed are never revealed or intentionally left vague. One point only is brought before the electors; relief for them and some imposition upon those with the most property. Such promises, unaccompanied by any distinct statement of equivalent burdens to be imposed, can only act as a direct bribe addressed to the great section of the electorate whose growing alienation from responsible government forms the soul of the Progressive Party. We are moving towards a state in which one class will impose the taxes while another will be compelled to pay them. It is obvious that taxation is more and more employed for objects that are not common interests of the whole community, and that there is a growing tendency to look upon it as a possible means of confiscation; to make use of it is to break down the power, influence and wealth of particular classes, to form a new social type and to obtain the means of class bribery. The danger and injustice is of dissociating the power of voting taxes from the necessity of paying them, and the fact that unqualified universal suffrage leads plainly and rapidly to this form of robbery. Progressivism, with its watchword of one man, one vote has made steadily successful efforts to place the property and liberty of the country under the complete dominion of the poorest and most ignorant. All contributes to the Decline of the Law.

Taxation is no longer for the purpose of discharging functions which are necessary or highly useful to the State; it has come to be regarded as a weapon of socialism, as an instrument of confiscation, as a levelling agent for breaking down large fortunes, redistributing wealth and creating a new social type. A graduated income tax, when those who are exempted form the bulk of the electorate, and thus are able to increase this taxation to an indefinite extent, is a direct penalty imposed on savings and industry and a direct premium offered to idleness and extravagance. It discourages the very habits and qualities which it is most in the interest of the State to foster. It is a strong inducement either to cease work or cease saving. It is at the same time perfectly arbitrary; the scale may be at first very moderate, but at any time it may be made more severe until it reaches to the point of confiscation. No fixed line or amount of graduation can be maintained upon principle, or with any chance of finality. The whole matter rests with the party politicians competing for the votes of the very poor and the very ignorant. Such men will have no difficulty in drawing impressive contrasts between the luxury of the rich and the necessities of the poor, and in persuading ignorant men that there can be no harm in throwing great burdens of exceptional taxation on a few men. Yet no truth of political economy is more certain than that a heavy taxation of capital, which starves industry and employment, will fall most severely on the poor.

Graduated taxation is certain to be contagious and it is certain not to rest within the limits that its originators desired. It cannot be otherwise when political power is placed mainly in the hands of the ignorant and poor, when professional politicians are continually making changes in the incidence of taxation a prominent part of their electioneering programs. When almost every year sees an enlargement in the functions, and therefore the expenditure, of the State; when nearly all the prevalent Utopias take a socialistic form and point to an equalization of conditions by means of taxation, under such conditions the temptation to enter upon this path becomes almost irresistible. A system of graduated taxation will never produce a real equality of fortunes, or prevent the accumulation of great wealth, but will certainly, in aiming at those objects, ruin the national credit, and bring about a period of rapid commercial decadence. Far-seeking, productive men hesitate to commit themselves to undertakings which can only slowly arrive at maturity when they see the strong bias of popular legislation against property, and the readiness with which a considerable number of modern statesmen will purchase a majority in Congress by allying themselves with the most dishonest groups and countenancing the most subversive theories. Every influence which in any way is restrictive of industrial life, that increases risk and diminishes profits must necessarily divert capital. Highly graduated taxation realizes most completely the supreme danger of democracy, creating a state of things in which one class imposes on another burdens which it is not asked to share, and impels the State into vast schemes of extravagance.

It was the belief that the power to tax ought to be under the sole control of the representatives of those who give it. The old principle of connecting, indissolubly, taxation and representation has probably never been more loudly professed than in the present day; but it is only one of the many instances in which men cheat themselves by repeating forms and phrases, while the underlying meaning has almost wholly passed away. In the great changes that have taken place in the disposition and balance of powers, many of the old constitutional checks have become obsolete, inoperative or useless; but the whole tendency of modern politics has only increased the provision that matters of taxation only increase the income and scope of the government rather than confine it within its proper bounds. The whole drift of democratic government is to diminish or to destroy the control which property once had over taxation. The justification for the special political powers vested in large taxpayers is in the idea that those who chiefly pay should chiefly control; that the kinds of property which contribute most to support government should have the most weight in regulating it. It is the duty of a legislator to provide that one class should not have the power of voting the taxes, while another class were obliged to pay them. It is plain that this fundamental element in the Constitution is rapidly being destroyed.

It would be difficult to conceive a stagnation either more dangerous, or more absurd, or more humiliating than this. According to all rational conceptions of constitutional government, it should be object of the legislator to strengthen the influence of intelligence, loyalty, and property in the representation and, in every change, to improve the character of Congress. If such ideas are discarded as obsolete and behind the age, if the new worship of mere numbers prevails, to the utter disregard of all the real interests of the State, then the electorate will get the government it deserves. Very few men can realize distant consequences more than one removed from the primary one. National interests continually give way to party or class interests; proximate ends overshadow distant consequences before withering away themselves. All classes are liable to such mistakes but especially those who have passed out from below the empire of old habits and restraints. They are insensitive to the complexity of the social fabric and the close interdependence of its many parts, and to the transcendent importance of consequences that are often obscure, remote, and diffused through many different channels. But even literacy is no real guarantee that a man will wisely exercise political skills. Only a wide diffusion of property, a system of representation that gives a voice to many different interests and types, and the sedulous maintenance of the connection between taxation and voting can maintain such wisdom. No graver error can be made by a financier than to institute a system which is so burdensome and so unjust that men will be disposed to employ all their ingenuity to evade it. Taxation is ultimately the payment which is made by the subject for the security and other advantages which he derives from the State. If the taxation of one class is out of proportion to the cost of the protection they enjoy; if its members are convinced that it is not an equitable payment, but an exceptional and confiscatory burden imposed upon them by an act of power because they are politically weak, very few will have any scruple in defrauding the government of what they demand.

When the Progressive party has shown itself incompetent to conduct the business of the country with honor, efficiency and safety; when public opinion has learnt more fully the enormous danger to national prosperity, as well as to individual happiness, of dissociating power from property, and giving the many an unlimited right of confiscating by taxation the possessions of a few, some great reconstruction of government is sure to be demanded. Arguments that are now dismissed with contempt may revive and play no small part in the politics of the future.

AFTERWORD

WILL DURANT
ARIEL DURANT

CONFUCIUS

"He was five hundred years before our era, the national conscience which gave precision and corroboration to the profound ideas of which the classic books of remote antiquity reveal to us only in first outlines...men were touched by the potent spirit coming from the distant past which summoned up in them the truths glimpsed by their fathers."

Professor Chavannes, 1918, speaking of Confucius

"At fifteen, I had my mind bent on learning. At thirty I stood firm. At forty I was free from doubt. At fifty I knew the decrees of Heaven. At sixty my ear was an obedient organ for the reception of truth. At seventy I could follow what my heart desired without transgressing what was right."

Confucius (551-479 BC)

"The Higher Man has nine things which are subjects with him of thoughtful consideration. In regard to the use of his eyes he is anxious to see clearly…In regard to his countenance he is anxious that it should be benign. In regard to his demeanor he is anxious that it should be respectful. In regard to his speech he is anxious that it should be sincere. In regard to his doing of business he is anxious that it should be reverently careful. In regard to what he doubts about, he is anxious to question others. When he is angry he thinks of the difficulties his anger may involve him in. When he sees gain to be got he thinks of righteousness."

"The Higher Man conforms with the path of the mean, for there is no end of things by which man is affected; and when his likings and dis-likings are not subject to regulation, he is changed into the nature of the things which come before him."

Confucius (551-479 BC)

"The ancients who wished to illustrate the highest virtue throughout the empire first ordered well their own states. Wishing to order their own states, they first regulated their families. Wishing to regulate their families, they first cultivated their own selves. Wishing to cultivate their own selves, they first rectified their hearts. Wishing to rectify their hearts, they first sought to be sincere in their thoughts. Wishing to be sincere in their thoughts, they first extended to the utmost their knowledge. Such extension of knowledge lay in the investigation of things."

"Things being investigated, knowledge became complete. Their knowledge being complete, their thoughts were sincere. Their thoughts being sincere, their hearts were then rectified. Their hearts being rectified, their own selves were cultivated. Their own selves being cultivated, their families were regulated. Their families being regulated, their states were rightly governed. Their states being rightly governed, the whole empire was made tranquil and happy."

Confucius (551-479 BC), from *The Great Learning*

"The rule of moral conduct which should direct our actions is so obligatory that we cannot escape from it on a single point, or for a single instant. If we could escape it, it would no longer be an unchangeable rule of conduct. That is why the superior man, he who follows the right path, keeps watch in his heart over the principles which are not perceived by the many, and he meditates carefully on that which is not openly proclaimed or recognized as doctrine."

Confucius (551-479 BC)

There is something in the Confucian idea that if a man only sets himself right, the rightness will extend to his family first of all, and finally in widening circles to the whole community. The Higher Man is the keynote and substance of the Confucian philosophy. This is the essence of the matter and a complete guide to life. The world is at war, says Confucius, because its constituent states are improperly governed; these are improperly governed because no amount of legislation can take the place of the natural social order provided by the family; the family is in disorder, and fails to provide this natural social order, because men forget that they cannot regulate their families if they do not regulate themselves; they fail to regulate themselves because they have not rectified their hearts-they have not cleansed their own souls of disorderly desires; their hearts are not rectified because their thinking is insincere, doing scant justice to reality and concealing rather than revealing their own natures; their thinking is insincere because they let their wishes discolor the facts and determine their conclusions, instead of seeking to extend their knowledge to the utmost by impartially investigating the nature of things.

Let men seek impartial knowledge, and their thinking will become sincere; let their thoughts be sincere and their hearts will be cleansed of disorderly desires; let their hearts be so cleansed, and their own selves will be regulated; let their own selves be regulated, and their families will automatically be regulated-not by virtuous sermonizing or passionate punishments, but by the silent power of example itself; let the family be so regulated with knowledge, sincerity and example, and it will give forth such spontaneous social order that successful government will once more be a feasible thing; let the state maintain internal justice and tranquility and the world will be peaceful. If the state is in disorder the proper thing to do is not to reform it but to make one's life an orderly performance of duty. To the Chinese the ideal is not the pious devotee but the mature and quiet mind, the man who, though fit to hold high place in the world, retires to simplicity and silence. Silence is the beginning of wisdom, as wisdom can only be transmitted by example and experience. The great man, though abounding in achievements, is simple in his manners and appearance. Get rid of your pride and your affectations; your character gains nothing for these. Confucianism gives us a ladder to climb and is one of the golden texts of philosophy.

Confucianism survived so many rivals and so many attacks for twenty centuries, because it was felt to be indispensable to that intense and exalted moral tradition upon which China had founded its life. As these were the religious sanctions and ancestor worship, so the family was the great vehicle of this ethical heritage. From parents to children the moral code was handed down across the generations and became the invisible government of Chinese society; a code so stable and strong that society maintained its order and discipline through nearly all the vicissitudes of the unsteady state. What the Chinese, said Voltaire, "best know, cultivate the most and have brought to the greatest perfection, is morality." "By building the house on a sound foundation," Confucius said, "the world is made secure."

We ask of a thinker only that, as the result of a lifetime of thought, he shall in some way illuminate our path to understanding. Proof of worth comes in how little must be erased because of the growth of knowledge and change of circumstance, how it offers us guidance even in the contemporary world. Throughout the dialogues, we find Confucius putting together, piece by piece, his picture of the ideal man.

Wisdom begins at home, and the foundation of society is a disciplined individual in a disciplined family. Confucius and Goethe both said that self-development is the root of social development. What the Higher Man seeks is in himself; what the lower man seeks is in others. He moves to make his conduct in all generations a universal law. The Higher Man is not angered by the excellences of other men; when he sees men of worth, he thinks of equaling them; when he sees men of low worth, he turns inward and examines himself, for there are few faults we do not share with our neighbors.

None but such men can restore the family and redeem the state. The rules of propriety form the outward character; we become what we do. Confucius said: Politically "the uses of propriety serve as dikes for the people against excess; he who thinks the embankments useless, and destroys them, is sure to suffer from the desolation caused by the overflowing water." The stoic conservatism of Confucius sank almost into the blood of the Chinese people, and gave to the nation, and to its individuals, a dignity and profundity unequaled elsewhere in the world or in history. And today, as then, could no better medicine be prescribed for any people suffering from the disorder generated by the agitators of the left?

The intellectual discovery of China was one of the great achievements of the Enlightenment. "These peoples," Diderot wrote of the Chinese, "are superior to all other Asiatics in antiquity, art, intellect, wisdom, policy, and in their taste for philosophy; nay, in the judgment of certain authors, they dispute the palm in these matters with the most enlightened peoples of Europe." "The body of this empire," said Voltaire, "has existed four thousand years, without having undergone any sensible alteration in its laws, customs, or language; its organization is in truth the best the world has ever seen. It is indeed a social organization that has held together more human beings, and endured through more centuries, than any other known to history; a form of government which was almost the ideal of philosophers; a society that was civilized when Greece was inhabited by barbarians, that saw the rise and fall of Babylonia and Assyria, Persia and Judea, Athens and Rome, Venice and Spain, and may yet survive when Europe and the Americas have reverted to darkness and savagery."

In the primitive theology of China heaven and earth were bound together as two halves of the great cosmic unity; the order of the heavens and the moral behavior of mankind were kindred processes, parts of a universal and necessary rhythm called *Tao*-the heavenly way; morality, like the law of the stars, was the cooperation of the part with the whole. The Supreme God was this mighty heaven itself, this moral order, this divine orderliness, that engulfed both men and things, dictating the right relationship of children to parents, of wives to husbands, of vassals to lords, of lords to the emperor, and of the emperor to God. The political stability and spiritual continuity which ancestor worship gave to civilization allowed the nation to achieve a powerful spiritual unity in time; the generations were bound together with the tough web of tradition, and the individual life received an ennobling share and significance of timeless majesty and scope.

This simple and almost rationalistic religion never quite satisfied the people of China. Its doctrines gave too little room to the imagination of men, too little answer to their hopes and dreams, too little encouragement to the superstitions that enlivened their daily life. In the south, particularly, the Chinese soul inclined to mysticism; it was repelled by the frigid rationalism of the Confucian faith, and hungered for a creed that would give China, like other nations, deathless consolations.

Confucius is less concerned with the other world than with the art of living to the best advantage in this. To live to the best advantage in this word is, he holds, to live proportionately and moderately; so the Confucian tradition of the far East has much in common with the Aristotelean tradition of ancient Greece. Confucius aspired at most to be the channel through which the moral experience of his race that had accumulated through long centuries, and found living embodiment in these sages, should be conveyed to the present and the future; in his own words he was not a creator but a transmitter. No one has ever insisted more than Confucius on a right example and the imitation that it inspires as the necessary basis of civilized society. This insistence would seem justified by the force of his own example which molded for seventy generations-the ethos of a fourth of the human race-and that with little or no appeal to the principle of fear either in this world or in the next.

The special praise that Confucius bestowed on his favorite disciple was that he was "always progressing and never came to a standstill." What Confucius plainly had in mind was progress according to the human Law. What the Progressive means by the term is no less plainly material progress. He seems to have assumed, so far as he gives his subject any thought at all, that moral progress would issue almost automatically from material progress. Progress, though, if it is to make for civilization, must be subordinated to some adequate end which Progressivism does not supply. As a result, we have the type of men who are pursuing power for its own sake, men who do not care where they are going, provided they can get there faster and faster.

The very greatness of Republicanism, its utter dependence on the people, was at the same time its source of weakness. In a republic there was no place for fear; there could be no sustained coercion from above. It was axiomatic that no society could hold together without the obedience of its members to the legally constituted Authority. In a Republic, order, if there is to be any, must come from below. By resting the whole structure of government on the unmitigated willingness of the people to obey, the Americans were making a truly revolutionary transformation in the structure of Authority. The Revolution was designed to change the flow of Authority; the elected republican magistrate would be distinguished by his inherent worth and would know no good separate from that of his subjects. Such a change in the nature of Authority and the magistracy only mitigated the problem of obedience in a republican system. The people themselves must change as well, developing a public virtue which could only mean the sacrificing of private interests for the good of the community. Republicanism was delicate precisely because it demanded, and absolutely required, an extraordinary moral character in the people. No model of government can equal the importance of this principle nor afford proper safety and security without it.

The American Revolution was no simple colonial rebellion against English imperialism. It was meant to be a social revolution of the most profound sort. Americans who became committed to independence and republicanism were inevitably compelled to expect or at least hope for some amount of reformation in American society. Everyone was aware of the special character of republicanism and the social and moral demands it put upon a people. The greatness and very existence of a republic depended on the people's virtue, as demonstrated by the experience of the ages. Even the ancient republics, virtuous and grand as they were, had eventually crumbled. Despite their keen awareness of the failure of past republics and of the unusual delicacy of republican government, Americans took it up with an astounding ease, burying the monarchy and embracing the new ideology. The key questions were not any particular economic advantages or political rights but rather the kind of people Americans were and wanted to be. Such was their faith in the transformative power of republican government itself that their very anxieties about being virtuous enough in the end added to the urgency of their cause. It was in fact the most important stimulus to revolution. The pervasive fear that they were not predestined to be a virtuous and egalitarian people in the last analysis drove them to the events of 1776. Only separating from Britain and instituting republicanism could realize the social image that the Enlightenment had drawn for them. But it was more than Europe that the Americans rejected. It was the whole world as it had been, and indeed it was as themselves had been. An obsession with luxury, vice and corruption that hindered America's social development, the distribution of power and wealth, the way in which society was moving and maturing, the insolent domination of a powerful few, all contributed to republicanism becoming the ideological response to the great social changes that had crept into American society from England.

The people were largely a body of yeomanry, supported by agriculture, all independent, and nearly upon a level. But, due to the difference in the character, industry and virtue of men, inequality necessarily grows where men are left free to pursue their own ends There was no single ecclesiastical system, no oppressive established church, no aristocracy, no great distinctions of wealth, only a general equality; yet lacking that necessary social equality in nature, Progressives were compelled to press it artificially upon the society, thus destroying and perverting all personal liberty, in order to force into establishment Rousseau's version of political freedom.

"The side of Rousseau that moved the world is the side that exasperates and inspires revolt; it is the mother of violence, the source of all that is uncompromising. It launches the simple souls who give themselves up to its strange virtue upon the desperate quest of the absolute, an absolute to be realized today by anarchy and tomorrow by social despotism"

Lanson, *Annales de la Societe Jean-Jacques Rousseau*

BIBLIOGRAPHY

Aaro, David, *Nikole Hannah-Jones Claims Opposition to 1619 Project Not About 'Accurate Rendering of History'*, 2021

Adams, James Truslow, *Hamiltonian Principles,* 1928

Adams, James Truslow, *Jeffersonian Principles,* 1928

Adams, James Truslow, *The Living Jefferson,* 1936

Adams, John, *Thoughts on Government, Volume Four,* 1819

Aristotle, *Politics*

Babbitt, Irving, *Democracy and Leadership,* 1924

Buenano, Maria, *The 1619 Project: What It Is and Why You Should Not Let Your Child Read It,* 2020

Burke, Edmund, *Reflections on the Revolution in France,* 1790

Chohan, Usman, *Modern Monetary Theory: General Introduction,* 2020

Coit, Margaret, *John C. Calhoun American Portrait,* 1950

Coy, Peter, *Guide to Modern Monetary Theory,* 2019

Culbreath, Jonathan, *Modern Monetary Theory for Conservatives,* 2021

Daley, Beth, *Explainer: What is Modern Monetary Theory?* 2017

D'Souza, Deborah, *Modern Monetary Theory,* 2021

Ezrati, Milton, *What is Modern Monetary Theory,* 2019

Freitag, Nathalie, *Modern Monetary Theory,* 2020

Gasman, Marybeth, *What History Professors Really Think About 'The 1619 Project'*, 2021

Gilder, George, *The Spirit of Enterprise,* 1984

Gilder, George, *Wealth and Poverty,* 1981

Guelzo, Allen C., *Preaching a Conspiracy Theory,* 2019

Hannah-Jones, Nikole, *The 1619 Project,* 2019

Harris, Leslie M., *I Helped Fact-Check the 1619 Project. The Times Ignored Me.,* 2020

Hartley, Jonathan, *The Weakness of Modern Monetary Theory,* 2020

Hemingway, Mark, *1619 Project, Touted as Racial Reckoning, Ignores Democratic Party Racism,* 2021

Hill, Helen, *George Mason, Constitutionalist,* 1938

Horan, Patrick, *5 Problem with MMT,* 2019

Hogeland, William, *The Historians are Fighting,* 2021

Hutchens, Gareth, *Modern Monetary Theory: How MMT is Challenging the Economic Establishment,* 2020

Jefferson, Thomas, *Notes on the State of Virginia,* 1783

Jones, Nicole Hannah, *1619 Project,* 2019

Justice, Tristan, *'1619 Project' Founder Melts Down After Criticism of Her Fake History*

Ketcham, Ralph, *The Anti-Federalist Papers and the Constitutional Convention Debates,* 1986

Kirk, Russell, *The Conservative Mind,* 1953

Lake, Rebecca, *Modern Monetary Theory, Explained,* 2021

Lane, Rose Wilder, *The Discovery of Freedom,* 1943

Langdana, Farrokh, *Modern Monetary Theory and Covidonomics: How This Will End,* 2020

Lea, Jessica, *What is the 1619 Project and What are People Saying About It?* 2019

Lecky, W.E.H., *Democracy and Liberty,* 1896

Lewis, Nathan, *The Problem with MMT is that It's True,* 2019

Likos, Paulina *What is Modern Monetary Theory?,* 2021

Locke, John, *Two Treatises of Government,* 1690

Lockert, Melanie, *What is Modern Monetary Theory? Understanding the Alternative Economic Theory That's Becoming More Mainstream,* 2021

Magness, Philip W., *Fact Checking the 1619 Project and Its Critics,* 2019

Mahdjour, Nima, *Modern Monetary Theory,* 2016

Maine, Henry Sumner, *Ancient Law,* 1861

Maine, Henry Sumner, *Popular Government,* 1885

Mankiw, Gregory, *A Sceptics Guide to Modern Monetary Theory,* 2021

Mathews, Lipton, *How to Disprove the 6 Most Outrageous Myths of the 1619 Project,* 2020

Mathews, Dylan, *Modern Monetary Theory, Explained,* 2019

Mayo, Bernard, *Jefferson Himself,* 1942

McDonald, Forrest, *Novus Ordo Seclorum,* 1985

McLaughlin, Dan, *Sean Wilentz Fires Back on the 1619 Project and the Climate of Anti-History,* 2021

Milikh, Arthur, *The Real Goals of the '1619 Project',* 2020

Mitchell, William, *Countries That Run Continuous Deficits Do Not Seem to Endure Accelerating Inflation or Currency Crises,* 2021

Montesquieu, Charles, *The Spirit of the Laws,* 1748

Murphy, Robert, *A Rebuke of Modern Monetary Theory,* 2020

Newman, Alex, *In Chicago, Schools Re-write History with '1619' Lies*

Owsley, Frank Lawrence, Lanier, Lyle, Fletcher, John Gould, et al, *I'll Take My Stand,* 1930

Paine, Thomas, *Common Sense,* 1776

Paine, Thomas, *Rights of Man,* 1791

Paterson, Isabel, *The God of the Machine,* 1943

Pettinger, Tejvan, *Modern Monetary Theory Explained,* 2020

Phelan, John, *Modern Monetary Theory: Debunking the Latest Incarnation of Government's Magic Money Tree,* 2019

Prawer, S.S., *World Literature and Class Conflict,* 1976

Rand, Ayn, *The Virtue of Selfishness,* 1961

Rand, Ayn, *The New Left: The Anti-Industrial Revolution,* 1965

Rand, Ayn, *Capitalism: The Unknown Ideal,* 1966

Roberts, Michael, *Modern Monetary Theory: A Marxist Critique* 2019

Roche, Cullen, *Modern Monetary Theory Critique*, 2011

Rogers, Jon, *What is the 1619 Project?* 2021

Rossiter, Clinton, *Conservatism in America,* 1955

Rousseau, J.J., *Complete Works*

Sandefur, Timothy, *The 1619 Project: An Autopsy,* 2020

Scaringi, Mark A., *The Lies of the 1619 Project,* 2019

Serwer, Adam, *The Fight over the 1619 Project is Not About the Facts,* 2019

Shanthaarachchi, Aruna, *Does MMT Give Lousy Politicians the Right to Print Money?* 2021

Shor, Russell, *Modern Monetary Theory,* 2020

Simba, Malik, *The Three-Fifths Clause of the United States Constitution,* 2014

Strauss, Valerie, *Why I Teach the Much-Debated 1619 Project, Despite Its Flaws,* 2021

Streithorst, Tom, *The Radical Theory That the Government Has Unlimited Money,* 2018

Trenchard and Gordon, *Cato's Letters,* 1720

Wells, Buddy, *Ivo Vetger's "Magic Money Tree" is Full of Fantasy,* 2021

Wood, Gordon S., *The Creation of the American Republic,* 1776-1787, 1969

Woods, Chris, *What is the 1619 Project and Why is it so Controversial?* 2021

Made in the USA
Columbia, SC
15 September 2022